The Ethnohistory of Northern Luzon

Stanford Anthropological Series, No. 4

The Ethnohistory
of Northern Luzon

FELIX M. KEESING

STANFORD UNIVERSITY PRESS

STANFORD, CALIFORNIA

1962

STANFORD UNIVERSITY PRESS
STANFORD, CALIFORNIA

© 1962 by the Board of Trustees of the
Leland Stanford Junior University

Library of Congress Catalog Card Number: 62-9563
Printed in the United States of America

Published with the assistance of the
FORD FOUNDATION

Preface

At the time of my father's death, on April 22, 1961, *The Ethnohistory of Northern Luzon* was taking final shape. He had planned to deliver it to the publisher in mid-June. The first six chapters were in final form; the next five were virtually ready for typing. Chapter XII was being reshaped from an earlier draft with pen, scissors, and paste pot, and was largely completed. Only the thirteenth and concluding chapter—the most crucial of all—awaited a planned total revision.

At the risk of further delaying publication, I was forced to carry out this revision under difficult circumstances. During most of this revision I was without access to the body of the manuscript. The primary problem, however, was simply that the author's personal familiarity with the peoples of northern Luzon and their environment and with the vast masses of historical material he had sifted gave him insights which I could not hope to match. These insights had increased in complexity and sophistication as the manuscript progressed, and the final chapter was to have represented a final synthesis.

These ideas were never written; all that survived him were a brief early draft—which had not satisfied him at the time—and a series of cautious chapter summaries which had been largely eliminated in the final manuscript to make way for the revised and expanded conclusion. My revision was accomplished more with scissors and paste pot than with pen. It is hoped that it achieves its goal as a summary; as a final creative synthesis it could not.

As Felix Keesing's final work, this book may seem an enigma. What led so creative a scholar through this mass of detail? There is no simple answer; yet a partial and complex one may help to place the work in perspective. The book is in one sense an accident. It began with a study of a single group, the Isneg, and an examination of historical documents pertaining to them. The author describes in the opening chapter how the study grew until it encompassed all of northern Luzon. It grew partly because the narrower bounds, once established, seemed arbitrary and artificial; partly because it offered the fascination of a detective mystery or a complex puzzle; partly because the author believed a synthesis of the ethnographic data was long overdue, and felt constrained to try; partly because it offered a research outlet that could be continued piecemeal under the steadily mounting pressures of department administration; and partly because the long time span of the historical records offered rich data on the processes of cultural change which had long held his interest. But most of all he saw in the ethnohistory of northern Luzon as it emerged from the records an affirmation of the creativity of man, his capacity to reformulate his culture, often rapidly, to meet changing circumstances or a new environment.

On the author's behalf, the assistance of numerous colleagues on the various stages of the manuscript is gratefully acknowledged. Among the many who gave generously of their time and ideas are Harold Conklin, Edward Dozier, Charles Frake, William Nydegger, and William Henry Scott. Particular thanks are due to Fred Eggan, without whose enthusiasm and help the manuscript would not have been written, and to other members of the Philippine Studies Program of the University of Chicago. The research assistance of Stanford students Russell W. Coberly, Theodora C. Kreps, Hans Leder, Charles E. Mann, Charles Stortroen, and Thomas E. Voorhees in examining historical documents played an important part in the study. Above all, the author's wife, the late Marie M. Keesing, played a tireless role as editor, critic, contributor, and companion, as she did in all his work.

I owe thanks to Fred Eggan for his encouragement and suggestions on the final chapter, to Bernard Siegel, G. D. Spindler, and Mrs. Harriett Reid of the Stanford Anthropology Department for their assistance in bringing the book to completion, and to Leon Seltzer and others of the Stanford Press for help in matters of publication and editorial assistance. I wish particularly to thank David Pauly, who redrew the maps from the author's originals, Mrs. Morris Zelditch, who compiled the Index, and Shirley Nelson for her patient and painstaking editorial work.

ROGER KEESING

Cambridge, Mass.
November, 1961

Contents

List of Maps

The Ethnohistory of Northern Luzon

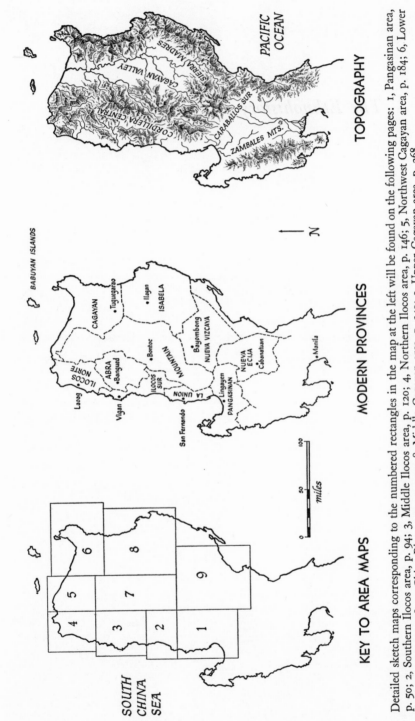

KEY TO AREA MAPS   MODERN PROVINCES   TOPOGRAPHY

Detailed sketch maps corresponding to the numbered rectangles in the map at the left will be found on the following pages: 1, Pangasinan area, p. 50; 2, Southern Ilocos area, p. 94; 3, Middle Ilocos area, p. 120; 4, Northern Ilocos area, p. 146; 5, Northwest Cagayan area, p. 184; 6, Lower Cagayan area, p. 208; 7, Chico River area, p. 222; 8, Middle Cagayan area, p. 240; 9, Upper Cagayan area, p. 268.

I. The Problem

INTRODUCTION

Historical documents are being put to increasingly effective use by anthropologists in reconstructing the longer-term dynamics of human groups. This ethnohistorical study of the interrelations of lowland and mountain peoples in northern Luzon represents an experiment in assembling and analyzing such documents to test various existing theories of migrations and relationships within the area. It is also designed to show how far, in the case of an unusually full documentary record, it is possible to use such materials to demonstrate processes of cultural persistence and change, with which anthropological theory is markedly concerned.

The problem of unraveling connections and contacts between adjacent lowland and highland groups is widely characteristic of ethnohistorical studies the world over, and is exemplified in such mountainous zones as New Guinea, Madagascar, Central America, the Himalayas, and the European Alps. In northern Luzon, the mountains are inhabited by so-called non-Christian peoples whose modes of living are very different today from those of their Christianized and Hispanized neighbors of coast, plain, and valley. Some are "dry" or natural-rainfall gardeners scattered out in small hamlets. Others are "wet" cultivators, growing crops in irrigated terraces sculptured in mountain pockets and up the sheer hillsides. These latter may also live in hamlets dotted through the fields, but more usually they cluster into villages. Regional distinctions in physique are considerable among these peoples, though with the lowlanders they fit into the general type of medium to short brown-skinned Southeast Asians. In some zones the mountain fringes also have bands of dark pigmy Negritos who hunt and glean, though their numbers have dwindled greatly in modern times. Dialect variations, together with differences in house styles, dress, and other matters of custom, mark off the mountain peoples other than the Negritos into ten major regional groups, and the lowland peoples into eight such groups.

One ready explanation for the presence in these mountains of peoples so different from their lowland neighbors has been that they are descended from groups who were earlier arrivals in the area. In the face of later, more powerful groups, they would then have chosen retreat to the heights as the alternative to destruction or absorption. Such a theory may apply to the Negritos, and it is tempting to go further and apply it at least to the dry-gardening groups. In the case of the wet-terracing peoples, with their more complex technologies and social structures, both popular and scientific speculation has pictured them as being descended from a separate migrant group, coming prior to the present lowland peoples according to some views, or else later according to others. They are visualized as having moved across the China Sea to northern Luzon from some mainland Asian area where mountain terracing was practiced. Another popular view of Spanish times was that some at least of these groups were descendants of Chinese or Japanese who were shipwrecked or who engaged in trade and piracy along these coasts, and sought refuge inland, carrying with them wet cultivation techniques.

In addition to these ideas involving different waves of migration, modern anthropological workers have noted the possibility that at least some of the mountain groups share with the adjacent lowland groups the same original ancestors and sources of custom. Almost four centuries have elapsed since the Spanish exploring expeditions ranged the northern Luzon lowlands. The initial records will show how the accessible groups faced a choice between submitting to the alien control or retreating into the interior. Some retreated into the interior, and others subsequently retreated to the mountains in the course of uprisings from time to time against Spanish control. In the light of such documented events, questions arise not only concerning how much the lowlanders and mountaineers may share common origins, but also to what extent the highland fastnesses were permanently occupied prior to Spanish times.

This second approach of hypothesizing common backgrounds calls even more than the separate migration theory for explanations of the variations in physique, language, and custom found in modern times. On the biological side, frankly, any opinions must be highly speculative. There is no way to control data, either through documents or in terms of present genetic knowledge, on the dynamics of human breeding in such an area. At most it can be said that the so-called Malay populations are as genetically diversified here as they are in other parts of Southeast Asia, so that the localized inbreeding of small mountain groups, combined with selective hybridization in some areas with Negritos and possibly with Chinese and Japanese, could account both for the range of types and for the intergradation to be observed today. In the same way the lowland populations have a complex genetic history, which has included considerable mixture with Asian and European elements in the later centuries, plus rapid multiplication of numbers, especially during the last century.

Dynamics of language are more open to analysis through methods of historical linguistics. As will be seen, older studies by mission scholars and others of relationships among the languages and dialects of the region are now being followed up by glottochronological and other investigations. It is in the spheres of custom, however, that the chances are best for reconstruction, by way of documents going back to the initial Spanish contacts. Explorers, missionaries, officials, travelers, and settlers reported in terms of their various interests what they did and what the places and peoples coming to their attention were like.

The great weakness of any viewpoint which reads out of modern observed differences a series of separate migrations is that it assumes human behavior to be overly static. Dry cultivators might not have been dry cultivators several centuries ago. In some cases records indicate that modern rice-terracing villagers were at one time scattered gardeners growing root crops. Recent anthropological studies of cultural dynamics reveal the complexity of the processes of innovation, loss, persistence, and reformulation in human custom. Hypotheses to explain the present likenesses and differences both among the mountain peoples and between them and the lowland peoples must take realistic account of the range of possibilities here. Sensitivity to such factors enables the documentary record to be approached with acumen.

In northern Luzon, as in so many other mountainous zones, migrants have moved not only up to the heights but also down again to settle in the lowlands, especially in the latter case the converts to Christianity. In the case of the principal mountain chain, the Cordillera Central, they have also moved to high country from a number of different zones around its margins. The ethnohistorical possibilities are correspondingly diversified. The simplest theoretical picture or model, apart from one involving separate migrants, is of an original group, of which part stays in the lowlands and part goes into the mountains. Each then undergoes subsequent ethnic reformulation, so that they become different. Continuing contacts, as in trade or even war, would affect them mutually. The upland migrating group might split and settle in different ecological settings, as, say, at varying elevations, diversifying the mountain opportunities for reformulation. With in-migrating groups entering from different localities in the lowlands, and then interacting, the human possibilities continue to multiply. The outmigration of segments to the lowlands presents other variants. Upon the bare framework of such models the rich variability of human behavior has vast scope to foliate.

GENESIS OF THE STUDY

This study is an outgrowth of field work by the writer and his wife in the northern Luzon mountains (Keesing and Keesing, 1934). It developed particularly as a result of contrasting two groups: the so-called Lepanto or northern Kankanai, who were wet-terracing villagers, and the Isneg or Apayao, who are dry-gardening hamlet dwellers. A brief glance at the ethnohistorical problems associated with these groups will serve to make clearer the objectives and methods of the study.

The Lepanto are part of a large wedge-like population of wet-cultivators extending into the mountains from the west side of northern Luzon, of whom the best known anthropologically are the Bontok. The adjacent lowlands comprise a generally narrow strip of the Ilocos coast, home of one of the most numerous Christian ethnic groups in the Philippines, the Ilocano. The Cordillera here rises high above the tropical forest line, and the large, compact villages of the Lepanto are in steep grass and pine forest country, where only terraced cultivation could maintain the surprisingly dense population of modern times. The principal ethnohistorical problem here is whether the differences between the lowland and the mountain peoples can be traced, through historical documents of the long Spanish period or through other evidence, to ecological and cultural dynamics operating upon an originally common population, or whether some theory of separate migrations is called for.

The Isneg are a dry-gardening group who occupy less elevated areas further north in the Cordillera. The mountains here are generally clothed in dense rainforest, and the waterways, though swift and subject to floods, are usually navigable by rafts and small boats. Rather permanent hamlets are dotted sparsely along the principal streams, from which the people range out to their annually shifting gardens; they also hunt and fish. Their river systems empty both to the north coast and into the great Cagayan valley, east of the Cordillera. The principal ethnohistorical problem here is to test out the possible relations between these dry cultivators and the Christianized lowland groups to the north and east. On this Cagayan side, the lowlanders show greater linguistic and other variability than do the modern Ilocanos, so that tracing past connections between them and their mountain neighbors is correspondingly more complex.

Both the Lepanto and the Isneg had continuous trade relations with lowland communities over the period of recorded history, even though war and headhunting were also prevalent. Sporadic military expeditions and mission work, too, provided some contact with things Spanish. Converts, especially from around the mountain fringes, were brought down to settle in the lowlands. These known happenings raise questions about what artifacts, what patterns of action and thought, really belong to the pre-Spanish period, and what are products of direct or indirect Spanish influence. Less capable of being traced through documents, yet at least equally important, are the diffusions and reformulations of custom that occurred as a result of contacts of peace and war among the mountain peoples themselves.

This study began, in a smaller way, with a detailed exploration of the records of Spanish times that had significance for interpreting the Isneg history and culture; that is, documentation on the extreme north of Luzon, including the lower Cagayan valley. The experiment appeared so rewarding that, after consultations with several anthropological colleagues interested in the northern Luzon mountain groups, the same method of compilation and analysis was applied to the rest of the Cagayan valley and its mountain hinterlands. With the northern and eastern parts of this zone so treated, it was decided to round out the picture by assembling corresponding materials on the south and west sides of the mountains, that is, the Pangasinan plains and Ilocos coast.

SOURCE MATERIALS

The attempt has been made to locate and analyze all available documents from Spanish and other sources relevant to ethnohistorical interpretation, and to set out the resulting record quite fully for the scrutiny of other workers dealing with the region or interested in collateral application of the method to other areas. The main period of concern will be from 1572, when the first Spanish expedition reached northern Luzon, to the end of the eighteenth century. Later records are used sparsely and selectively to provide demographic and cultural perspective, and to bridge over to modern official, ethnographic, and other information. The materials on both lowland and mountain peoples which are considered to have bearing on ethnohistorical problems are set out in summary form, and in critical matters verbatim. In general, for each region, they are presented in chronological order, and there is a running analysis to bring out their significance. Translations have been made as necessary from Spanish and other languages to keep the whole record in English.

The bulk of the materials has been sifted from a great conglomerate of documents translated from Spanish and other sources, including the archives of the "Indies," under the editorship of Emma Blair and James Robertson (*The Philippine Islands, 1793–1898*, 54 volumes). Another important source has been an extensive collection of documents assembled in Manila by Professor H. Otley Beyer, including many unpublished records, from which copious notes were taken there in 1932–33 through his courtesy. Of other sources, listed in the Bibliography if they have been of importance but otherwise referred to in the text where the materials have been used, those most notable are a collection of Augustinian mission documents assembled by Angel Perez (1904), Isabelo de los Reyes' *Historia de Ilocos*, Julian Malumbres' large three-volume *Historia* covering Cagayan, Isabela, Nueva Vizcaya, and Mountain Province, and Manuel Buzeta's encyclopedic *Diccionario* of the Philippines compiled in the mid-nineteenth cen-

tury. Of bibliographies giving leads to sources, those published by the Newberry Library in Chicago in relation to its important Ayer Collection of
Philippine publications and unpublished documents are outstanding. Some
useful materials, including translations of non-English documents, were
supplied by Professor Fred Eggan from the Philippines Studies Program
at the University of Chicago, and this scholar also gave much information
from his rich personal knowledge of northern Luzon. Phelan's recent study
of the "Hispanization" of the Philippines serves as a useful framework for
understanding Spanish policies and Filipino responses in the archipelago
as a whole. Old and modern maps have been examined painstakingly to
identify place names and other geographic data. Doubtless additional material could be brought to light through further search; yet the record as
compiled here is a rich and vivid one.

The study will not attempt to review the literature dealing with the
pre-Spanish period except as particular facets help in interpreting the historical documents. Except for very scanty archaeological materials, the re-
constructions by anthropologists and others of migrations and of cultural
sequences in northern Luzon represent speculative inferences from later
group distributions and ethnic characteristics. Past and present ideas can
be seen by reference to works cited in the Bibliography, notably by Beyer,
Cole, Kroeber, Keesing, and Eggan. In the same way, no review will be
made of literature relating to Chinese and Japanese contacts of pre-Spanish
times. The few records by early Asian writers that have been identified
as referring to northern Luzon, or are thought to do so, lack any ethnohistorical detail (see works by Beyer, Iwao, Laufer, and Zaide in the Bibliography).

THE RESEARCH DESIGN

As suggested in discussing the genesis of the study, a number of broad
problems open out for analysis so far as the records can illuminate them:

1. The numbers, distribution, and characteristics—racial, linguistic, and cultural—of the lowland populations at the time of initial Spanish contacts.

2. Subsequent changes among such populations in the course of Christianization and Hispanization.

3. The presence of any groups in the mountains when the Spaniards arrived,
and the retreat of lowlanders into the high country in the face of Spanish pressures.

4. River and ridge systems between lowland and mountain areas which could
best serve as migration pathways; trading routes which might be clues to such
pathways.

5. Varying ecological zones marked by differences in terrain, rainfall, natural resources, and other features which would have called for reformulations of
culture by groups occupying them.

6. The numbers, distribution, and characteristics of the mountain peoples
as records make them known.

7. Penetration of the mountain areas by Spanish military expeditions and missionaries, and the responses of the different populations.

8. Comparison of mountain groups with lowland groups at all periods, to weigh the extent of likenesses and differences, and to test hypotheses of possible relationships.

Within these larger perspectives, special note will be taken of a number of critical, or diagnostic, factors, of which the following may be mentioned here:

a) Stability and change in ethnic and linguistic boundaries.

b) Locations of gold where rivers enter the plains, which could have brought about occupation of the mountains to work this resource, wanted by pre-Spanish traders from neighboring Asian areas.

c) Scattered or concentrated settlement, taking account of early Spanish resettlement policies.

d) Dry and wet cropping, and the distribution of irrigated terracing.

e) Use of different crops, including plants introduced in historic times.

f) Distribution patterns of a number of specific cultural elements, such as use of work animals, the ceramic arts, tooth-blackening, betel-chewing, and ritual drinking of sugar-cane or rice wine.

g) Extent of development of leadership and class structures.

h) Value systems for the individual and group, as expressed in religious beliefs and other matters.

i) Warfare and headhunting as shaping intergroup relations.

j) Trading and other ties, especially between lowland and mountain peoples.

k) Anti-Spanish movements, including revolts and regressions to older cultural patterns.

Prior to the nineteenth century, northern Luzon was subdivided into three provinces: Pangasinan to the south, Ilocos to the west, and Cagayan to the east. Though, as will be seen, these jurisdictions were cut up into smaller provinces, they continue to provide a broad geographic nomenclature which will form the general frame of the study. The Pangasinan-Ilocos, or western, region will be dealt with first, as being the scene of the initial Spanish penetration, and materials on the Cagayan, or eastern, region will follow.

Each region will be introduced by a general survey, and then will be examined in more detail by way of a series of area studies: four in the case of Pangasinan-Ilocos, and five in the case of Cagayan. These areas have been established through consideration of geographic, ethnic, and historic factors as outlined above. In advance of more specific definition, the framework of regions and areas, and the rationale for their delineation, may be seen in the following tabulation of basic features. It will be noted that all of northern Luzon is covered in a clockwise direction:

I. *The Pangasinan-Ilocos Region:* The northern Pangasinan area, and the narrow Ilocos coastal strip stretching north, backed by the Cordillera Central mountain range.

1. *The Pangasinan Area:* The Agno and other river systems linking plains and mountains; the ethnic group called Pangasinan predominant in the lowlands, that called Ibaloi on the adjacent Cordillera heights, Negritos and various groups called collectively Ilongot in mountains further east.
2. *The Southern Ilocos Area:* The Amburayan and upper Abra river systems; southern Ilocano in the lowlands, three related groups—Kankanai, Lepanto, and Bontok—in the mountains.
3. *The Central Ilocos Area:* Short coastal rivers, and the Abra river system and valley back of the coastal Ilocos range; central Ilocano in the lowlands, Tinguian in the mountains.
4. *The Northern Ilocos Area:* The Laoag and other river systems; northern Ilocano in the lowlands, northern Tinguian and western Isneg in the mountains.
II. *The Cagayan Region:* The Cagayan river valley, with many tributaries descending from the Cordillera Central to the east, the Sierra Madre range to the east, and the Caraballo Sur range to the south.
5. *The Northwest Cagayan Area:* The Abulug-Apayao river system; remnants of an old coastal population, along with immigrant Ilocano, in the lowlands, Negrito remnants in the foothills, and Isneg or Apayao in the mountains.
6. *The Lower Cagayan Area:* The generally swampy zone around the Cagayan river mouth, and the Sierra Madre mountain zone to the east; Ibanag in the lowlands, Negrito remnants in the foothills.
7. *The Chico River Area:* The Chico tributary of the Cagayan, draining most of the northeast sector of the Cordillera Central; Itavi in the lowlands, southern Isneg and various groups called collectively Kalinga in the mountains.
8. *The Middle Cagayan Area:* The middle reaches of the Cagayan river, with tributaries draining mountain zones to west and east; Ibanag and groups collectively called Christian Gaddang in the lowlands, non-Christian Gaddang, Negritos, and other groups in the mountains, a Christian group called Palanan on the bay of that name on the eastern, or Pacific, coast.
9. *The Upper Cagayan Area:* The headwaters of the Cagayan, and its major tributary, the Magat; Christian Gaddang, Yogad, and Isinai in the lower valley zones, Ifugao and Ibaloi on the Cordillera Central heights to the west, and scattered small groups called collectively Ilongot, together with some Negritos, in the mountains to the east and south.

The final chapter presents a review and interpretation of the materials seen as a whole. Extant migration theories are discussed in the light of the ethnohistorical records, and leads are given to show how the latter not only illumine anthropological information on the present-day peoples but also open out leads for further research. The concluding section suggests possible applications of this study to other zones of the world where lowland-highland relationships challenge investigation.

II. The Pangasinan-Ilocos Region:
General Perspectives

PLACE AND PEOPLE

The southern and western zones of northern Luzon, that is Pangasinan and Ilocos, with their mountain hinterlands, may be usefully considered first as a broad unit. This is because many significant records deal with them in an over-all way, particularly those delineating Spanish administrative and ecclesiastical activities, and the general responses of the local people —variously friendly or hostile.

The narrow lowland strip of the Ilocos coast stretches from north to south for approximately 160 miles. Back of it, the rugged mountain mass of the Cordillera Central rises at its highest points to nearly 10,000 feet. Its southern abutments drop away rather sharply to great plains, bordered by the Lingayen Gulf, and extending southward to the Manila area. Eastward, the Caraballo Sur mountains form a cross-range linking the Cordillera heights with the Sierra Madre range on the Pacific side of northern Luzon.

The foothills and flats south of the Cordillera Central comprise the northern part of Pangasinan Province. Those further east, that is, south of the Caraballo Sur range, lie in Nueva Ecija Province. The latter was created partly out of old Pangasinan, and partly out of Pampanga Province, which in earlier Spanish times extended into this region. The Ilocos coast, at first a single province, now comprises three such jurisdictions: from south to north, La Union, Ilocos Sur, and Ilocos Norte. The Cordillera heights mostly fall within Mountain Province, created in American times.

The river systems that drain to the south and west are generally swift-flowing, with deep gorges in their mountain reaches. Most notable are the Agno and Pampanga, passing southward to the plains, and the Abra, flowing to the sea about midway along the Ilocos coast. Other important waterways are (from south to north) the Bued, the Aringay-Galiano, the Naguilian, the Amburayan, and in the north the Laoag. Because water utilization is vital to the mountain peoples, the rivers played a key role in their upward migrations and in the establishment of their modern settlement patterns.

Climatic conditions in the area are defined by two major factors: the annually reversing direction of the monsoon winds, and the lie of the northern Luzon mountains across their path. The summer season, especially from June to September, is marked by rainfall along this coast, with precipitation tending to increase from south to north, so that Ilocos Norte has the third highest average rainfall during this season of any province in the Philippines; Ilocos Sur has the fourth highest; La Union has the fifth highest; and Pangasinan has the seventh highest. The western slopes of the Cordillera (Abra and the western side of Mountain Province) also have a very heavy precipitation—the southwestern heights around Baguio have the highest summer rainfall recorded for any part of the Philippines. By contrast, in the winter season, especially from December to March, the northeast monsoon is dry as it blows down over the Cordillera heights. Ilocos Sur, the central coastal province, has the lowest average rainfall for this season of any Philippine province, and droughts of more than a hundred days have been recorded. La Union has the second lowest, Ilocos Norte the third lowest, Pangasinan the fifth lowest. Further inland, however, the western sections of the Cordillera have a considerably higher winter precipitation (Philippine Census, 1918, and other sources).

Because of the extreme seasonal alternation in rainfall, the Ilocos coast flora is predominantly of the monsoon forest type rather than the tropical rainforest type. Only in the lower northern section of the Cordillera, comprising eastern Ilocos Norte and the Apayao subprovince of Mountain Province, are the monsoon winds moisture-laden through both seasons of the year, so that rainforests thrive. Approximately above the 3,500 foot level, the heights open out into grasslands, with pine forests on the higher ridges and peaks.

The Pangasinan and Ilocos lowlanders begin the annual cycle of their irrigated or wet rice crop with the opening of the wet season around the middle of the year. If, additionally, they plant nonirrigated or dry (upland) rice, it must be grown in the same season; as will be seen, it is rarely more than a very minor crop. In later times, a second wet rice crop has been grown in the dry winter season, but this is limited by water scarcity, and, except in northeast Pangasinan, production is minor compared with the main crop. Different types of rice require from about five to seven months to mature, staggering the harvest. Sugar cane is a significant crop here as elsewhere in north Luzon. Old-type root, vegetable, and fruit crops have been supplemented by a number of American plants, particularly sweet potatoes, maize, and tobacco. Here, too, precipitation is often a crucial factor. Notably the old cultivated or wild root crops, *gabe* or taro (*Colocasia antiquorum*), *ubi* or yam (*Dioscorea alata*), *tugue* (*Dioscorea sativa*, L.), and some others, require wet soil, and so are mainly rainy-season garden or forest products rather than field crops. Tolerating drier conditions, the *camote* or sweet potato (*Ipomoea batatas*) and maize, both of which were introduced in very early historic times, have become important crops. Even so, it is rare for more than one maize crop to be grown yearly. Tobacco, a major commercial resource, is a dry-season crop to be harvested before the rains damage the leaves, that is, in April-May.

The mountain peoples, while variously using all these crops, are less seasonally bound. The rices of the wet terracers are grown in the winter season from December on. Second cropping of rice in the summer is a very recent practice, and religious conservatism still makes its adoption a selective matter. Sweet potatoes, which thrive in the high country, are for some communities the principal dietary staple. The modern crop patterns by provinces are shown in the Appendix.

Barrows, visiting the Ilocos coast at the beginning of the American occupation, expressed amazement at the "narrowness of the Christian strip, a mere ribbon in width." Behind the towns, usually at most "two to five miles from the coast," were "rancherias of the *infieles*"—that is, the first of the "non-Christian," or "pagan," settlements (*A Preliminary Report*, p. 8). At the south end of the coast, and in the adjacent plains of Pangasinan Province, the basic ethnic group is called "Pangasinan," or in linguistic terms speakers of the "Pangasinan" language. Northward the coastal people are classed as "Ilocano," or in linguistic terms speakers of "Iloko." In modern times, land-hungry Ilocano migrants have spread southward into the Pangasinan area, where in many remoter districts they have come to outnumber the indigenous population, or *naturales*. They have also swarmed into the Cagayan region to the east of the Cordillera, and to quite an extent into other sections of the Philippines.

As the terrain rises, the Christian lowlanders thin out, giving place to the so-called non-Christian peoples, though many of the latter are now also Christianized. Scattered groups live in the mountain sections of the coastal provinces, but the bulk of them are within Mountain Province, with settlements occasionally up to the 8,000-foot level. They are often called by the over-all term "Igorot," meaning in the Tagalog language of the Manila area "mountaineer." More narrowly, this term has been applied to the mountain populations in the high south and central zones of the Cordillera.

The ethnic affiliations and characteristics of the mountain groups will emerge more fully as the study proceeds. On the southern heights are the "Ibaloi," with a language called by the variants "Nabaloi" or "Inibaloi." Northward along the western side of the Cordillera are the "Kankanai," sometimes referred to as "southern Kankanai," with next the "Lepanto" (a district name) or "northern Kankanai." Deeper in the mountains are the "Bontok." Where the high country falls away in elevation in the Abra valley area, the people are classed as "Tinguian" or "Tinggian." In the mountains of the extreme north are the "Isneg" or "Apayao." Similarly along the east side of the Cordillera are the "Ifugao," the "Gaddang," and the "Kalinga," this last name being in Cagayan dialects the word for "enemy." Other than Ibaloi, these are also used as language names. In foothill zones several pockets of Negritos have survived up to modern times. Among general surveys of these ethnic and linguistic groupings are publications by Beyer (Philippine Census, 1918), Keesing (1936), Kroeber (1943), and Le Bar and Graham (1955).

The derivation of the names Pangasinan and Ilocos cannot be established with certainty. Of Ilocos, Isabelo de los Reyes sums up in 1890 the views of Spanish historians by saying that the "general belief is that it was given to the area by the first Spaniards." He and others trace it to a root word of Luzon dialects (*ilog* in Tagalog, *alog* in Iloko), meaning "small waterway." From this, Spaniards supposedly first developed the name "Tagalog" for the groups around Manila, i.e., *taga-ilog*, "people of waterways." Correspondingly, this north coast area with its many streams was spoken of as an area of "ilogs," or "Ilocos." Pangasinan is supposedly derived from the root word *Pang-an*, meaning "river-bank."

De los Reyes cites another name "Samtoy," considered by some writers to have referred to the Ilocos region, but by others to a supposedly once prominent settlement there, or else to the Iloko language. The term is said to be derived from *sao-mi ditoy*, literally "one's own dialect," hence meaning to later Ilocanos their own speech.* This latter point raises the question whether there were significant linguistic or dialectal differences leveled out by the subsequent common use of a lingua franca. De los Reyes, after citing opinions of various church fathers and other linguists of his time, agrees with the "illustrious P. Carro" (*Vocabulario de la lengua ilocano*, 1849) that early Ilocos had "diverse dialects": Carro himself suggested that there were eight to ten such dialects. These differences were almost wholly leveled out by the standard Iloko idiom, though north and south Ilocos still have "many words" not mutually understood (de los Reyes, 1, 9, 66–72). How far the records can shed light on this linguistic problem will be seen.

De los Reyes also summarizes the existing knowledge of a syllabic script, with fifteen characters, which was employed in Ilocos apparently during pre-Spanish times, and was related to various similar scripts in southeast and east Asia. It was lettered on bamboo or leaves, and the extent of its use is not known. This historian of Ilocos also pictures the early popula-

---

* E.g., H. P. Williams and A. B. Guerrero, *English-Ilocano Manual and Dictionary*, Manila, 1929.

tion as spread out in "rancherias," comprising "a hundred families more or less, according to the size of the land they occupy." Secular leadership of each rancheria was provided, he says, by a chief, who acquired his title "by force" and governed with the aid of the "old respected men." Spiritual leadership, however, was in the hands of "priestesses," and religious beliefs pictured an array of deities and spirits, the latter including ghosts of the dead. His fairly lengthy reconstruction of pre-Spanish life, however (Volume One of his *Historia*), is so obviously based on interpretations from later Ilocano custom in the area that it needs critical sifting in ethnohistorical terms, as will be done in this study so far as records are available.

No detailed studies have been published of the modern Pangasinan people, though various comments on their characteristics will appear in the records. The Ilocanos have been delineated in general terms by Christie (1914) and Cole (1945), while specific communities are described by Orr (1942) for Ilocos Sur and by Nydegger (1960) for Ilocos Norte. In both Pangasinan and Ilocos there are large towns which are hubs for smaller settlements or pueblos, and especially in the Ilocano areas these in turn have scattered adherent hamlets or "barrios" and even individual homesteads in zones of newer colonization. Towns are centered on the plaza, with public buildings and the church, also the market and the more substantial homes, near by. A wealthy class provides the *principales* or "caciques," called in Iloko *baknang*, and at the other end of the scale are tenants and laborers; formerly there was peonage verging on slavery. Christie says that "at least two towns of considerable size" existed on the Ilocos coast prior to the coming of the Spaniards, indicating some degree of political cohesion—but this assertion will need to be tested by the records. Further descriptive materials will appear in the documents to follow.

When the Spaniards arrived, the northern Luzon peoples were not without sophistication as regards groups coming by ships from overseas lands. Chinese had been trading for centuries at suitable landing points along the coast, here as elsewhere in the Philippines. Japanese traders competed with them, and indeed an anchorage at Agoo near the south end of the Ilocos coast on the Lingayen Gulf is spoken of in the first Spanish records as the "Port of Japon." Inward trade included cloth, ceramic ware, semiprecious beads, and worked and unworked metals, while among goods taken out were gold, deerskins, carabao horn, beeswax, and fibers. In general, relations appear to have been those of friendly convenience. But the coastal settlements also suffered from severe raiding by pirates, both from the China-Formosa area and from Islamic zones further south in Malaysia, marked by looting and the capture of people for sale in the slave trade.

Spanish penetration and control of the Philippines was motivated particularly by the hope of locating rich gold deposits. A prime concern, therefore, of the initial Spanish expeditions to northern Luzon was that gold was being traded all over the area from "mines" located in the south and south-central sections of the Cordillera. The "Mother Lode" country comprised various localities on the heights, still worked today by commercial mining companies. Alluvial gold was also washed from streams along the southern and southwestern margins. Indigenous use of gold was mainly for ornaments and ceremonial insignia. For these purposes, too, copper was mined from extensive deposits in the Mankayan area in the south-central parts of the Cordillera.

It will be seen as a fair hypothesis that one of the major factors, if not the major factor, leading to the original settlement of these highest sections of the mountain chain by Filipino groups was this working of metals. Additionally, throughout these highlands, hunting and gathering could draw people in, particularly ranging after deer, wild carabao, wild pigs, honey and beeswax, and lumber, as the early records for both the Ilocos and the Cagayan sides of the Cordillera will show. To such factors will be added, from the beginnings of Spanish contact, the retreat of lowland groups to the mountains to escape Spanish pressure and control, which will be a major continuing thread, to be seen in the subsequent history of "runaways" and "rebellions," particularly on the Cagayan side.

INITIAL SPANISH CONTACTS

Spanish penetration of northern Luzon began in 1572, that is, some seven years after Legazpi's occupation of the Manila region. The first reference to Ilocos appears to be in a *Relation of the Conquest of Luzon,* dated April 20, 1572, which takes note of "a province called Yloquio, which is said to be very rich in gold mines; but the Spanish have not seen it as yet" (Blair and Robertson, to be abbreviated from here on as B&R, III, 171). The subject of gold comes up again and again in the early records, with Ilocos and Pangasinan named as among the principal sources of gold (see B&R, Index Volumes, "Mines, Mining, . . . Gold"). Copper mining, however, is not mentioned in the records until much later.

The initial exploration and pacification was carried out by Juan de Salcedo, youthful grandson of Legazpi, and "master-in-camp" of the Spanish military forces. As told by the historian Martinez de Zuñiga, whose *Historical Review* of the Philippines was published in 1803, Salcedo proceeded with 45 Spanish soldiers in small boats rowed by Indian oarsmen up the coast from Manila. Rounding Cape Bolinao,

he coasted the whole of [Pangasinan Province] . . . and that of Ylocos, until he arrived at Cape Boxeador, examining all the ports, bays, and landing places. . . . He was desirous of preserving a good understanding with the Indians, and most of the towns on the coast received him in a very friendly manner, and supplied him with provisions . . . ; but on his entering the rivers and creeks, he found great resistance from the inhabitants of the districts bordering on them. He attacked them on several occasions, putting them to flight with great ease, and sent to them, desiring them to leave the mountains, with a promise of his friendship. Some, however, . . . could not divest themselves of their apprehensions, while others readily came down, submitted, and agreed to pay the tribute.

Opposition broke out within Salcedo's party when he was about to round the north coast to Cagayan, so he moved south again to "Bigan" (Vigan, the present capital of Ilocos Sur Province), and built a fort. He then left his second-in-command there with 25 soldiers, and with the others resumed his journey in three boats to Cagayan and ultimately down the east coast to circle Luzon (Maver's English translation of Martinez de Zuñiga, i, 127–32).

Fuller materials on Salcedo's contacts with the different settlements along the coast, and on the flight of people to the mountains, will be given in the later area studies. They come primarily from records assembled by an Augustinian chronicler, Gaspar de San Agustin, in his *Conquests* (1698), and cited with additional comments by Isabelo de los Reyes (1890, ii, 9–20). These and other records indicate that Salcedo stayed over not only in Ilocos because of his interest in the local gold, but also on the east coast opposite Manila, where there were also mines from which gold was being extensively traded. He brought back to Manila, according to an Augustinian father, Ortega, writing in mid-1573 to the Viceroy in Spain, "a thousand taes [a tae being a weight of an ounce or a little more] of gold in addition to as many more which he shared between himself and the soldiers." Salcedo was then sent back by the Governor with an additional party of soldiers to "colonize Ylocos" (B&R, xxxiv, 257–59, 286–87).

Another Augustinian father, Rada, writing in 1574 to the Viceroy, gives an account of Salcedo's methods of entry, as seen through ecclesiastical eyes:

[Although the people] never attacked the Spaniards, still they defended themselves in all their villages, and would not surrender unless conquered by force of arms. Consequently all those villages were entered in the same way, by first summoning them to submit peacefully, and to pay tribute unless they wished war. They replied that they would first prove those to whom they were to pay tribute, and consequently, the Spaniards attacking them, an entrance was made among them by force of arms, and the village was overthrown and whatever was found pillaged. Then the Spaniards sent to have the natives summoned to submit peacefully. When the natives came, they asked them to immediately give them tribute in gold and to an excessive amount, for which they promised to give them writs of peace. (B&R, xxxiv, 286–87.)

Legazpi died in 1572, and his successor as Governor, Lavezaris, decided to dispatch a follow-up expedition to Ilocos. The stated purpose was to "inspect the population and the villages which were to be divided up into repartimientos," that is, holdings for the collection of tribute, following the *repartimiento* or encomienda pattern established already in the American colonies. Disliking Salcedo, he put Colonel Martin de Goite in charge. The Augustinian quoted above, Ortega, reports of this expedition:

[With him was] Captain Lorenço Chacon with more than 130 soldiers and more than 800 Indians who rowed the boats in which they went. Without discovering any new lands or seeing any new villages besides those which . . . [Salcedo] had discovered and pacified, they collected in tribute three thousand taes or more [of gold].

Ortega explains indignantly to the Viceroy in Spain that such tribute collection was being done before the proper time and "contrary to the law of God and the directions of his Majesty [the King of Spain]." "The first thing they do when they reach any village or province is to send them an interpreter or two, not with gifts or presents, not to preach to them . . . , but to order them to bring tribute immediately and to be friendly with the Castilians." As such people are not accustomed to being "vassals of any native king or lord," he continues, all this is "confusion to them and causes them much evil." Lacking other wanted property, they are forced to "give as tribute the necklaces which they wear about their necks and the bracelets they and their women wear on their arms."

When these evil abuses are inflicted upon them, some of them refuse to give the tribute or do not give as liberally as those who ask it desire. Others, on account of having to give this and of their fear at seeing a strange and new race of armed people, abandon their houses and flee to the tingues [i.e., hills] and mountains. When the Spanish see this, they follow them, discharging their arquebuses at them and mercilessly killing as many as they can. Then they go back to the village and kill all the fowls and swine there and carry off all the rice. . . . After this and after they have robbed them of everything they have in their miserable houses, they set fire to them.

In this way, Ortega claims, the expedition burned and destroyed "more than four thousand houses" and "killed more than five hundred Indians"— and boasted with pride of having "committed that exploit." As a consequence of such "killing and robbing . . . and collecting as enemies," the region will take at least six years to "reach its former state," or in the opinion of some more than "a lifetime" (B&R, xxxiv, 259–61).

Shortly after these happenings, a memorandum was prepared by the Augustinian fathers covering "matters to be discussed with his Majesty or his royal Council of the Yndias" by one of their number who was returning to Spain. This statement reiterates the charges made above of the tribute "exactions" and the "pillaging of villages" where the people "abandon their houses."

We Spaniards are held in ignominy . . . and our name is held in abomination. . . . [We] are considered as the usurpers of others' possessions, as faithless pirates, and as shedders of human blood, because we illtreat our own friends, and harass and trouble them; while many acts of violence are used toward them both to their own houses and to their wives and daughters and possessions. . . . There has been no punishment inflicted for all the above. . . . Consequently, great dissoluteness has reigned.

Among the specific instances cited, the memorandum tells how along all the coast of "Ylocos" and "Bulinau," the two principal gold sources known at the time in Luzon, "raids have been made twice in one year." Of the initially established encomiendas, and the encomenderos to whom they had been allotted, it says:

With no greater pacification than the above, the land is assigned and divided, whereupon the encomendero, taking some companions with him, goes to the village or villages which have been given to him, and makes them the following speech: "Take heed that I am your master, and that the governor has given you to me to protect from other Spaniards who annoy you." This is the universal reasoning of most of them, and they make no mention of God or the king. Then they immediately demand the tribute. . . . They have generally asked three or four taes [of gold] apiece from the Lusones [Luzon island peoples]. . . . If some of the people do not wait for the encomendero in order to agree to give him the tribute, their houses and village are burned. Many of the encomenderos stay in their encomiendas all or the greater part of the year . . . where they prove a great hindrance or obstacle to their Indians. (B&R, xxxiv, 273–78.)

The division of the Ilocos region into encomiendas was done by Salcedo, with whom the new Governor became reconciled, so that he was named Lieutenant-Governor of Ilocos. Rada, the Augustinian quoted previously, judges the Governor to have been "very partial," in that of "three companies" of soldiers who had come together from New Spain, holdings here were granted to Salcedo's company only. He reiterates "how unjust has been the affair of the Ylocos, for they have done nothing there for two years back but make raids," and "now they have gone to collect the tribute for the third time." In a document written a little later he asks: "With what right have three extortions, of large amounts of gold, been made on the Ylocos, without having any other intercourse with them, beyond going there?" (B&R, iii, 255; xxxiii, 287–88.) Governor Lavezaris, however, in a 1573 report to the King, tells his side of the Ilocos situation:

I shall continue the *repartimiento* of this land, in those places discovered by Captain Juan de Salcedo. . . .—on the coast of Yloco; for it would be impossible for this fleet to sustain itself in any other way, on account of the great privation and poverty endured in the past and present by the soldiers, especially since they are not now permitted to make raids. These were wont to be made formerly in order to support themselves; but they proved of great harm and prejudice to the natives. (B&R, iii, 188.)

The reference here is to the production of income not only for private encomenderos but also from certain encomiendas allotted to the Spanish

Crown, in order to produce income for such public purposes as the maintenance of war vessels, forts, public works, ecclesiastical establishments, and hospitals. The private holdings were allotted to officials and military veterans or their surviving families. Both the Royal and private tributes had to be paid in part for support of the Church.

In 1574, an official, Mirandaola, in a letter to the King, discusses the gold sources of "Ylocos." There are mines, he states, "in the neighborhoods of Balatao, Turrey, Alingay, and Dinglas. . . . These are very rich mines, from which, it is said, much gold is extracted, and there are many metals and rivers which have not yet been examined." "Balatao" (Baratao) and "Alingay" (Aringay) are names of villages in an encomienda established on the Ilocos coast adjacent to the gold-bearing southern heights of the Cordillera; "Turrey" probably refers to an encomienda called Purao (later Balaoan) somewhat further north; and "Dinglas" or Dingras was an encomienda in what has become Ilocos Norte. Mirandaola also discusses three kinds of gold traded "around Manila," one of which is called "Lunguinquin." By this could be meant gold from Lingayen, the principal center of Pangasinan, and if so it would also have come from sources in the southern Cordillera (B&R, III, 223–24).

In a later communication to the King, Lavezaris tells of his activities in colonizing the area with Spaniards:

Inasmuch as this island of Lucon is so large, and as, for the preservation of the natives, we need some settlements of Spaniards to protect and defend them, and teach them our holy Catholic faith, it seemed best to send Captain Juan de Salcedo with seventy or eighty soldiers to people the coast of Ilocos, on the shores of a river called Bigan. There I ordered him to found the town of Fernandina in memory of the prince, our master (may he live many happy years); and I continued to apportion, in the name of your Majesty, all that had been discovered and won over thereabout, reserving for your Majesty what you had ordered me through your royal decree. (B&R, III, 276.)

Fernandina, or Villa Fernandina, was named for the first-born son of Felipe II, born in 1571. It is the present Vigan, capital of Ilocos Sur, and site of Salcedo's initial fort.

A *Relation* by Governor Sande (1576) tells how the authorities sent a "galliot" from Manila in 1574 to follow up Salcedo's initial contacts along the Cagayan coast, and the latter, who was in Ilocos at the time, got it to put in for provisions at "some villages of Cinay" (the Sinait area), north of Fernandina. This ship, however, was sacked by a famous Chinese corsair or "pirate" of the time, Limahon or Limahong, so that the permanent settlement of Cagayan did not commence until five years later. Sande tells how Salcedo sent a message to Manila with information on Limahon's presence in the area by a *virey*, a "small boat" used by the "natives of these islands" (in Iloko *viray* means "sailing boat"). Meantime Limahon directed his large fleet of 62 vessels southward in an attempt to capture Manila. En route he plundered the settlement at Fernandina. He then attacked the capital and succeeded in setting fire to it. But a relief force from Ilocos headed by Salcedo helped to save the city from investment. Limahon then withdrew his forces to Pangasinan. As told by the historian Martinez de Zuñiga (1803), he made an "amicable arrangement" with a local chief "on an inlet of the river Lingayen," and then formed an encampment, which he fortified "with a strong stockade."

The Governor, after putting down some disaffection among the people around Manila, sent a military force by sea against Limahon. In 1575 the squadron, with 250 Spanish soldiers and 1,500 "friendly Indians," entered the Lingayen river by night. The Chinese fled from their ships, which were captured, and a "most sanguinary engagement" followed. The Spanish forces invested the outer part of the fort; but busy with plundering rather than pressing the attack, they were expelled by the hard core of the corsair's forces. A siege was instituted, but after four months Limahon and his followers escaped in thirty boats built inside the fort (Maver's translation of Martinez de Zuñiga, 1, 145–52; B&R, IV, 38–44; V, 109).

Out of this Limahon affair came an item of lore, which gathered credence among later Spanish chroniclers, namely, that some of Limahon's men escaped by fleeing to the Cordillera heights, becoming the ancestors of the "Igorots." References occur to the supposedly lighter skin color and slanting eyes of the mountaineers in the southern part of the Cordillera. A statement, for example, from Antonio Mozo, an Augustinian historian writing in 1763, illustrates this view:

It is said that the Igolot tribe are a caste of those Chinese who had come over with the pirate Limahon . . . ; being conquered, he escaped with those whom he could gather, those who could taking refuge in these mountains in which they multiplied exceedingly. . . . [They] greatly resemble the Chinese in the light color and gracefulness of their bodies, especially in the eyes. (B&R, XLVIII, 82.)

An alternate version is that these southern mountaineers were descendants of Chinese who were "shipwrecked" on the coasts "long before the Spaniards arrived" (quoting here Baltazar de Santa Cruz in 1676, B&R, XXXVII, 243). In the same way, some Spanish writers asserted that the Tinguians of the Abra valley resembled Chinese, and were the descendants of early Chinese settlers. Assertions were also made that the Isneg or Apayao people of the north end of the Cordillera, and the Ifugao on its southeast side facing the upper Cagayan, were wholly or in part descendants of Japanese. Only with studies by anthropologists in modern times, in which all the mountain peoples were placed within the normal physical and cultural range of the Philippine population at large, were such ideas countered. Undoubtedly, however, sporadic unions did occur with Chinese and Japanese shipmen and settlers, especially along the coasts. Chinese mestizo groups also developed in the towns.

Records of this time describe the mountain peoples in very general terms, usually applied to the Philippines as a whole. Sande possibly includes the northern Luzon mountain peoples in a description of this broad kind, though the principal reference appears to be to zones further south:

Inland in the islands, and away from the rivers, dwells another race who resemble the Chichimecos of Nueva España, very savage and cruel, among whom are some Negroes. All use bows and arrows, and consider it meritorious to kill men, in order to keep the heads of the slain as ornaments for their houses. They are the most despised people in these islands and are called *Tinguianes,* or "mountaineers"; for *tingue* means "mountain." They have quantities of honey and wax, and trade these commodities with the lowlanders. (B&R, IV, 68–69.)

"Chichimeco," though a regional name, was often applied by the Spaniards at the time to the remoter mountain Indians of Mexico. Sande also records the death of Salcedo in 1576. While "collecting tribute," he had an attack of "the sickness that kills old and young." Sande adds: "It is not safe to go unarmed or carelessly in that country." Martinez de Zuñiga fills out this account by saying that Salcedo died while "visiting a mine in his domains," through drinking cold water during a bout of fever (B&R, IV, 24–26, 118; Maver's translation of Martinez de Zuñiga, I, 157).

EARLY DESCRIPTIONS

The first account of the resources other than gold in the Ilocos area seems to be in a letter from Moldinaldo to the King in 1572: "Ylucos . . . is very fertile, abounding in provisions: rice, fowls, swine, goats, buffaloes, deer, and many kinds of lake-birds, all in great abundance" (B&R, III, 297). About three years later an encomendero complained of receiving no tribute from his encomienda except 176 "pieces of white cloth" collected by his agent. The Ilocos cotton textiles, including "blankets," were later to become an important trade product, even being sent to America (B&R, III, 310–11; XXIII, 280; XXVII, 177). In 1582, Miguel de Loarca gives a remarkably full description of the area and peoples (B&R, V, 81–151). Of the "province of Pangasinan," he says:

Its bay is about six leagues around. Three large rivers, which flow from the mining district of the mountains, fall into this bay. This province has a peaceful population of four thousand. The land is allotted to six encomenderos; but the best portion of it, which has one thousand men, belongs to his Majesty. . . . This province abounds in food supplies, such as rice, goats, and swine; and many buffaloes are hunted. . . . [The lowland people] sell their articles of food and clothing to the miners; the gold that they obtain in return for these they barter with the Spaniards.

The population figure given here clearly refers to the pacified sections of the privince only; as will be seen, much of the region was still not under control. Loarca also notes that an alcalde-mayor, or civil magistrate, had been governing it for "two years," that is, since about 1580, located at Lingayen, and that "from the province one can go by land to Manilla, over a very smooth and good road." He speaks of the Pangasinan people as "more intelligent" than their western neighbors in the Zambales mountain area, "for they are traders and traffic with Chinese, Japonese, Borneans, and the natives of other islands."

Where the coastal flats of the Lingayen Gulf narrow at the southwest abutment of the Cordillera, Loarca places the settlement of Agoo, otherwise called "the Port of Japon" because Salcedo encountered Japanese trading vessels there and it was apparently a regular port of call for them. A short distance north were the "villages of Aringuey" (modern Aringay) and "Baratao," with a combined population of 2,000. In this area, he says, the people were "of the same race as those who inhabit Pangasinan." Next up the coast came the "villages of Purao," whose inhabitants "differ from the Pangasinan people . . . in language but resemble them in customs." Loarca notes, however, that "these people do not kill their children, as do the people of Pangasinan." This reference cannot be clarified for want of information on the handling of children in old Pangasinan: it could refer to deformed infants or to the killing of one of twins. No mention is made, in the recital of "villages," "valleys," and "provinces" along the Ilocos coast, of any other linguistic breakline.

Loarca gives a total population count from Purao northward of 26,100. This represents a denser pattern of settlement, or at least a higher proportion of people pacified, than in Pangasinan. Between the most northerly known locality, Vicagua (the later Bacarra) and the mouth of the Cagayan river, a distance of "twenty leagues," were "some rivers and settlements, but the inhabitants are not pacified or even known." The Spanish measure of a league varies, but is usually nearly four miles. Cagayan, as will be seen, had been settled by the Spaniards in 1581, that is, just previous to this account.

Of the "people of Ylocos" in general, Loarca says: "[They] resemble the Pintados [of the central Philippines] in their manner of living, but they eat raw meat. They are a quiet and peaceful people, dislike war, and are humble and well-disposed." He tells of their trade with the Cagayan peoples, and also with the Babuyan Islands north of Luzon. Of the latter, he says that "many swine are imported therefrom into the province of Ylocos," so that the islands are named after the "word for swine in the Ylocos language" (*babuy*). This is the first reference to a distinctive Ilocos speech. It suggests that, whatever local dialectal variations existed, Iloko was becoming, or had already become, the trading lingua franca of northwestern

Luzon. Loarca also discusses the "Tinguianes" or mountain peoples. His references are generalized, however, so that it is not clear how far they apply to peoples in the northern Luzon Cordillera: "The inhabitants of the mountains cannot live without fish, salt, and other articles of food, and the jars and dishes of other districts; nor on the other hand can those of the coast live without the rice and cotton of the mountaineers."

He cites an origin myth by which the "Tinguianes" explain human differences:

[Those] who fled to the most hidden rooms [the mountaineers] are the chiefs . . . ; those who remained nearer the outside are the timaguas [ordinary people]; those who hid themselves in the walls are the slaves; those who hid themselves in the fireplace are the blacks; and those who fled out to sea through the open door are the Spaniards . . . [and] they had no news of us until they beheld us return through the sea.

The mountaineers consider it "a point of honor to take revenge" when wronged: "[They] set out [on raids] after they have gathered the harvests, and since their custom is to be enemies to those who are such to their friends, they do not lack opportunity for fighting." The account goes on to say that enemies are taken alive, to be sold as slaves, and also that while the chiefs monopolize any captured "booty," a small portion is given to the "timaguas" or ordinary people who "go with them as oarsmen." Certainly this part of the narrative could hardly apply to peoples living along the rarely navigable streams of the Cordillera.

In 1583, Fray Domingo de Salazar, in an account of *Affairs in the Filipinas Islands,* speaks of "La Pampanga," the Pampanga river area southeast and south of Pangasinan, as a region from which "all this country used to be supplied with rice, wine [possibly both rice wine and sugar-cane wine], and fowls."

[From here] a great number of Indians went to the mines of Ylocos, whence they remained during the time when they ought to have saved their grain. Many of them died there, and those who returned were so fatigued that they needed rest more than work. As a result, in that year followed a very great scarcity of rice, and for lack of it many of the Indians died from hunger.

Salazar notes that another debilitating factor was that "many" of the Pampanga men were employed by the Spaniards to man galleys and cut timber for shipbuilding, and therefore they might be absent for four to six months. Others would "run away and hide in the mountains, to escape from the toils imposed upon them." Much of this document is a diatribe against the continuing evils of the encomienda system, with "confiscations" and "forced collections" of rice, at times "even all" being taken, so that the people "sow little and reap less." Encomenderos might even include "tortures" as means of getting tribute (B&R, v, 211–26). This delineation, even if somewhat colored by a churchman's viewpoint, gives a vivid glimpse of early acculturative events. The movements of refugee groups from Pampanga back into the mountains, combined with a kind of gold rush triggered off by the Spanish mania for gold, doubtless swelled the populations later to be called broadly "Igorot" along the southern face of the Cordillera, or else "Ilongot" further east in the Caraballo Sur mountains, of which more later. It is not made clear, however, whether some at least of the people who went to the "mines of Ylocos" were impressed by the Spanish to do so, as part of their early attempts to control and develop the mines, or whether the movement was voluntary.

An unsigned and undated document of the time in the archives of the Indies fills out this picture in some other respects:

Ylocos . . . contains a Spanish settlement, Villa Fernandina. . . . That province is densely populated and contains larger settlements than the other provinces. The people are however more barbarous. . . . They are husbandmen and possess very large fields. Consequently it is a land abounding in rice and cotton. . . . [There is] considerable gold. . . . Those people enjoy it for they have more communication with the miners than anyone else.

Of the gold, this document says, Governor Ronquillo is "hot after it"; but the search had already "cost him many men" as the "land is very rude and food is scarce." Governor Ronquillo de Penalosa, referred to here, was in office from 1580 to 1583. Ilocos had by then "many churches and Christians." In sum, the anonymous writer judged the people to be "very simple, domestic, and peaceful" (B&R, xxxiv, 382–83). Even so, a writer in 1586 could still say that the Ilocos people were "pagan and idolatrous—worshipping the devil, offering sacrifices and payment for the quantities of gold that [the devil] gave them" (B&R, vi, 146). A factor contributing to the peacefulness of the Ilocos peoples appears to have been the difficulty these coastal dwellers, with their narrow ribbon of flat land and relatively dense settlement pattern, would have had in resisting Spanish military control. Such control was exercised by sea as well as by land, while back of them were hostile mountain peoples.

MISSIONS, COMMERCE, AND POLITICAL CONSOLIDATION

The story of the initial mission work in Pangasinan and Ilocos is surprisingly obscure, considering the voluminousness of ecclesiastical records of early times. The Augustinian Order is usually given credit for sending the first resident "religious" (used as a noun for a priest or brother) to the northern Luzon area. The historian de los Reyes, however, reviews an interesting controversy among later ecclesiastical chroniclers as to whether or not they were preceded by Franciscan fathers. He himself accepts the view that Franciscans opened the first church establishment in Vigan, and pioneered the initial conversions. First to arrive, he believes, was Fray

Juan Bautista Pizarro, who came in 1578 to Vigan, and then was followed by fathers Ortiz and Ayora. He acknowledges, however, that there were other authorities who claimed that Augustinian fathers founded a "convent" in Vigan in 1575, while some considered that Pizarro was really an Augustinian rather than a Franciscan (de los Reyes, II, 93–44).

The Franciscan records of the early work of their Order set out in the Blair and Robertson volumes do not mention Ilocos. Augustinian archives, too, apparently do not refer to any workers in northern Luzon prior to 1584. At that time, fathers of the Order opened mission work in Pampanga villages and then continued northward into Pangasinan and Ilocos. In 1587 they were joined in Pampanga and Pangasinan by Dominicans, and a division of territory was made soon afterward between the religious Orders by which the Dominicans took over the Pangasinan work while the Augustinians continued to hold the Ilocos coast.

In 1586, a *Memorial* notes that some of the "provinces" of Luzon "have never been conquered" to that date, or if once subdued "have revolted again." Included in the list is Pangasinan, along with the mountainous Zambales region to the west and southwest of it (B&R, VI, 185). This reference suggests that the area was marked by unrest, such as was recorded above for adjacent Pampanga to the southeast. Somewhat in contrast, a *Relation* by Salazar (whose earlier *Affairs* was quoted previously), who was writing with other commentators in the period 1586–88, says of Pangasinan that it was "pacified." It had at the time 5,000 "tributarios" (the tribute-paying population), of whom 1,500 were held by the King and the rest by five private encomenderos. The region was still "without instruction," that is, no mission work had been started there.

"Ylocos," this document continues, "is inhabited for forty leagues inland," which apparently means up the coast for the approximately 160 miles to the Cape Bojeador area. It had 27,000 tributarios, of whom 6,000 were held by the King and the rest by fourteen encomenderos. In addition, "there is a considerable population of mountaineers who recognize no master." The calced (shod) Augustinian Order had started mission work, and had five "religious" in four "houses" or districts. The province had an alcalde-mayor, and the small town of Fernandina had some resident Spaniards. Another document of the time remarks that the "magistracy of Ylocos," when put up for "auction," had brought in only 300 pesos, and so was "unprofitable" (B&R, VII, 35–37, 86).

Various records of this period relate to trade with visiting Chinese and Japanese merchants. Frequently, it was said, rather than making the sometimes stormy voyage down the coast to Manila, they discharged their cargoes at Lingayen Gulf or Ilocos coast landing places, to be carried by local trail or sea transport to the capital. At the same time "many Chinese" were coming from China or from Manila to the provinces of "Pangasinan,

Ylocos, and Cagayan." Cloth was a principal trade article, doubtless reflecting in part the missionary insistence on wearing clothes appropriate to Christian converts. There is even a special report on this phase of trade which has a modern ring: "When the natives . . . saw these large quantities of cloth brought by the Sangleys [Chinese], and that these were so cheap, they were unwilling to weave cloth, as they were wont to do before the Spaniards had come and before the Sangleys had brought cloth to them." Japanese interest in the Philippines waxed high at this period, and a document reports that the Japanese were seizing Chinese vessels in Ilocos and Cagayan in an attempt to gain both political and commercial advantage. "Thefts and damages" by Japanese were also reported, especially in Ilocos and the newly opened Cagayan area. Forts were built at this period in Cagayan for "protection against Indian, Japanese and Chinese robbers" (B&R, vii, 165; ix, 74).

In 1591, three Spanish military expeditions crossed from northeast Pangasinan over the Caraballo Sur range to explore the headwaters of the Cagayan valley. As will be seen in the Cagayan study, they called the upper Magat river valleys into which they struck "Tuy," in its later form usually Ituy. The initial expedition reported being "attacked by the Zambales" en route. This name has its stricter application to the peoples of the Zambales mountains west and southwest of Pangasinan. But it was also used by some early writers to apply more generally to uncontrolled mountain peoples in the Pangasinan area. The records indicate that the Zambales took every opportunity to "impede the general traffic" both across the plains and down the coast by robberies and killings (B&R, viii, 200–225, 241, 251, 305).

De los Reyes devotes several pages of his history of Ilocos to a critique of the encomienda system in the region, including disputes between the Church fathers and the encomenderos regarding "abuses" (ii, 46–54). In 1591, an "Encomienda List" for the Philippines gives a brief survey of each encomienda in the region, and these materials will be presented in detail in the sections that follow. In its over-all significance, the survey shows Pangasinan as still having six encomiendas, which were yielding "about 6,000 whole tributes" from 24,000 persons—the rate of four persons to each tribute being an old method of estimating population totals under the encomienda system. By then the area had eight Augustinian mission workers, servicing "2,400 souls," the reference here being apparently to converts of ecclesiastically responsible age. All encomiendas were said to have "justice" in the sense that the province had a civil administration under the alcalde-mayor, though not all had "peace" in the sense of being fully pacified.

In Ilocos there were correspondingly seventeen encomiendas, yielding 17,130 tributes from 68,520 persons. All had "peace" and "justice." Eight had resident Augustinian workers, whereas some of the others were "visited" from the "monastery" centers where in all 20 ecclesiastics were in residence. Notably the two principal settlements Vigan (Fernandina), and Laoag in the north, which later was to become the capital of Ilocos Norte, were among the King's holdings (B&R, I, 40; VIII, 104-8).

In 1593, Governor Dasmarinas ordered that the annual encomienda tribute be raised from its initial rate of "ten reals" to "twelve reals," eight reals being equivalent at the time to one peso. This was a principal factor in generating a major "rebellion" in Cagayan, and it caused unrest even in the more settled districts (B&R, IX, 243-44).

By 1594, or about a decade after the Augustinians had opened their mission work in the area, one of the fathers, Ortega, wrote that of "about seventy thousand souls" under encomienda control in the provinces of Ilocos and Pangasinan, "very few . . . are baptized." He estimated the number at less than 8,000. Pangasinan and Ilocos, he said, required a further "thirty ministers" for their "conversion and instruction." In Pampanga, to the southeast and south, baptized persons were also "few" (B&R, IX, 101-3).

In 1587, it was said above, Dominican fathers joined the Augustinians in an attempt to convert the stubborn Pangasinan people. Shortly afterward, this Order took over the main Pangasinan field, leaving the work from Agoo northward up the Ilocos coast to the Augustinians. At the request of the Governor, too, the Dominicans assumed responsibility for the Cagayan mission field, including the provincial capital at Nueva Segovia where Augustinians had worked for a time. In 1595, a "Bishopric of Nueva Segovia" was formed, with its seat in that capital, and all ecclesiastical work in Pangasinan, Ilocos, and Cagayan was placed under the jurisdiction of the Bishop. The seat was to be transferred in 1755 to Vigan in Ilocos, not least of all for greater accessibility.

One of the most outstanding early Augustinian fathers, Fray Esteban Marin, was particularly known for his activities among the mountain groups. After a period in Pangasinan, he was stationed at various points in Ilocos. In the course of his work he is said to have compiled a Zambal-Spanish dictionary and a grammar and dictionary of the Igorot language. He is also credited with baptizing "more than 2,000" Igorots. Such converts were drawn out of the high country and so became assimilated into the lowland milieu (B&R, XXXVII, 244-45; de los Reyes, II, 55).

Marin is described as "establishing" villages of converts. This hints at a pattern of resettling hitherto more scattered residential groups, which is made explicit in other ecclesiastical records as a feature of mission policy in the area, in cooperation of course with civil authorities. It is illustrated by a Dominican historian, Diego Aduarte (1640), writing of communities at the southern base of the Cordillera, San Jacinto and Manaoag (B&R, XXXI, 140, 258-60):

[The] church and village [of San Jacinto] was formed here of people from different regions, on a very pleasant river named Magaldan, the inhabitants gathering to it from several villages and some from the mountains of the region.

The first entry [to Manaoag] was by Augustinians. . . . But the village was so small [that it did not justify continuous residence, hence] it was seldom visited and little good resulted. . . . Fray Juan de San Jacintho [went there in 1605, and] the fact was spread abroad among the villages. . . . Some other hamlets were added to that one, and the village of Manaoag was made of reasonable size.

An Augustinian historian, Juan de Medina (1630), in reviewing the initial establishment of missions at the various centers in Ilocos, also speaks of such resettlement. He is explaining why the early fathers could not "be neglectful": "For scarcely has one left them for any short space of time, when they return to their natural way of life . . . just like a bow which, when strung, is bent; but, when unstrung, at once straightens and regains its former position." He then goes on to say:

The Ilocans lead all the other Indians in being clean and neat and in having large settlements. However, that is due to the early religious, who settled them in villages, and the people have remained settled so thoroughly. Had the like been done in other provinces, the religious would not have suffered so greatly.

A late-nineteenth-century father, Coco, who edited an edition of Medina and added many notations, is quoted by Blair and Robertson as making the following footnote observation:

Unless the Father is vigilant, nothing useful is done. . . . If he relaxes, all the good . . . disappears. . . . The greater number of the Ilocan plains are crossed by irrigation canals, brought to completion by the initiative of the fathers, and preserved until now by the watchfulness of the same persons.

Medina clearly believed that concentration of settlement, with technological advances over their "natural way of life," resulted from the initial mission work and was not the pre-Spanish pattern (B&R, XXIII, 247, 276-79).

Various attempts were made by Spanish military expeditions and by missionaries during the late sixteenth century to penetrate the Cordillera heights. But these met with consistent failure, as will be seen in the appropriate chapters to follow. With pacification and Hispanization of the lowland groups, and resistance by the mountain groups, the lines were drawn between Christian and non-Christian, which were to last up to modern times. At most, mission workers were able to whittle away at the edges of the mountain populations, transferring converts down to the lowland communities. Not until the nineteenth century could inland mission centers be established with more than ephemeral existence. In the same way, the few military expeditions that tried to establish permanent bases had to be withdrawn because of logistic difficulties and the hostility of the mountaineers. Most expeditions were merely hit-and-run affairs for "punitive" purposes.

An early example of such a venture occurred in 1601, when Mateo de Aranda commanded a force that was sent by order of the Governor against the "Ygolotes." The particular coastal zone where the party struck in is not specified in the records. The Augustinian Marin was appointed as interpreter because of his knowledge of the language and the supposed "confidence" the "insurgents" reposed in him. An attempt to make peaceful contacts failed, and the party was ambushed by a large group of mountaineers. Marin was among those killed by a flight of arrows, and the survivors had to withdraw (B&R, xxxvii, 244–45; de los Reyes, ii, 72).

In 1609, a *Relation* by Dr. Juan Manuel de la Vega reviews the sketchy knowledge to that time of the "Ygolote" country and people. These materials will be analyzed in the Pangasinan chapter to follow. Here it need only be noted that he speaks of gold as being traded both into the upper Cagayan valley and into "certain towns of Pangasinan." In the latter, the "Ygolotes . . . exchange it for food—hogs, carabaos, and rice. . . . The natives do not cultivate the land—for one reason, because of its great sterility, and the lack of ground to cultivate" (B&R, xiv, 301–6, 315). In the same year, Morga, in a notable account of "events" in the Philippines, comments on the gold trade as seen from the Ilocos side:

On the slopes of the mountains, in the interior, live many natives, as yet unsubdued, and among whom no incursion has been made, who are called Ygolotes. These natives possess rich mines, many of gold and silver mixed. They are wont to dig from them only the amount necessary for their wants. They descend to certain places to trade this gold . . . with the Ylocos; there they exchange it for rice, swine, carabaos, cloths, and other things that they need.

He goes on to say that the Ygolotes "do not refine or prepare" the gold, this being done by the "Ylocos," who then handle its distribution. If this statement is true, the mountain peoples at the time were washing out the raw metal only, and their methods of refining gold and copper, which will be noted later, would be subsequent acquisitions. At least, with the vigorous demand for gold, the simplest way for handling the product, so far as it was to be traded to the lowlands, would be to sell it unworked. Morga reports that in his time, nearly four decades after the Spanish began their attempts to locate and control the mining areas, the mountain people were still thwarting such efforts. "The Ygolotes fear that the Spaniards will go to seek them for their gold, and say that they keep the gold better in the earth than in the houses." It will be noted that the coastal peoples were being called the "Ylocos" by Morga, who was thus applying the geographic name as an ethnic appellation.

In 1612, a survey was made of the "Status of Missions" throughout the Philippines, as the result of a Royal order requesting information on progress to that time, and on further needs for ecclesiastical establishments and personnel. For Pampanga Province the Augustinians reported a total of 28,200 Indians "in confession," paying 9,500 tributes, and being served by 26 ministers from ten mission centers, along with their "visitas" or visiting places. On the Ilocos coast they had thirteen centers, with their visitas, in which 31 ministers were serving a total of 42,800 Indians "in confession," these paying in all 14,600 tributes. The Dominicans by then had four centers in Pangasinan, with eight fathers and two lay brothers serving about 3,630 Indians and also the "new conversion in the tingues (i.e., mountains) of the Manaoag district" (B&R, XVII, 193, 195–97, 211). The details of this useful survey will be set out in the regional sections to follow.

The problem of achieving stability in northern Luzon during these early years cannot be appreciated fully apart from at least passing reference to the larger power struggles in the western Pacific, which at times rendered Spain's hold on the Philippines a precarious one. Drake's expeditions, and conflicts with the British over possession of key points in southeast Asia, are part of this picture (e.g., Bartolomé Leonardo de Argensola, *Discovery and Conquest of the Moluco and Philippine Islands,* in English translation, 1719). For example, an expedition of 300 Spaniards and about 1,500 Filipinos, including bowmen from Ilocos and Cagayan, was sent to the Moluccas in an attempt to recover forts in those islands from the British. The Japanese and Chinese threatened invasions, and outbreaks among resident Chinese led to fighting and massacres. Struggles between Spanish forces and "Moro" groups in the southern Philippines and Borneo were to drag on to American times, and Moro pirates "infested the seas," as de los Reyes put it. Struggles also set in with the Dutch in the seventeenth century.

An interesting set of instructions was issued in 1592 by the Philippine Governor, Gomez Perez Dasmarinas, which spelled out precautions to be taken in the face of an expected invasion of Luzon at that time by Japanese forces. Officials were directed to send word of the menace "throughout the coasts," including those of "Ylocos," while the religious Orders were given instructions that would help to "protect" the indigenous population. One measure suggested was that gold ornaments of the local people be taken into protective custody and sent for "safety" to Manila; this, the Governor says, would have the added usefulness of discouraging them from turning against the Spanish and so forfeiting the wealth. Another measure proposed was to exempt certain chiefs from tribute, and otherwise "make much of them," to ensure their loyalty. It was also suggested that "a quantity of rice, swine, fowls, and other food" be "stored in the mountains" to keep them from the Japanese, and also to have emergency means of support if loyal groups had to retreat inland. Perhaps the most interesting section of these instructions reads:

And since, if the enemy came, . . . it would be necessary for the Indians who have their villages and houses on the seacoast, or along the rivers or estuaries, where the enemy could penetrate easily, to retire inland to live, it seems that it would be advisable for the fathers . . . to have the natives warned and persuaded immediately to move to more retired and secure places; . . . they should commence their sowing, since there are many virgin and unoccupied lands. . . . [If the enemy did not come,] they would lose nothing in harvesting their rice; [and] it would be necessary to abandon their hamlets and comforts, if the enemy did come. . . . [By] withdrawing from each varangay [settlement] ten men, or the number that may be deemed sufficient, these fields and new settlements may be commenced. (B&R, VIII, 289-90.)

It is not made clear in the records how far this policy directive was actually implemented at the time, especially whether communities did shift away from exposed points. Notable, however, is the fact that nearly all the principal Luzon settlements which date from early times are placed somewhat away from the coast or exposed river edges.

THE EARLY SEVENTEENTH CENTURY

In 1618, an unsigned *Description of the Philippinas* (B&R, XVIII, 97-100) says of Pangasinan:

There must be . . . between ten thousand and twelve thousand half-pacified tributes, two thousand belonging to his Majesty, and the rest to private individuals. The capital . . . is a place called Binabatonga. It formerly contained about three thousand houses, or, according to other estimates, a greater number; but it now has only about two thousand.

The wording here suggests that a city-sized center existed in Pangasinan—a puzzling item in the record. The old Binabatonga or Bina Lato-gan in the 1612 mission survey, was later called Binalatongan and then San Carlos. It is nearly ten miles inland from the Lingayen Gulf coast. The 1918 Philippine census, in a brief account of Pangasinan, says that the seat of an old pre-Spanish Kingdom called "Layug na Caboloan" was located near here (1918, I, 234-35). But the contemporary records give no indication of such a history. It did become the center of a Royal encomienda, and it will be seen as the headquarters of an indigenous "King" in a rebellion of 1660-61. The 1612 mission survey showed it as having 1,300 Indians "in confession" and a Royal tribute list of 1605-9 counted it as paying 431 tributes, both figures suggesting that it was not an unusually large center.

The natives of Pangasinan and Zambales, according to this 1618 *Description*, were "chiefly those called Negrillos." They "are mountain Indians and are either very tawny in color, or black." The writer judged that they were the "real aborigines," and that "they belong to the same race as those living farthest in the rugged interior." He describes them as "restless," "warlike," and "averse to trade and communication with other people," making the "cutting off of heads" their "whole happiness." "Very few of them have fixed settlements, nor do they plant crops; but they live upon camotes, a kind of potato, other herbs and roots, and the game which they hunt."

This description appears to be double-barreled in the sense that it covers the hunting and gathering of wild products characteristic of the Negrito, and also the shifting natural-rainfall (dry) cultivation of Malayan-type mountain peoples. Fuller descriptions of both these economies will be forthcoming in the area chapters to follow. They will also show that the *camote* or sweet potato, introduced to southeast Asia by Portuguese and Spaniards probably early in the sixteenth century from America, had become by this time a staple food. The reference here goes on to speak of the killing of as many as 60,000 to 80,000 deer a year within Pangasinan province: "The Indians pay these deerskins as tributes, while trade in them is a source of great profit for Japon, because the Japonese make of them good leather."

This document also includes a useful account of the "province of the Ilocos." The people here were "on the whole more settled and tractable."

[Although] there have been some disturbances among them, they are now very peaceable. They are well supplied with provisions, especially with rice—a great quantity of which comes to Manila every year during February and a part of March, for at this time the winds are favorable for going [by sea] from Ilocos to Manila and back again. . . . Fernandina is the capital. . . . This province must have between fourteen and fifteen thousand tributes which are collected without resistance. . . . There used to be in it, also, a great quantity of gold, but the Ygolotes Indians diminished the amount [because of] using it for their ornaments.

By 1621, a *Memorial and Relation* by Coronel states of this whole region that "there are none unconverted except the Zambales . . . and those in the mountains where the mines are, and a few villages behind those same mountains, which are called the province of Ituri," i.e., Ituy, at the head of the Cagayan valley (Thèvenot, 1673, ii, 22). Various ecclesiastical estimates of the time count the Bishopric of Nueva Segovia, overarching Pangasinan, Ilocos, and Cagayan, as ministering to 128,000 "souls," of which 58,000 were under the charge of the Augustinians in Ilocos, and the rest under the Dominicans (B&R, xix, 287; xx, 235; xxii, 86).

In 1624, King Felipe IV addressed anxious inquiries to the civil and religious authorities regarding progress in exploring the Cordillera gold mines. Four years before, Governor Fajardo had initiated correspondence with the King relating to the mines. "The Ygolotes," he wrote, were "extracting only what they need" for trade to get cattle, salt, iron, and other goods. "When we secure efficient management of these mines, and the duties from them," he said, it could be of help in meeting the many administrative expenses in the islands. An initial attempt by a Captain Aldana to penetrate the region at this time ended, however, in his death, so that the "work of pacifying and reducing" the highlanders failed to get ahead. Coronel, in the work quoted above, states that these "warlike Indians . . . never permit anyone from the plains to visit" the mountains. He also speaks of the mission fathers who were in touch with the mountaineers as having advised them to keep the mines sealed off in order to prevent "abuses" such as had occurred elsewhere. The government, however, gave "assurances" that the people would receive proper protection. The King then issued orders to "explore the mines and the lands of Ygolotes." Two expeditions followed, in 1623 and 1624, the second under Alonzo Martín Quirante reaching the mining areas and reporting elaborately on the people as will be seen; but both had to withdraw (B&R, xix, 159–60; xx, 262–301).

In discussing earlier the mission-sponsored resettlement of lowland groups, the Augustinian Medina (1630) was quoted as using the name "Ilocans"—approximating the modern name Ilocano. They were leading, this author says, "all the other Indians in being clean and neat and in having large settlements." The province was producing "rice in abundance." Among sources of prosperity was the fact that Chinese traders, when unable to go to Manila, "enter some port or river of Ilocos," and traders come from Manila to buy their wares. Ships from "Macan [Macao] and India" were also "accustomed to anchor" there. The "town of Fernandina, which now exists only in name," had become Vigan, the capital and "best town in Ilocos," and the center of civil and ecclesiastical affairs. The Augustinian establishment had "thirteen priorates." "The Indians are all Christians, and are the humblest and most tractable known. The entire province lies along the coast, and has fine rivers, which descend from the mountains." Some of the "converts," however, with their adherents, were suffering greatly "from the Igolotes," and one midway up the coast, Tagudin, "on that account is almost depopulated."

Medina describes the "Ygolotes" as "light-complexioned Indians," more "unconquerable" than even the "Zambales and Negrillos."

When peaceful, they bring down gold, which they extract from their mines; and they exchange it for cattle, which those along the coast own. They trade also for abnormally large and completely white swine . . . [and] blankets which the people in Ilocos make of excellent quality from cotton. . . . But when the Ygolotes are hostile . . . [they] come down to hunt heads, in which they take great pride. This is a remarkable inclination of all these Indians, for they are all bloodthirsty. (B&R, xxiii, 276–80, 296.)

ANTI-SPANISH UPRISINGS

From this point, records of the settled areas in Ilocos and Pangasinan thin out, and much of what is said up to the nineteenth century on both the lowland and mountain peoples repeats essentially what has been covered. The most notable exceptions are various disturbances and "rebellions" centering mainly around the desire to gain self-government and to end the tribute and forced labor systems. These were to culminate in the major uprisings which preceded the entry of the Americans into Manila Bay in 1898.

In 1645, following a great earthquake throughout Luzon, an uprising occurred in the upper Pampanga river area south of the Caraballo Sur mountains. This was led by a local visionary who claimed that the entire city of Manila had sunk into the earth (B&R, xxxviii, 95–98). The story of this "delusion," and the difficulties the Spanish had in suppressing it and getting its adherents to return from the high country to which they fled in the face of Spanish vengeance, will be covered in the Pangasinan chapter. In 1660 a major anti-Spanish outbreak occurred in Pampanga, and in turn spread into Pangasinan and Ilocos. The general course of events may be traced here, though specific local incidents can be held over to the chapters which follow.

As pieced together by Blair and Robertson (xxxviii, 141–215) from Bernal Díaz's *Conquests* and other sources, the "Pampangos" were "harassed by repeated requisitions for cutting timber for the continual building of galleons." They also "received no satisfaction for many purchases of rice for which the money was due them." Besides being "the most warlike and prominent people of these islands," they had leaders "trained in the military art" in "our own schools," that is, in Spanish military service in the southern Philippines and elsewhere. An "exasperated" group, which had been kept woodcutting in a camp for eight months under the forced labor system, burned their huts and raised the standard of revolt. The insurgents occupied key settlements. They also "wrote letters to the provinces of Pangasinan and Ilocos, urging them to . . . throw off the heavy yoke of the Spaniards."

The Philippine Governor of the time led a Spanish force from Manila against the rebels. Then by an offer of an amnesty and of redress for wrongs, he brought this critical situation under control. Official dispatches were sent to the Pangasinan and Ilocos authorities to be alert for similar disturbances. Almost immediately "sedition" did break out in "the village of Malanguey" in Pangasinan, but was apparently "quieted" by the alcalde-mayor with a party of soldiers. "[Yet the] fire, covered during two months, steadily spread, through the hidden passage of the intercourse between different villages. . . . A spark [also] flew over to the province of Ilocos . . . the mine [then exploded] . . . with a fearful crash."

In Lingayen, the Pangasinan capital, another Indian "master-in-camp," Don Andrés Malong of Binalatongan, touched off a first incident of "mob ferocity" by killing the alguacil-mayor and his family. From here the "multitude," growing as they went, sailed along the coast, forcing villages to surrender where they would not do so voluntarily. The alcalde-mayor and other Spaniards fleeing from Lingayen were all killed except two small children.

Malong . . . caused himself to be acclaimed king of Pangasinan. . . . In order to perpetuate by might his new but tyrannical dignity, he summoned to his aid the Zambal tribe. . . . They accepted the invitation more by the desire to plunder than by friendship. . . . Malong easily persuaded himself that he was invincible; his arrogance therefore led him to send letters to all the chiefs of the provinces of Ilocos and Cagayan, commanding that they immediately acknowledge him as their lord, and slay all the Spaniards . . . unless they wished to experience chastisement.

Similar letters sent to Pampanga leaders were seized by the Spaniards en route, so that Spanish land and water forces were appropriately mustered. A military party made a surprise landing by sea and captured Lingayen without Malong's knowledge.

Malong had already sent some of his men on a minor "raid" into south Ilocos. He still felt strong enough to divide his forces and send a large expedition northward through Ilocos to Cagayan. Apparently he hoped that such a move would win the adherence of the peoples of these areas, and bolster their courage to oppose Spain. This unit comprised "four thousand men, Zambals and Pangasinans." The personnel that remained, thus weakened, were pushed back to Malong's headquarters in Binalatongan. Faced with defeat, they "burned the church and convent," smashing and trampling the images, and then those who could escape capture retreated to the mountains. Troops caught Malong, and he was imprisoned. So was "finally extinguished this fire" in Pangasinan.

Meantime, what the record calls a "melancholy tragedy" was taking place in Ilocos. The rebel force struck up the coast, smashing the opposition of the Spanish commander and his "Ilocan" troops. It was able to invest Vigan, killing or "taking as slaves" those who resisted, and capturing the mission personnel. Moving on northward toward Cagayan, the expedition was halted through a determined stand by "a troop of Ilocans and Cagayans" at Badoc in southern Ilocos Norte. The rebels made particular efforts to obtain the "church silver" of the ecclesiastical centers. The captured fathers were generally spared, yet were harassed, plundered, and even forced to accompany the rebel troops. Some "three hundred Ilocan Indians" joined the insurgents, some forced, and others as "traitors." A message then came from Malong requesting that the expedition return to Pangasinan and instructing it to "destroy the villages with their churches and convents" as it moved back. Meantime, Spanish troops, by then victorious in Pangasinan, were advancing into Ilocos. When the two forces met between Candon and Tagudin, the rebels were defeated and scattered or taken prisoner.

At this juncture a new outbreak flared up in the Laoag area of northern

Ilocos. Acting upon letters received from Malong, a "very rich chief," Don Pedro Almazan, rallied various local community leaders. He also called on the "heathen barbarians" of the mountains, the "Calanasas," to "join the conspiracy," and the movement even spread to settlements on the north Cagayan coast. (The Calanasas will be seen as western groups of the Isneg or Apayao ethnic group.) Almazan was "crowned" king, using a crown taken from an image of the Virgin in the Laoag church. A Spanish force then moved up the coast, and with loyal Ilocan and Cagayan forces put down the "conspiracy," and chased the "Calanasas" back into their mountain fastnesses. It takes a full page in Blair and Robertson to list the various hangings and shootings of Malong, Almazan, and many other leaders, either in the Philippines or in Mexico, for their part in these uprisings (B&R, xxxviii, 141–215). One commentator of the time adds that 500 persons were also consigned to "slavery," presumably in the galleys (B&R, xxxvi, 193).

Díaz, reviewing these events of 1660–61, claims that such rebellious uprisings, aimed at gaining "liberty," could not have achieved such an objective, even if successful; on the contrary, he asserts, it would have been "their entire perdition." He bases this view on an account by an old north Ilocos chief of the time, Don Pedro Anas, of the "confusion," "lawlessness," and "tyrannical" acts of the leaders:

[In] escaping from their civilized subjection to the Spaniards, they would have fallen back into the barbarous tyranny of their own people—which, like chips from the same log, is what most hurts, as experience shows. . . . [Some] of them could not unite with the others, and, although all desired liberty, they did not work together to secure the means for attaining it, and therefore they experienced a heavier subjection.

Díaz throws into some contrast the potential tyranny of such newer leaders with the leadership situation in the pre-Spanish setting, at the same time extending his remarks to cover the Philippines as a whole:

[When] the Spanish arms conquered them with so great facility they were living without a head, without king or lord to obey—being only tyrannized over by him who among them displayed most courage; and this subjection was continually changing, other men, of greater valor and sagacity, gaining the ascendancy. (B&R, xxxviii, 197, 205–12.)

Doubtless, in all such troubled times, some of the lowlanders took their chances of retreating back into the mountains for safety, especially when they had trading relations with the upland peoples.

CONTINUING RECORDS: 1662–1762

A *Description* by Latona in 1662 says both of Pangasinan and of Ilocos that "the natives have their own language" (B&R, xxxvi, 193). Whatever varying local dialects existed prior to Spanish days, the mission-written lingua franca of each of these zones was evidently well established by this time. The known early grammars, dictionaries, and texts have been listed in various historical bibliographies, notably those compiled by Doris Welsh as being in the Newberry Library (1956, 1959).

Around 1663—dates cited by different authorities vary—a major expedition led by Admiral Duran de Monforte penetrated the central Cordillera from the Candon area. As will be seen in the chapter on the southern Ilocos area, it established a fort and mission center at Cayan. Numerous settlements were recorded by name as having been visited, but no success was achieved in mining the local gold. Some "obedience" was secured, Díaz says in his *Conquests*; but as the occupation "dragged on," it proved "very costly and very remote," so that after some five years the Spanish forces were withdrawn. "Many Igolotes," however, were led "to settle in villages of Ilocos and others in those of Zambales." Gold, Díaz states, is "the great stumbling block," and because of the "greed" of the Spaniards, "God does not reveal to us" its sources (B&R, xxxvii, 246-49). An attempt followed to combine control over both the northern mountain peoples and the equally troublesome Zambales mountain peoples by establishing a fort at "Orori," possibly Urorin or Palosapes, in northeast Pangasinan. But it was also quickly abandoned. As Díaz put it: "[The] Igolotes, [who] are today friendly and subject, rebel tomorrow, and their villages disappear; and we controlled a few only, who were gathered in the villages of Bauang, Bangar, and Narbacan, where many souls of those who were baptized were obtained." Of the communities named, Bauang is in La Union, Narvacan near the Abra river mouth, and Bangar in between (B&R, xxxvii, 278-80).

In 1676-78, various civil and ecclesiastical consultations were held in Manila and elsewhere on the problems of handling the uncontrolled groups and dealing with their incursions upon the settled communities. As told by a Dominican chronicler of the time, Baltazar de Santa Cruz, it was generally agreed that "those infidels and apostates" could not be reduced by military force. The only method open, therefore, was to "attract them by love," that is, through mission effort (B&R, xxxvii, 145-46). As a result, during the decade or so that followed, a series of "active missions" (*misiones vivas*) were created in buffer zones of northern Luzon and other parts of the Philippines (Phelan, 1959, pp. 140-42). Their activities will be seen in both Ilocos and Cagayan.

In 1681-83 a new series of rebellions broke out in sections of Zambales to the west. Their principal significance for this study is that, in the hope of "reducing" the Zambals of these mountains and the adjacent west coast of Luzon, settlements were established subsequently at Cabangan, Subic, and other points to which Pangasinan families were also transferred in order to expedite their peaceful assimilation. A Recollect mission historian,

Juan de la Concepción, records in 1788 that it had become possible to get Pangasinan groups to shift in this way because the province was "abounding with people" who had "become so numerous and there is no room for all." In one instance, the resettlement of the Zambals of an island in the Cape Bolinao area, the people became "so angry" at the inadequacies of a mainland site to which they were taken that "many families retired to Ilocos" (B&R, xxxviii, 226-40; xl, 240-41; xli, 238-39; xlviii, 292-99).

In 1697 an Italian visitor, Dr. Giovanni F. Gemelli Careri, speaks of Ilocos Province as the "best peopled and richest in the islands." He also takes note of the "Igolloti," a "warlike people" living in the mountains and "not subdued." The latter, he says, exchange their gold in Ilocos and Pangasinan for tobacco, rice, and other commodities. The Pangasinan mountains produce much "Brazil Wood," used in "dying Red and Blew." "Wild Indians" wander there: "They Sow a little in their Valleys, and what more they want, they get in the Conquered Country [the lowlands], in exchange for small bits of Gold" (from *A Voyage Round the World . . . ,* pp. 433-34). This reference to "wild Indians" apparently applies to dry-cropping groups at the southern end of the Cordillera and in the adjoining Caraballo Sur mountains. The documentary records on these zones, which were partly within the sphere of the Dominicans working in Pangasinan, and partly controlled by Augustinians who moved northward up the Pampanga river to develop mountain missions in its headwaters, will be set out in the next chapter.

During the last twenty-eight years of the seventeenth century, according to de los Reyes, eighteen new pueblos had been founded in Ilocos, indicative of more effective organization of the lowland peoples. But "Igorrotia," as he calls the "land between Ilocos and Cagayan," was merely being "nibbled at" in terms of effective penetration and control. There were even at the time many scattered Ilocano barrios which had not yet been "established in pueblos." The "public calamities," he says, which had been castigating Ilocos, were not the only factors in producing this "backwardness."

Various other causes exist, and among them was perhaps the laziness or fault of the encomenderos and the local authorities who failed to concern themselves more with reuniting the many groups of Ilocanos and the rancherias of Igorrotes and Tinguianes, attracting them with paternal treatment, enlightening them with knowledge which can invigorate them and stir their dignity.

The reduction of the Igorrotes, he says, had not succeeded because of a "false belief" that they could be handled with arms rather than with the persuasive and beneficial methods which the missions employ (de los Reyes, ii, 143-44).

Several decades were to pass before any strong move was made to improve administrative methods. Jumping chronologically, it can be noted that one of the most distinguished eighteenth-century Spanish administrators, José Arzadun y Revolledo, visited northern Luzon in 1743 on an inspection trip. His report on Ilocos, as summarized by Paul Leitz from an Ayer Collection copy, spells out various "ordinances" relating to Indian rights. Only the legal tribute could be collected, and the people were not to be forced to labor apart from the required *polo* [labor] services (Phelan, 1959). Their lands were inviolable, and they were not to be punished for killing marauders. Women could not be forced to work, except for girls who had the task of cleaning the church. Boys also could be used to help at church services. Elections for *gobernadorcillos* (justices of the peace) were to be free. At the same time, the Indians could not change their names or move without permission, and they were forbidden to sell their belongings except at auction and with officials present. They had to keep prescribed rules as regards sanitation and fire prevention. Their dress was to be based on considerations of health, and cleanliness had to be maintained in the distribution of food. Domesticated animals had to be kept from injuring crops. Judicial officials were to stay within the limits of their authority (Leitz, Ayer Collection, Document 74).

In 1735, Ilocos Province was reported to have a population of 48,950. A total of 10,041 tributes were collected in wholes or fractions from 20,082 persons (de los Reyes, ii, 161). For approximately the same area, the 1591 encomienda list had shown a total population of 68,520, paying 14,600 tributes, while in 1621 the Augustinians counted 58,000 "souls." In the decades to follow, however, the population was to rise with increasing momentum.

An ecclesiastical survey, *The Religious Estate in the Philippines,* published in 1738, shows the religious geography through the northern Luzon region as of that time. Ilocos Province was still under Augustinian control and had "three curacies": "Vigan, Bangued [in the mountains of Labra], and that of San Diego, a mission of the Tinguianes." The specific localities of churches and missions will be discussed in the area chapters that follow. "Labra," however, will be recognized as the inland valley of Abra, while San Diego was apparently Santiago in the Laoag valley further north. In all, the Augustinian "administrations" in Ilocos numbered 51,453 "souls." Additionally, the Augustinians controlled the section of Pangasinan comprising the southern extremity of the Ilocos coast strip, including Aringay, "whence religious go to the mountains." Here they ministered to 8,875 "souls," bringing their total in the region to 60,328 "souls" (B&R, xxviii, 158–59).

The Dominicans correspondingly had control of the rest of Pangasinan. The 1738 survey, after listing the ecclesiastical centers, adds that they have "some visitas, and missions of blacks." This last reference was evidently to Negrito groups both on the Zambales side and in the east Pangasinan area. The total number of "souls" under Dominican administration in Pangasinan was by then "about 48,000."

In 1754 another ecclesiastical survey was made of the area. But it repeats essentially the same information as that given in the 1738 survey, and evidently used the latter as its direct source (B&R, xxviii, 161–64). A 1760 census of Augustinian parishes and missions lists 18 lowland centers in "Ylocos" Province, in which the total number of the "tributes of men and women" was 17,283, and the total indigenous population was 57,258. The southern section of the Ilocos coast, politically within Pangasinan Province, had 5 centers, with 3,064 tributes and 9,742 people. This meant a total of 67,000 people along this lowland coastal strip. In addition, the mountain missions among the "Igorrots and Tingyans" belonging to Ylocos showed a total of 605 "new Christians" and 426 "catechumens." The Augustinians working northward up the Pampanga river also served 217 Christians in the Tayng area of east Pangasinan, together with an "Igorrot" mission which had 343 new Christians and 60 catechumens (B&R, xlviii, 53–57).

An Augustinian chronicler, Antonio Mozo, presents in 1763 an unusually detailed account of mission work carried out by his Order in the first half of the eighteenth century. He quotes one of his colleagues, Juan Bautista de Olarte, as having attested in 1702 to a number of mission exploits by Augustinian fathers, of which the following are relevant here:

[I] certify that the religious of the said my order who serve in the villages of Agoo, Bavang [Bauang], and Bacnotan in the province of Pangasinan have converted to our holy faith, and instructed and baptized, in the period of two years twenty-six natives of the tribe called Igorrots, who dwell in the said mountains.

I also certify that the ministers who serve in the province of Ilocos have in the period of two years converted to our holy faith and baptized one hundred and fifty-six natives from the infidel Tinguians who are in and belong to the said province, and live in its mountains and hills.

Mozo comments on the degree to which the lowland areas had become populous: Settled "in villages, and maintained in a very civilized and Christian society, [they] hold their own on the frontier of the infidels; for their territory allows them no alternative, shut in on the one side by the sea, and on the other by very rugged mountains."

This writer, as will be seen, characterizes very extensively the mountain peoples of the Caraballo Sur range, where he himself worked. He also summarizes knowledge to his time of the mountain "tribes" occupying the Cordillera Central. Three of them, he states, are "very extensive and populous": the "Igolot," occupying the "lofty and rugged ranges" for about 30 leagues northward between north Pampanga and Ilocos; the "Tinggian," not less numerous and extending about 40 leagues further along the same mountains; and beyond them the "Apayao," extending another 30 leagues, and consisting of "many thousands of souls." Finally, "at one side" in "a more restricted territory," is a fourth tribe called "Adang," with "fewer souls." Being less powerful, this last group has its dwellings in "places almost inaccessible." "Of the said four tribes, the first and third are to a great degree cruel and barbarous; but the second and fourth, although sufficiently obstinate, are more tractable" (B&R, xlviii, 68–69, 80–84). Mozo's fuller descriptions of these peoples will be set out in the appropriate chapters to follow.

Augustinian chroniclers including Mozo use the year 1755 as a special marker because a spurt of vigorous mission effort developed along the western slopes of the Cordillera at that time. For a brief period, as will be seen, the situation looked promising for massive conversion of "infidel" groups; but then it lapsed back. De los Reyes says of the years 1756–58 that "difficulties continued" because military measures were put ahead of all else in the attempted control of the mountain populations, hence confidence was not fostered. Under these circumstances, the Igorot "escapes to the forest, where his footprints are searched for in vain." In 1759, for example, a major force from Pangasinan and Ilocos ranged the heights for some days, burning villages and destroying fields, but without any significant results other than to cause the new Christians to flee to the fastnesses (de los Reyes, ii, 166–71; also a collection of Augustinian documents in Perez, 1904).

FURTHER REVOLTS

In the early 1760's, British naval forces took over Manila temporarily. The Spanish-British struggles of the time were reflected in various outer areas of the Philippines in attempts to throw off Spanish rule. Uprisings occurred almost immediately in the Cagayan valley, but were suppressed. In Ilocos, as Martinez de Zuñiga puts it, "sedition . . . [took] a still deeper root" in a major outbreak of 1762–63, usually called the Silang (or Silan) rebellion.

Diego de Silang, a young man originally from Pangasinan, spoke Spanish well, and had been serving as a church messenger between Vigan and Manila. According to Martinez de Zuñiga, his initial objective was not to advocate a break with Spain, but to oust oppressive local Spanish functionaries and replace them with Ilocano officials as a basis for more just self-government, with himself serving as head of the loyal forces against the British. The alcalde-mayor of Ilocos panicked, and resigned his powers to the Bishop of Nueva Segovia, who had transferred his seat to Vigan some eight years previously. The Bishop was then asked to exempt the people from tribute. Meantime Silang gathered "troops," who camped on the hills around the "fortified" headquarters of the Bishopric. After an engagement with some "loyal Indians," the rebels "burned down part of the city."

Silang, rendered vain by these successes, despatched emissaries towards the north, who, raising all the native towns, committed many robberies and atrocities, directing their vengeance in particular against some of the chiefs and

Augustine friars, insisting on its having been their fault that the tribute had not been abolished. . . . The authority of Silang being acknowledged by the towns of the north, his emissaries proceeded to those of the south, directing each of them to name a chief as their representative, who was ordered to Bigan, where their powers were to be ratified.

Silang "now found himself master of the whole province," and assumed the title of "Alcalde Mayor for the Protection of the Catholic Religion, and of the Dominions of the King of Spain." He issued a manifesto on the true Christian spirit, "obliging the Indians to hear mass, ordering them to confess, and to take care that the children went regularly to school." At the same time he "robbed the estates of cattle," "obliged the proprietors to ransom their lives with money," fined each "friar," and otherwise forcibly levied revenues.

Rumors circulated that Spanish forces were advancing, and the friars responded by withholding "absolution." Anti-Spanish feeling then showed especially in the "northern towns," and in consequence many of the clergy were brought as prisoners to Vigan. Silang then exchanged presents by sea with the British, who appointed him governor of Ilocos on their behalf.

A break here into this account of Martinez de Zuñiga may be taken to note a series of documents in the Ayer Collection representing exchanges between the British commander and Silang. The first of these communications acknowledged his "submission to British authority." It also notified him that a British warship was being sent for his protection, with troops and arms to follow soon, on their arrival in the Philippines from India, to destroy the Spanish forces. Silang was reminded of the humaneness of British policy: freeing the people of all tribute and personal services, and assuring them of freedom of worship and security of property. The communication claimed that the Augustinians had been participating in armed activities contrary to their profession, and were causing much bloodshed. "Manifestos" were enclosed for distribution in Pangasinan by Silang to make the people aware of the "fairness of British intentions," and also a "patent" for the signatures of Silang and other newly named officials. Another communication followed, inviting Silang to send trading vessels to Manila with "fruits" and other products of Ilocos. Silang forwarded a reply reaffirming his loyalty to the British cause, and saying that he had published the British communications in the "towns and pueblos" of the province (Ayer Collection, Documents 127, 128, 131).

The account by Martinez de Zuñiga continues with the statement that Silang became a "despot." He used some troops recruited from the "mountaineers of other provinces, who had taken refuge at Ylocos," to make all the fathers prisoners, promising the people that English clergy would come to minister to them. The Bishop then "declared Silang excommunicated."

At this point a secretly planned "murder" of the clergy was averted by the action of a Spanish mestizo, Miguel Vicos, who volunteered to kill Silang, and did so at his house "with a blunderbuss." The fathers scattered again to their "towns," and the arrival of a Spanish force "tranquillized such as were in any way discontented."

Meantime, Silang's wife, a mestiza named Gabriela, gathering his loyal followers, had fled inland to the fastnesses of the Abra valley. There she rallied fresh support from the people. But her forces, marching back to the coast, were defeated and dispersed. De los Reyes tells how Gabriela was hanged along with "more than a hundred persons." Nevertheless, some of the "other chiefs" who were supporters of Silang were able to escape by taking refuge in Abra (Martinez de Zuñiga, Maver's translation, ii, 213–21; B&R, xlix, 160-68, 174, 300–302; de los Reyes, ii, 171–90).

Two further documents in the Ayer Collection can round out the story of this outbreak. The first consists of a message of "appreciation" sent by the Spanish Governor to the "pueblos of Santa Catalina, Vigan, Bantay, and San Vicente," that is, the people of the Vigan area, for having "aided" Vicos and an associate in putting down the Silang revolt. The other is addressed by him to the Bishop of Ilocos asking that he arrange to have Vicos given the "promised remuneration for his distinguished service" in killing Silang (Documents 136, 137).

In Pangasinan, meantime, the "most obstinate" of all the rebellions of this period broke out. Characteristically, it started in the Royal encomienda of Binalatongan, the leader being Juan de la Cruz Palaris, often known as "Palaripar." Here, too, it centered around the goals of ending the tribute system and replacing the Spanish functionaries by indigenous personnel. A small party of Spanish officials had arrived at this time to investigate possible "tampering with the English," but quickly fled. An assembly of the Dominican fathers then declared that unless the people submitted to Spanish authority, they too would leave. A Spanish expedition from Pampanga engaged an entrenched force of "ten thousand" Indians, and after putting them to flight found it wise to retreat. A reversion to older customs, in this instance headtaking, is recognizable as one of the alternative patterns that such a vigorous movement may take. As reported by Martinez de Zuñiga: "Four Spaniards and four Indians were killed [in this engagement], whose heads the rebels carried off to the towns, where they amused themselves with dancing, according to their custom, and became bolder than ever." An uncertain situation continued, with the priests under constant threat. Then, with the end of the Silang outbreak, and with the Bishop from Vigan helping, a group of Pangasinan leaders were persuaded to go to the Spanish headquarters in Pampanga for pardon, and a new Spanish alcalde-mayor was appointed.

The latter was "not long in discovering that the flame of rebellion was only smothered, not extinguished." He was besieged in a fortified church by a rebel group that had "assembled tumultuously" in the town of Calasiao. A Spanish military party made a forced march to relieve him, and occupied Lingayen; there it was joined by "a body of Indians" brought by land and sea from Ilocos. A series of engagements followed. "[By] the beginning of 1764 nobody opposed our authority in the towns, [but] the rebels had retired to the mountains, taking with them the friars [who could not escape]. . . . [Each] group of rebels had its particular chief, and the rebellion could not be quelled merely by one battle." More than a year ensued before punitive measures—"hanging the leaders of the mutiny as they took them, pardoning the great mass of their followers"—had resistance under control. Martinez de Zuñiga concludes his particular account of these events by saying that

of the rebels more than ten thousand perished. . . . [Many,] too, died of hunger, or passed over to other provinces, and in the first enumeration that was made of the province after the rebellion, it was found that twenty-six thousand nine hundred and twenty-seven persons were deficient of the proper number, composing nearly half the population. (Maver's translation, ii, 221–29.)

The actual figures on which this demographic statement is based are given in a contemporary document, which says that prior to the insurrection Pangasinan had 60,383 "souls," but in 1776 the total had fallen to 33,456—the loss of 26,927 cited above (B&R, l, 24).

Fresh disaffection broke out at various points in the Philippines with the imposition by the government in 1780–84 of a tobacco monopoly. In Ilocos, major hostilities were barely averted, and the Cagayan valley was the scene of a full-size "rebellion." Tobacco not only was being grown profitably in the coastal provinces, but also was traded down from the mountain peoples, especially in Apayao, Kalinga, and Lepanto. From this time on, illicit mountain tobacco became an article of contraband. Yet it continued to be traded extensively to both the Ilocos and the Cagayan sides of the Cordillera, in spite of periodic Spanish military raids inland in the attempt to destroy growing fields of tobacco.

LATER PERSPECTIVES

In northern Luzon as elsewhere in the Philippines the religious Orders shifted at times the boundaries of their fields of work, voluntarily or through government directives. In 1773 the settlements from Agoo north to Bangar were transferred from Augustinian control to that of the Dominicans. Fathers of the latter Order, notably Fray Francisco Panadero, attacked in turn the problem of "catechizing the mountain tribes"—though apparently with no higher rate of success than their predecessors. In 1790, however, this ecclesiastical arrangement was reversed, and the Augustinian boundary was once more established at Agoo (de los Reyes, II, 194, 201).

An unsigned document in the Ayer Collection (No. 251), dated by Leitz at "*ca* 1794," gives a description of the province of Ilocos as of 1793. By then it contained 38 pueblos of Christians, 40,861 native tributaries, and 499 mestizos. Altogether the population comprised 170,000 inhabitants. Royal revenues from Ilocos totaled "probably 25,000 pesos," and over the previous half century the tribute total had risen by 60,000 pesos in spite of several epidemics of yellow fever and a great plague. The population was growing, even though some people had been "expelled" or else had "gone to Manila" to find jobs. Landholdings were close to the pueblos, and there were "innumerable lawsuits" before the judicial authorities. The boundaries of pueblos, the writer states, should be settled immediately to avoid lawsuits. He also suggests making a division of Ilocos, into two provinces, with Vigan and Laoag as their capitals. Laoag was expanding in size, and because it had "much space for new pueblos," it should be larger than Vigan within twenty years. Measures are proposed in this document to step up colonization of new land in the Laoag area.

In 1810, 1812, and 1816, additional revolts occurred in "various towns in the province of Ilocos." A document of 1827 titled *Reforms in the Filapinas* by Manuel Bernaldez Pizarro attributes them to the immense number of "plebeians," by contrast to the paucity of leaders or aristocrats, with the result that they can be easily stirred by "a seditious person, a few drunkards, or the superstitious tale of some old man." Pizarro reports that because the province had too many people for effective administration, he had recommended that Ilocos be divided into two jurisdictions, with each town "controlled more closely," and that this had been done by Royal order (B&R, LI, 199). This division was effected in 1818, with Vigan being made the capital of Ilocos Sur, and Laoag of Ilocos Norte.

In 1850, Manuel Buzeta published an encyclopedic survey of the Philippines containing extensive materials on the peoples and affairs of northern Luzon, as other regions, including a description of all named localities and communities. This source will be used considerably in the chapters that follow. Here a summary may be given of his census figures, comprising counts for 1818 and 1847, by provinces:

Pangasinan: 1818, 119,322; 1847, 242,476, paying 48,321½ tributes.

Ilocos Sur: 1818, 147,095 controlled people, plus 530 Spaniards and 875 "new Christians"; 1847, 192,272, paying 38,517½ tributes.

Ilocos Norte: 1818, 135,748 controlled people, plus 5 Spaniards and 65 "new Christians"; 1847, 157,559, paying 31,512½ tributes.

In 1848, the eastern boundary of Pangasinan was realigned with the formation of Nueva Ecija Province, and in 1850 its northern coastal strip was combined with the southern part of Ilocos Sur to form La Union Province.

From the early decades of the nineteenth century, the Spanish authorities launched renewed efforts to open up the high country and bring the still little-known mountain peoples under control. Military expeditions under Galvey, Oscariz, and other notable leaders ranged through the mountain settlements. The ecclesiastical Orders similarly produced some fresh pioneering fathers—though as of 1843 a work on the "Character and Influence of the Friars" could still state that because of "mortality" and "scarcity" of workers, "the spiritual conquest of the Igorrotes and other infidels who inhabit the interior of the islands has been almost abandoned" (B&R, xxviii, 238).

In 1846, Abra was detached from Ilocos Sur and made into a separate province, under "politico-military" administration. At the time, it extended over the main Cordillera ridge to include most of the present subprovince of Kalinga. Its known population at the time of Buzeta's survey (1847) was 31,815, paying 3,763½ tributes. South of Abra, a politico-military "Comandancia" or "Distrito" called Tiagan was formed in 1847 along the coastal Ilocos range between the Abra river and the coastal flats for control of the "infidels" back of the Christian population. In 1852, the higher country further inland, ranged nearly two centuries before by Admiral Monforte's expedition, was made into a politico-military Comandancia of Lepanto, with its capital at the old fort center, Cayan. A separate district was in turn created for Bontoc in 1859: this had special problems of control because of the warring propensities of the Bontok ethnic group.

Meanwhile, at the south end of the Cordillera, another politico-military district had been formed in 1846 called Benguet, roughly covering the area of the present subprovince of Benguet. This was particularly affiliated with La Union Province, where Ibaloi and Kankanai settlements extended in the more rugged sections almost down to the coast. In the separate Cagayan survey a similar series of commands or districts will be seen as being carved out along the eastern side of the Cordillera and in the Cagayan headwaters, serving as agencies of pacification and, in the meantime, as buffers between the mountaineers and the lowland communities. As will be seen in the following chapters, various changes in the organization and alignment of such districts was to occur, notably the consolidation of the mountain jurisdictions in 1908 to form Mountain Province.

A useful survey of the later Spanish policies toward the mountain peoples is given in the Taft Commission Report of 1900, particularly in statements by Scheerer. Of the Cordillera as a whole, he says:

[The region] was divided . . . into a number of small "distritos," with rather uncertain boundary lines, and more or less dependent upon the adjacent Christian provinces. . . . The most rudimentary manifestation of Spanish sovereignty . . . was a "cuartel" or blockhouse garrisoned by a Spanish lieutenant and a native police force, with orders to hold at bay the head-hunting savages of the surrounding valleys. [This marked Spanish dealings with the Ifugao and most of the northern Cordillera groups.] . . . Other districts—the so-called "Comandancias Politico-Militares"—were established to attract, with the help of the Catholic friars, the heathenish . . . Igorrotes in a gentle way toward civilization. Of this order, the most important and advanced are Tiagan, Lepanto, and Benguet. Other districts again, like Bontoc . . . held the middle between the two classes aforementioned.

Scheerer speaks of Spanish efforts to resettle the mountaineers in "Towns," the principal ones being called "pueblos" and the smaller ones "rancherias." Here they were accessible for labor services, and in more advanced localities for collection of monetary "poll-taxes."

The Madrid government repeatedly issued strict orders to employ . . . a policy of suave attraction, and the Igorrotes were allowed to live in the towns, into which they were gradually gathered from the small, primitive rancherias under headmen of their proper race, preserving all of their peculiar habits not in open contradiction with a gradual advance in civilization. . . . All towns govern themselves in the old style under "gobernadorcillos" and "tenientes," assisted by a "directorcillo" or secretary (and some had a schoolmaster). . . . It was one of the duties of the [Spanish] comandante carefully to watch the permanence of the towns once established, and in view of the well known tendency . . . to take to the mountains, such a movement came to be looked upon as an offence or crime. (*Taft Commission Report,* pp. 155–56.)

In 1898, when the Spaniards were ousted from the region in the course of the Philippine revolution, the Filipino leader Aguinaldo issued a provisional decree abolishing the military aspect of this administrative system. A disturbed period ensued throughout the Cordillera until the Americans took over and brought civil administration into effect.

The outstanding demographic fact revealed by modern censuses has been not only the very great increase of population numbers and settlement density in the lowland areas, but also a major outward migration of the Ilocano group. In the 1948 census, speakers throughout the Philippines reporting Iloko as their "mother tongue" totaled 2,340,221. The three coastal provinces of Ilocos Norte, Ilocos Sur, and La Union had a combined population of 765,073, of whom 678,426 counted Iloko as their mother tongue. Abra had 66,412 such Iloko speakers out of a total of 86,600 people, so that its Tinggian-speaking indigenous population of 22,348 comprised a minority. In Pangasinan, with 920,491 people, 440,264 were Iloko speakers, being barely outnumbered by the 443,923 counting Pangasinan as their mother tongue. Only Mountain Province was holding its own, with 44,700 Iloko-speaking immigrants, but the bulk of its total population of 278,120 still comprising the so-called "non-Christian" groups.

REVIEW

This chapter has provided the general geographic, ethnic, and historical frame for the region as a whole. The lowland peoples were seen assuming their later identities as "Pangasinan" and "Ilocano," expanding in numbers, and reformulating their ways of life particularly through Christianization and selective Hispanization. The Spanish colonial administration and the work of ecclesiastical Orders were vividly delineated. So far, however, the "infidel" mountain peoples have been seen in general terms only. In the area chapters that follow, rich detail will be filled in, notably so regarding these mountain groups.

III. The Pangasinan Area

PLACE AND PEOPLE

The southern abutments of the Cordillera Central rise from the Lingayen Gulf area with extraordinary abruptness by way of rugged, water-gouged slopes to the heights of Benguet, in places nearly 10,000 feet above sea level. The Ilocos coastal strip is here very narrow, with foothill spurs coming in places almost down to the sea, and between them meager flats where rivers and streams have built out the coastline and valley floors.

Eastward, the Cordillera heights continue by way of the Caraballo Sur range to merge into the Sierra Madres paralleling the Pacific side of Luzon. South of these mountains, the Pangasinan plains extend inland for more than thirty miles. Some foothills separate this area from more flats of the upper Pampanga river valley. On the eastern coast, the Sierra Madres fall away to Baler Bay.

On the southwestern side of the Cordillera, as would be expected, the rivers and streams fall swiftly to the coast. The heights are drained particularly here by the Angalacan-Bued, Aringay-Galiano, and Naguilian river systems. Further south, flowing into the plains and Lingayen Gulf, is the extensive Agno river system arising high in the nuclear area of the Cordillera around Mt. Data along with the other principal rivers which drain this mountain chain. Two deep gorges cut north to south, one carrying the Agno and the other carrying its tributary, the Ambayabang, which rises in the Kayapa valley area. The southward runoff of the Caraballo Sur and Sierra Madre mountains conjoins in the Pampanga river.

In modern jurisdictional terms the western part of the area consists in its lowland and foothill districts of the northeastern part of Pangasinan Province, and roughly the southern half of La Union Province. The adjacent Cordillera heights comprise the central and south sections of Benguet subprovince, one of the five divisions of Mountain Province. On the eastern side, the upper Pampanga river area is in Nueva Ecija Province, while the Baler Bay area on the Pacific coast is in Quezon (formerly Tayabas) Province.

As noted already, the southern Cordillera region was the principal source for gold in northern Luzon. The mining areas were in the high country, but alluvial gold was also panned in the lower streams. Old trade trails connect the Benguet heights with the Pangasinan plains, the Ilocos coast, and the Magat river headwaters in Nueva Vizcaya. The modern focus of Benguet is at the small city of Baguio, established at the beginning of the twentieth century by the Americans as the summer capital of the Philippines in the great amphitheater of the Benguet valley.

The lowland population northward to the Bauang area is basically Pangasinan, as seen in the preceding chapter. But members of this ethnic group have become vastly outnumbered in southern La Union and in many outlying northern Pangasinan districts by the vigorously colonizing Ilocano. Apart from linguistic differences, the distinctions between these two ethnic groups have undergone a leveling process in historic times. Yet their traditional characteristics, which will be brought out by the historical records, show considerable persistence. The upper Pampanga river area will be seen as having an ethnically heterogenous population of converted mountaineers, and of more or less recent Pangasinan, Ilocano, and Tagalog colonists. The Baler Bay people, who are a northern extension of Tagalog speakers, will not be dealt with in this study.

The southern and eastern two-thirds of Benguet subprovince is inhabited by the Ibaloi or Inibaloi, sometimes called by the Spaniards "Benguetanos." This ethnic group also occupies adjacent mountainous areas of Pangasinan in the south, La Union in the west, and Nueva Vizcaya in the upper Cagayan valley to the east. Further east, along the Caraballo Sur range, are scattered non-Christian groups called by the general ethnic name Ilongot. In the Sierra Madres, along with peoples of this type, there are also Negritos.

The Ibaloi number today about 40,000, of whom some two-thirds live in Benguet. They occupy approximately 110 settled localities in Benguet, and what appears to be close to a hundred in the adjacent mountain zones. Though considerably resettled by the Spaniards in what are called "towns," they continue for the most part to space out their houses singly in their fields or on hillsides within the settlement area. This is in marked contrast to nearly all other Cordillera groups, who cluster their houses either in villages or in hamlets. The main Ibaloi house type is rectangular and built with cogon grass or plank walls in a style different from the houses of neighboring groups; clothing styles, use of colors, and many other cultural characteristics also mark them off.

Administrators have rated the Ibaloi as unusually submissive, passive, and shy as compared with the Cordillera peoples generally. In the face of pressures, as will be seen, many have pushed back into deeper fastnesses. Yet to the old resource of gold have been added large livestock herds, coffee

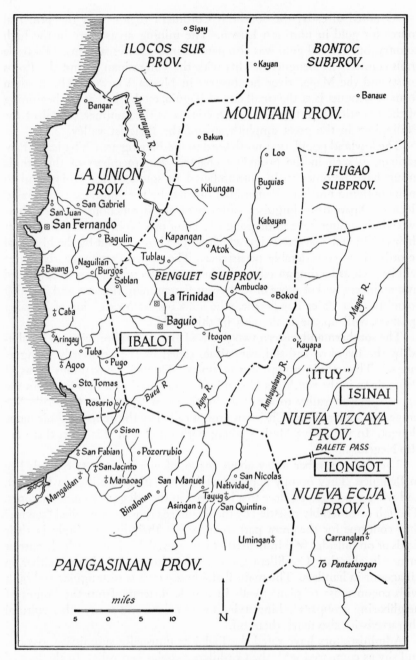

PANGASINAN AREA

plantations, and intensified agricultural production. These resources are largely controlled by wealthy and powerful families who have emerged as aristocrats to a degree matched nowhere else among the mountain communities. The city of Baguio, mentioned above, has become the major marketing center for the Ibaloi, largely obviating the long treks to the lowland communities. Many are now Christianized, but the old religion is very persistent. Male priests provide the main religious leadership, but female shamans or mediums may be called in to treat sickness and other ills. A distinction is often made between the "river settlements," especially along the Agno and its tributaries, which stress rice growing, and the "mountain settlements" on the ridges and slopes, which stress root cropping. The principal ethnological writings on the Ibaloi are by Otto Scheerer and C. R. Moss, but information is scanty, particularly on the settlements outside Benguet. Of the varied Ilongot groups, further east, no preliminary description seems necessary; they will be covered in the appropriate local records of eastern Pangasinan and the upper Cagayan valley.

Recent glottochronological studies of linguistic relationships by Pittman and associates of the summer Institute of Linguistics (1953) and by workers in the Philippine Studies Program of the University of Chicago (Fox and others 1953; Anderson 1960) indicate that the Ibaloi speech, usually called Inibaloi or Nabaloi, has become very markedly distinct from all the neighboring languages: Pangasinan, Kankanai, Ifugao, and the upper Magat languages of Cagayan. It also has local dialect variants. The Pittman group noted a particularly marked contrast between the speech used on the Benguet heights and that in the Kayapa valley area away to the east.

The Pangasinan and Ilocano groups grow their traditional wet rice crop in the rainy summer season, as noted in the last chapter. The Ibaloi, however, follow the general mountain timetable of growing the traditional crop in the winter, from December or January on, the grain ripening with the summer warmth. Where water is available both groups have added in modern times a second crop. But it is proportionately very minor except in northeast Pangasinan, where the Agno river system has a strong winter flow, and on the Benguet heights during the wet summer. The terrace walls built by the Ibaloi, like the walls often built around their hillside gardens, are nearly all of earth (D. C. Worcester in 1906 spoke of them as made of "mud"), and tend to be crude compared with those of the Ifugao and Bontok. In slope and other construction features, the more elaborated terrace systems, as in the Agno valley, appear to show marked influence from the adjacent Ifugao.

Dry (upland) rice has a very minor place in the lowland economy, and is almost nonexistent on the Benguet heights. But moderate amounts are grown along the western and southern slopes of the Cordillera. For the dry-gardening Ilongot of the Caraballo Sur mountains it is a major crop.

Sweet potatoes (*camote*) are grown in great quantity throughout the Benguet area, and for the "mountain towns" they are likely to be the predominant crop. Moss, in his *Nabaloi Tales* (1924), cites a story of the "origin of rice" which begins by stating: "Long ago the Igorot had never seen any rice. Their food was always camotes." Such tales also include frequent mention of "gabe," or taro, which is also grown in fair amounts in the damp high country. Yams (*ubi*), tugue, and other cultivated and wild roots, little used in the high country, have notable importance in many lowland districts in carrying the poorer people over between rice harvests. Vegetables and fruits are in greater use in the lowlands than in the mountains, while maize is almost wholly a lower-level crop (Philippine agricultural censuses, and other sources).

The prime ethnohistorical problem here is to define the relation of the Ibaloi and Ilongot to the lowlanders of Pangasinan and Nueva Ecija. In this connection, one of the early American governors of Mountain Province, John C. Early, departs from the usual theory of a separate origin for the Cordillera peoples by writing of the Ibaloi that "he is no doubt a cousin of the Pangasinan." He also states, on the basis of his inquiries into their history: "The Ibaloi considers Kabayan as his seat or home, and from there has spread to Bokod, Tublay, Trinidad, a part of Kapangan, and a part of Atok" (*Manila Daily Bulletin,* February 1, 1929). Kabayan is one of the gold-bearing districts of the middle-upper Agno river, and it will appear in the records to follow.

EARLY PERSPECTIVES

Spanish penetration of this zone started with the initial explorations by Salcedo's expedition in 1572. As recounted by de los Reyes in his *Histoiria de Ilocos,* drawing principally upon Gaspar de San Augustin's *Conquistas,* his flotilla passed up the Zambales coast and into the Lingayen Gulf in late May of that year. Salcedo's first contacts in Pangasinan were friendly. "The Pangasinanes received the Spaniards with good grace, and learning of the objective of civilizing them, and leading them into religious ways, by instruction, assured the visitors that they would be well treated. The Pangasinanes presented the Spaniards with rice, chickens, hogs, and pieces of gold."

Salcedo decided to explore the extensive waterway of the Agno. Directing his boats inland, his party encountered some "poblaciones," but these had been deserted. Going further, they reached the "pueblo of Malimpit," presumably near the modern city of Lingayen. The inhabitants there engaged in a treacherous attack, and the Spaniards "subdued them with arms."

From this area the party moved along the coast to the landing place of the "Nakarlan" river, apparently the Angalacan in the Mangaldan–San

Fabian area. After passing the night there, they "ascended the river to the pueblo." The inhabitants, armed with bows and arrows, tried to obstruct the way, discharging them from hiding places along the banks. Embarking once more, the Spaniards arrived on the same day at a port "three leagues" further on. Here three Japanese vessels were encountered, presumably adumbrating the early name of this place, "Port of Japon," the later Agoo. A fight ensued between the Salcedo party and the Japanese, and the latter fled with some casualties. The Spaniards again ascended the river to the settlement, which here was of hamlet size (*caserío*). Finding that this had been "reduced to ashes," they returned to the sea.

By the night of the following day, the party encountered another pueblo called "Atuley." This was probably in the settlement area at first called "Balatao," and later Bauang. The settlement was located on high, rough ground which the inhabitants could defend from above. Salcedo, avoiding a direct assault, broke his party up into small groups and these worked up to the summit from various sides, so that the defenders abandoned the pueblo. The record speaks of the beauty of this settlement with its "well placed streets and houses." From two of the people who were captured, Salcedo ascertained that it was the "capital of that district," and that in the interior there were "many barrios or pueblos." These captives were released with a message that the people would not be harmed, and that a truce was desired. Two hours later, some of the inhabitants returned, including several of their leaders. Being well received, they proposed to return the next day to celebrate a treaty of peace; they also asked the Spaniards to retire to their ships in the meantime. But these people failed to return, and Salcedo resumed his course, abandoning the plan until a later occasion. From "Atuley," the flotilla proceeded to "Purao," or Balaoang, in the coastal zone (de los Reyes, II, 10–12).

Following this not too auspicious beginning, Spanish authority was established particularly through the carving out of encomienda holdings in the area. The first general description is given by Loarca in his 1582 survey of northern Luzon. He speaks of Pangasinan as having a "peaceful poulation" of 4,000. The "best portion" of its land, containing one-fourth of the people, was by then allotted to the King, and the rest to "six encomenderos." The specific location of the encomiendas is not given, but presumably one was at Lingayen, where the alcalde-mayor of the district was located. Where the Ilocos coastal region narrows, Loarca places the "Port of Japon," that is, Agoo, where "there is a settlement of Indians of the same race as those of Pangasinan." "Six leagues" further up the coast were the "villages of Alinguey and Baratao," with a population of about 2,000. These, he says, were the most northerly of the groups of "the same race as those who inhabit Pangasinan." The people of this district had been allotted first to a private encomendero, but "now they belong to the Royal Crown"

(B&R, v, 105–7). "Alinguey" or Aringay still exists, but "Baratao" is not a recognizable place name of modern times. It was probably the area to be called in further records Bauang. "Four leagues" further north was the next encomienda, "Purao," or modern Balaoan, where the people "differ from the Pangasinan people . . . in language, but resemble them in customs"; this district will be dealt with in the next section.

An *Account of Encomiendas,* published in 1591, gives somewhat fuller information on holdings in Pangasinan. For the zone being dealt with here, two are listed:

Magaldan (the modern Mangaldan): "has" 800 tributes, and a population of 3,200; has "justice" and "instruction"—that is, civil control and mission personnel.

Baratao (evidently covering settlements from Agoo to Bauang): "collects" 1,500 tributes from a population of 6,000; has "justice," and "one convent with 2 religious."

The total estimated population in the controlled districts was therefore 9,200. Tributes were "collected" along the Ilocos strip, but the more southerly area merely "has" them, suggesting collection difficulties. Where for some other Pangasinan encomiendas it is specified that they are "peaceful," mention of peace is pointedly absent in the Magaldan and Baratao listings (B&R, VIII, 104–5). A 1605 report on receipts from Royal encomiendas speaks of the "villages of Agoo and Alingayan" as yielding a lower figure of 824 tributes (B&R, XIV, 245).

For additional demographic perspective, a survey of the "Status of Missions," dated 1612, may also be included here. It tabulates the establishments in this zone as follows, the first two being Dominican and the others Augustinian:

Magaldan (Mangaldan): 2 ministers for 900 Indians.

Mauazug (Manaoag): 2 ministers, one a lay brother, for 400 Indians, "or a trifle less," and also undertaking "the new conversion in the tingues," i.e., the adjacent mountains.

Agoo: a "convent" with 2 ministers serving it and its "visitas," that is, outer settlements which were visited; 1,500 tributes, and 4,500 Indians "in confession."

Alingayen (Aringay): called a "province," and served with its visitas by 2 ministers; 800 tributes, and 1,400 "in confession."

Bavan (Bauang): served with its visitas by a "convent," with 3 ministers; 1,200 tributes, and 3,600 "in confession." (B&R, XVII, 195, 211.)

Recognizing fully the hazard of using such early population estimates, we may venture some analysis. For the Mangaldan area of Pangasinan, a marked discrepancy shows between the asserted total of 3,200 persons in 1591 and the 1,300 or "a trifle less" in 1612 in Mangaldan and Manaoag together. With due allowance for a possible toll of disease, it looks as if some people of this coastal area had moved back eastward or possibly up into the hills to escape the Spanish pressures and controls. By contrast, the southern Ilocos coast strip offered no such hinterlands for refuge other than the formidable Cordillera heights. Where the 1591 encomienda list shows a total of 1,500 tributes and 6,000 persons, the mission figures of 1612 indicate 3,500 tributes and 12,500 "in confession," apparently meaning of ecclesiastically responsible age, or on the four-to-one basis a total population of 14,000. It will be seen that in later times the northern Pangasinan plains had a marked growth of population: an 1845 figure shows 44,047, and the 1903 census 114,166. The Ilocos coast section north to Bauang, however, had no comparable space for intensified settlement, so that as population similarly increased, many of its people had to migrate elsewhere: the 1845 population figure was 25,123, and that for 1903 was 60,613.

THE PEOPLE THROUGH MISSIONARY EYES

The initial efforts of the Augustinians were far more successful in Ilocos than in Pangasinan. Aduarte in his Dominican *History* of 1640 gives a perhaps somewhat colored interpretation of the Augustinian record in Pangasinan when accounting for the entry of his own Order in 1587 to work there. When the Dominicans reached the Philippines, he says: "the Indians of Pangasinan were given over to idolatry, and so detested the gospel that, though the ministry of some religious was brought to the Indians on both sides of them (who are those of the provinces of Pampanga and of Ylocos), these Indians always refused to admit them."

Some Franciscans, too, trying to gain converts along with Augustinians, "had no success with them" as a result of their "determined resistance." On the contrary:

the Indians were wretchedly victorious, obliging the ministers by their perversity, to go away and leave them in the darkness which they loved. There was only one place—the principal village called Lingayen, where the alcalde-mayor resided—in which some of the religious of our father of St. Augustine had been able to persevere. . . . The Spaniards who lived there . . . were able to compel the Indians to treat the fathers properly—not as they had in other villages where they were not only treated discourteously but came near to being killed.

In the face of this opposition by the Pangasinan people, the Augustinian fathers "came to the conclusion that it was best to leave them." Aduarte, always a good raconteur, tells how this resistance had been "commanded" by "the devil . . . on occasions when he had spoken" to the Indians. He then cites a specific instance, which is illuminating by its reference to travel between lowland settlements and the mountaineers:

One of these occasions occurred while some Indians were on their way from the villages below to the mountains of the Ygolotes, on their ordinary business. As they were going through a thicket . . . they heard a very loud and dreadful voice lamenting and complaining pitifully. The Indians retreated in great alarm but, as they were many, they ventured to follow it to see who had uttered it, and in this way they came near to the place where it had sounded.

The lamenting voice then declared itself to be "Apolaqui," the *anito* or "god" to whom they prayed for success in war, for safe traveling, and for good fortune in "business." Apolaqui then explained why he was aggrieved, namely, that: "[You] should receive among you strangers with white teeth, wearing cowls, and that they should place in your houses some sticks of wood laid across each other to torment me." The spirit then announced that he was "going from among" them. The Indians, Aduarte states, still called the locality in his time Pinabuenlagan, meaning in the local speech "at the cross." The reference to white teeth indicates here, as also in similar references by Aduarte to protests by the devil in Cagayan communities, that tooth blackening was a prevalent custom: it is still practiced among some of the non-Christian groups of northern Luzon.

The Augustinians, as seen in the general chapter, kept control of the Ilocos coast mission work from Agoo north where the people were more amenable to conversion, but transferred the main Pangasinan area to the Dominicans. The latter then bore the brunt of the opposition which had been generated. The fathers "suffered greatly from hunger and from hardships," as the Pangasinan people refused them even "the necessities of life" for proffered payment. "Many times" the fathers had to "carry on their backs" their wood, water, and beds as they "went from one village to another." For "three years" the first six fathers experienced such hardships, and at one time five of them were sick at once, yet "no one was converted." Even the Bishop of the Philippines, at the request of "many Spanish captains" asked that they "leave the Indians." It was true that these Indians were of all the tribes in the country the worst, the fiercest, and most cruel —an unconquered tribe who celebrated their feasts by cutting off one another's heads."

As, however, the Indians perceived that the fathers "not only did them no harm, but came to their aid in their necessities," they "began to be mollified." Aduarte then relates a "story" of how a chief went by night to one of the fathers, and said that he was "persuaded" that such persons as he was, without desire to obtain gold or silver, and full of the virtues, could not be deceivers. Then came a kind of mass conversion:

When the leading men of the tribe began to consider becoming Christians— their headmen being already so, as well as some others—they came to the religious, and persuaded them that, in order that all of them might be converted together, they should first of all give up in a single day everything which they held in commission for the devil; these things which they used for their sacrifices . . . [So] there were given up an infinite number of pieces of earthen ware and a great deal of very old wine . . . [used] at the time of the sacrifice . . . like holy water. . . . [After instruction and fasting] general baptisms took place.

Aduarte's account tells of various healings, dreamings, visions, fastings, and other "marvels" which happened at this period of mass crisis. In fact, "no day passed without a miracle."

All the Spaniards and religious of other orders are amazed at this conversion, and especially at seeing them give up vices so enticing as drunkenness, which used to be very common among them. . . . The very friars who are their ministers are amazed to see such a conversion in a tribe so barbarous, so cruel, and so completely given over to vice.

Here follows an account of how their minds were even "set upon preparing themselves for death" through virtual excesses of devout behavior. A report written eleven years after the Dominicans began their work claims that Pangasinan by then was "composed of Christians—there being, of course—a heathen here and there" (B&R, xxx, 180–90).

The Blair and Robertson translation of Aduarte follows up this sequence of events with further sections that relate to this early mission work in Pangasinan. Items of special ethnohistorical significance refer to "their greatest idol, who was called Ana Gaoley," and worshipped in shrines or temples called *anitoan*.

The priestesses had been accustomed to invoke these oracles, for the ministry of idols among them was given over to women. These women, called *managanito,* were dressed in vestments dedicated to this sole use, and employed certain vessels esteemed among them, containing oils, unguents, odors, and perfume. With all this they placed themselves in a retreat where they used to conjure the devil; and there the devil spoke to them, giving them answers with regard to their wars, their sicknesses, and their undertakings. Whatever the devil asked by the mouths of these women, however costly it might be, the Indians brought immediately; and if through them he commanded the Indians to kill [they did so].

This delineation of female shamans virtually duplicates accounts of such religious leadership and practice that will appear in the early records of the northern Cagayan coast and at various points in the Cagayan valley. It stands in sharp contrast to the later accounts of important male priesthoods among the non-Christian rice-terracing peoples of the high Cordillera, though female shamans are still found among the latter with limited "practices," mainly in the field of sickness. The dry cultivators, however, such as the Isneg in the northern part of the mountains, still lodge religious leadership in the hands of women shamans as in this Pangasinan account. Unfortunately, the early Augustinian historians had no interest in recording such matters as regards the Ilocos coast peoples, so it can merely be said that among modern rural Ilocanos, female shamans have importance in the considerable spheres where old-style beliefs and practices have persisted, even though male priests carry their predominantly Christian traditions.

One of the Indian women of "highest rank," when about to be married, was found to be pregnant. Her parents intended to "execute upon her their ancient law, which was to bury her alive, together with the malefactor." She made a "false accusation" of paternity against one of the priests, which though proved wrong led to her being pardoned by her group. Of "bereavement" the record says:

The devil . . . required them to do the most painful things. . . . For the first three days they did not have a mouthful to eat; for three more days they had only a little fruit; after this, for a long time, they had only boiled herbs or roots, without wine to drink, and with nothing savory to eat. During all this time they wore around the neck a little gold chain, which was a mark of mourning . . . and this they were not allowed to put off during all this period, unless they killed someone. As soon as they committed a homicide, there was an end of the mourning and the fast.

This description is reminiscent of mourning ritual among some of the non-Christians in modern times.

"Worst of all" were the wars they were "constantly waging among themselves, and the great oppressions inflicted upon the people of the lower class by those . . . above them in rank." These latter took away their possessions, and "made them slaves," at their "mere whims." Aduarte cites the case of a very old chief, Cabanday, who was "very tyrannical" and therefore "the most esteemed," who gave his accumulated "gold and riches" to a father in asking for baptism. Another great chief, Casipit, of the village of Mangaldan, was at first so insistent that the fathers should be ousted from his community that he "offered his encomendero half his property" if he could get rid of them. But his wife was baptized, and he followed "with the whole of his family and his large retinue." These "good people" subsequently "directed their slaves" to pay as much attention to their religious duties as to their work.

The parents of a child who was born blind "planned to kill her." But instead they sold her for "eight reals" to a father, who baptized her. Her sight was restored, so that many children were brought for baptism. The healing of sickness by the fathers created a strong impression, especially as they "ordered houses to be built in all the villages to serve as hospitals." Among such an "agricultural tribe," Aduarte says, "the sick suffer much," and often die for want of care "because their kinsmen are obliged to go out to their fields." Two reports occur of a "plague of locusts," which miraculously "spared the fields of the Christians." The Pangasinan people "being farmers," this also impressed them. A heathen, as the result of a vision, "put away all his wives but the first, though he loved another and better one"; that is, polygyny was practiced, as among some of the mountain peoples today.

One of the Dominican fathers, Fray Marcos de San Antonino, is described as "walking about among these little villages and fields." This raises the vital matter of settlement patterns in the Pangasinan ethnic area prior to the growth of town centers, and application by civil and mission authorities of the concentration policies discussed in the previous chapter. While the topic is always somewhat vague, an impression is gained that some larger communities existed at coastal and river trading centers, but that otherwise the settlements tended to be of hamlet size (B&R, xxx, 180–215).

Aduarte, in addition to presenting this rather generalized record, gives some specific accounts of happenings in the northern Pangasinan area that are of special concern to this study. Already quotations have been cited describing the founding of the communities of San Jacinto and Manaoag from scattered population elements. Of Magaldan (Mangaldan), Aduarte states that this was "the most obstinate of all Pangasinan villages . . . in their errors." The people at first had refused to admit the Augustinians, or to "listen to a secular priest" who had been assigned to them, even though the alcalde-mayor of Pangasinan "fined and punished them." The Dominicans, taking over in their turn, sent Fray Pedro de Soto to work there. "The people of this region still lived in their ancient villages and rancherias in the hills and mountains, without civilization, order, or system, any more than if they had never known Spaniards." Fray Pedro, who lived in Magaldan three years, "conquered them in the end." He was "particularly hateful to the hostile natives because he was the first one who learned the language of the Indians"—he spent a "whole year," Aduarte tells, in translating the gospel, the lives of the saints, and other material into Pangasinan. This father had a technique of paying money for "information as to those who continued to sacrifice to the devil."

[He] immediately went in haste to the place, sometimes alone, and caught the sacrificers in the very act. Without waiting an instant, he upset everything, and broke the dishes and bowls and other vessels which they used in their rites; poured out their wine; burned the robes in which the aniteras or priestesses dress themselves on such occasions, and the curtains with which they covered up everything else; threw down the hut, and completely destroyed it. In this way he made them understand how little all those things availed, and how vain were the threats the devil uttered against those who would not venerate him. . . . Many were thus aroused and undeceived, while others, and not a few, were angry, so that it was a wonder that he was not slain.

Other fathers, Aduarte says, adopted this same drastic plan for combatting idolatry, but Fray Pedro "led them all" (B&R, xxxi, 145–46).

THE MOUNTAIN POPULATIONS

Some of the converts who resettled at Manaoag, Aduarte says, were drawn from the "mountains of the region." In his continuing record he states: "The Negrillos and Zambales who go about through those mountains were continually harassing this village, partly because of their evil desires to kill these men, and partly for robbery. . . . [They use] bows and arrows. . . . [These] enemies come when [the villagers are] out in the fields." The "Negrillos and Zambales" referred to here were hardly likely to be raiders all the way from the Zambales mountain range away to the west on the other side of the Pangasinan flats, though these did plague lowland settlements (B&R, VIII, 200–225 *passim*). Rather, they appear to be groups living along the southern Cordillera margins, and perhaps especially Negritos occupying the foothill country between the Agno and Pampanga rivers, as will be seen later.

The account goes on to tell of an Indian chief named Dogarat, who was an infidel of Anbayaban, a "village of Ygolote Indians who inhabit some high mountain ridges" about "four leguas" from Manaoag.

[He] used sometimes to go down to the village . . . and listen out of curiosity to the preaching of the religious. . . . [As a result, he] began to incline . . . toward becoming a Christian. He therefore learned the prayers, and knew them by heart; and the only thing which held him back was the necessity of leaving his vassals and his kinsmen if he was baptized, and going away from the washings of a river of his village, where they used to gather grains of gold, which come down with the water from the hills and ridges where they are formed. . . . [Falling severely ill,] he sent to call the religious who resided at that time in Manaoag, Father Fray Tomas Gutierrez, who visited the sick Indian, giving him thorough instruction. . . . [The father then] baptized him and named him Domingo. . . . [He] recovered, and used to attend church on fast days.

This account of an infidel leader and his settlement on a gold-bearing river is rich in implications of mountain-lowland interaction. The name "Anbayaban" appears to correspond with Ambayabang, applied today to the major branch of the Agno river which is east of Manaoag and has its source in the Kayapa valley area. The account spells out the mission policy of the time of bringing mountain converts down to the lowland communities in order to sever their "heathen" ties. In this instance, however, Domingo seems to have stayed on. He is described in a continuing story as having experienced a minor miracle. His rosary and a purse, which held a "trifle of gold," had been hung on a tree when he was "hunting," and survived a fire (B&R, XXXI, 258–62).

In 1620, two of the Dominican fathers, Juan de San Jacinto and Francisco de Ugaba, petitioned the alcalde-mayor of Pangasinan to certify their authority to evangelize the "Igolotes," and to confirm their exclusive rights to the ecclesiastical administration of the "provincia de los igolotes." This petition was approved, and San Jacinto, then serving as vicar of Manaoag, said Mass "on a river just inside the province" in the presence of both Spanish and Indian representatives. Several days later, Mass was also celebrated in an Indian community called "Goa" (Ayer Collection, Document 25).

A number of references were made in the previous chapter to the mining and trading of gold, and to various Spanish attempts to penetrate and control the high country. The first actual account of an expedition into the southern Cordillera seems to be in Governor Sande's *Relation* of 1576:

Because it is reported that the best mines are those in the province of Ylocos, I sent thither the sergeant-major from this camp with forty arquebusiers. He reached those mines, and reports they are located in a very rough country, twenty leagues inland; that the way thither is obstructed by great forests; and that the country is very cold, and has great pine forests. He brought some metal [back]. . . . [The] country is hostile. (B&R, IV, 116.)

This terse report is remarkable for its delineation of essentials. The fact that such a small party could reach the heights, where later much larger military expeditions failed, could suggest various possibilities: the powerful first impression of Spanish guns, a sparseness of population in the mountains at that time, or relative lack of opposition on the part of the mountaineers in this period of early contacts.

In 1609, a compilation was made by Dr. Juan Manuel de la Vega, a member of the Philippine judiciary, of "what has been known from old times" of the "rich mines of the Ygolotes." It comprised a special section of a report on early expeditions to the "Province of Tuy," that is, the headwaters area of the Cagayan valley. But the writer says that the materials were based on knowledge available from the various districts bordering on the area, including information from Spaniards and Indians who had visited the mines. Of the region and people this account says:

[The] mountains and ridges . . . [are] so lofty, it is cold, although its inhabitants go naked except for some garments made from the bark of trees. This region lies btween the provinces of Cagayan, Ylocos, Pangasinan and Tuy. The people are light complexioned, well-disposed, and intelligent. It is reported that about eighteen or twenty thousand Indians use lance and shield. They are at war with their neighbors up to certain boundaries. Beyond those boundaries those peoples trade with one another. . . . These mountains contain large pines, and other trees found in Castilla.

As regards the mining and distribution of the gold, the account states:

[The] Ygolotes descend to certain towns of Pangasinan with their gold, and exchange it for food—hogs, carabaos, and rice, taking the animals alive to their own country. Until that food is consumed, or but a little time before, they pay no heed to securing any gold. Then each man goes to the mine assigned to him, and they get what they need, according to what they intend to buy, and not any more. They are a people as void of covetousness as this; for they say that they have it there at hand for the times when they need it. . . . [Almost] daily those Ygolotes go to a village of the province of Pangasinan, as to an emporium, to buy provisions in exchange.

As a result of his survey, Vega judges that "the mines are very numerous and rich," and that they had been worked for a long time.

[It] is a well-known fact that for these many centuries the greatest quantity of gold, and that of the finest quality, in these islands has been and is still obtained there; and at the present time this industry is as active as ever. . . . Consequently one cannot doubt that a great treasure could be secured with expert men and the order to work those mines, since rude Indians, without any skill except in washing, obtain so great a quantity.

Geographically, the "wealth of these mines" was reported as lying "in certain mountains, in a district of four or five leagues in extent," and "included between two large rivers which flow into Pangasinan." This represents a reasonably accurate placement of the main gold deposits as known in later times, the two large rivers evidently being the Agno and the Bauang-Naguilian systems to east and west, respectively.

Vega's account goes on to say that the "natives do not cultivate the land," presumably meaning here the employment of wet cultivation techniques.

[On the one hand, this is] because of its great sterility, and the lack of ground to cultivate; and, on the other hand, which can more easily be believed, because, confident that in their gold mines, they have thereby sufficient to purchase what ever they wish from Pangasinan, where the nearest abundant supply of provisions is to be found. The richest and chiefest among them is he who has more heads hanging in his house than the others; for that is a sign that he has more food, and gives more banquets. . . . [They] are pagans, and but little given to pagan rites at that. On the contrary they are very lukewarm in their idolatry, and consequently it will be easy to inculcate in them the holy Catholic faith.

This last confident statement was, of course, to prove false, since even into the twentieth century the main body of these "Ygolotes" proved resistant to Christianity. Returning to the topics of leadership and warfare, Vega says that as with the inhabitants of "Tuy" in the Cagayan headwaters, and "those of many other provinces and mountains," the Ygolotes

have a cruel, barbarous custom, which they call "the cutting off of heads." This is quite usual among them, and he is considered as most valiant who has cut off most heads in the civil wars waged among themselves and with their neighbors. This race are ruled by certain superiors whom they call "chiefs," who are the arbiters of peace or war.

Vega was critical of the official attempts to that time to penetrate the mining areas. Governor Ronquillo, he says, had sent Juan Pacheco Maldonado to "discover" the mines, the date being about 1583. So lacking in diligence and intelligence did he prove that he "remained two months amid the mountains," and in the period "could not catch a single Indian except only two women." A quantity of earth which he carried back was poorly handled by an "assayer" brought from Spain, who proved to be such a "charlatan" that the test was "worth nothing." Some bars, supposedly of "very fine gold" taken from the mines, when pulverized, proved to have no gold in them. A military expedition under Captain Clavijo, sent into the mountains in 1595 from the Tuy side as will be seen, turned back after an engagement with a force of "more than one thousand Indians" because his guide was wounded.

This compiler concludes his survey by proposing to the government that he be given the task of pacifying the people and assigning them to encomiendas:

That, if by our care and diligence, we allure the chiefs of the Ygolotes together with the other chiefs by means of presents, kind words, and mild treatment, to descend to the plain, or to live quietly in settlements in their natural habitat, submitting to his Majesty, paying their tribute, and abandoning the barbarities that they have been wont to practice on their own children and those of the lowlands; and if they accept the faith and are quiet and pacified: we receive permission to distribute and apportion them in encomiendas.

Vega then proposes that such encomiendas be allotted in three ways: one-third to the "royal treasury," one-third to the "soldiers engaged in the conquest," and the remainder to him as "our exclusive property" (B&R, xiv, 301-7, 317-18). The authorities, however, did not accept this offer.

In the early 1620's, as seen in the previous chapter, the Philippine authorities were being pressed by the King to take control of the mountain mines. In 1623, a military expedition climbed the heights from the Ilocos side. According to Martinez de Zuñiga (1803):

This expedition, under charge of Francisco Carreño de Valdes, head of the provinces of Pangasinan and Ylocos, marched in good order seven days, and on the eighth day arrived in the town of the mines, where the natives received them well; but the Spaniards placed too much confidence in them. The Igorrotes, when least expected, rose on them, and treacherously murdered the chief of the friendly Indians, on which de Valdes retired, to wait a better opportunity. (Maver's translation, i, 247-48.)

In February 1624, a new expedition led by Captain Alonzo Martín Quirante struck inland from Aringay, north of Agoo. His force included 70 Spanish officers and soldiers, some Negro slaves, 2 Japanese miners, 47 Chinese carpenters, smiths, and sawyers, 2 priests, and 1,748 Indians, about half each from Pangasinan and Ilocos. The report of this venture gives a surprisingly detailed picture of the mountain conditions and peoples.

The expedition struck inland from Aringay in late February, the cool drier season. The Indians, however, soon began to "desert." As the heights were scaled, the "Ygolotes" tried to block the advance by burning off the terrain, building defensive stockades at narrow points, and cutting down trees in the passes. At Galan, a locality with "new mines," there were "about two hundred houses around," all deserted. Here a fort called Santiago was built.

The mountains were almost everywhere devoid of forests; for except in the very damp ravines, reed-grass does not grow, or any tree except pines. For that reason, wherever one looks from the height, very many mountains are to be seen, so jagged, steep, and near together that it seems impossible for men or any other living thing to exist on them.

The Ygolote settlements, the expedition report states, were "established on the peaks of the mountains, and on the roughest of them" for defensive reasons: this could still be said of some Ibaloi settlements in the twentieth century. Sentinels were maintained day and night, and sharp pointed stakes and stones were also placed along the trail approaches for defense. Their "miserable huts" were very small, and made of straw and short wood with no walls but with roofs to the ground and low doors. The people slept "high up on boards or planks"—such plank "beds" were being used by the mountaineers into modern times. Hair was worn long and both men and women had bark-cloth clouts; to these the chiefs added "Ilocan blankets, which they have inherited from their ancestors," and sometimes gold in their teeth. Chiefs were differentiated only by "more bones of animals killed in their feasts, more clothes, and greater age." There "is one in every ten or twelve homes, who is head of the kinsfolk. They inherit from father to children, or by blood, and do not recognize one as greater than the other." This may be interpreted as a pattern of leadership by senior elders of prestige in extended family and kin groups, with individual inheritance from parents, and no strong class distinctions. It is fully in line with the expected social structure of the time, though later the Ibaloi were to develop strong aristocratic tendencies through Spanish commercial and other impetus (Moss and others).

Fighting weapons were lance and shield, and when a head was taken a feast was celebrated. Skulls were made into cups from which the people drank at "feasts and revelries." They were also left as "household effects" to their heirs. At the death of a member of the group itself, the corpse was tended for "many days," and body fluids were drawn off until it was "dry." The body was then interred with blankets and other goods for the journey to the spirit land, either being lodged in a sitting position in caves fronted with stones, or "set in trees." Among the ritual goods were *buyos* (betel nut), suggesting that betel-chewing was prevalent in the southern Cordillera at the time, though it has been subsequently replaced here by the use of tobacco. Betel-chewing is still practiced among dry cultivators such as the Isneg further north, and was also a custom in parts of the Cagayan valley when the Spaniards arrived.

The "Ygolotes," the report continues, were "idolatrous." They "say god is the sky, whom they call Cabunian, and they offer and sacrifice to him, in their banquets and feasts, swine and carabao"—Cabunian is still the name of a major deity of the southern Cordillera peoples. "Old men or women" conducted the sacrificial ceremony, "which is called *magunito*" (*maganito,* which means to have dealings with an *anito* or spirit). He who kept up the feast longest and killed most animals was "most respected." "Sages or philosophers," comprising the "oldest men and women," were especially given respect at such times, as they were "said to talk with the devil."

The people could not read or reckon time, but they "govern themselves" by one star rising in the west, called *gaganayan*. "On seeing the star they attend to the planting of their waste and wretched fields in order to sow them with yams and camotes, which form their usual and natural food. They do not have to plow or dig, or perform any other cultivation than that of clearing the land where they are to plant." Together with this vital quotation may be taken another, in which the report accounts for the diffi- culty in making demographic estimates:

It is not very easy to ascertain the number of those people, who are scattered, for they are so intractable, and do not let themselves be seen, moving from one place to another on light pretext, without any hindrance; for their houses, to provide which would be the chief cause of anxiety, they easily build anywhere, with a bundle of hay, while they move their fields of yams or camotes (on which they live well) from one place to another without much effort, pulling them up by the roots—for, because of the dampness of the country, these take root wherever they are placed. If they reach one thousand men that is a great number. They can scarcely gather in one body or live on friendly terms with one another.

The picture afforded by these two quotations is of a scattered settlement pattern with great potential mobility, of cogon grass houses, and also of the practice of dry cultivation. Strikingly absent is any reference to rice cropping, or to terraced and irrigated fields. Yet this was the period from late February, when modern Ibaloi have transplanted their rice from the seedbeds to the flooded terraces, with the harvest ripening in June (Moss, 1920*a*, pp. 221–22). It will be seen that another "exploring" expedition led by Galvey which traversed the area two centuries later (January 1829) also failed to report wet rice terracing. The presumption is that it was adopted by the Ibaloi during the nineteenth century, and indeed in the twentieth century, as will be seen, government reports tell of the first terraces being built in remoter northern zones of Benguet.

The reference to *camotes* as being grown along with yams at this time is particularly interesting. If the botanical identification is correct—and there is little reason to doubt that the Spaniards would recognize the sweet potato which they themselves used extensively—this American plant had already spread as a staple into the mountains. This also happened in the New Guinea highlands well ahead of European penetration; there, the sweet potato provides the essential basis for subsistence among the mountaineers, and without it, indeed, the relatively barren highlands would perhaps not have been settled.

Quirante's report, in discussing the lack of unity among the people, says that those living on the southern Cordillera heights had "little or no communication" with mountain groups living in "Banaco" (possibly Bauko, a village in Lepanto further north). The same was true as regards "Aytuy" (Ituy) and "Panaquy" (Paniquy), that is, the peoples of the upper Magat valley area on the Cagayan side, though "it is said that they pay a sort of tribute or recognition" to these latter groups. All were hostile to "those" of "Alrade," "Vigan," and "Orraya," so that "all those Ygolotes being so separated, cautious, malicious, and treacherous, no message can be sent to them." By the "Vigan" Ygolotes referred to here were evidently meant mountain populations on the Ilocos coast side further north toward Vigan, while the "Orraya" Ygolotes were still uncontrolled mountain groups to the northwest in the middle Cagayan called Irraya by the early Spaniards. The name "Alrade" is not identified; it could well refer to a district either in Pangasinan or in Ifugao.

In the rainy season, this "wretched race, most of whom are miners," along with "wives and children," washed sand in the streamlets to recover gold. This entailed less work than mining the ore, which was done a "little" in the dry season. The mined areas were found to be on "five elevations." Galan, the Spanish base, was evidently located in the gold-bearing Tublay area in the Naguilian river headwaters. Beyond Galan, at a distance of three leagues, were Arisey and Bugayona and a league further was Baranaban; these presumably comprised the gold-bearing Ambuklao area of the upper-middle Agno river. Next came Antamog, two leagues on, which is the rich modern Antomok mining area; and finally Conog, a further half league, presumably the modern Balatoc-Itogon mining area. The account describes pickaxes tipped with iron, used by the local miners to chip the ore while sitting in the passages. This in turn was crushed "with a stout rock in receptacles" and then carried to "washing places," where the gold was recognized by its gleam in sunlight. By crushing again and by washing and rewashing, the metal was recovered. In trading the gold to the lowlands, it was measured not by weight but "by sight."

The emphasis in the gold trade on obtaining livestock from the lowlanders is explained by Quirante as being linked to the killing of animals for "solemn feasts." On their part, the mountain people "only breed small and wretched dogs." The account adds:

Besides, those Igolotes are indebted to the natives of the village who are our friends [i.e., the lowland trading settlements], and are unable to pay those who give them credit; the wealth and wit of both peoples being so small and restricted that, although those people have no other kind of expenses, or other things to attend to, than the product of their mines, they are generally in debt.

This credit and debt relation, by which the mountaineers became to a point dependent on lowland traders, is paralleled on other frontiers, where isolated peoples provided the larger world with a special resource which they commanded: for example, the North American Indian fur trade; the exploitation of sandalwood, pearls, and seaslugs in the Pacific islands.

The expedition miners, including Japanese mining specialists, opened numerous tunnels in the gold-bearing areas during "many months" of prospecting. But they failed to locate major gold deposits. Specimens of the ore were carried to the plains in "four hundred small rice baskets," and samples sent on to Mexico for examination. This failure, together with the high costs of maintaining the enterprise logistically and in the face of hostility by the mountaineers, led to abandonment (B&R, xx, 262–301).

CONTINUING RECORDS: NORTH PANGASINAN

Medina's Augustinian *History* of 1630, in contrast to the full and leisurely texture of Aduarte's Dominican record, has almost nothing specific to say of the missions on the southern Ilocos coast, which formed the panhandle, so to speak, of Pangasinan Province. But its statements quoted in the last chapter on the largeness and neatness of settlements, and the effectiveness of mission concentration policy, presumably apply to this area as well as to others further north. Medina notes tersely that "religious were placed in Bauang." The "Igorrotes" are referred to as coming down to "hunt heads, in which they take pride," and also to trade "a great quantity of gold" from their mines. They are, he says, "unconquerable," and vacillate between friendliness and enmity; when they "rebel" their "villages disappear." "We [have] controlled a few only," and along this part of the coast they were "gathered" in Bauang, and thus absorbed into the Christian lowland population (B&R, xxiii, 276–80).

From this time on, the lowland districts and settlements receive little specific mention except at times of civil or ecclesiastical censuses and other surveys, or when "rebellions" flared up. Pangasinan, it was seen, was the locale for a major outbreak in 1660–61, when disaffection spread to it from Pampanga. The self-declared "King" Malong had his principal headquarters in his home town of Binalatongan in west Pangasinan. One of Ma-

long's "associates," however, was a "native of the village of Agoo": Don
Pedro Gumapos, whom he made a "Conde" or "Count." In the course of
rebel operations, Gumapos led a force north as far as Bauang. Subsequently
a major military force of four thousand Pangasinans and Zambals, under
another leader, Macasiag, moved on northward through Ilocos Province.

The operations of Gumapos are the subject of a considerable exposition
by Díaz in his *Conquests*. After occupying Agoo, his rebel force, which included "Zambals and Negritos," advanced on Bauang. The "vicar-provincial" was conducting a service in the local church as they approched:

He found at the door of the church two Indian chiefs of that village. . . .
[They] told him not to be afraid, as they were there determined to defend the
father from the fury of the Zambals, who were already near, even if it cost them
their lives. . . . While he was saying mass, the Zambals arrived . . . [under]
their leader or captain . . . Gumapos. . . . [They] waited very quietly for
the father to finish saying mass.

Gumapos then came up to kiss the father's hand, accompanied by armed
"Zambals and Negritos," and "told him absurd things about his rebellion
against the Spaniards." Then, on the excuse of looking for Spanish refugees, the convent was looted. The father was also asked to pay a ransom
to spare the life of the priest in charge of the Agoo church, who had been
captured. Unable to extract the ransom, Gumapos ordered his men to kill
the prisoner, as had already been done in the case of a Spanish "tax-collec-
tor." But, instead, "a chieftainess of the visita of Balanac" and others of
the faithful collected gold to have his life spared. The two fathers were then
imprisoned.

All the while the Zambals remained in Bauang, they were engaged in plundering and robbing the poor Indians, and did all the damage they could. . . .
[When they left, the fathers] emerged from their prison, half-dead from weakness . . . but the Zambals had left nothing in the convent, and the religious
therefore had to send to the Indians to beg food. . . . On the following day
. . . nearly all the people in the village of Bauang confessed and received com-
munion, most of those who had taken part in the murder of the Spaniard . . .
doing penance . . . especially the headman.

One of the Bauang leaders, Don Dionisio Maricdin, who had shown
great loyalty where others had "conceived so great fear," was shortly afterward made "sargento-mayor of the villages of Aringuey, Bauang, and
Agoo." The picture suggested here is that these marginal Pangasinan communities of the north were both prosperous and under mission control to
the point where they were for the most part out of sympathy with the anti-
Spanish movement of their ethnic fellows living further south in Pangasinan. At least they must have felt caught between fear of both the Spaniards and the rebels with their respective military forces to the north and
the south.

In the face of anticipated further hostilities, a military force of 1,500 "Ilocans" under a Spanish commander moved down the coast into Bauang. The vicar-provincial went to meet the party, but failed to encounter them, so that when they arrived they "found the village without inhabitants, because for fear of the Zambals they had fled to the woods." The "drums" being beaten, the village was quickly "full of people" again, and notice was sent to Agoo that aid was at hand. A troop under an Ilocan master-in-camp was then dispatched to Aringay to deal with the father of Gumapos, Don Miguel Carreno, who was the "head of the conspirators" and was communicating to his son "all the operations of the loyal Indians." Carreno was seized and hanged, and the "Zambals of his command" were defeated and took to flight.

The Spanish alcalde-mayor of Ilocos then came south, and the Spanish force moved on to Agoo. Soon faced, however, with Macasiag's rebel army of more than three times their number, and realizing that the Ilocan troops were "all undisciplined" and "somewhat timid," the Spanish commander advised retreat. But the alcalde-mayor, confident of the superiority of firearms, set up instead an ambush south of Agoo. When the fight joined, the Ilocan master-in-camp was killed, and a precipitate retreat followed, in which not only the Ilocan soldiers but also men, women, and children attached to their camp left the area "in flight." The rebels captured the arms and gunpowder, and in turn put them to busy use. The Spanish leaders attempted to "rally the Indians" at Agoo, and afterward at Bauang, but they were pushed back northward. Subsequent happenings will be reviewed in the later chapters, including the final defeat of the rebel forces. The churches and convents of the Agoo-Bauang area were undoubtedly looted in accordance with insurgent policies, as was done elsewhere in Ilocos (B&R, xxxviii, 176, 181–91).

An ecclesiastical chronicler of 1676, Baltazar de Santa Cruz, reviews both Augustinian and Dominican mission progress in Pangasinan, Ilocos, and Cagayan. He notes how lowland Christians were suffering from the deceit, cunning, and cruelty of the "Igolotes." They "harm villages" in both Pangasinan and Ilocos by "setting fire to them" or "by means of safe ambushes," and "regard theft as great cleverness." He says of them that they are "very superstitious" and "practice divination." They also "practice bigamy, for they marry many women." "Arrows" were their usual weapons, and they also "carry lances and *balaros* (daggers) which they buy in other villages with gold."

Baltazar also speaks of the great extent of "rough land" which stretches by way of some "high mountain chains to the coast." He is evidently talking of the Caraballo Sur and Sierra Madre ranges to the east and northeast. This region, he says, contains "heathen settlements," although there are "some Christians among them." In spite of "many" attempts by military parties and missionaries, Baltazar continues, it "has not yet been possible" to bring the region under control (B&R, xxxvii, 88–99, 243–44).

From this time, ecclesiastical and other documents begin to fill in the story of these eastern areas, which so far have received almost no specific reference.

THE EASTERN AREAS

The extensive Pangasinan flats bordering the southern Cordillera face stretch inland for a little more than thirty miles. They are mostly drained by the Agoo river system. To the southeast, through broken foothill country, are further flats of the upper Pampanga river system. The heights of the Caraballo Sur and Sierra Madre ranges to the north and east, respectively, discharge their water runoff into the Pampanga. Before the formation of Nueva Ecija province in the nineteenth century, this latter river area comprised the northern part of Pampanga Province.

Vague references were noted in the general chapter to "Zambals" and "Negritos" in the region. As the ethnic geography becomes clarified, it will be seen that Negrito groups were widely distributed through the foothill country, and the mountain peoples were of the type blanketed by the general term "Ilongot." In the early records, the Negritos are often called by the popular Spanish name for this group, "Balugas." The Ilongot peoples mostly appear under local names derived from mountain river systems on which they were encountered: e.g., "Italon," "Abaca," "Irapi," "Iruli," "Ibilao."

Mission workers approached these populations from two directions: the Dominicans from adjacent zones of Pangasinan, and the Augustinians working northward into the Pampanga river headwaters. Through their territories, too, ran old trade trails between the Pangasinan-Pampanga flats and the headwater valleys of the upper Cagayan. It was by one or more of these trails that several initial Spanish military expeditions passed in 1591–94 to explore so-called "Tuy" or "Ituy," the valleys of the upper Magat river. From about 1630, Dominican mission fathers used them to carry on sporadic work among the Ituy peoples, as will be seen in the Cagayan study. Their records show that they made some converts among the "infidels and apostates" living along the southern faces of the Cordillera and Caraballo Sur heights. The "apostates" were evidently runaways from the lowland settlements, such as were spoken about by Baltazar in the quotation given above. Two small mountain settlements, Carranglan and Pantabangan, the former on a trail going over the Balete Pass, became gathering places for Christians.

These settlements, with some others lower down the Pampanga river, broke into the news in 1646, when northern Luzon experienced a very severe earthquake. An "Indian of evil disposition," as Díaz puts it, plotted an uprising:

[He exhorted] the natives to rebel and restore themselves to their former liberty, by slaying the Spaniards and the religious. He assured them that in Manila there were no Spaniards left, because the earth had swallowed them, with the entire city . . . and that the demon, with whom he had compact and intercourse, had promised . . . that they might maintain themselves without paying tribute, and might enjoy much prosperity. . . . The delusion of the Indians of [the settlement of] Gapang went so far that they seized arms, and summoned to their aid many heathen Zambals [i.e., mountain people], and burned the churches of Santor and Pantabangan.

The local encomendero hastened there with his collectors and some "friendly Indians" to try to stop the movement, but he was mortally wounded and most of his party were slain. The people then "fortified themselves in the mountains." A mission father well known to them then went in with a strong military party, and after various "perils" the "sedition was finally quelled" (B&R, xxxviii, 95–98).

In 1668, after a prolonged yet futile attempt to control the Cordillera peoples from a fort placed at Kayan on the Ilocos side, as will be seen in the next chapter, the Philippine Governor of the time had a fort built instead at a "a sitio called Orori." This, according to de los Reyes, was located "on the heights of the rancherias of Pantabangan and Karranglan" (ii, 128–29, 147). It could possibly have been at the later Urorin or Palosapes, a Christian settlement point to be mentioned below—that is, Palusapis near the modern town of Muñoz. The purpose of this new fort was, hopefully, to control both the Igorots and other mountain peoples to the north, and the Zambales mountaineers to the west, against whom campaigns were being waged at the time. This project, however, came to a quick end. Díaz (1718) tells how a new Governor who took office in 1669, just after the fort was completed, ordered the Spanish commander, Don Pedro de la Peña, "to withdraw from the presidio of Orori on the frontier of the Igolotes, as that presidio was entirely useless, and only an object of expense, without any profit" (B&R, xxxvii, 278–80).

From 1632, as will be seen in the upper Cagayan chapter, Dominican fathers had been crossing periodically from Pangasinan to work in Ituy, the upper Magat river valleys. As told by Aduarte (1640), the pioneering Dominican, Fray Tomás Gutiérrez, in crossing the mountains had noted "a tribe of Indians called Alegueses" who were "a vagabond people having no settled places of abode." This father proposed to "settle" them on a new site, but died before he could carry the plan into effect (B&R, xxxii, 201). The records indicate that they lived in the Ambayabang river area, and they could have been either shifting dry cultivators or else Negritos.

About 1685, according to Salazar's Dominican *History* (1742), this

Order opened a mission center to "accomplish the reduction" of this tribe, and also of "Igorot" groups living in adjacent zones of the Cordillera. This work had its headquarters at a mission center called San Bartolemé. Though not on modern maps, it is shown in later records to have become a stopover point, with the name Malionlion, on a Pangasinan-Cagayan "road" built in 1739 by civil and ecclesiastical authorities. Early-eighteenth-century mission maps to be referred to below place Malionlion between the forks of the Agno and Ambayabang rivers.

The subsequent history of the San Bartolemé mission is told in several Dominican chronicles. The work there lasted for "more than twenty years." Many people were baptized, "especially of the Alaguetes, who were more docile than the Igorots," although some of the latter were also converted. By 1698, it was reported that the Alaguetes were intermarrying with the Pangasinans, and the "idiom" of Pangasinan was becoming the common language. As summarized by Blair and Robertson from Salazar, the later story of this mission may be set out here:

In 1709 or 1710, because of disputes that arose between those of the village [of San Bartolemé] and the Igorots, who lived in the mountain, the latter descended the mountain at night and set fire to the village. . . . Consequently the village is deserted, and the father and the inhabitants removed to San Luis Beltran [possibly the later Asingan, as this is the name of its patron saint], which being further from the mountains is safer. After six years there, a government decree removes them to Maoacatoacat. Later the mission is moved to Pao, and finally to Manaoag. But since the natives dislike to leave the site where they are settled, and also enjoy a life of freedom where they are not molested by the tribute, many of the inhabitants refuse to move at the successive transfers. Falling into relaxation in consequence, many become infidels, and their number is increased by those who flee to them to escape the tribute and the restrictions of religion.

Here are seen at work the contra-acculturative tendencies that resettlement tends to generate. In 1732, in response to Dominican pressures, a new mission village was opened on almost the same site as the old San Bartolemé "at a location called Maliongliong," for "the conversion of the Igorots," and this village was called San José. Few new converts, however, appear to have been made (B&R, XLIII, 76–77).

Meantime, from 1695 on, Augustinian fathers had been moving northward up the Pampanga river to develop missions in its headwater areas. From 1702 they made the old settlements of Pantabangan and Carranglan their major bases for work among the Ilongot groups in the Caraballo Sur mountains and in the upper Magat (Ituy). They also moved westward into the foothill country to establish missions among the Negritos, and on to the Agno river flats around Tayug, where they made "Igorrot" converts. These efforts are described in considerable detail by the Augustinian chronicler Mozo (1763), who was one of the workers, and in a series of documents written by other participating fathers and edited by Angel Perez (1904). Perez also gives three mission maps drawn at the time.

As told by Mozo, the pioneer father, Fray Antolin de Arzaga, worked initially among settlements of Italon and Abaca north and east of Pantabangan. After arriving at the settlement in 1702, he sent a message to an Italon village called Lublub, some twelve miles east of Pantabangan toward Baler Bay, asking that he be allowed to enter it. The chief, with a party, met him and he was able to visit the village, which he reports as having "about one hundred and fifty persons." Of the "Italon tribe" more generally, he states:

[It] consists of fifty-six villages—so far as I have yet ascertained—which lie on the shores of two deep rivers, toward the north. They have a general language which is entirely separate from those of Tagalos and Pampanga; they have well-kept villages, with high houses. They take great care of their fields, and keep their grain in . . . granaries. . . . The fishing, as also the hunting, is abundant and good. . . . The people are kindly, but very warlike and of courageous dispositions; they are quite ingenious, and are hospitable. . . . They understand that there is a God . . . to whom they offer sacrifices. . . . They have a contract of marriage with one wife only, which lasts until death; they do not allow concubinage; and they do not marry their relatives.

Fray Antolin then compares the Italon with the Abaca, consisting of "ten villages," evidently in the region of the present Abaca river. Having been visited at Pantabangan by some Abaca people, he found on his first trip to the nearest Abaca village, Diama, that "arches" had been built over the trails and a large cross erected at the "entrance of their jurisdiction" and also one in the village. The Abaca, he says, though warring with the Italons, and having a "different language" from them, were almost of the same type. But "some of them have several wives, and this is not so liberal a people." He notes that Diama village had "over a hundred persons." One Abaca had "continued forty years in apostasy"—indicative of earlier mission contacts in this general region from both the Dominicans in Pangasinan and the Franciscans in Baler Bay.

Following this initial work extending outward from Pantabangan, the Augustinians began mission activities among the Italon from the second center mentioned above, Carranglan. It is described by Mozo as an old settlement point for Christians, but "for lack of a minister . . . going without administration." The initial Augustinian, Fray Baltazar de Santa Maria Isisigana, met with a general willingness in the region to accept Christianity. By 1704, he and Antolin had established five new mission villages of Italon and Abaca converts on more accessible sites in the lower country: Santo Tomas de Villanueva (80 families), Santo Cristo de Burgos (100 families), San Augustin (160 families), San Pablo (140 families), and San José (70 families). The mission authorities sent "220 cattle" from Manila for distribution in the area.

Fray Antolin tells of making an arduous trip by "wretched roads" to Tablayan, a village of the "upper Italons" some 50 miles northward from

Pantabangan, which took him well into Cagayan. Sickness forced his return, but he was accompanied by the chief and his family. This was possibly the modern Ilongot settlement area of Tanayan, on the Conwap tributary of the upper Cagayan river. Fray Antolin died in 1707, and in his place was sent Fray Alejandro Cacho, who was to work in the upper Pampanga and Ituy regions for "more than forty years." Angel Perez says of him that he "formed villages, opened roads, established schools, built churches, and felled groves; and what was but a little before a gloomy and impenetrable forest . . . [became] a broad plain . . . a fertile field and beautiful province, the pride and hope of the new converts" (B&R, XIV, 70, footnote 18). Mozo draws upon Cacho's writings in giving an account of the ferocity and cruelty of the mountain tribes, which he compares to the Huns:

If they succeed in killing a person they try to drink his blood; and cutting off pieces of his lungs, together with . . . other parts . . . [they] divide these among themselves and eat them raw—not only to make themselves terrible, but also because they say it is a powerful medicine for exciting courage, fierceness, and fortitude in their battles. They also cut off the head, and carry it away in order to celebrate their festivals, with great gluttony and carousing, with a sort of wine they make from sugarcane. . . . Afterward, they take the grinders and teeth and set these in the belts of their cutlasses. . . . [Hardly] anyone . . . has not in his hut a collection of the skulls from human heads. . . . [At] their feasts, and in the superstitious rites which they practice, they utter a thousand execrations against [sorcerers or wizards]. . . . [On a war party] they throw into a hole in some creek a root and herbs which they carry, provided, and by their using various magic spells [gain the aid of the demon].

Mozo goes on to contrast the life of the mountain groups with that of the lowlanders further south:

The tribes converted by the early missionaries were more civilized, dwelt on the plains, and had a more orderly mode of life, sowing grain and gathering enough for their support; but those of whom we speak, besides being rough in their behavior, hardly know any tillage of the soil, living generally by hunting. Their mode of cultivating what little they plant is as follows: They first clear some little piece of ground from the brush and weeds on it, with their knives . . . then with the point of the knife they make holes in the ground, in rows, and throw into each a few grains of seed; they know no plow, or any other thing that might serve as one, for which reason the harvest they gather is always very small.

In other words they were dry cultivators, using shifting gardens. Mozo goes on to describe their cultivation of sugar cane, from which they "make wine for drinking at their feasts." Because such peoples had "to go wandering about," the fathers, as soon as they began "to confer baptism," endeavored to "find animals and other necessaries for the cultivation of the land." They had to teach not only how to "plow and sow," but also how to cut the crop with a sickle and to winnow it instead of "picking the grain spike by spike." Mozo notes the attachment of these peoples to the mountains and their abhorrence of life on the plains, the latter increased by their dread of small-pox, from which they could quarantine themselves in the mountains by shutting off trails, and also by their dislike for the hotter climate of the low country. Hence the missionaries "made no further effort to change their dwellings," but went to their home areas (B&R, XLVIII, 69–80).

In the course of these records, additional local names appear for the mountain groups, especially the general term Ilongot. It is also made clear that the foothills between the Agno and Pampanga flats, empty of Negritos today, were inhabited by "Balugas" at the time. Cacho, in a document published by Perez (1904), speaks of them as a "most vile nation," eating roots and hunting with bow and arrow (Perez, 1904, pp. 36–39). Mozo, who worked among them himself, includes in his account a description which could apply to Negrito remnants of today:

They have their own territory, within which they go about in bands, and from which they never go out; but they do not have any fixed dwelling place in it, for they remain a short time in one place hunting, and afterward they remove therefrom four or five leguas away. In whatever place they arrive, they make their hut in an instant with four rough sticks, and with a sort of grass, very long and flexible, . . . or with the leaves of palms. . . . They live entirely in common, and therefore when they capture any deer or wild swine (by hunting which they live) they immediately share it equally—except the head and neck, which parts they set aside for the dogs that they have, who start the said game. Each band, usually containing twenty-five to thirty persons, goes by itself, with one man to whom the rest pay respect, generally the one who is most daring and valiant.

The account goes on to describe their gathering of "honeycombs" from trees, so that they could eat the honey and sell the wax in order to buy tobacco. They also dug for tubers of *sucbao* (apparently an edible pond lily, *Nelumbium speciosum*), which they roasted. Their weapons comprised the bow and arrow and "half-cutlass" and their "arrows were poisoned with a decoction of the bark of the *camandag*" (the croton shrub). They also used herbs as medicines and "love philters." Mozo tells how he himself made "more than 150" Negrito converts during a three-year period, and established "two small villages" of these people. He does not specify whether these were between the Pampanga and Agno rivers or on the Sierra Madre side. The main mission center for the Negrito work in the former area was Lupao.

Out of this Augustinian effort, the essential demographic patterns of eastern Pangasinan and northern Nueva Ecija became established. Mozo tells of two sets of mission villages taking form, one group "within the mountains" and the other group "in the valleys." The mountain communities, besides the older Carranglan and Pantabangan, are named as Puncan, San Miguel, Santa Rita, Bolo, San Juan, and Santo Tomas. The valley communities were Tayog or Tayug, Umingan, Lupao, San José, Palosapes or Urorin, San Agustin, and Santa Monica (B&R, xLviii, 60–78; see also the mission maps in Perez). Cacho describes how the people were taught by the fathers to construct "irrigated fields," and how their pueblos were being enlarged by families descending from the mountains to receive baptism (Perez, 1904, pp. 30–55). Across the Caraballo Sur, similar successes were occurring in the upper Magat valleys of Ituy, as will be seen in the later chapter on that region.

Among the communities listed above is Tayug, which is on an eastern tributary of the Agno river not far from the Dominican-controlled settlement of Asingan. It will be seen by fitting together the mission geography of this early-eighteenth-century period that the breakline between the Dominicans and Augustinians along the Cordillera was between these two centers. Back of Tayug, the Augustinians also developed another center, San Nicolas. Cacho refers to Tayug as a "pueblo of recent converts," from the "Igorrot nation," with "much gold." In 1780, Fray Benito Herosa describes the "Igorrotes" of the area as comprising "many people, divided into rancherias."

The ordinary foodstuffs of these infidels are gabi [taro], camotes [sweet potatoes], ubes [yams], gourds, all of which they plant in abundance; they also eat much flesh of hogs, cattle, carabao, and deer, which they hunt on the slopes of the mountains; all these products they eat simply, without mixing one with another; they also use no condiments. . . . They also plant sugercane, which they crush for the juice; something of rice, though not for maintenance, but in order to have with that juice, brewing it into wine, which they call basi, and which induces great bouts of drunkenness, especially in their gatherings and feasts. They also plant some maize, but it ordinarily grows poorly, because of the heavy rains.

It is notable that rice is deliberately described as used not for a general food, but for brewing wine. A similar statement will appear in Augustinian records of the mid-eighteenth century relating to groups on the southwest slopes of the Cordillera back of Agoo. In neither instance is reference made to the irrigated terracing of later times. Herosa speaks also of "an old *Maganitera*," or female shaman, conducting religious rituals, but makes no mention of male priests (Perez, 1904, pp. 30–31, 236–43). The two mission sketch maps in the Perez collection show written on the southern Cordillera heights ethnic rubrics which on one is written "Igorrotes de Abiag" and on the other "Igorrotes de Albiag": the name perhaps suggestive of the modern appellations "Ibaloi" and "Nabaloi."

In the 1730's, as will be seen, pressure developed among the Cagayan peoples to have an overland "road" or official trail built to connect that province with Pangasinan. This project was completed in 1739, the southern base being at Asingan, and the northern one at Bugay. It could be traversed in approximately two days by horseback, and construction was done under joint government and mission (both Dominican and Augustinian) auspices, using "Indian" labor. The work was supervised by a Dominican father, Fray Manuel del Rio. The latter, in a chronicle that records the building activities, tells of meeting opposition at first from "Igorrotes" in the intervening mountains. He describes them as "a bloodthirsty and very treacherous people." Finally, after liberal distribution of presents, they gave their consent to the construction work. The bargain was then ceremonially sealed:

In the presence of all, a hog was killed, and, as soon as the knife was thrust into it, profound silence reigned [during its dying struggles]. . . . After a long time, a Christian Indian who was experienced in their ceremonies came forward, and, collecting in his hand some of the animal's blood, went, with loud cries and a swaggering step, and smeared with the blood the feet of the Igorrot chiefs; at this they were well pleased. . . . This done they were given something to drink, and the cattle, *carajays* [jars], salt, and other [gifts] . . . [and] returned to their villages contented.

Roadhouses were built at intervals "in the places called Colong, Malalapang, and Malionlion." Malionlion, between the Agno and Ambayabang rivers, is referred to as the last town on the border of Pangasinan. Here "a missionary was stationed to serve some Igorrot Christians," and to extend conversion and peace in the region. This center was spoken of earlier as the site of the old San Bartolemé mission. Del Rio refers to an attempt made by a Governor of the Philippines twenty years previously to open such a road, which had proved unsuccessful in spite of heavy expenditures (B&R, xlviii, 134–36).

In 1740, the Augustinians will be seen as transferring their work in Ituy to the Dominicans, who had been moving into adjacent areas of the upper Cagayan valley. Then in 1753 the mountain missions of the Pantabangan and Carranglan areas were transferred to the Franciscans. This Order had been working since 1609 among the Tagalog-speaking people on the Pacific Coast side at Baler and several points further north. Martinez de Zuñiga, in his *Historical Review* written in 1803, was to report that the "missions of Pantabangan" had at that time "two or three" Franciscan fathers in the area. Pantabangan had 60 houses, Carranglan 82, and Puncan 56. "Very little progress is made in these missions," he says, "on account of the misgovernment among the Indians and the lack of policy on the part of the Spaniards." Those groups not converted by that time were evidently to continue on as non-Christians to form the Ilongot and Negrito groups of modern times (B&R, xlviii, 67).

THE MIDDLE PERIOD TO 1840

In 1744 a notable map of the Philippines drawn by Fray Pedro Murillo Velarde shows the provinces of Pangasinan, Ilocos, Cagayan, and Pampanga, with a rough delineation of the Cordillera and its principal rivers between them. For the area being discussed here, the map shows in Pangasinan the settlements of San Fabian and Magaldan, or Mangaldan, then up the coast one called "Ravon," evidently the present small community of Rabon on the border of Pangasinan and La Union provinces, followed by Santo Tomas, Agoo, and Balanac, the last an unidentified name in the Aringay area. No place names appear within eastern Pangasinan or the southern Cordillera, though "Ygolotes" is written along the mountain chain. Only the lower section of the Agno river and gorge is shown, and its eastern tributaries are confused with headwater streams of the Pampanga river. In the old Pampanga province, Pantabangan and Bongabon are shown, with Puncan deeper in the Caraballo Sur mountains; here the "Ytalones" are recorded.

An ecclesiastical survey of the Philippines in 1738 shows the Dominicans as having nineteen "administrations" in Pangasinan. Listed as in the northern parts of the province were Mangaldan and Manaoag, and others seemingly recognizable there are Anguio, apparently San Fabian, and Baruc, possibly Asingan which has a constituent settlement called Baro. The record speaks of the principal centers as having "some visitas," and there were also "missions of blacks." The Augustinian establishments in northern Pangasinan were listed as being

in the village of Agoo, with Santo Tomas and Aringay, whence the religious go to the neighboring mountains to the conquest of the barbarous Igorrote people; in the village of Bauan [Bauang], with those of Boua, Dalandan, Caua, and one other fine mission; in the village of Bagnotan, with that of San Juan, and another fine mission. These administrations number 8,875 souls.

Caua is the present town of Caba, while Boua, or Bona in an alternative spelling, may be Rabon; Bagnotan, San Juan, and Dalandan (an old settlement from which San Fernando took form) will be dealt with in the next chapter. The total figure for "souls" cited here is an extraordinarily low estimate, as will be seen from other records to be cited below. A corresponding Augustinian ecclesiastical survey for 1754 speaks of the "convents and ministries" of Agoo, Santo Tomas, and Aringay, with "several missions of Igorrotes in the mountains," and those of "Bauar [Bauang], Bona, Dalandan, and Caba, with another mission of mountaineers" (B&R, xxviii, 158, 159, 167).

The Augustinian Mozo (1763) was seen in the general chapter to have classed the "Igolotes" as the southernmost of "four very noted tribes." He speaks of them as having "multiplied exceedingly."

[Igolot] fierceness and cruelty is unequalled; their only desire is to take captives, in order to have slaves for their service, and when they have enough of these, to kill whomever they encounter. For this reason, without a strong escort one cannot pass, except with great danger, through the upper part of these mountains; and even the villages are so infested with them that as a precaution they always keep some men armed to resist these marauders—at night stationing a sentinel with his drum, who is changed during the daytime—through that mountain range.

Such conditions, Mozo says, had proved a constant trial to the "patience" of the lowland villagers:

[Because] in every place our natives—especially if they are away from the village—are so harassed by the Igolots; therefore when they go to sow their grain or gather their crops they erect high sentry-posts, from which they can see if the enemy are coming; and those who work keep the sickle in one hand and a weapon in the other—as we are told of the Israelites when in the time of Esdras they were building the walls of Jerusalem. . . . And even when they do this, they are not safe from the fury of those savages. Such was the ferocity of this tribe . . . [that they tried] the patience of all those villages.

Mozo gives a vivid account of Igolot funeral ceremonies:

It is a usage among these people not to give burial to any of their dead, especially if he was a chief, until whatever he may have left has been consumed in gluttony and carousing among his relatives and others belonging to him; with some chiefs this is commonly no small amount, because in the rivers there some gold is found, and all the people endeavor to obtain it for their chiefs. For, expending for cattle, hogs, rice, and wine whatever the dead man possessed of this sort, they make enormous bonfires about the corpse, which they lay on the ground; and, having killed the animals, they . . . prepare barbecues which are savory to their taste. Afterward, beginning to dance around the corpse, they keep this up night and day, one set giving place to another. They eat and drink frequently; and if any one is inclined to sleep he squats on his haunches, with his head resting on his knees, and needs no other bed. Thus they remain, ten, fifteen, or twenty days with the corpse, without interring it; and even [the stench] . . . does not drive them away. They reserve some gold and some food, which afterward they inter with the deceased, so that he may have it, as they say, for his journey.

The Igolotes, Mozo continues, would not allow the missionaries to settle among them, and any who tried were threatened with death if they did not leave. Mission work had therefore to be confined to making conversions along the fringes of their territory, where "outside missionaries" could establish contact with them. The Igolotes were "not disturbed by this."

[Rather] they were pleased, because their relatives or friends who had removed to Christian villages were thus able to supply them with articles of comfort or luxury which they themselves had not—blankets, wine, hogs, and cattle, of whose flesh they are very fond, and use it continually in their feasts and "banquets."

Such trading gave the missionaries opportunity for contacts that might lead to conversions.

Mozo then goes on to report a shift in the attitudes of the Igorots of the southern Ilocos coast area in 1755 toward mission activity. This came about, he says, through the work of Fray Francisco Cordoba, who had been sent in 1747 to Agoo, "on the frontier of the Igolots."

[This father] soon secured their good-will, although they long refused to allow him to live among them. Finally, after seven years of this apparently unfruitful labor, a miraculous change occurred. During the visitation of the provincial . . . while he was conferring with Cordova at Aringay, five chiefs came down from the mountains and asked [the provincial] to send missionaries among them. He sent a deputation of them to Manila to ask this favor from the governor [who granted their request. . . . They were] baptized while in Manila, and returned to their tribe, who eagerly sought baptism also. Cordova was made superior of the new mission, with . . . [two] assistants; they built two churches, and baptized many hundreds. In other Igolot villages, missions were also conducted by [three other fathers]. (B&R, xlviii, 80–82, 87–90.)

This new mission effort is reported in a particularly rich set of additional Augustinian documents assembled by Angel Perez (1904). Manuel Carillo, in his *Brief Relation* of 1756, speaks of the principal center of work as at Tonglo, a mission-established Christian pueblo in the mountains back of Agoo, and locale of the "most celebrated front of Catholic action" at the time. The fullest records, however, are those of Pedro Vivar, who established this center, and tells of his visits to 59 named mountain settlements in the area.

Vivar, in a report on "the district of Benguet" dated 1755–56, weighs what is "good" and "bad" in the "Igorrote" character and custom. He speaks of "avarice" reigning among them; of their "slaves," including captured or refugee lowlanders, some of whom have lived among them for many years; of their ability to carry loads of "camotes" and other goods on the steep slopes; and of their beliefs and festivals. Wine is made, he says, by fermenting a mixture of "rice and sugarcane." The rice is "sown in the mountains" (a phrase suggesting dry cultivation), while the sugar cane is "grown around their houses." This passing statement on rice cropping for the making of wine repeats one given earlier regarding the "Igorrotes" in the Agno river area. When Vivar was traveling inland to establish the Tonglo center, he reports being "well regaled" at one of the settlements with a meal of "bananas, camotes, and aba [apparently *ubi,* or yams]," suggesting that rice was not in use as a staple food.

In October 1755, Vivar used the implied invitation of a leader who came to Tonglo from the high valley of Benguet to make a trip to that area. Though this is the first located record of a visit by a Spaniard since the Martín Quirante expedition of 1624, the fact that he speaks of this valley as "famed" for its "uniqueness" suggests that others may have explored it in the meantime.

It has a plain four leagues in circumference in the form of an O, and is surrounded with moderately elevated hills covered with pines. At their bases are the houses, of which there are some two hundred or more. There are plentiful springs, which feed a lake half a league in circumference, abounding with eels and varied birds. There are four rancherias in this locality; Benguet, Bugao, Acaba, and Pijo, and many more are in the neighborhood.

He then gives the population totals in the four named settlements as 28, 76, 75, and 43, respectively, suggesting that for the most part the houses were spread out among the fields as in the characteristic Ibaloi residential pattern of later times.

These population figures are typical of the very precise statistics given for the settlements under the influence of the Tonglo mission. Francisco de Cordoba lists 32 rancherias in the area, with a total of 126 Christian and 1,996 "infidels," that is, 2,122 persons, or an average of 66 to a rancheria. Vivar, in his tabulation of these settlements, shows the largest to be Aputut, one of several around Tonglo, with 135, while the smallest had 12. He also lists the names, though not the population numbers, of 28 more settlements in the high Benguet area, including the upper Agno valley north to Buguias; for some, even the names of the leading men appear.

A striking point is that none of the 32 rancherias under Tonglo mission influence still exist, at least under the same names. An exception might be Tonglo, if it is a locality called "Monglo," near Sablan. Of those deeper in the mountains only Buguias, Ambusi, and Lutab in the upper Agno valley are recognizable. This seems to indicate in vivid fashion a later dispersal of the accessible settlements in the face of Spanish tribute collections, and of punitive military expeditions to be seen below.

As part of the mission activities, the fathers persuaded the leaders to construct new fields for the growing of crops, including "sugarcane, cotton, and other products," as Carillo puts it, "just the same as the naturales of Ilocos." This author pointed out also how readily the new converts returned "to their old asylum" in the mountains, and "resumed their former idolatries." One of the problems of adjustment to the lowlands was that mountaineers "get sick," and are also exposed to epidemics such as one that swept the coastal area in 1754, killing some 14,000 people. There were also problems of security, as those who were pacified and resettled became prey to still hostile groups in the deeper mountains.

Vivar gives in his account of the district of Benguet a lively description of a "fiesta" to which neighbors were invited as guests. For the feast, two carabaos were killed and thirty jars of wine were on hand. Music was supplied by two "bells of Sangleys" (i.e., Chinese bronze gongs) and a large drum, and continued deafeningly throughout the night. An *anitera,* or shaman who was an elderly woman, arrived in the morning. Using various paraphernalia of blankets, a lance, two "crowns," and a jar of wine, she carried out a complicated ritual of constructing an "altar," jumping, shouting, and brandishing the lance, praying, offering wine to "her god," decking the owner of the house and herself with the crowns, and consecrating a number of trussed pigs prior to their sacrifice and cooking. The heads of the hogs were subsequently hung in their houses. It is noteworthy that accounts of the time picture women rather than men serving as shamans or mediums (Perez, 1904, pp. 104-58).

In spite of these mission advances, lowland settlements continued to be harassed by marauding mountaineers. In 1758, to the unhappiness of the fathers, as told in the general chapter, the Philippine Governor ordered Don Manuel Arza y Urrutia, then alcalde-mayor of Pangasinan, to join with the Ilocos authorities in conducting a military expedition against them —a resumption of the older patterns of punitive action. As additional objectives, this force was to make them "pay tribute," and to require them to "form pueblos," and live in a "social manner." Even if the missionized settlements were not among the original offenders, they soon became involved.

According to de los Reyes' account of this undertaking, pressure was first brought to bear upon the immediately accessible rancherias—the ones under mission influence—to comply with the government policies. One leader, Lakaaden, of the settlement of Butiagan, back of Agoo, did undertake such consolidation, and the resulting new pueblo paid 77 tributes from its 336 residents.

The main body of the expedition which assembled under Arza consisted of 12 Spaniards, 1,959 Pangasinans, 15 mestizos, and "some miners." It left San Fabian in February 1759, and the plan called for other parties from Agoo, Bauang, and Bacnotan, numbering 250 men, to join it en route to the Benguet heights. The latter group became engaged in various fights with mountaineers and was delayed. As a first act, the Pangasinan party "burned the rancheria of Balangabang and its cultivations," as its inhabitants had committed many depredations in San Jacinto. On the next day the same was done to the rancheria of Sokiao. Finally in March the sections of the expeditionary force effected a junction, and on their further march burned the houses and destroyed the fields and animals of "Bonoy, Kaoeng, Luat, and Paonay," fifteen rancherias in Lumtang, and also the rancheria of Boa. All these names are on the mission lists of visited settlements. Various engagements were fought with the mountaineers, who battled valiantly. After a week of such activity, the party reached the mission center, Tonglo, but found it deserted. Here and in neighboring areas they burned 35 more settlements. The expedition then returned to the coast: as de los Reyes puts it, "as always! without any effective results." The historian Juan de la Concepción, in a recital of these events says that the expedition "destroyed fields of camote, gave [gabi], sugarcane, and tobacco," and "killed pigs"—significantly omitted is any reference to rice, though the date was February, the growing season (de los Reyes, II, 168-71; Juan de la Concepción, XIV, 361-81).

The later historian Malumbres (1919, pp. 226-30) says that Arza's main party entered the mountains by proceeding northward from Manaoag, taking the trail used by the mountaineers to bring gold from the mines down to Magaldan. He also says that Arza was helped by some "Igorrote leaders who had been baptized and were living in Manila." In addition to making his fruitless sortie into the mountains, Arza tried to bring pressures on the troublesome groups by "prohibiting all communication and commerce in gold, wax, iron, and other goods with the infidels"—a directive which seems to have been equally futile. No further mention was found in the records of the Tonglo mission, so that it seems to have come to an end except as conversions might be made in nearer settlements.

The peoples of northern Pangasinan Province were somewhat marginal to the events of the Silang rebellion of 1762–63 in Ilocos. Nevertheless, the revolt that followed in Pangasinan must have drawn them in, though the major engagements with Spanish forces took place in the large town areas in the central and west sections of the province. By 1764 many groups of rebels had fled to the mountains, leaving the towns to the Spaniards. Some undoubtedly went west into fastnesses of Zambales, while others presumably moved up into isolated zones along the southern face of the Cordillera and Caraballo Sur mountains. As peace was restored, and the greatly reduced Pangasinan population reassumed a stable settlement pattern, many of these rebels probably stayed on in the sparsely settled districts eastward from Manaoag. Though the later history of this area does not appear to be well recorded in published works, such districts and centers as Asingan, Tayug, and Umingan in northeast Pangasinan, and Lupao, San José, and Puncan in the later created Nueva Ecija Province eastward from them, may have built up their modern populations in part from these refugee groups. Sawyer in 1900 was to describe the "Pangasinanes" as still having as "one of their characteristics" a decided propensity to "*remontar*," i.e., to leave for the mountains so they could be "out of reach of authority" (1900, p. 249).

In 1785, a boundary adjustment was made between the old Pangasinan and Ilocos provinces. The border of Pangasinan was pushed northward to take in the communities of Agoo, Aringay, Kava or Cava, Bauang, San Fernando, San Juan, and Bacnotan (de los Reyes, II, 198). This area in turn, with a northern segment added, was to be constituted in 1850 as a separate province, La Union. With this latter was associated an adjacent mountain jurisdiction of Benguet, formed in 1846 as a politico-military district or Comandancia.

In 1829 one of the pioneers of nineteenth-century exploration in the northern Luzon Cordillera, Don Guillermo Galvey, led an expedition to the heights of Benguet. Because his *Diary,* published in 1842, offers significant comparisons with the 1624 expedition of Martín Quirante, and includes some critical perspectives for ethnohistorical reconstruction, it may be reviewed quite fully here. On an earlier occasion Galvey had penetrated "the first mountain chain" to destroy tobacco fields "planted clandestinely." "Igorrotes" there had spoken of a very large and rich "town" that made war from the high interior upon the "pagans of the foothills." Galvey assembled a force in Agoo consisting of 61 officers and soldiers, with 200 "polistas" (forced carriers). He left the coast in early January, the same month that Martín Quirante did, so that any wet rice crop in the area should have been mostly planted out.

On the fifth day, following the bed of the Aringay river, the party passed through two villages abandoned in each case except for the headman. In one of them, "Luceng," which had "eight houses," Galvey was given a "basketful of camotes and other tubers." On the next morning's march, only one village was encountered, indicating a sparse settlement pattern, and here the party crossed "fields of sweet potatoes." Resting overnight, they encountered next day barriers of sharpened stakes and bow-and-arrow traps, while a "crowd" of armed Igorots threatened from the heights. The latter launched an attack with a "shower of stones" but were driven off. By night a "village" was seen on the heights of Mt. Tonglo round which the party had come, and also "immense pine forests with here and there a hut." Moving eastward next day, small valleys were seen on all sides, "some of them well under cultivation," and also large herds of "carabaos, cows, and horses." The valley of Benguet, "about five miles in circumference," was reached in the afternoon. A "great many people" were running in all directions and shouting, and in the bottom of the valley were "beautiful fields."

[It] is surrounded with springs, and forms a basin. The soil was very well cultivated, with immense fields of sweet potatoes, gabe [taro], and sugarcane, but I saw no paddy [rice field] in this tract of land. All was well irrigated and fenced in by dividing lines of earth after the manner of Spain, and provided with wells.

The valley contained "some 500" houses, of "broad pine board," and "very dirty." The party had trouble with two drunk Igorots, who attacked them, and several hiding men were captured and released with messages suggesting peace. After a night ringed in by armed parties that lit fires on the heights, there followed an inconclusive series of attacks on the Spaniards in which some drunk Igorots were captured. On the ninth day, Galvey decided to take drastic action, and "arriving at the houses," burned down "some hundred and eighty." The party then moved southwest with its prisoners toward the coast, and after encountering three days later a "village of twelve houses," came to the familiar terrain of the coastal mountains. On the evening of the fourteenth day, Aringay was reached (Galvey, translated in Scheerer, 1905, pp. 173–78). This account, it is seen, tells of root crops being grown in gardens "fenced" with earth walls, and specifically notes the absence of wet rice "paddies." No mention is made of gold, but this could be explained by the fact that the Benguet valley is not one of the mining areas.

In 1829 and 1831 according to Malumbres' useful accounts of nineteenth-century explorations in the Cordillera, a Dominican father, Fray José Torres, who was stationed at Magaldan, made two trips to the southern heights of the Cordillera. The first took him from San Nicolas through the Kayapa area to Aritao in the Cagayan headwaters, and the second into the "Valley of Benguet." The date of the latter journey was February-March, the growing period for the wet rice crop. Fray José, evidently with some indigenous companions, traveled from Manaoag up the Aliong river to "Lebang," where there were "gold mines"—these gold deposits are still known in modern times. Two settlements were encountered, one with "6 or 7" houses, the other with "12 or 14," that is, a hamlet type of residence. At "Cabuleo," however, a "large pueblo" was encountered, and "contrary to the custom of the Igorrotes" a large crowd of both sexes had gathered. They were given at Cabuleo and other places "much sweet-potato, taro, and great pieces of pork." The father visited various mining areas, including the "celebrated mine of Aucupang" (Acupan, near Itogon), and then moved on into the valley of Benguet. "The party was given a feast at which were consumed great quantities of stewed meats mixed with sweet-potatoes and taro, which the Igorrotes supplied in abundance." At "Irisan" (still a settled area today, located northwest of Baguio), "many people were occupied in harvesting sweet-potatoes and taro, the principal foods of these Benguet Igorrotes." Proceeding to "Cagalin," they encountered "much tobacco." From here the father's party followed the Aringay river down to "Tabao," the present Tubao, which "had some Christians dependent on Agoo," where they reached the coast (Malumbres, 1919, II, 279–91).

Malumbres tells of further expeditions by Galvey in Benguet and "Quiangan" (Ifugao). The ethnohistorical materials on Ifugao will be dealt with in the Cagayan section of the study, but here it may be noted that Galvey's journals rightly speak of the "immense quantities of palay [rice] which are produced" in that ethnic zone. In 1833 Galvey traveled to "Cabayan," the Ibaloi district of Kabayan on the upper Agno river near the mountain ridge that forms the ethnic border between that group and the Ifugao. The date, according to his journal, was early March. As he passed from Agoo up through the mountains "eight Igorrotes" came at one point to visit him, bringing sweet potatoes, eggs, and ginger as a gift. Reaching the eastern section of Benguet, Galvey records that "the pueblo Lutab," which is an alternative name for the principal settlement of Kabayan, had 97 houses made of "planks." Two other pueblos, "Dada" and "Samangan," had 36 and 32 houses, respectively. That is, the district had settlements of fairly large size.

Lutab, Galvey's journal states, had "many fields of palay and herds." The reference here to "palay" grown in fields suggests the practice of wet cultivation (Malumbres, 1919, II, 233–36). It would seem to be a fair hypothesis therefore that wet rice terracing was becoming established by this time in the upper Agno valley of eastern Benguet, though not yet in the main parts of that district where root crops still provided the vegetable staples. Moreover, the technique could well have come from adjacent Ifugao, as will be seen later.

Galvey, writing in 1842, tells how subsequent to his first visit the Benguet people "asked" for peace and became his "friends."

On different expeditions I have passed eight or ten times through their valley, and . . . they have treated me with kindness, providing me with rice, cows, and other food. Still, as a consequence of this [first] expedition and of smallpox, this town has been reduced to about a hundred houses.

The implication here seems to be that, subsequent to 1829, a considerable number of the Benguet valley people retreated further into the fastnesses. Galvey notes that he had built a "highroad" to it, and this may have been a factor in stimulating conservatives to move away from prospective Spanish control. The ethnographer Scheerer was to say later of the Ibaloi:

Whenever these people experienced some trouble (from the Spanish authorities or their own powerful rich men) . . . their unfailing expedient has been to leave the rudimentary towns, to the formation of which a kind government has conciliated them, abandoning their poor huts and fields, and migrating with their families to other higher and lonelier mountains, swelling the hordes of head-hunters, into whose savage life they fall back. (Scheerer, in *Taft Commission Report,* 1900, p. 152.)

This scholar has recorded a story of a past leader, Kidit, who cooperated with the Spaniards at first, but later defeated a Spanish punitive expedition. He introduced, so the story says, the first "civilizing" influences into Benguet, and the later wealthy leaders with their extensive rice fields and herds are said to be his descendants (Beyer Collection, Igorot Paper 43). In a footnote to his translation of Galvey's journal, Scheerer (1905, p. 178) states that by the end of the nineteenth century the whole Benguet valley, where Galvey counted some 500 houses, had only 9 houses left in it.

LATER PERSPECTIVES

As early as 1705, a governor of Pampanga Province had applied the name Nueva Ecija to the military command that controlled the upper Pampanga river area, honoring in this way his home city. In 1848 it became a separate province, though a complicated series of status and boundary changes were to occur before it assumed its modern form. In the process, the old Pangasinan and Pampanga boundaries were cut back. The population of the area remained extraordinarily sparse until well along in the nineteenth century.

Buzeta's encyclopedic survey of the Philippines (1850) gives a remarkably full description of the principal communities in the lowland zones around the middle of the nineteenth century. The following is a summary of his statistical and related materials, first for the northern Pangasinan and Nueva Ecija areas, and then for southern La Union, the settlements being grouped by localities.

San Fabian to Binalonan. Mangaldan was the largest settlement here as of 1845, with 2,392 houses and 14,355 people. San Fabian on the coast had a population of 11,498, Manaoag 9,247, San Jacinto 7,385, and Binalonan, 6,260.

Agno River Area. The largest settlements in 1845 were San Nicolas with an 1845 population of 5,100, and Umingan with 4,634. Colonization of these districts by Ilocanos was already under way, so that the older centers of Tayug and Asingan were being outnumbered—the former having 4,370 and the latter 3,832.

Upper Pampanga River Area. An 1818 census showed Puncan with its "annex" Carranglan as having 719 people, and Pantabangan 535; in 1845 the totals were: Pantabangan 1,073; Carranglan 1,066; Puncan 339. Northern Nueva Ecija was still sparsely populated, but later it was to be extensively colonized by Tagalogs, Pangasinans, and Ilocanos.

Southern Ilocos Coast. Agoo was the principal settlement, with an 1845 population of 6,936, occupying 1,156 houses. This was a notable salt-making area. Aringay and Santo Tomas were visitas of Agoo, the former together with its dependency Caba having 6,923 people, and the latter 4,524. Bauang, further north, had 6,740.

The northern Pangasinan zones, therefore, had a total counted population of 48,681, the Pampanga river headwaters 2,478, and the southern Ilocos zone had 25,123.

This author speaks of rice and maize as being the principal agricultural staples of the lowland settlements, and also of the important forest resources of the high country. Gold, he says, is panned from the lower Agno, where it debouches from the mountains, by people in the Tayug and Asingan areas. On the Ilocos coast, Santo Tomas, Agoo, and Aringay are market places to which the "Igorrotes" bring their gold from the mountains of Banguet (Benguet). Alluvial gold is also extracted from the Bauang-Naguilian river system, inland from Bauang. Of the "Igorrotes," Buzeta says:

These people make up a great population which occupies the whole width of the cordillera. . . . [They] are corpulent, robust, and well built people. . . . They have the custom of painting themselves with different colors, and they wear a figure representative of the sun on their hands. . . . The men wear a loincloth, called a baaé and made from bark, and a type of cape which covers their backs or which they wear over one shoulder. The women wear a type of bodice or jacket about their breasts and a piece of cloth or bark, which covers their body down to the knees. The leaders are distinguished by adornments on their baaé. Their mourning clothes are white. . . . Those who live in the valley of Banguet [Benguet] live in bamboo huts which are shaped to form a triangle with the ground. They are covered with a grass which is called *cogon*. . . . Those who live in the center of the cordillera construct their houses somewhat better, employing pine which they cut by hand with their *tatibong* . . . [which] is a two edged blade with a Roman point and has a hilt made from carabao horn. They also use the bow and arrow. . . . The food of the Igorrotes amounts to forest fruits, sweet potatoes, létaro [taro] roots, rice, which they cultivate, and meat from the carabao, boar, and deer which they hunt and whose meat they preserve. Also there are some cannibals. (Buzeta, 1, 52.)

Buzeta also speaks of the "vast territory" of the Caraballo Sur and Sierra Madre mountains east to Baler Bay on the Pacific side. He identifies the "numerous settlements of Infidels" occupying them, variously "Ibalao" and "Ilongot." These groups were "living a miserable life," "maintaining themselves by pillaging," and ambushing wayfarers on the "more frequented trails" with "well-aimed, poisoned darts." He also places Negritos in the Sierra Madre forests. In 1856 a politico-military district called Principe was formed as an adjunct of Nueva Ecija, comprising in general this mountainous area with Baler as its headquarters. Buzeta shows the Baler area as having in 1845 a population of 1,280.

A map of the southern Cordillera region drawn in 1852 by Antonio Murata, and seen in the Beyer Collection in Manila, shows twenty settlement names in the Benguet area, of which only five are recognizable today. This indicates again the mobility of residential patterns in the face of Spanish penetration.

In the second half of the nineteenth century, the commerce in gold from the mountains to the lowlands dwindled. Cavada, writing of Pangasinan Province in 1876, fails to mention gold as a resource, and says that it is "poor" in mines. Of La Union Province with its adherent Benguet District, he merely says under "Mining": "There are indications that a gold mine exists." In his list of exports, however, he includes "600 onzas" of gold. Cavada's accounts of Pangasinan and La Union make no separate mention of the non-Christian population elements. He does note, however, that Benguet had a population of 19,113. Angel Perez (1902) says of the Pangasinan area: "Some Igorrote villages are found in the Christian towns of Pozorrubio, Alava, San Nicolas, Tayug, and Nueva Ecija."

The Taft Commission Report of 1900 included Benguet among the "most important and advanced" jurisdictions of the Cordillera. It says of Pangasinan Province that it contained "a few Igorrotes" who were living along its northern and eastern boundaries. Furthermore, the Igorrotes on the higher Cordillera could speak the Pangasinan language as a result of trading with its inhabitants. "Gold and copper," the report says, were being marketed in the Pangasinan towns. Of La Union Province, it states that besides the coastal towns and villages there were a multitude of "little hamlets" of Igorots within the jurisdiction of the Christian towns. Benguet had 15,734 inhabitants, of whom the number of Christians "does not exceed 1,000." Its capital and principal town was La Trinidad, in the Benguet valley somewhat north of where the Philippine summer capital, Baguio, was to be developed; it had a population of 2,980. Though the non-Christians spoke "Benguetano," they could also "understand and speak the Ilocano tongue" (Philippine Commission Report, 1900, III, 31, 37–38).

Further records of Benguet during the early American period show continued dynamics in settlement patterns and modes of living. David Barrows, who explored the Cordillera extensively in the initial years, writes for example of sparsely populated northern Benguet: "Apparently to escape outside authority and exactions [its people] have abandoned the lower slopes and, retiring to the very crests of the mountains, have scattered through the forests in little hamlets of three or four to a dozen houses" (1903, p. 12).

In the more accessible areas, however, the people were at this time expanding their rice terraces and herds, tending coffee plantations established in Spanish times, and growing vegetables for the market at newly founded Baguio. Several powerful families had become fabulously rich by Ibaloi standards and, indeed, exceedingly well-to-do by Filipino standards more widely. Important mining areas were sold to American companies, and modern Benguet subprovince was in the making.

The American agricultural records notably show that the wet rice terracing system of cultivation was still in process of spreading at this time into northern zones of Benguet. They also attest to the rapidity with which terraces can be built up, contravening the assumption made by some modern ethnologists that these step-like systems require long periods of time for their construction. The 1931 annual report of the Governor for Mountain Province, seen by the writer in the records at the capital, Bontoc, states for example regarding the Loo valley, in the headwaters of the Agno river: "[In] the last two years [it] changed from entirely camotes to rice, and new fields are constantly under construction." The 1932 annual report of Benguet subprovince also states that its people are "all the time looking for more land to make into rice paddies." Extensive terraces have also been built in recent years for vegetable growing to supply the Baguio market.

MODERN CENSUS DATA

To throw the earlier demographic materials into perspective, selected statistics can usefully be reviewed from the twentieth-century censuses. The first American census in 1903 showed the northern Pangasinan districts treated in this study as having a combined total population of 127,370. By 1948 the figure had risen to 288,148. Correspondingly southern La Union had totals of 60,613 in 1903 and 114,876 in 1948.*

---

* In northern Pangasinan the 1948 population totals by municipal units in the lowland zones were as follows (from west to east): San Fabian, 23,997; Magaldan or Mangaldan, 26,103; San Jacinto, 10,313; Manaoag, 34,304; Pozorrubio, 21,675; Bina-

The first point to become obvious is the tremendous southward surge of Ilocano migrants into the Pangasinan ethnic area, particularly the northern districts. By the 1948 census, in which respondents were classed for the first time by their declared "mother tongue," Pangasinan Province as a whole had, along with its 443,923 Pangasinan speakers, 440,264 Iloko speakers. In La Union Province, most of which was within the Pangasinan ethnic area when the Spaniards arrived, there were 222,716 Iloko speakers but only 4,855 Pangasinan speakers.

The mountain zones of these two provinces continued to have their non-Christian "Igorot" populations. The first American census of 1903 showed Pangasinan as having 3,403, of whom 17 were classed as "civilized" and the rest "wild." La Union contained 10,215, of whom 165 were "civilized"; perhaps half of this number were in the southern part of the province being considered here. Benguet, the adjacent mountain jurisdiction, had 21,926 Igorots, of whom 98 were classed as "civilized." Subsequently, with the formation of Mountain Province, the boundaries of Benguet sub-province were extended to take in more of the non-Christian settlements. By the 1948 census, the number in Pangasinan counting the southern "Igorot" or "Inabaloi" dialect as their mother tongue totaled 755; most of them were in the San Nicolas district. La Union had 5 specified as speaking Inibaloi, plus 7,619 speaking unclassified "Igorot" dialects, perhaps half of them Inibaloi speakers and the rest Kankanai speakers, with which the next section is concerned. Nearly all of them were in the mountain districts of Burgos, Naguilian, Pugo, and Tubao. For the southern and eastern sections of Benguet subprovince inhabited primarily by Ibaloi, the population in 1948 was 88,083, of whom 29,262 were in the cosmopolitan city of Baguio, 16,970 were in the gold mining Itogon area, and the remaining 41,851 were scattered in seven other municipal units. The census figures on the Mountain Province languages do not separate Ibaloi consistently from a larger "Igorot" category, but members of this ethnic group in Benguet appear to number about 30,000.

REVIEW

The record to this point makes plausible a hypothesis that the mountain Ibaloi are offshoots of the adjacent northern Pangasinan lowland people. Entering the high country, it would seem, well before Spanish times to work gold, they could have adjusted their way of life to the new ecological

---

lonan, 23,361; Asingan, 24,701; Tayug, 19,782; Umingan, 29,729. For the units along the mountainous Cordillera face they were: Sison, 13,480; San Manuel, 15,330; San Nicolas, 18,218; Natividad, 11,780; San Quintin, 15,330. In southern La Union the lowland units had populations as follows: Santo Tomas, 12,897; Agoo, 16,638; Aringay, 13,079; Caba, 7,320; Bauang, 22,441. The mountain unit totals were: Rosario, 12,869; Tubao, 9,105; Naguilian, 15,227; Pugo, 3,952; Burgos, 1,348.

circumstances. The coming of the Spaniards brought not only consolidation and Hispanization of the Pangasinan ethnic group, but also drew the line sharply between Christian lowlander and non-Christian mountaineer. In the nineteenth century, with the opening up of Benguet, Ibaloi life entered a dynamic phase which apparently turned former dry cultivators into wet rice terracers, and otherwise produced the combination of old and new elements described by modern ethnographers.

In the same way, it is plausible to think of the varied Ilongot (Italon, Abaca, etc.) peoples as mainly derived from migrant or refugee lowlanders who moved up the Pampanga river into the Caraballo Sur mountains, becoming hybridized more or less with older Negrito groups in the process. The Negritos, however, have tended to become extinct: certainly those who were formerly widely spread between the Agno and upper Pampanga rivers are completely gone.

For both these mountain groupings, however, the story is not complete. The Ibaloi must be compared with the Cordillera peoples adjoining them to the north, while Ibaloi groups must be followed eastward into "Ituy," that is, the Magat river country in the Cagayan valley head. Here, particularly, their possible relation to an ethnic group called the Isinai must be examined. In the same way, the Ilongot groups on the Pangasinan-Pampanga side of the Caraballo Sur must be seen in relation to widely spread dry cultivating groups throughout the Cagayan headwaters eastward from the Magat river. It will remain, therefore, for the final chapter to place these southern mountaineers in complete perspective.

IV. The Southern Ilocos Area

PLACE AND PEOPLE

This zone is separated out for study in order to understand the southern Ilocanos of the coastal region and also three mountain groups: the Kankanai or southern Kankanai, the Lepanto or northern Kankanai, and back of them the Bontok. The coastal districts comprise the northern half of La Union Province and the southern half of Ilocos Sur. In Spanish times the inland areas comprised four politico-military Comandancias: Amburayan in the south, Tiagan in the north, and further inland Lepanto and Bontoc. Today the inland districts lie within Mountain Province, that is, northern Benguet subprovince and Bontoc subprovince.

The Cordillera Central heights are centered upon the nuclear area of Mt. Data. From here the Abra and Chico rivers gouge their way northward, the former system descending to the Abra valley before reaching the Ilocos coast, and the latter to the Cagayan valley. On the west, the most notable river is the Amburayan. Between the Abra and the sea lies the secondary Ilocos range, with heights up to nearly 6,000 feet. In general the Kankanai live in the Amburayan area, the Lepanto occupy headwater streams of the Abra and Chico systems, and the Bontok are somewhat further down the Chico, that is, to the east and northeast of the Lepanto.

Old trading trails exist between the coast and the interior. The most important are those linking the mountain communities with Balaoan and Tagudin to the south, and with Candon to the north. In the nineteenth century a main Spanish "road" passed from Candon across the Bila Pass to Angaki in the Abra valley, and on to Cervantes. From there it went on up to Kayan in Lepanto, and over the Cordillera ridge to Bontoc. Another extended inland from Tagudin to the copper-mining area of Mankayan and on to the gold-mining area of Suyoc, both worked extensively by the local mountain peoples. From there a connecting "road" passed northeast by way of the Bauko area to Kayan, with a branch to Sabangan and on down the Chico to Bontoc. Gold existed in workable quantity not only at

Suyoc but also in streams of the Tagudin and Santa Lucia areas on the coast.

Anthropological information on the Kankanai, or southern Kankanai, is scanty. Modern censuses show them to number about 30,000, of whom about one-third live in northwest Benguet subprovince and the rest in the old Amburayan area, now comprising the high country of northern La Union and southern Ilocos Sur, together with adjacent southern sections of Bontoc subprovince. They occupy approximately 150 settled localities, of which some 40 were Spanish resettlement points or "towns," about one-quarter of them in Benguet. Some of their settlements are almost inaccessible because of steep terrain. Moss (1920b) says that their houses are spread out more or less singly like those of the Ibaloi, and their ritual life and other customs are fairly similar. Their terraces and gardens have "mud" walls (Worcester, 1906). Aristocratic leaders have come to the fore, though in general they are unlikely to be as "rich" as those among the more acculturated Ibaloi. Women's dress is visibly different, Moss notes, and magical practices are more elaborated among the Kankanai. Modern linguistic studies, as stated in the preceding chapter, show a very marked contrast between the Kankanai and Inibaloi languages.

To the north, the Mankayan area shows a transition toward large compact villages with intensive wet rice terracing, such as were described for the Lepanto or northern Kankanai in the first chapter. The Lepanto number approximately 35,000, and occupy about 35 major settlements and some smaller outliers on the upper Abra river system and in the Chico river headwaters. The largest communities are in the Kayan-Bauko-Besao area. The Lepantos are industrious, group-minded, and ceremonious farmers with extensive terracing systems.

The Lepanto people, for all their contrast in culture with the Kankanai further south, are classed linguistically as Kankanai speakers. Various writers, however, note that a marked dialect difference exists between the two groups; e.g., Worcester termed the northern or Lepanto dialect "Kataugnan" (1906, p. 862). Recent glottochronological studies show this to be so, and they also reveal further local dialect variation in each of the two zones. The Kankanai dialects also vary from district to district and differ from the Ifugao language spoken across the mountains on the eastern Cordillera slopes. The contrasts with Tinguian, spoken in the Abra valley, and with Bontok, are less, yet are still very marked. No study was available showing relations of the Kankanai dialects to the Iloko of the adjacent coastal communities.

Further north, along the coastal Ilocos range in the old Tiagan Comandancia, which was centered on San Emilio, the mountain people are conventionally classed with the Lepanto. But no precise ethnological or linguistic information exists to place them accurately. Modern census figures

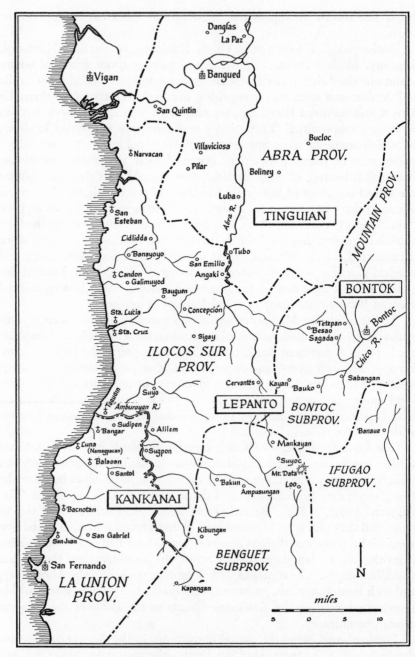

SOUTHERN ILOCOS AREA

are obscured by the progressive assimilation of these people into the Ilocano colonies that have filtered into these lower, forested zones. Perhaps 20,000 of them could still be traced back to mountain origins, though those who are still non-Christian have fallen in numbers to around 5,000. They are distributed in well over a hundred settled localities. Apart from several small-town concentrations, the families appear to scatter out in clusters of a few houses or in houses set at a distance apart, much as in Amburayan. The region also has a number of Tinguian settlements made up, as will be seen, by people who moved from the Abra valley toward the coast. Until modern times it also had Negritos living in the forested districts.

Inland from the Lepanto, the Bontok occupy the steep gorge country of the upper Chico and its adjacent tributaries. This group totals about 30,000, and has some 30 principal villages, also set compactly among surrounding terraces, plus some small outliers. The writings of Vanoverbergh, Keesing, Eggan, Scott, and others on the Lepanto, and of Jenks, Keesing, and others on the Bontok show extensively shared cultural characteristics, along with well-marked differences. Both have "ward" divisions in their villages, with political and ritual life centered on "men's houses"; marriages are generated mainly through associations of the unmarried youth in "girls' houses"; the house group is usually an independent nuclear family; male priesthoods provide the main religious leadership, and the pig is the central sacrificial animal. Agricultural techniques are closely similar, including terrace construction with almost perpendicular walls built up of stone, and trampling of fields with carabao to break up the soil. Yet house and clothing styles are quite distinct, while aristocratic class distinctions and political unities are less developed among the Bontok. The latter, too, are more warlike, aggressive, even bumptious. Very limited glottochronological studies to date indicate that there are the usual local dialect differences. They also suggest that the Bontok speech contrasts in about the same very marked degree from the Kalinga dialects to the north down the Chico, and from the Ifugao, as it does from the Lepanto. The Fox group in 1953 suggested as a preliminary step in classification that the Kankanai, Bontok, Kalinga, and Ifugao be taken together as forming a "Central Division" of the mountain languages.

The lowlanders grow their traditional wet rice crop in the rainy summer season, from about June on. The mountain terracing groups have their corresponding cycle in the drier winter season, from December–January on. Little second cropping is possible in the lowlands, but the Kankanai and especially the Lepanto have adapted in early American times to a double cropping system by which they grow extensively in the summer what they call the "Ilocano" crop. This second cycle is devoid of the elaborate ritual which marks their traditional planting and harvesting. The Bontok further inland have been much slower in adding this secular crop to their religion-bound one-crop system, but in 1929 infestation of the first crop by slugs caused some to do so, and by 1948 it had been adopted considerably in all but the remoter northern districts of Sadanga and Barlig.

Very little dry rice is grown in this zone, and that almost exclusively by the peoples of the Ilocos range rather than in the high Cordillera. Maize, featured in the lowlands, is almost non-existent on these latter heights. By contrast, sweet potatoes are grown extensively, and where a second wet crop is not produced they are the principal everyday plant staple for all but the "rich" families, so that output is very large. This is especially so among the Kankanai of northwest Benguet, where in 1948 the Kapangan district alone produced 4,355,000 kilos, or more than three times the total output of Ilocos Sur Province. Taro is a ceremoniously grown crop in the mountains, but yams and *tugue* are important only in the lowlands, where along with vegetables and fruits they tide the poorer households over between rice harvests (Philippine agricultural censuses, and other sources).

The American Governor Early, who was quoted in the previous chapter as considering the Ibaloi to be a "cousin" of the Pangasinan, expressed in the same source a corresponding opinion that the "Kankanay" is a "cousin of the Ilocano." "[He] considers Suyoc in old Lepanto his seat from whence he has spread to old Amburayan, including the barrios of Tagudin, Buguias, Kibungan, and parts of Atok and Kapangan" (*Manila Daily Bulletin,* February 1, 1929). Early evidently has in mind here the Kankanai in the narrower sense of the southern Kankanai. Suyoc is the gold-mining area of this part of the Cordillera, and is in the transitional zone between this southern group and the Lepanto.

EARLY PERSPECTIVES

The record of Salcedo's initial expedition, as given by the historian de los Reyes, tells of the advance of his boats up the coast in early June, 1572, from "Atuley" (apparently the Bauang area) to enter the zone being dealt with here. Arriving at the landing point at the mouth of the "Purao" river, he "jumped ashore" with a party of soldiers. "Purao" will be seen from later records to be the initial name given to Balaoan. Apparently no populated point was encountered along the intervening coast where San Fernando, capital of La Union province, is now located.

The Purao inhabitants received the Spaniards "as friends." But as Salcedo and his party advanced to the "población," they "encountered no women or children," which indicated to them from previous experience that the people were ready to dispose of them with their lances. Not intimidated, they continued to advance. Meantime a group attempted to surprise the boats, but they were driven off by arquebus fire. The people accompanying the Salcedo party then stampeded, and "everyone fled to the mountains," leaving behind the dead and wounded.

On the following day, the Spanish flotilla moved on from Purao to "Dumanguake," a "pueblo of the same region." De los Reyes judges this to be Kaog, later called Santa Lucia, and an encomienda with the name "Lumaquaque" or "Dumaquaque" will be noted shortly as being subsequently developed in the Santa Lucia–Tagudin region. The account says that "this province had extensive pueblos and many peoples. It contained mines of gold, which Japanese and Chinese merchant ships came to exploit." Here, too, the Spaniards were "well received" by the inhabitants, but the indications were that they were rallying forces to fight. Salcedo therefore sent a party into the "enemy pueblo," sacking the houses, while the "indigenous allies" who were accompanying the Spaniards carried off as their loot many supplies. No resistance was met in this "población," but as the party was returning, the local people tried to engage them. They were driven off by a volley of arquebus shots.

Salcedo would not permit pursuit of the fugitives. Nevertheless, a chief named Silata was captured and brought before him. On his knees Silata implored clemency, saying that he had had no part in the fight. Salcedo not only pardoned this leader but gave him presents, then sent him back to his fellows with a message asking that peace be made. Silata reciprocated by bringing many provisions to the Spaniards, and also some gold. After securing their submission, the expedition moved on northward out of this zone (de los Reyes, II, 12–13). The reference to trade in gold with Japanese and Chinese merchants is particularly significant as indicating that mining in this Cordillera zone had been developed prior to Spanish times.

Following these not very auspicious initial contacts, three encomiendas were formed along this section of the coast: one at each of the two points where Salcedo landed, and the third at Candon. They are identified in the Loarca survey of 1582, which also gives the first general description of the region.

In the previous chapter, the northernmost of the Pangasinan settlements identified by Loarca was seen to be "Baratao," the later Bauang. "Four leagues" further north were the "villages of Purao," which "differ from the above in language, but resemble them in their behavior and customs." As already noted, this seems to have been the breakline between the Pangasinan ethnic group and the southernmost of the Iloko speakers, the later Ilocano. "Purao" is seen from later records to be the Balaoan area, in the northern part of La Union Province. The continuing lack of mention of settlements in the intermediate San Fernando area, now the most heavily populated section of La Union, suggests that it might have been an unsettled buffer zone or no man's land between the two ethnic groups. The Purao villages, Loarca says, comprised an encomienda under two private encomenderos, and had a population of 2,000.

"Three leagues" north of Purao lay the "villages of Lumaquaque," in a valley of that name. The population of "about" 1,500 were organized in an encomienda, with its revenues going half to the King and half to a private encomendero. De los Reyes, as noted above, identified this location as Santa Lucia. "Two leagues" further were the "villages of Candon," with "about" 1,800 people under two private encomenderos. Loarca says that the villagers of both Lumaquaque and Candon "resemble those of Purao," indicating his impression of ethnic and linguistic uniformity along this coastal strip. The total population according to this initial estimate was 5,300 (B&R, v, 107).

The *Account of Encomiendas*, dated 1591, fills out this picture some-what, and gives a further population estimate. The following were the encomiendas recorded, from south to north:

Purao (Balaoan): "has" 2,000 tributes, and a population of 8,000; a private hold-ing, with "peace" and "justice"; an Augustinian "convent."

Dumaquaque (Tagudin): "has" 900 tributes, and a population of 3,600; changed to a wholly private holding, with "peace" and "justice"; an Augustini-an "monastery."

Candon: "collects" 900 tributes from a population of 3,600; "peace" and "jus-tice," but "no instruction," i.e., no church establishment.

The tribute wording quoted here in which Candon "collects" the specific number of tributes, while Purao and Dumaquaque each "has" them, prob-ably indicates that these last two counts included groups not yet controlled enough for tribute paying. The 8,000 figure for Purao, particularly, could have included an estimate of mountain populations back of this area. This 1591 survey indicates a total population of 15,200, nearly three times the Loarca estimate, and they paid, or were capable of paying, 3,800 tributes (B&R, viii, 104).

To round out these early demographic perspectives, relevant materials from the ecclesiastical survey of 1612 used earlier may be added here. The following were the recorded "convent" centers:

Purao: served with its visitas by 2 ministers; 1,000 tributes, and 3,000 Indians "in confession."

Tagurin (Tagudin): the former Lumaquaque or Dumaquaque, served with its visitas by 2 ministers; 1,000 tributes, and 3,000 "in confession."

Santa Cruz: served with its visitas by 2 ministers; 900 tributes, and 2,700 "in confession."

Candon: served with its visitas by 2 ministers; 800 tributes, or 2,400 "in con-fession."

The four mission centers, therefore, served communities paying in all 3,700 tributes, and having 11,100 persons "in confession," that is, of ecclesiastical-ly responsible age. If the tribute total is transposed to the four-to-one ratio used in official estimates of the time as a basis for reckoning total popula-tions, the over-all figure rises to 14,800 (B&R, xvii, 195–96).

It seems fair to assume from the 1591 and 1612 figures that the people along this section of the coast, later to be called southern Ilocanos, numbered around the latter part of the sixteenth century about 15,000. By demographic perspectives of the time, this was an unusually high density of settlement, and the Augustinians established more centers to serve it than was done in any other part of Ilocos comparable in size. Whether its original "villages" were in some instances large prior to the application of Spanish concentration policies is not clear, though the Salcedo materials suggest it. At least the encomienda and mission operations enhanced the importance of the principal centers, especially Purao (Balaoan), Tagudin, and Candon. For comparison it may be noted (anticipating the later population materials to be presented at the end of the chapter) that by 1818 the coastal districts had approximately three times as many people, that is, 44,912. In 1847 there were more than five times the number, or 77,362, and by the first American census in 1903 over seven times the number, or 109,448.

CONTINUING RECORDS: THE COASTAL DISTRICTS

Loarca, in 1582, stated as a distinguishing mark of the "Purao" peoples that they "do not kill their children as do the people of Pangasinan." Presumably he is referring primarily here to female infanticide, and in the minds of the Spaniards of the time it could have been seen as a factor making for denser populations along this coastal strip. He also says of the Purao way of life: "They till the land; and possess much gold, on account of being near the mines." His deliberate references to the "tilling" practiced by this group could imply that agriculture was more featured and efficient here than further south. Along with the population figures, it suggests that wet cultivation techniques existed on these coastal flats in pre-Spanish times. A hypothesis that the wet terraced cultivation of the adjacent "wedge" of mountain peoples is a reformulation of lowland agricultural techniques, and that their large and compact village communities could also have a historical relation to lowland village settlement patterns, seems to draw strength from these records so far as they go. No hint appears, however, to shape an answer to the associated question of whether the mountain populations established permanent inland residence prior to Spanish times, except perhaps in mining areas, or whether they were refugees escaping from the troubled conditions of initial Spanish contacts. These problems will be discussed more fully when the total record has been examined.

The records cited in the general chapter describing lowland conditions during the early period of Spanish control doubtless have over-all application in this southern area. Yet there is a dearth of specific references. The rapidity with which its people assumed an orderly, prosperous, and passive character evidently made it rarely newsworthy. A 1577 note of payments into the Royal treasury lists the Purao encomienda as having been at first one of its revenue sources. The Augustinian chronicles record little except the comings and goings of church personnel. One of the fathers achieved notoriety by stealing the monstrances of Tagudin and Candon (B&R, IV, 112; XIV, 168; XXIV, 39, 51, 71, 89, 140). In 1599, a settlement called Bacnotan, or Bagnotan, was formed in the apparent no man's land between "Baratao" (Bauang) and "Purao" (Balaoan). This became a visita of the Bauang mission, so that if it was a new settlement it could represent a northern migration of Pangasinan people. De los Reyes, in his later history, says of Bacnotan that its inhabitants at first refused to receive baptism because of the death of many babies being baptized: that is, they could have been a conservative group who moved into this unoccupied territory to escape Spanish pressures. In due course, Fray Pedro de la Cruz, who was stationed there, miraculously restored the sight of a child through baptizing it, and as a result "many Indians were baptized (de los Reyes, II, 68).

In 1630 the Augustinian historian Medina speaks of Purao (Balaoan) as being "the first village in the province of Ylocos after leaving the province of Pangasinan. This village belongs to the bishopric of Cagayan, and is a district of about one thousand Indians, although it is unhealthful. Two religious live there usually." Medina goes on to speak of Tagudin and Candon as being included among a series of ecclesiastical jurisdictions in Ilocos given in 1610–13 the status of "priorates." Of them he says: "That convent [Tagudin] suffers greatly from the Igorrotes, and on that account is almost depopulated. . . . Candon [is] an important priorate of that [Ilocos] province and the best, although without a vote. It ministers to more than one thousand five hundred Indians" (B&R, XXIII, 277, 296).

Either Medina is here very careless with his population figures, or else a drastic reduction had occurred from the earlier totals. If Tagudin was "almost depopulated," and Purao and Candon together had somewhat over 2,500 Indians as in his count, the total population would then have been only about 3,000 instead of the 15,000 noted earlier in the century. The tempting idea emerges here, as in other areas, that many of the coastal people under the stress of increasing Spanish pressures became remontados, moving back into fastnesses of the coastal range or even beyond to the high Cordillera. Some of this upland movement could have been involuntary, for the mountain peoples in their attacks upon the coastal settlements took back with them slaves as well as heads.

In 1660–61 southern Ilocos does break spectacularly into the records with the great Pangasinan insurrection of "King" Malong. As noted in the previous chapters, an account by Díaz in his *Conquests* tells how the zone between the Pangasinan Bauang settlements and the "Ilocan" Balaoan settlements became something of a battleground. At first the commander of the Spanish forces in Ilocos, Arqueros, was able to move down the coast to free Bauang, Aringay, and Agoo temporarily of rebel elements. After being routed south of Agoo, however, the Spanish forces retreated precipitately northward through this whole section of Ilocos. No stand was made short of Narvacan, further up the coast, as will be seen in the next chapter. The Balaoan, Tagudin, Santa Cruz, and Candon communities were left to be sacked by the Pangasinan and Zambal forces, and their inhabitants scattered out as far as they could to seek refuge in forest and mountain hideouts. The fathers resident in their convents had meantime been ordered to retreat to Vigan. Of this, the record says: "Some fathers thought that they ought not to obey this mandate; and one of them made his way through the middle of the enemies, to go to his ministry of Taguding, and others to the hills, to which the Ilocans had retreated, for fear of the Zambals" (B&R, xxxviii, 190). As elsewhere, attempts were made to save the church "silver," sometimes by burying or otherwise hiding it, and equally strenuous efforts were made by the rebels to locate it. The "silver belonging to the church at Taguding" was taken for safety to Vigan, but was seized there.

When finally, in early 1661, the rebel army retreated in defeat from northern Ilocos, it burned the villages and churches in its wake. Candon was destroyed in this manner, and from there the rebels proceeded southward to Santa Cruz. Correspondingly, pursuing Spanish forces reached Santa Lucia only two miles up the coast.

[When the rebels] learned that the Spaniards were at Santa Lucia . . . they collected many of the valuables and cloths which they had plundered and set fire to them, and they set out in search of the Spaniards, who also were coming with the same object. . . . The armies came into sight of each other between the villages of Santa Cruz and Santa Lucia. . . . The Zambals twice engaged our men, with fierceness and loud shouts; but they were finally conquered by the Spaniards—more than four hundred Zambals being killed, and the greater part of their force taken prisoners.

This battle marked the end of the Pangasinan and south Ilocos phases of the insurrection (B&R, xxxviii, 190–205).

THE MOUNTAIN POPULATIONS

Shortly after this disturbed period, a major expedition led by Admiral Pedro Duran de Monforte penetrated the mountains back of this section of the coast. An account given by Díaz in 1718 places the starting date of this venture as 1668. But the later historians de los Reyes and Malumbres give it as 1666 and 1663, respectively, while other dates in this decade are also used elsewhere in the records. In all, some three to five years were spent exploring the region and its resources, and attempting to pacify and convert its peoples. Finally the troops were withdrawn, and such converts as were made were transferred to the lowlands.

As told by Díaz, the Admiral assembled an army of Spanish, Pampango, Zambal, and Ilocan soldiers under veteran Spanish officers. Three Augustinian fathers were appointed by the church authorities to accompany him, and some "civilian Spaniards" also went along. The expedition proceeded inland from Candon by short marches, for fear of ambushes. Ahead it "always had spies" who knew the road. "Without notable happenings [it] reached the first two villages of the Igolotes—called Cayang . . . [which had] one hundred and fifty houses; and Lobing, with a few less. These they found deserted."

Cayang and Lobing are known from subsequent records to be the Lepanto villages of Kayan (or Cayan) and Lubon, which still exist on the heights east of the Abra river. In modern times they each have about twice the number of houses, set, as noted earlier, in a compact cluster with terraced rice fields around them. It seems a fair assumption that what the expedition found was a smaller version of the modern type of village. A total of 150 houses, assuming that figure was approximately correct, would have contained some 500 to 600 people, and in the barren and steep terrain of that area a wet rice crop as well as dry cropping would have been needed to support a group of this size.

The Admiral judged that "Cayang" would be a suitable place for a military post, since it was "pleasant," and "nearest to the villages that had been subdued." The latter reference could mean either nearby Lepanto villages or settlements, if there were any at that time, on the Ilocos range nearer the coast, which might not have been counted "Igolote." A fort was therefore built "until by means of the Zambals and Ilocans, the Igolotes should become quieted and reduced to their houses." "Gradually many of the chief Igolotes came, and showed themselves to be obedient, and friends of the Spaniards, and well inclined to profess the evangelical law and be baptized." A church was then built of "available materials," presumably the locally used stone and cogon grass, with a pinewood frame. This was "because of the difficulty in finding bamboo." "The same and greater difficulty was experienced in building a fort of palisades and a terreplein; for all of that land was bare, and had no forests of timber . . . [so that wood] had to be brought far."

Díaz says here that "only short and confused accounts remain" of the expedition's activities. Reports told, however, that it "explored one hundred and fifty villages" from "the heights of Cayan to the mountains of Cagayan." Most of them were "located on the shores of large rivers, all of which flow into the great river of Cagayan." Díaz then lists by name 38 villages "which rendered obedience," adding that 9 more in the "valley called Loo" did the same. This list is followed by 15 additional names of villages that "paid something as recognition" of the Spanish authority, with the further statement that there were "others" as well. Díaz then says that the expedition made contact with over a hundred more villages of "little importance." Most of the 53 specific village names listed by Díaz are still used by communities or for localities in the Lepanto, Bontoc, Kankanai, and northern Ibaloi areas. Or, to put this in another significant way, many of the present-day settlement areas of these ethnic groups are recognizable by name in this seventeenth-century list. This great stability in residential patterns stands in marked contrast to the more ephemeral nature of settlements in most of Benguet.

Besides the objectives of pacification and conversion, the expedition "did not neglect to look for gold mines, for the working of which they took along miners and plenty of tools." "But although they found mines in the latitude of 17 degrees, from which the Igolotes extract very fine gold, our miners could not obtain any in all the assays that they made; for all went up in smoke. That was one of the reasons that made the conquest drag on, as it was very costly and very remote."

This gold-bearing area was evidently Suyoc, in the Abra river headwaters. Missing here is an expected reference to copper, for presumably this latter metal was being mined by then in the Mankayan area near Suyoc. Either the record is defective, or the Spaniards were not at that time interested in the less valuable metal. Díaz speaks a little later in his record of gold being the "great stumbling block" in Spanish relations with the mountain peoples, and of God "not revealing it to us" because of Spanish "greed."

More success, Díaz says, marked the efforts of the fathers to obtain conversions, for their "fruits . . . in that conquest were considerable." In some instances "entire villages" were "reduced" to the faith. "Prudently," however, the father felt that it would be "difficult to preserve that field of Christendom unless those people were reduced, and removed to a more suitable site, secure from the continual wars which some villages waged against others. Thus many were led to settle in the villages of Ilocos, and others in those of Zambales [Province]." The Díaz account here speaks of parallel military efforts to subdue the mountain headhunters in the Zambales area. He indicates that the garrison forces lodged in the Kayan area became needed in those operations, which were nearer Manila, and this led to their withdrawal (B&R, xxxvii, 245-49).

Malumbres is more specific in telling of the venture's end. The Spanish forces, he says, were unable to secure fields for planting, and the supplies which the "Igorrotes" could allot them were "insignificant." "Bit by bit" they were withdrawn, so that after some five years of occupation only the fathers were left. Because of the "inhospitable" atmosphere, they in turn transferred their "neophites" to the "pueblos of Ilocos." Malumbres quotes a letter from the Governor of the time indicating that defenses against the mountain peoples could best be developed further south where they could deal with the Zambales mountain peoples as well as those of the northern Cordillera; moreover, the mines were not "beneficial," hence they did not justify continued occupation (1919, ii, 220–24).

The Augustinian historian Mozo (1755) gives a quite different version of this penetration, stressing its ecclesiastical phase almost to the exclusion of the military phase. He places its date erroneously as 1660, and says:

Two religious escorted by some soldiers entered the territory of the Igorrotes, and in a place called Cayam they established a small military post with a church, which they dedicated to the archangel St. Michael; and from this place they began with apostolic zeal to preach to those tribes the holy name of God, but the harvest of souls which they could obtain was exceedingly small. A little while later . . . the soldiers became sick through insalubrity of the region, and the barbarians threatened to cut them to pieces if they did not immediately go away from that place. Accordingly, not having sufficient force to resist, the fathers were obliged to yield to this opposition, and retired with much sadness, taking with them such persons as they had baptized. From that time until recent years, none of the various attempts to found a mission there had been successful, although occasional converts were made among those tribes. (B&R, xlviii, 85–86.)

In the general chapter, Díaz was quoted as saying of the "Igolotes" that groups seemingly friendly and subject "rebel tomorrow, and their villages disappear." The few that were "controlled" had been "gathered in the villages of Bauang, Bangar, and Narbacan" (B&R, xxxvii, 279–80). It could be significant that Bauang in La Union and Narvacan in central Ilocos Sur are roughly the southern and northern boundaries of the mountain areas from the Amburayan Comandancia to the Tiağan Comandancia, that is, the Kankanai-speaking groups. Such converts are seen from the records to have drawn kinsmen down for trade and resettlement. In doing so, the latter would have had to adjust to ecological conditions on the lower, forested, and humid slopes, including presumably scattering out more than in the large and compact mountain villages. Bangar is a settlement to the south of Tagudin, and may have been formed with mountain converts at this time. Its establishment as an independent pueblo, however, is dated by de los Reyes from 1700 (ii, 128–29, 147).

THE MIDDLE PERIOD TO 1840

As with Bangar, the names of other communities not mentioned to this point appear from time to time in the records. Undoubtedly some of them were already existing segments or dependencies of the older centers, so that their so-called "founding" represents acquisition of the status of independent "pueblos." In 1738 an ecclesiastical survey of the Augustinian establishments shows that, for the zone considered here, "administrations" existed in Dalandan, San Juan, Bacnotan, Balaoan, Namagpacan, Bangar, Tagudin, Santa Cruz, Santa Lucia, and Candon. Of the new names here, Dalandan or Dalangdang is the original settlement which in 1764 was to become Pindangan, or San Fernando, the later La Union capital. San Juan, said by de los Reyes to have been formed in 1590 through a division of the old "Baratao" into two settlements, apparently dates its independent status from 1707 (de los Reyes, II, 60, 68; Cavada, p. 234). Namagpacan, now Luna, dates from 1690. The ecclesiastical survey speaks of Bacnotan, Balaoan, and Tagudin as each having a "fine mission," by which evidently was meant work in progress among the mountain peoples back of the settlements (B&R, XXVIII, 158–59). A similar survey for 1754 shows no significant changes in this religious alignment (B&R, XXVIII, 167). A census of the "Igorrot" missions "belonging to the province of Ilocos" for the year 1760 lists 35 "new Christians" in the territory of Candon, 79 in Bangar, and 12 in Namagpacan.

The Murillo map of 1744, referred to in the previous chapter, is not strong on the geography of this area. Along the coast it places the settlements of Bacnotan, Tagudin, Santa Cruz, and Candon. The Cordillera heights are indicated, with the ethnic label "Ygolotes," but there are no place names. The southward course of the Abra river back of the coastal range is entirely missing, a point which will be discussed more fully in the next chapter. Instead, the Chico tributary of the Cagayan is traced through the mountains into that zone, suggesting that the upper Abra was believed to be the Chico headwaters.

As seen in the preceding chapter, the 1750's were marked by a vigorous though temporary period of mission work along the southwest face of the Cordillera. These efforts carried north to the Candon region, as shown in the Augustinian documents assembled by Perez (1904). Manuel Carillo, in his *Short Relation* of 1756, lists the names of eight mountain settlements back of the Bauang-Bacnotan area which were mission targets, and says that "many Igorots" were led to "descend" from the mountains back of Tagudin and Candon. In a further report, he tells that in the following two years 165 persons were baptized in these areas. As further south, the converts were pressed to develop larger communities and permanent irrigated fields. The Vicar Prior of Bacnotan, Juan Sanchez, certifies in records of 1755 that three "Igorot pueblos" back of that center, with 165 persons who were Christians, went in October "to live and found their houses in the sitio of Acpatac," a league and a half away, and were developing cultivated fields and herds. Another group settled at Bomboneg, a little more than a league away from Bacnotan (Perez, 1904, pp. 111, 120, 155).

In 1797-98, de los Reyes tells, the northern part of the coastal area experienced a period of disturbance as a result of a popular protest by the "commoners" (*kailianes*) against abuses and oppressions by their leaders (*principales*). This first emerged in Santa Lucia, and spread to Santa Cruz and Candon. The Santa Lucia people had sent representatives to Manila with their complaints. The local *gobernadorcillo,* in revenge, brought "false accusations" to the alcalde-mayor of the province against these representatives, and he was authorized to "take action against them." He arrested the principal representative, Josef Gaspar, and had him imprisoned at Candon, while two others were put in the Santa Cruz jail. When, "on a Sunday," the people assembled in Santa Cruz "according to custom," they respectfully asked the *gobernadorcillo* to explain what wrongs the prisoners had committed. They were told that "only the alcalde-mayor knew this"; but this answer did not satisfy them. The following day, more than two hundred persons assembled and repeated the request, but received no satisfaction. At this, "all the pueblo," yelling for the freedom of the prisoners, advanced on the government office, stormed the door with "lances," and, overwhelming the officials, set the two representatives free.

The crowd then proposed to proceed to Candon to release Gaspar. But instead they sent a message to the alcalde-mayor at Vigan presenting their case. He in turn sent the teniente-mayor of Vigan, a prominent Ilocano leader, to investigate the matter. As a result of his successful negotiations the people retired peacefully to their homes, the representatives went free, and the "abuses were curbed" (de los Reyes, pp. 201-5).

Angel Perez, in a useful history of the mountain peoples (1902, pp. 23-33), tells how in 1811 the Spanish authorities gave the title of "Teacher of the Camp" to "Soliman, Captain of the Mountain Igorrotes, of the town of Cayan." Soliman, he says, went to Manila to ask that his "title and authority" be extended over "all the Igorrotes," and to request that troops be established "in all the passes." He also proposed that new Christians should not have to pay tribute, and that alcalde-mayors and others in power should not be permitted to "deprive them of their lands and places inherited from their ancestors." This early progressive leader, however, failed in his attempt at larger consolidation. In a revolt which followed, only nine "rancherias," all located near Cayan, supported Soliman and other Spanish-appointed officials. Perez lists the names of seventeen rancherias that opposed them, including prominent communities of the other Lepanto districts nearby: Besao, Bauko, and Sabangan. In the period that followed, Perez says, many Spanish expeditions were sent to the mountains to punish the people for raids, and to restore peace. At this time, the inner mountain zone occupied by the Bontok people and also the high northern sections of Benguet were still virtually unknown.

In 1833, Guillermo Galvey, on one of his exploring expeditions in the south and central Cordillera, ranged from the upper Agno river to the Suyoc and Kayan areas. His journal, as summarized by Malumbres, speaks of Suyoc as having "40 houses," and "immense landslides and excavations" as a result of mining activities. "Cayan" had "250 houses," and "excellent sementeras of palay," evidently referring to its rice terraces. Southeast of Kayan was "Magecimuy," with "280 houses." This place name is no longer recognizable, but a "Maguiney" does appear in the de Monforte village list of the 1660's, and in the list of villages loyal to Soliman; it was evidently one of the present-day communities between Kayan and Mankayan, and its size suggests that it could have been Guinsadan (Malumbres, 1919, II, 243–44).

LATER PERSPECTIVES

A brief description may be given of the principal settlements, summarized from Buzeta's statistical and other information. Buzeta includes census figures for 1818 in the case of Ilocos Sur, that is, from Tagudin north, but not for the old Pangasinan section that became part of La Union in 1850.

San Fernando area. San Fernando, capital of La Union, was still small in 1847, with 870 houses and 5,225 people. It was an important communication and trading center, with a noted daily market for agricultural and fisheries products. To the north were San Juan and Bacnotan, with 1847 population totals of 5,405 and 5,794.

Balaoan-Tagudin area. Bangar was the largest settlement here, with 1,324 houses and 8,105 people (1847). The corresponding population totals for other centers were Balaoan 7,572, Namagpacan 7,397, and Tagudin 7,207. The last named had 6,550 in 1818.

Candon area. Candon in 1818 had 9,270 people, and in 1847 a total of 3,075 houses with 16,347 people. Buzeta speaks of it as a trading center for "rancherias of Igorots and Tinguians," and for "Negrito infidels." To the south, Santa Lucia and its "dependency" Santa Cruz had a combined population in 1818 of 9,225, and in 1847 the former had 9,590 and the latter 4,720. Gold, Buzeta says, was obtained in some waterways at Santa Lucia, including some "nuggets."

By Buzeta's 1847 count, the coastal zone had a total population of 77,362.

Buzeta notes that in the mountains back of San Fernando were "various westerly tribes of Igorrotes," the nearest being only a half-hour journey from the población itself. These were evidently settlements in the lower reaches of the Naguilian river. He also speaks of a barrio called Tundingan near San Fernando which was "formed from a rancheria of Igorrotes reduced to Christianity." A pueblo called "Naquilian" seems to have been a trading center on the edge of the "Igorrote" country, and may be ancestral to the modern settlement of Naguilian further down river near Bauang, which the ethnographer Moss later described as a principal trading point for the upland peoples (1920*a*, p. 227). San Juan also had some "rancherias of Igorrotes" called Nagyubuyuban, a name still used for one of the Kankanai hamlets on the Baroro river eastward from San Juan.

Further north, the old coastal towns also had their adherent groups of Christianized and non-Christian mountaineers. Bangar was an organizing center for various mountain missions, including "San Raphael," which became the modern Sudipen. Among the missions operating out of Tagudin were "Sevilla" and "Argaguinan" (later Agaguman). Santa Lucia had a mission called "Ronda." Candon was a major center for mountain trading and for mission work.

Buzeta also gives impressionistic descriptions of the various mountain groups as they were known and classified in the mid-nineteenth century. North of the "Igorrotes" of the Benguet area were the "Buriks," comprising the southerly Lepanto settlements where the spread-out residential pattern is giving place to larger villages:

These are somewhat different from the Igorrotes, having a rather larger and more vigorous physique. They tattoo their bodies with a coat of mail design. . . . They are more industrious and wealthy than the [Benguet people] . . . and their customs are more humanitarian. They regularly cultivate rice and irrigate their fields with fresh water brought in canals. The water supplies their crops and livestock, and makes possible the gold mining at Sucju [Suyoc] and the copper mining at Yamcayan [Mankayan].

Further north were the "Busaos," the name presumably derived from the important northern Lepanto community of Besao, overlooking the great valley of the Abra. Bounded "on the west by the Tinguianes and on the east by the Itetapanes," they "are distinguished from the other tribes by their mild character and less savage habits."

They only paint themselves on their arms, where they draw diverse flowers. Some wear large earrings and others suspend pieces of wood amounting to a good deal of weight from their ears . . . they wear a cylindrical cap which is open on the two sides and wrapped many times with feathers. It is made of wood or cloth fabricated from tropical vegetation. . . . They use an *aliva* as a weapon. It is like an iron ax, nearly square, with a point on the rear and a short handle. They make this weapon in the village of *Benang*. . . . They cultivate much rice and use a system of irrigation which never fails the crop.

Further inland still were the "Itetapanes," or Bontok ethnic group, the name being taken from the first Bontok village encountered on the old trail from Kayan, and still called Tetepan:

[This] group has a comparatively smaller population. . . . They are of short stature and fine build. The color of their skin is darker. . . . It is as difficult to take them away from the savage life as it is the Negritos. . . . They borrow the cylindrical headwear from the *Busaos* but they paint it a very bright red color—as they do their weapons: the spear, arrows, and the *aliva*. . . . Also in the season of the north winds and rains they use a palatina made of . . . leaves [i.e., a shoulder cover].

The Murata map of 1852, referred to in the previous chapter, shows the regional differentiation of the "Buriks" in the south and the "Busaos" in the north. It also marks several district clusters of settlements, but the only one named is "Yamcayan," that is, Mankayan.

Various abortive attempts were made by Spaniards during the early part of the nineteenth century to get control of the copper and gold mines in the Mankayan-Suyoc area. In 1856 a Spanish enterprise called the Cantabro-Filipino Company received a concession to develop commercial copper mining in the Mankayan area, and began operations four years later. This company is reported to have extracted two and a half million pounds of copper during its first fifteen years of activity.* Spanish officials were assigned to Mankayan in 1862, and maintained residence there to supervise labor conditions and other affairs. Perez (1902) says that the firm employed more than 600 Chinese workers as well as local mountaineers. He quotes two visitors, Prat and Ruiz, as speaking of how "magnificently imposing" the local scene then was from the official residence on a hill above Mankayan: "[The] Chinese colony, the barrio of the Christians, the making of carbon and the cutting of wood that the Igorots practice in nearby pine groves—in a word from this watchtower the administrator's eyes can reach all parts."

In general the Igorot men carried the minerals from the mines to the foundry, the Chinese attended the foundry, while Igorot women helped with the "washing" of the metal. Working conditions were extolled by those observers, payment was prompt, and through the efforts of the Spanish administrators these "savages" were being transformed from their "traditional customs . . . into constant servers of this establishment." Some Spanish settlers had started coffee plantations in the vicinity. This mining enterprise later waned, Perez says, "partly due to a decline in the value of copper," so that by 1892 "hardly forty persons" were employed, though the coffee plantations were continuing. In the nearby gold-mining area of Suyoc at that time, as pictured by Perez, the government was wrestling with the problem of trying to stimulate agriculture on the potentially rich local lands in the face of the traditional habits of mining gold for sale in other districts. He describes its people as buying rice not least of all to make wine. In 1886–88, during which time two of their outstanding leaders died, months were spent "without doing . . . work and in continuous intoxication." In the second instance, government police were sent to compel burial of the corpse, and they, too, joined in the ceremony, so that a Civil Guard force was dispatched to punish both the Igorots and the policemen (Perez, Chapter VI, translated in the Beyer Collection).

* A review of the historical records relating to these mines is given in A. J. Eveland, "Preliminary Reconnaissance of . . . Mancayan-Suyoc . . . ," *Bulletin, Philippine Islands Mining Bureau* (1905), No. 4.

In 1847, a year after the Abra valley was made into a separate province, the Ilocos range mountain region between it and the Ilocos Sur coast was made into the politico-military Comandancia of Tiagan. The name was taken from a settlement point just south of San Emilio, which became its capital. In 1723, according to Cavada, Tiagan had become the first "rancheria" established, in the sense of coming under Spanish control, within this area. Two other rancherias, Ampayao and Ananao, had subsequently been established, in 1776 and 1791, respectively, while thirteen other settlements came under Spanish control in the first half of the nineteenth century.

In 1852 a corresponding politico-military jurisdiction was formed further inland and to the southeast, the Comandancia of Lepanto. Cavada gives 1837 as the initial date for the official "establishment" of "rancherias" in this area, and includes Kayan, or Cayan, the old center used by the Monforte expedition, as among six brought under control in that year. Kayan became the first capital of Lepanto. In 1875 Tiagan was linked administratively with Lepanto, and a new capital was developed at Cervantes, a more accessible center with a combined Ilocano and indigenous population.

In his 1876 survey, Cavada lists 22 principal "rancherias" in Tiagan, and 60 which "were paying tribute" in Lepanto. Their combined "Igorot" population was 29,791, of whom 18,701 were "under control." The people were characterized by him as "pacific, obedient, and timid, easily governed and susceptible to moral and material uplift," though they continued to be "infidels" (Cavada, pp. 114–15). Perez, in his "ethnographic dictionary," quotes a report of 1877 on Tiagan, made by the Comandante of the time, D. Mariano Rojo. The rancherias of the district, he states, are "comprised in major part of the race of the Tinguians." They are located near the lowland flats, because their inhabitants are accustomed to trading with the Christian pueblos. "As much for that reason as because of the fertility of many of their little valleys and mountains, they outstrip in culture and well-being the rest of the rancherias of the districts of Cayan and Bontoc." This report shows Tiagan as having 24 rancherias, with 9,037 inhabitants (Perez, 1904, p. 351).

In 1881, the Augustinians reestablished a mission in Kayan, and spread their work from there to other principal settlements (B&R, xxxvii, 247; Perez, 1904, index). Perez describes Cervantes in 1891 as a "cosmopolitan" official and marketing center. Its role was enhanced with the building of a road from there directly to the coast near Tagudin, largely replacing communication by the older trails.

Further inland and across the main Cordillera ridge, a third politico-military Comandancia, "Bontoc," was formed in 1857. This was designed to control and pacify the Bontok communities of the upper Chico river. Its headquarters center was at the present small town of Bontoc, capital of

Mountain Province. Cavada records this Comandancia as having 31 "ran-cherias," with a total population of 10,134. Surprisingly, in view of their repute as particularly ferocious headhunters, he characterizes the Bontok as being "in general good, hard-working, and mutually helpful people," except as they become involved in death feuds which lead to fighting (Cavada, 1876, pp. 121–22). In 1886, a Spanish expedition was sent to punish Bontok communities for burning houses and taking heads in Lepanto. Though a pardon followed, a Bontok raid was made in the same year on Abra, and thirty heads were brought back (Perez, in Beyer Collection). Besides having a substantial garrison at the capital, the Spaniards found it necessary to maintain blockhouses at three points in the district. Part of their task was to circumvent raids by the western Ifugaos into Bontoc and Lepanto (Perez, 1902, pp. 60–77; A. E. Jenks, 1905).

In 1890, the Amburayan Comandancia was formed further south between the Benguet district and the Ilocos coast. Its purpose was to control the scattered Kankanai groups in the general region of the Amburayan river system. Its first administrative center was Alilem. But early in the American period the coastal town of Tagudin, on which its settlements depended heavily for trade and ecclesiastical leadership, was incorporated into it and made its capital. The Beyer Collection includes a useful set of documents relating to the formation of Amburayan. An official report recommending its establishment says in part:

[These peoples] since the remote date of their submission to the Government of the sovereign country have been living abandoned to themselves, receiving but feeble sparks of civilization from the Christian pueblos to which they belong and which far from conducting them along the path of progress do but increase the chaotic condition of their false beliefs and devices.

The report states that Amburayan had 40 settlements, and "12,150 souls according to the tax lists," but "probably 16,000 in all." Perez speaks of the Kankanai of the area as "differing very little from the Igorots" of Benguet except that they "celebrate their festivals more splendidly" and "drinking and gambling are more frequent" (Perez, Chapter IV, in Beyer Collection).

The Taft Commission report of 1900 gives a useful statistical survey of the four Comandancias. Tiagan had 7,793 inhabitants living in 53 "villages" and 25 "hamlets." Its administrative center, San Emilio, had a population of 1,658, so that the rest of the settlements were mostly small, averaging less than 80 persons each. Lepanto had 16,152 "registered" inhabitants, living in 5 towns and 40 villages, obviously of much larger size than the Tiagan aggregations. Along the northern margins of both Tiagan and Lepanto the Igorot population showed intermarriage and cultural penetration with the Abra Tinguians. Bontoc had 13,985 registered inhabitants, though some estimates placed the population total of this less-known area much higher. Amburayan had an estimated population of 30,000 "pagans" and 150 Christians occupying 34 "towns" and 76 "hamlets," so that its principal centers were of large size. In addition to its "Igorot" population, a settlement of Tinguians had been established in the Sigay district of north Amburayan.

THE HISTORICAL PERIOD THROUGH MOUNTAIN EYES

In 1911 the American Governor-General issued instructions throughout the Philippines for local authorities, that is, the indigenous officials, to write down so far as possible the "entire history" of each community. Robertson subsequently edited and compiled the records submitted by the eleven municipal districts of Lepanto, and his resulting publication provides a most useful sample of how mountain peoples view their earlier relations with the lowland peoples. The following is a summary of those items of most ethnohistorical interest, the districts concerned being treated from south to north:

Ampusungan. The Spaniards did not organize this settled area as a "town" until 1878, because of its "sparse population." For many years the people "promptly deserted their homes" whenever any of the Spanish Civil Guard appeared.

Mankayan. This mineral-rich center had three barrios, of which Mankayan (Aban) has had copper deposits and Suyoc gold. Mankayan was formed by people who "came from very distant rancherias" in "time immemorial." Spanish officials were stationed there from 1862 until the insurrection. Some of the old inhabitants, when hunting, made a fire for cooking, and were astonished to see the stone melt, yielding dark red copper. After various trials they were able to make jars of it, and they also took lumps to Tagudin for sale. "After some years" several Spaniards and an Englishman, two of their names still remembered, came as a commission and a year later they "took possession" of the mines, "telling our ancestors that they had been given the title" by the government. Thereupon some of the ancestors went to other pueblos or to nearby places, while some stayed on as "workmen for these men." At Suyoc, gold was discovered when a man, in bathing, was rubbing earth on his head (as with soap) and "saw that his hands had become tinged a saffron color." This turned out, when the earth was shaken in wooden vessels, to be "small particles of dust." After talking the matter over, the group decided to try to melt this dust by putting some in a broken jar over hot coals, and after some hours they got gold, though in an impure state. After greater control, they converted some of the gold into earrings. They found these could be sold to other rancherias and in Tagudin. They continued to work the gold subsequently, in spite of its difficulty.

Kayan (Cayan). In 1844 its seven barrios "sent to the capital of Abra" a request that a Spanish official be stationed there to deal with hostile attacks and stealing by neighboring "towns." This led to its becoming, for a time, the capital of Lepanto. The "first friar missionary" came in 1881. No records back of that time were cited, as for example, its use as headquarters by the Monforte expedition.

Cervantes. In 1883 this became the capital of Lepanto because Cayan lacked "good building sites." It consisted of three barrios inhabited by "Ilocanos and other Christians," and four inhabited by Igorots.

Sabangan. One of its six "barrios," Pingad, laid claim to "great antiquity and size." During the Spanish regime, however, many of its inhabitants moved to other barrios. A second barrio was formed by a group who migrated en masse from "another place because of the frequent visits of their neighbors, who were their enemies." A third barrio was formerly "nearer the river" (the upper Chico), but moved "higher up the mountain" for protection from its "more savage neighbors." The Spaniards, when they came, established a Civil Guard Post at Sabangan barrio because of its central position.

Besao. Of its eight barrios, Besao itself was founded, according to its origin story, by a man and his wife who could no longer "make a living" in an earlier locality nearer the coast. The man's sister, however, decided instead to go down to a barrio of Candon in the lowlands, where she married. When the population of Besao reached 300, they considered themselves "strong enough" to send 50 persons to the coast to buy salt. Near Santa Lucia they had a small boy left on their hands by his father who ran away. He later married a Besao girl, and in due course contacted his kinsmen, who were really descendants of the sister, to provide a link with the coastal people; he was also appointed master-of-camp of Besao by the authorities at Vigan. As a token of relationship, the kinsmen of the sister "granted to the Besao people half of the plain which lies between Santa Lucia and Candon" in case they should want to make homes there. From then on they collected rent of salt and cotton. But after many years, in renewing the arrangement, the people of Candon made out a false paper denying these rights. Enmity between Igorots and Christians originated in the killing of some of the former who were looking "for work" in Santa Maria on the coast, and whom the Christians asserted had stolen their dog for food. As a result Besao with another barrio took a young man's head at Santa Maria. Later peace was made through the intervention of the Santa Lucia kinsmen.

Bauco. The Spaniards established a government, after "several campaigns," in each of its four barrios.

Angaki. The first inhabitants of Angaki itself came from two small mountain settlements of the Ilocos range in 1836, and these settlements had been formed in previous generations from people who came from other places. The first Christians settled there in 1884. Initially taxes were paid in wax and baskets. Of its five outer barrios, Malideg was formed from people who migrated from the Ilocano town of Santa Maria, "in order to escape the baptism which the Spaniards were forcing on them, and in order to live in accordance with Igorot customs." The ancestors of Patiacung barrio trace back to 1793, when they "went to a place called Balaoa, west of Santa Lucia" in Ilocos Sur. They were compelled to pay a tax for the privilege of living in the town, and had to promise to help the Christians should "harm threaten from other Igorots"; this led to their migration further inland.

San Emilio. This district had eight principal barrios, each divided into two or more parts. Some formerly belonged to Ilocos Sur and some to Abra. Seventeen additional living sites were remembered, but "these places were deserted because of sickness, in accordance with Igorot custom." In Spanish times, memories of which went back to 1829, a garrison was stationed at San Emilio. "One friar" worked there from 1890 to 1897. In 1894, the politico-military commandant "enforced baptism" upon two of the towns in the area, San Emilio and Concepcion, so that all the people were baptized. But "the customs of the Igorots, such as performing canaos [ritual feasts] and other habits, had not been forbidden up to date." Since the revolution, no more of their children had been baptized.

For Concepcion, another of the Tiagan districts, the only significant reference was that just given. For two Lepanto groups, Bagnen and Bana-ao, no comments were recorded on the history of Spanish times. Along with these historical and pseudo-historical memories were written down stand-ard myths of the region: a flood incident from which a brother and sister were saved on high mountains; the founding of a community by a man looking for his pregnant sow, camping to care for the litter, and, because he liked the new place, sending for his relatives and friends to come and settle it (Robertson, 1914).

MODERN CENSUS DATA

As in the previous section, selected data from modern censuses may usefully be presented here to give demographic perspective. The 1903 census showed the northern La Union districts as having a combined total population of 67,176, and by 1948 the figure had risen to 111,464. Correspondingly the southern Ilocos Sur districts being dealt with in this chapter had totals of 42,272 in 1903 and 85,383 in 1948.*

The coastal zones show the expected dense populations, overwhelmingly Ilocano in their ethnic composition. The mountainous inland districts still have their quotas of non-Christians. These groups and their languages are labeled differently in the various censuses, and comparison of numbers from count to count is difficult because of periodic boundary changes, including those which accompanied the formation of Mountain Province.

The 1903 census showed all La Union as having 10,215 "Igorots," of whom 165 were classed as "civilized" and the rest "wild." As suggested in

* The following were the populations in 1948 by municipal units:

NORTHERN LA UNION

Lowland				Mountain	
San Fernando	28,742	Balaoan	14,274	Bagulin	3,101
San Juan	12,521	Luna	11,258	Santol	5,060
Bacnotan	13,793	Bangar	14,988	San Gabriel	5,805
				Sudipen	6,922

SOUTHERN ILOCOS SUR

Lowland				Mountain			
Tagudin	15,637	Sugpon	2,159	Cervantes	4,346	Angaki	3,130
Santa Lucia	10,021	Alilem	3,049	Concepcion	1,819	San Emilio	3,245
Santa Cruz	13,799	Suyo	3,012	Bauguen	4,771	Banayoyo	2,572
Candon	22,362	Sigay	1,571	Galimuyod	3,418	Lidlidda	1,673

the preceding chapter, approximately half seem to have been in the zone treated here. Ilocos Sur Province, as a whole, had a corresponding 1903 count of 13,578 Igorots, of whom only 2 were classed as "civilized" and the rest "wild." Nearly all of them would have been in the mountains of this southern zone. Further inland, the Lepanto-Bontoc jurisdiction of the time had 70,426 Igorots, of whom 143 were "civilized."

The 1939 census shows the mountain margins being penetrated vigorously by Ilocano settlers, but in the higher country the mountain peoples still vastly predominated. Census takers sometimes distinguished the mountain languages in the area as "Kankanai," or "Bontok," but for the most part grouped them as "Igorot" (unclassified). For all La Union, the figures showed 513 "Kankanai" speakers in the Bagulin district inland from San Fernando, and otherwise 6,561 in the general Igorot-speaking category, or 7,074 in all. This figure, as seen in the previous chapter, includes many Ibaloi to the south. Ilocos Sur had a total of 17,940 Igorot speakers, nearly all of whom lived in the area being treated here. The largest groups, as would be expected, were in the furthest inland districts: Cervantes 4,051, San Emilio 2,839, and Sugpon 2,010.* Nearer the coast, Ilocanos consistently outnumbered the mountaineers. In the Galimuyod district near Candon, there were at the time 642 speakers of "Tinggian" (Tinguian), and a few were scattered in other districts. There were also a few Bontok counted along the coast.

The 1948 census showed La Union as having 7,636 people returning an Igorot dialect as their mother tongue, while Ilocos Sur had only 4,208. Statistics on religious affiliation showed in the category "pagan and not belonging to any religious group" corresponding totals for the two provinces of 2,099 and 9,881.

In Mountain Province, back of these areas, three southern districts primarily inhabited by members of the Kankanai ethnic group had in 1948 a combined population of 16,256, while the five Lepanto districts had 36,430. The five districts comprising approximately the Bontok ethnic area had a combined population of 32,403, this figure including the small Mountain Province capital town of Bontoc with a cosmopolitan population. Here, too, the statistics on language speakers are complicated by the frequent use of some census takers of the general category "Igorot" (unclassified) and by others of the more precise "Kangkanay" or "Kankanay," which covers both the Kankanai and Lepanto. The province, in terms of mother tongues,

* Until the 1948 census, the schedule did not request respondents to identify their mother tongue. A considerable number of people with bilingual competence, therefore, reported both languages. For this reason the total number of language speakers tends everywhere to be higher than the total population. In the case of old interaction points such as Cervantes and San Emilio, both Ilocano and Lepanto respondents probably made bilingual returns in numbers of instances.

showed 100,680 in a combined "Igorot-Kangkanay" category, though this figure evidently included many Benguet Inibaloi and Bontok speakers. The census identified 22,001 Bontok speakers.

The census figures for the southern Ilocos Sur districts were analyzed in detail to see if they could give any clues for interpreting the settlement patterns of the Lepanto and Bontok, with their large compact villages. Here, however, the demographic happenings of the last four centuries in the Christianized communities make any long-term interpretation dubious. The records show how the lowland Ilocos peoples were concentrated by the early missionaries and civil authorities into unusually large communities in terms of wider Philippine perspectives. Later population increases, on the one hand, tended to make the towns and poblaciones (administrative district centers) bigger; yet, on the other hand, they caused Ilocano colonists to spread out in smaller barrios and, where security permitted, into separate farmsteads as they pioneered new areas of settlement.

The 1903 census, which is the first to give population statistics in detail by poblaciones and barrios, shows most clearly these later phases of settlement. Old centers such as Candon and Tagudin are sizable rural towns, whereas the newer settled districts typically have many small and scattered barrios. From an analysis of several of the municipal units, the following is the 1903 settlement picture for some of the older districts:

Balaoan: total population 10,008; población 1,629; 33 barrios, averaging 254 per barrio.

Luna (Namagpacan): total population 11,116; población 574; 26 barrios, averaging 405 per barrio.

Tagudin: total population 8,503; población 3,174; 19 barrios, averging 286 per barrio.

Santa Cruz: total population 5,678; población 1,405; 14 barrios, averaging 305 per barrio.

Candon: total population 18,828; población 2,643; 30 barrios, averaging 540 per barrio.

Such coastal zones, by these figures, show barrio sizes to be smaller on the average than the sizes of Lepanto and Bontok villages. While the 1903 census does not give specific populations for the latter, as conditions were too disturbed for counts to be made, statistics for 1932 seen at the Mountain Province capital showed the average size of Lepanto and Bontok villages at that time to be around 700 persons, and nearly all ranged between 300 and 1,200.

A further pertinent question is whether the modern pattern of settlement along this stretch of the Ilocos coast differs from that in neighboring lowland districts in any way which could suggest that the distinctiveness of the mountain village pattern traces back to a distinctiveness in the old local coastal community pattern. The statistics are negative here. The

Agoo-Bauang districts to the south, and the districts to be seen north of Candon, show settlement patterns essentially similar to those seen here, e.g., Aringay 387 per barrio; Bauang 484; San Esteban 222; Narvacan 597. In the rich and now crowded Pangasinan flats from San Fabian eastward, the barrio averages run from around 500 to 1,000 persons.

REVIEW

As the further sectional studies continue, this southern Ilocos zone will be seen as probably the most complex and puzzling region of northern Luzon. This is so despite the apparent simplicity of what has been called a "wedge" of wet-terracing peoples extending back from the coastal mountains to the upper Chico, or Bontok, country.

As a central hypothesis, it might be assumed that the mountain populations derive from the coastal peoples who became, with consolidation and Hispanization, the southern Ilocano. As in Benguet, the first settlers might have moved inland to work gold in the Suyoc area, possibly well before Spanish times. Though speaking what could be termed proto-Kankanai, their ecological-cultural adjustments could have been similar, and related, to those of the Ibaloi. This would explain the close likeness between the modern Kankanai (southern Kankanai) culture of the Amburayan area and Ibaloi culture. Further north, proto-Kankanai speakers from communities up the coast, perhaps with a different version of the dialect, could then have struck inland to settle the Tiagan and Lepanto areas. Tiagan, little known ethnographically, seems to show marked ethnic affiliations with the Kankanai of Amburayan. Higher in the mountains, the Lepanto or northern Kankanai then developed their large wet-terracing communities, possibly under Spanish influence.

Given these speculative vistas, the Bontok must now be brought on the scene. Where the Lepanto extend from the western Cordillera slopes on to the headwater streams of the Chico, which flows to the Cagayan valley, the Bontok are wholly on the Chico side. For all their linguistic and cultural closeness to the Lepanto, the question must therefore arise whether as a population group they derive from west or east. Here the record to this point is quite incomplete, since it will be necessary to see their possible relation to the Kalinga peoples further down the Chico and to the Ifugao on the eastern slopes of the Cordillera. These latter groups are also wet terracers, though with markedly differing technological practices.

Modern ethnographers pick up hints, too, that dry cultivation of root crops may have preceded wet rice cropping in Bontok and Lepanto, as will be seen in the final chapter. Such dry gardening, noted already in Benguet, is also found among mountain Tinguian, northern Kalinga, and Isneg groups further north, and in Gaddang groups on the east side of the Cordillera. The question arises, therefore, whether the central heights were occupied by dry cultivating groups prior to the development of terracing. In this case, the marked ethnic differences between the Bontok and Lepanto could trace back at least in part to local variation in earlier times, rather than being thought of as later specializations, or as the result of their ancestral groups having come from different regions in the lowlands. Clearly the unraveling of all these threads will need to await the over-all analysis to be made in the final chapter.

V. The Middle Ilocos Area

PLACE AND PEOPLE

This zone constitutes the central part of the Ilocano ethnic area, that is, the northern half of Ilocos Sur Province, together with the great enclosed valley of the Abra river system, roughly corresponding to Abra Province. It is focused on two administrative capitals, Vigan in Ilocos Sur, and Bangued in Abra.

The coastal flats rise quickly to the first line of mountains, the Ilocos range. The Abra river empties its great volume of water through a gorge called the Banauang Gap. Until the development of modern roading, a day's journey by raft or on horseback was required to get from the coastal area through this gorge into the open river flats of the Abra valley. The Spanish word *abra* means "gorge," "breach," "pass," or "dale," all of which could apply here.

The main course of the Abra river flows from the south, as seen in the previous chapter. But great tributary systems rise around the valley flanks, most of them along the Cordillera heights, which form the eastern border of Abra. Notable are the Tineg to the northeast, and the Binongan, Malanas, Ba-ay, Bucloc, and Ikmin to the east and southeast. Trails lead by way of some of their headwater streams into Lepanto, Kalinga, and Apayao. They also cross from the middle Abra valley westward to the coast at Narvacan and other points, and from north Abra into Ilocos Norte.

In ethnic terms, the coastal areas of this zone have as their indigenous population the main body of the Ilocano. During the modern decades, too, colonizing Ilocano families have moved inland and up so far as land has been available and their lowland farming technology and trading have gained them a living. The Abra area has as its indigenous inhabitants the Tinguian, or Tinggian, ethnic group, the name being derived as already seen from the Tagalog word for "hill." An alternate ethnic and linguistic name is Itneg, apparently derived from the name of the Tineg river in northeast Abra. The Tinguians number today approximately 26,000.

Cole, Eggan, and other modern scholars have distinguished two broad

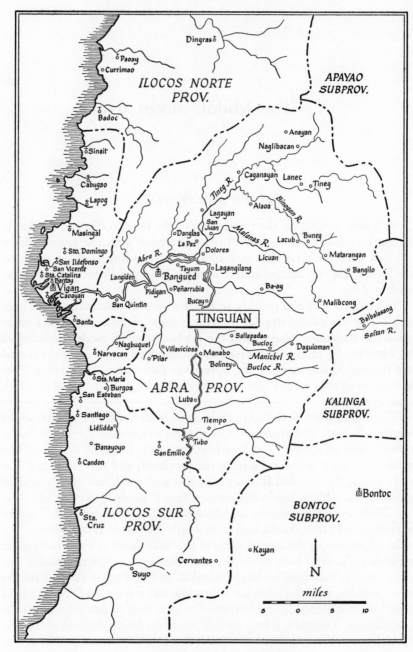

MIDDLE ILOCOS AREA

groupings: valley or "civilized" Tinguians who are wet cultivators living in village communities, and mountain or "wild" Tinguians who are dry cultivators with hamlet-sized settlements. The latter are sparsely scattered in the high country of north and east Abra, and northward into Ilocos Norte. Some of the valley Tinguians have also moved westward over the Ilocos range to form settlements on its coastal side, as seen in the preceding chapter. Cole says of this: "Many towns and districts now recognized as Ilocano are but Christianized Tinguian" (1945, p. 149).

Up to modern times, groups of Negritos have lived along the Ilocos coast range. By the 1903 census, however, their total number had fallen to 105, and by 1948 to 9. Small numbers of the Isneg, or Apayao, ethnic group have filtered over the Cordillera into northeast Abra from Apayao sub-province. Similarly some Kalinga have settled in eastern Abra from the subprovince of Kalinga, while the Balbalasang area of western Kalinga will be seen as showing Tinguian penetration and influence. The great majority of the Tinguians live in grassy hill country along the Abra valley floor at elevations of several hundred feet above sea level. Their villages are of considerable size, with the houses usually distributed in "barrio" clusters, and often rather scattered out among gardens and seed beds. The typical Tinguian house is a variant of lowland patterns, but there are character-istic styles of dress and ornament. No ward divisions or men's and girls' houses exist as among the Lepanto and Bontok. Child betrothal rather than sanctioned sex play is the usual prelude to marriage. Leadership is pro-vided by wealthy "headmen" or aristocrats. Ceremonial wealth in the form of Chinese jars, copper gongs, and precious beads vies with rice fields and livestock in defining the status of being "rich." Ritual and festival life is highly elaborated, with female shamans or mediums taking important re-sponsibilities in religious affairs. The dry gardening mountain Tinguian have less complex ceremonial, and much less differentiated, class structure.

Cole speaks of the valley Tinguian as "nearly identical in physical type to the coastal Ilocano," and of the Tinguian language as having "only dia-lectical difference" from Iloko (1945, p. 149). He hypothesizes that they have continuity with the pre-Spanish coastal population now counted Ilo-cano, and were fairly recent arrivals in the valley. The mountain Tinguian, by contrast, are "nearer the Igorot" physically, and show ethnic affiliations with older mountain populations. He and others have noted that the Tin-guian wet-terracing techniques show both mountain and lowland elements, along with local specialties. The walls, while rather Lepanto-like, are gen-erally low and of earth rather than stone. The fields are not fertilized, as is the Lepanto and Kalinga fashion. The carabao is used with a Chinese-style plow and harrow rather than for trampling the field. The Tinguian use a rice-knife to harvest grain instead of breaking off the stalks by hand, and their granaries are like those of the Ilocano (Cole, 1922, pp. 394–95; 1945, pp. 149–73).

Linguistic studies by glottochronological methods of the Tinguian speech and of its relations to Iloko and other neighboring languages are still inadequate. The Pittman group recorded dialect variations between east and south Tinguian groups, but found no very marked distinctions in basic words between Tinguian and Iloko, northern Kankanai, Kalinga, or Isneg. The Fox group gave Tinguian preliminary placement in a "Northern Division" of languages along with Isneg, and also with Ibanag, the speech of the lower Cagayan valley people.

In the Ilocos lowlands, it has been seen, the traditional wet crop is grown in the rainy summer season, from around June on. The Tinguian wet terracers, according to Cole (1922), also start the cycle "when the rains begin," a timetable which contrasts with that of the neighboring Lepanto and other mountain terracing peoples. Double cropping is minor, with a second wet crop slightly more extensive in Abra, which has somewhat greater rainfall than Ilocos Sur. Dry rice is grown in small quantity, especially along the Ilocos range adjacent to the coast. According to the district-by-district figures in the 1948 census, the mountain Tinguian settlements in the high country of eastern Abra along the main Cordillera grow almost none. Maize, too, is essentially a lower elevation resource. In Abra it is often possible to grow two crops annually, which is rare along the coast. Cultivated and wild roots, especially sweet potatoes, have considerable importance. Taro is grown more extensively in the damper soils of Abra than in the coastal districts (Philippine agricultural censuses, and other sources).

EARLY PERSPECTIVES

The historical record of this region opens, as with that for zones further south, when Salcedo's exploring party moved up the coast in 1572. As told by de los Reyes, the party left "Dumanquake" in early June of that year, and by nightfall reached the coast at "Kooayan," or Caoayan, near the mouth of the Abra river. Next morning they proceeded upriver in the direction of the "pueblo of Vigan." On both banks parties of the local people brandished lances, and shouted in hostile fashion. The Spaniards drove them off, and they "followed in a yelling crowd."

The flotilla anchored near Vigan, and the inhabitants tried to block a landing, so that it was necessary to fire arquebuses at the bank. Salcedo, through the medium of indigenous interpreters "brought from Manila," offered to make peace. But the overtures were rejected, and the men assembled in battle formation. The Spaniards then landed and attacked, forcing them with volleys of arquebus shots to fall back. In this way the party entered Vigan, while the inhabitants retreated to the adjacent "población" of Bantay, abandoning some of their women and children. These latter were subjected to no harm, though a limited amount of needed supplies were seized. Bantay was noted as having a "well sheltered port," and de los Reyes says in an aside that by local tradition it was a "very old pueblo." Once the Vigan people had seen that the Spaniards were "inoffensive people," they returned from Bantay and presented themselves to Salcedo. He received them well, and they "offered homage." From here the party moved on northward to the Laoag area, as will be seen in the next chapter.

Instead of going on from Laoag to Cagayan, Salcedo first returned to Vigan. He sent ahead a lieutenant, Don Antonio Hurtado, with twenty soldiers and six boats. They were well received, and given plentiful foodstuffs. Hurtado told the people of his mission to establish a Spanish colony there in order to aid them in their struggles with the surrounding settlements. The local people accepted this idea enthusiastically, and allotted workers to cut lumber for construction of a fort, with a stockade and various houses. Salcedo, after having "reduced many pueblos" in the north, joined Hurtado at Vigan. He agreed to the building of the fort "on a hill called Tamag, between the river and the sea, but somewhat away from the [Vigan] pueblo." When it was finished, Salcedo put Hurtado in charge, and continued on his journey northward around Luzon (de los Reyes, II, 13–15, 19–20). As seen in the general chapter, Salcedo returned to Vigan a short time later to establish there the Spanish "town" of Villa Fernandina, or Fernandina, and made it his headquarters.

The first comprehensive delineations of settlement patterns and population numbers in this zone, as in those treated in previous chapters, are provided by the Loarca description of 1582, the encomienda survey of 1591, and the ecclesiastical review of 1612. Loarca lists as the first locality north of Candon, discussed in Chapter IV, the "Province of Maluacan," with a population of "about" 1,800 Indins organized as an encomienda, Described as "three leagues" north of Candon, it was evidently the Narvacan area. "Two leagues" further, hence around the mouth of the Abra river, was the "Valley of Landan," with about 1,000 Indians, whose encomienda revenues "belong to the hospital of Manila." Next came the "Valley of Vigan," opposite which was the "village" of Vigan, with about 800 Indians. This encomienda area "belongs to the King." "Not far" from the indigenous village was the town of Fernandina, in which "twenty or thirty" Spaniards lived "as if in banishment." "A league" further on was the "Valley of Sinay," with about 1,600 Indians; both of these were under the same encomendero. These 1582 figures show a total population estimate of about 6,800 (B&R, v, 109).

The *Account of Encomiendas* in 1591 shows the following coastal holdings, from south to north, all spoken of as having "peace" and "justice":

Narbucan (Narvacan): private holding; 1,490 tributes from 5,960 people; served by "one ecclesiastic."

Narandam (Landan): provides revenue for the Manila hospital; 390 tributes from 1,560 people; has religious "instruction."

Bigan (Vigan): Royal holding; 800 tributes from 3,200 people; "one religious."

Bantay and Batanguey: Royal holdings; 1,000 tributes from 4,000 people; no "instruction," but visited from Bigan.

Panay (Masingal): private holding; 700 tributes from 2,800 people; "no instruction."

Cabugao and Sinay (Sinait): Royal holdings; 1,000 tributes from 4,000 people; "no instruction."

The encomienda list continues on here to give the holdings in Ilocos Norte, maintaining the general south-to-north order. In the middle of the list the name appears of a small encomienda, "El Abra de Bigan." This holding by a private encomendero "collected" 150 tributes from 600 people, and had "justice" but no "instruction." The place name "Bigan" is not found in the Laoag-Bacarra zone where this encomienda appears in the list. It seems certain that the encomienda was really in the Vigan area, with the "Abra" referring to the Banauang Gap—this, incidentally, the first use of the name located in the records. De los Reyes places it inside the Abra valley. It is doubtful, however, that the Spaniards could have penetrated the interior zone to this extent by 1591; the first mission workers will be seen as breaching it seven years later. Possibly, therefore, it could have been on the seaward side of the Abra river gorge. With this 600 people added in, the total population estimate of 1591 was therefore 22,120 (B&R, VIII, 105–8).

The ecclesiastical survey of the Agustinian missions as of 1612 makes no reference to the coastal zone from Narvacan to Vigan. But a major "Convent" was located at Bantay, just north of the Fernandina-Vigan area, with 3 ministers serving "visitas" throughout this central region. Bantay was to become the Augustinian headquarters for work in Ilocos, and at the time served 3,000 Indians "in confession," paying 1,000 tributes. Further north a "convent" at "Sinay" (Sinait), with its visitas, had 2 ministers serving 3,600 "in confession," paying 1,200 tributes. If the total of 2,200 tributes shown here is translated at the one-to-four ratio by which populations were reckoned at the time from tribute figures, the 1612 population total becomes 8,800 (B&R, XVII, 116–17).

A review of these early demographic leads, for what they are worth, points up a surprising discrepancy between the 22,120 in the 1591 encomienda count and this 1612 mission figure of 8,800. The latter, of course, could be a careless or garbled return. Yet if it was even approximately correct, an interpretation could be that the Vigan zone, which had the most direct and intensive contacts with Spanish military, civil, and ecclesiastical personnel, had been particularly hard hit by the introduced diseases, which took a toll virtually everywhere. Possibly, too, encomenderos might sometimes have exaggerated their estimates of the size of less controlled populations, thus opening the way to collect larger tributes than the authorized amounts. But in these areas adjacent to Vigan, which were under close control, such loose statistical records would not be expected. It may have well been, instead, that in this one part of Ilocos which had great inland valley zones to which coastal populations could escape from Spanish pressures, the apparent falling away of population numbers came about through extensive movement of people into the interior. The Banauang Gap would have been a ready escape hatch, so to speak, for people of Vigan and other settlements around the Abra river mouth to retreat from Spanish control. The lack of specific record in the mission figures of populations in Narvacan and other areas south of the Abra mouth suggests that here, particularly, coastal groups could have moved higher into the Ilocos range and perhaps on into the southern Abra valley. Peoples along the northern coastal strip to Sinait, too, could have crossed the mountains back of their settlements into northern Abra. Unfortunately, the records do not give specific answers regarding such possible early population movements.

To throw these demographic materials into perspective, it may be noted that the coastal strip from present-day Santiago, south of Narvacan, to Caoayan on the north bank of the Abra river mouth, had by 1847 a combined population of 50,431, compared with the 1591 encomienda total (Narbucan, Landan, and Abra de Bigan) of 8,120. The first American census of 1903 showed a slightly decreased figure of 50,102, a fall brought about by the shrinkage in the boundaries of Ilocos Sur with the formation of the separate mountain jurisdictions. The Vigan-Bantay area, which in 1591 had 7,200 people listed in its encomiendas, had in 1847 (north to Santo Domingo) a total of 47,709, of whom 18,532 were in the town district of Vigan; in 1903 the total was 44,915. The northern coastal area on to Sinait, with 6,800 in 1591, had later totals of 33,651 (1847) and 32,174 (1903). The early population figures seem high enough to suggest that the middle Ilocos coastal peoples, as those further south, were practicing wet rice cultivation at the time the Spaniards arrived.

THE COASTAL DISTRICTS

The general section on Ilocos has already dealt with much of the early history of this zone, including the founding of Fernandina, the uncertainty whether the Augustinians or the Franciscans pioneered church work in the Vigan area, the relations with Chinese and Japanese traders, and the depredations of the pirate Limahon. Sande's *Relation* of 1576 tells how Salcedo sent a "galliot" north to be provisioned at "Cinay," evidently the Sinay or Sinait encomienda, where it was burned by the pirate Limahon, who was en route to attack Manila at the time (B&R, iv, 26). Limahon also sacked Fernandina, as Loarca notes in his 1582 description of the settlement:

Not far from [the village of] Vigan is settled the town of Fernandina. . . . [The Governor] appointed there six regidors, two alcaldes, and one justice for all the province of the Ylocos. . . . At the coming of Limahon, Fernandina was plundered, and there remains now one alcalde-mayor, with twenty or thirty Spaniards, who usually dwell there as if in banishment. The alcalde-mayor receives a salary of three hundred pesos, and appoints notaries at his pleasure. (B&R, v, 109.)

In 1583 a *Report of Saleable Offices* in the Philippines notes that "the town of Fernandina in the province of Ylocos" had "proved to be so un-healthy a region" that, from being "the richest town of these islands" pre-sumably because of the gold trade, it "has now only a few inhabitants with no organized cabildo or government" (B&R, v, 203). The 1591 encomienda survey, dealing with the "Bigan" holding, appears to show this center passing its low point, and beginning to assume its future role as capital of Ilocos. It states: "The town of Bigan is called Villa Fernandina. Five or six Spanish citizens are settled there. It has one parish priest, one alcalde-mayor, and one deputy" (B&R, viii, 105).

Nearly twenty years later, Morga (1609) could still say of the town that though it was "settled by Spaniards . . . very few remain there." He notes that ships could enter over the "bar of Bigan" so that it was one of the ports of the coast (B&R, xvi, 109, 149–50). As seen in the ecclesiastical survey of 1612 above, the Augustinians established their principal center at Bantay, a little north of this secular capital.

EARLY PENETRATION OF ABRA

Once the coastal areas had been brought fully under civil and ecclesi-astical control, attention turned hopefully to the inland populations, particu-larly those living in the lower Abra valley. In 1598, according to de los Reyes, the Augustinian fathers Marin and Minon were able to penetrate the valley and found a "mission" at Banged. This center was evidently in the locality of the later capital of Abra Province, Bangued. Its purpose, de los Reyes says, was to serve as "the point of departure from which the infidels of Abra could be catechized on a major scale" (ii, 67). As noted above, it is uncertain whether the encomienda "El Abra de Bigan" was in this lower valley area.

Some rivalry developed at this time over which of the Cordillera popu-lations within the newly formed Bishopric of Nueva Segovia were properly targets for the Augustinians working out of Ilocos or for the Dominicans moving up the Cagayan valley. Bishop Soria, the first incumbent, judged that the "extensive pueblo" of Narvacan, south of the Abra mouth, "could serve well as the base for the conversion of the numerous infidels who inhabited those mountains and virgin forests, opening up, as their conquest progressed, pathways for communication with Cagayan."

A major reason for working in from the Ilocos side, according to de los Reyes, was that the "Dominicans did not have knowledge of the Ilocano dialect"—that is, the mountain peoples of the Abra region spoke, or knew as a lingua franca, the Ilocos coastal speech. According to this historian the Narvacan ministry was transferred briefly to the Dominicans (1612–13). One of the notable Dominican workers in the Cagayan mountain missions, Frey Tomás Gutiérrez, spent a year there at the time, apparently to familiarize himself with the language.

In 1612, the Augustinians, not wanting to be outdone in zeal by the Dominicans, made the mission at Bangued into a separate ministry. The father assigned to it was Fray Pedro Columbo, whose "evangelical labors," de los Reyes says, "achieved good results, as is registered in the Augustinian records in Manila." In 1614, another Augustinian, Fray Juan Pareja, started work in the "mountains of Abra" and "converted many infidels, concentrating them in pueblos during the six years he worked there."

In 1626, de los Reyes' account continues, Pareja returned to continue his work among these tribes, by then being called "Tinguianes." As such they were distinguished from the "Igolotes" who were on the more inaccessible heights. Between these two ethnic groups a state of "continual war" existed. The father made every effort to convert everyone in the Bangued area. The account here credits him with expanding the mission work eastward by establishing three visitas, "Tayum, Sabangan, and Bukao" (the last identified as the modern Dolores). These Christianized centers, it also states, engaged in bitter wars with Tinguian rancherias further inland: Talamuy, Bataan, Kabulao, and others. In all, Pareja was reported to have baptized more than 3,000 people, including their outstanding chief, Don Miguel Dumaual. De los Reyes says that this "famous Tinguian" contributed much to the progress of the pueblos then under Spanish influence, and he also left descendants who were still exercising authority in the late nineteenth century, the time of this historian's account (de los Reyes, II, 67, 75–77, 81–82).

In spite of these active beginnings toward penetration and control of what was to become Abra Province, the work fell away soon after this time. No further mention of the Bangued mission was found until the 1680's, when a controversy broke out among ecclesiastical and secular authorities because the Bishop of Nueva Segovia was living in Vigan rather than at his bishopric seat in the Cagayan valley. The "pretext" used by the Bishop, according to a record by Díaz of this so-called "Pardo controversy," was that he was "administering *ad interim* to the natives of the village of Bengues." This ministry "had for many years remained vacant," so that the people there were "becoming uneasy and disturbed." Díaz says that Bangued had been "abandoned" as having provided a "very poor living" for any incumbent father, and also as having "an unwholesome climate" (B&R, xxxix, 149). No effective work was really being done, however, in the interior at this time, and it would appear from the presence of Tinguian settlements along the coast from the Narvacan area southward to Santa Cruz that converts who did not apostatize moved for safety out of the war-torn valley during the later seventeenth century. Mission work, as will be seen, had to start again in Abra more or less from scratch during the early eighteenth century. Even then it tends to lapse once more, so that Christianization and Spanish control do not become really effective until the nineteenth century. The modern town of Bangued, capital of Abra Province, reckons its founding date, according to Cavada, as 1704, while Tayum, mentioned above, counts it as 1803.

CONTINUING RECORDS TO THE PANGASINAN INVASION

From records of the coastal zone, the year 1592 marked the birth of a "famous" person of the Vigan area, Don Pedro Bukaneg. As a baby, tradition holds, he was found by an Indian woman floating in the river of the settlement of Bantay. A blind child, he had been abandoned by his parents as being defective. He was baptized and brought up by the mission fathers. Of "rare intelligence," he helped with preparation of works on the local language. He was also renowned for his faith and moral leadership, and his example "led to many conversions" (de los Reyes, II, 63–64).

Reference was made in the general chapter to the leveling out of former dialectal variants on the Ilocos coast through the spread of an Iloko idiom. If this happened in early Spanish times, it is a fair assumption on the basis of comparable situations that the lingua franca which is now Iloko developed from the dialect of the Vigan area, since this was the administrative and mission center, and also the major focus for commerce. In this connection de los Reyes cites some stanzas written in the early seventeenth century by Pedro Bukaneg in the Iloko of the time (from Francisco Lopez, *Arte de la Lengua Iloca*, 1627) which indicate that it was "somewhat different" from modern Iloko. He also says that "the Chinese mestizos of Vigan" corrupted some words. Southern Iloko, he considers, has become more changed from the "primitive" form in later times than the northern Iloko (de los Reyes, I, 67, 71).

Various records cited in the general chapter that describe conditions around the first half of the seventeenth century—the abundance of rice and other products, the large settlements, the peacefulness and tractability of the population—may be taken as having special reference to the Vigan area, since Vigan was the center where visitors usually based themselves. As with similar capital towns, it was a focus for divergent official, commercial, and ecclesiastical interests, and particularly was open to conflicts between secular and religious authorities. It was presumably out of such conflicts that a complaint came, written by the Fiscal of the Philippines in 1606 to the King, regarding the "notoriously unjust practices of the ecclesiastics," which included taking "silver from the mission churches," and specified "Vantay" as one of the centers to have suffered (B&R, xiv, 168).

Most of the specific records of the seventeenth century for this region, as others in Ilocos, consist of terse references in the Augustinian records to the names of priests who served in the area. Sometimes the places where they were stationed are mentioned: the older centers of Narvacan, Bantay, and Sinait, and two new ones established in 1625, Santiago and San Esteban, both south of Narvacan. Medina's somewhat fuller *History* of 1630 speaks of Narvacan as a "priorate." He also describes it as "greatly exhausted by the burning of the church and convent"—possibly by marauding mountain peoples, as happened in the case of Tagudin further south. Medina refers to Bantay as the principal ecclesiastical establishment, with two resident "religious," and "more than one thousand Indians in charge"—a low figure if referring to more than the immediate Bantay area. By this time, the Spanish name Fernandina was becoming obsolete, giving place to the use of the older district name, Vigan. Medina says: "Vigan, or the village of Fernandina, . . . [is the residence of] the bishop, to whom this town has been given as his dwelling. . . . It is the best town in Ilocos, although it has suffered from damaging fires. It is also the residence of the alcalde-mayor of this province" (B&R, xxiii, 276–79, 296). This reference to the "Bishop" evidently is to the Bishop of Nueva Segovia, whose permanent residence was still in the provincial capital of Cagayan. Ilocos being part of the Bishopric, incumbents spent a portion of their time visiting or in residence at Vigan.

The orderly round of "Ilocan" life, as seen in previous chapters, was suddenly upset in 1660 with the invasion of Ilocos by rebel Pangasinan and Zambal troops under Don Jacinto Macasiag. Taking up the story of the victorious northward march of the large army from Pangasinan after their defeat of the Spanish defensive force near Agoo, the record shows an attempted fresh Spanish stand in the Narvacan area. Díaz, in his *Conquests,* tells how the retreating Spanish commanders ordered the Indians of Narvacan, with those of Santa Catalina, a visita of Bantay, to "erect a stockade and rampart in Agayayos." This was a narrow pass between cliffs through which the coastal "road" ran, and barely wide enough for a horse to traverse. Having garrisoned the pass with a "body of Indians," under command of one of their Santa Catalina leaders, the Spaniards then hurried to Vigan. Meantime the Spanish officials, the encomenderos, and the Augustinian fathers had been gathering at that center.

It was known that the rebel "King" Malong had been in communication with "some Indian chiefs" in the area, so that their loyalty in the face of the advancing rebel force was uncertain. The prudent action, therefore, seemed to be to "place in a ship all the father ministers and all the Spaniards who were there," and dispatch them to Manila. An alternative view was put forward by the fathers that "if the ministers were to retreat, it would be utter ruin to the province, in regard, not only to God, but to the king; for the Indians who yet maintained their faith and loyalty would abandon all if they had not the fathers—either through fear, or carried away by their heathen customs." The last phrase points to the awareness of the fathers that the old usages still had a persisting hold even in these extensively acculturated communities. An official decision was made to build a fort at Vigan in order to hold out until relief forces could arrive from Manila. This project was started, but was not completed, since "the Indians who worked at it were continually disappearing."

The alcalde-mayor then decided to leave by ship, and embarked with two fathers, though the Bishop, who was in residence there at the time, stayed on with the rest of the religious personnel. The flight of the top official "caused great injuries to that poor province." By this time, the central government was organizing both military and naval forces to meet the emergency.

The rebel force, on its arrival at Narvacan, "waited for some time" there, because of the problem of getting through the fortified "pass of Agayayos." The problem was solved, however, when the indigenous force "tore down the stockade, and very gladly went to offer them a free passage." The in-vaders then rapidly advanced on Vigan. As they entered the town, the Bishop sent word that he would "say mass" for their benefit, and their leaders with some others attended, and even "confessed to the priests." Most of the force, however, proceeded to loot "the village," and "the people took refuge in the Bishop's house and the church."

After two days, the fathers persuaded the rebels to allow these refugees to return to their homes. Permission was given, but they were quickly seized "to be their slaves." The church was then plundered of "all orna-ments and cloth," and the sacristans were killed, together with a Negro who was hiding there. "Many Ilocans died in various places on that day" —Díaz says that 80 were killed in Bantay alone, and another historian, Juan de la Concepción, makes the figure 800.

In those villages all was confusion, outcries, the discharge of arquebuses, and shouts; and among the ecclesiastics all was affliction and grief. . . . Some In-dian chiefs, for greater security, had brought to the Bishop's house the gold, silver, and other valuables which they possessed; and the amount thus brought together was so great that there was not space in the rooms above, and much property was even placed below the house. The Zambals cast their eyes on this wealth with eager desire.

The Bishop and other fathers, trying to protect this Indian property, along with the ecclesiastical property, approached the rebel leader, Macasiag, to guarantee its safety. Meantime his forces, "plundering and killing," had reached Badoc, in the southern part of what is now Ilocos Norte. Here they were turned back by a "troop of Ilocans and Cagayans," the Cagayan soldiers having been sent to intercept the intended march on along the north coast into that province. Contact was also made by one of the fathers with a naval force approaching from Manila. The Bishop then "summoned" the insurgents to meet him, so Díaz says, and "when most of them were assembled," he accused them of "the abominations, thefts, and murders which they had committed in the churches," and "publicly cursed and excommunicated all those who should thereafter kill, or meddle with things belonging to the churches or to his house."

Much of the "silver" of the church centers had been buried prior to the arrival of the rebels, together with "silver and gold of private persons." The rebels now began to locate and sieze this hidden wealth. One group at this time also "rushed to the house of the bishop, and pillaged whatever hampers and chests they found under the house." The Bishop, with the other fathers, was then removed to Santa Catalina, northwest of Bantay, so as to make possible complete looting of the establishment. On their way the party saw "many corpses" of the slain, and the burned-out village of Bantay. The rebel escort, on arriving at Santa Catalina, could not refrain from plundering and burning it. The party had to sleep out, begging some rice from the rebels for their food. For the remainder of the campaign these ecclesiastics were forced to travel with the withdrawing rebel army, and though some litters were reluctantly provided, much of their journey on the retreat southward was done on foot. Some "three hundred Ilocan Indians" had joined the rebels, so that in all they numbered at this time "about three thousand."

The vanguard of this force, after passing back through the defile at "Agayayos," approached Narvacan at night. Here they were suddenly attacked by "the Indians of that district, who, allied with the Tinguianes, did all the harm they could." This use of the name "Tinguian," evidently for people who came from the inland zone back of Narvacan, is the first specific application of that term found in contemporary records of the region.

In this encounter, "more than four hundred Zambals" were killed. So great was the daring of the attacking force that they even "seized and carried away one of the men who were escorting the fathers," and "cut off his head" in the manner of the headhunters. Moreover, they had "thickly planted the road" with "sharp stakes," in the traditional way of defense. The fathers, on arriving in Narvacan, found the headman hostile; they were detained at his house by "him and his blacks," and only under pressure from the Bishop were they permitted to go to the "convent." The reference here to "blacks" in the service of the headman, just after that to the Tinguians, suggests that these were Negritos. As noted at the beginning of the chapter, Negrito bands were still living back of this area of Ilocos up to modern times.

At Narvacan, the rebel leader Macasiag found a letter from "King" Malong telling him of the arrival of Spanish forces in Pangasinan, and ordering his return. The rebels left Narvacan largely unharmed, Díaz says, out of fear of the district people who were threatening them "from the woods." The local leader, Don Felipe Madamba, "a native of the village of Bringas," especially won their respect: "[He] was so loyal to His Majesty, and so valiant, that he dashed alone, on horseback, among the Zambals and Calanasas, cutting off their heads, without anyone being able to resist him. He was able to escape from these affrays, but his horse and he were covered with arrows."

The place name "Bringas" is not recognizable, but this vigorous head-cutting suggests that he was a non-Christian. The ethnic name "Calanasa" will be seen in the next chapter as used at the time to designate non-Christian Isnegs or Apayaos of the Ilocos Norte and Apayao mountains. If the rebel forces had been conjoined in the north by some of these mountaineers, it demonstrates still further the complicated ethnic character of the anti-Spanish movement.

The fathers insisted on staying at Narvacan, and said they would not go on "even if it cost them their lives." After some argument among the rebel leaders about whether they should be killed, they were left behind. The alcalde-mayor had meantime returned by boat to Vigan, and Spanish army and navy units converged on the area. The rebel force moved south, burning and sacking the convents and villages of Santa Maria, San Esteban, and Santiago in the southern part of this zone. From there they proceeded through Candon to Santa Cruz for the decisive battle in which they were defeated at the end of January 1661. The rebel leaders were variously hanged or shot at Vigan or in Pangasinan. One, Gumapos, who had taken the Bishop's staff from him, had his "sacrilegious hand" cut off and "fastened near the house of the Bishop." The people of this zone took no part in a further independence movement which followed immediately in northern Ilocos, and which will be described in the next chapter.

THE MIDDLE PERIOD

The decades from this time to the beginning of the eighteenth century yield almost no records of ethnohistorical interest regarding this zone other than those contained in the general section. The Monforte expedition of the 1660's, which attempted to pacify the interior peoples, evidently visited some of the settlements of southeast Abra. When the fathers who established the Kayan mission finally withdrew, the converts whom they took down to the coast settled among other places in Narvacan (B&R, xxxvii, 280). In 1676, the settlement of Masingal or Magsingal was founded north of Vigan, indicating growth of population along the coast toward Sinait. Two other communities were to be formed in this area in 1722, Lapog and Cabugao. With Santo Domingo and San Ildefonso, previously visitas, becoming independent pueblos in 1742 and 1769, respectively, the chain of towns along this northern coastal strip was completed. Correspondingly, south of Vigan, Santa was formed in 1713 and Santa Maria in 1760, these north and south of Narvacan, respectively.

The ecclesiastical survey of 1738, used in previous chapters, lists the Augustinian coastal centers in this part of Ilocos as "Narbacan," Santa Cruz (apparently Santa, north of Narvacan), Santa Catalina, Bantay, San Ildefonso, Masingal, Lapog, Cabugao, and Sinait. The survey speaks of Vigan as one of three "curacies" in Ilocos province, the others being "Bangued" in "the mountains of Labra," that is, Abra, and "San Diego," which is apparently Santiago in the Laoag valley of Ilocos Norte. Essentially the same list is given in a similar survey of 1751–54 (B&R, xxviii, 158, 164).

The Murillo map of 1744 shows some of the coastal settlements: Santa Maria, Narvacan, Vigan, "Calofitan" (perhaps Cabaritan, adjacent to Santo Domingo), Cabugao, "Salomague" (a settlement at the coastal point of that name), and Sinait. The Abra river is shown extending inland little more than the short coastal rivers, though three forks are indicated in the locale of the main Abra valley floor. A name "Solonsolong" is written here, though with no indication of its precise locality or significance. Bangued is not shown. As noted in the preceding chapter, the upper reaches of the Abra river are apparently confused with the Chico headwaters. Furthermore, the Abulug river to be seen in the northwest Cagayan section as draining much of Apayao subprovince is shown extended much further toward the Ilocos-Abra side than is really the case.

In the 1750's, as noted in previous chapters, the Augustinians launched determined efforts to Christianize the Cordillera peoples. The study of northern Ilocos will show that they struck into the mountains to the north as well as to the south. It therefore seems extraordinary that virtually no mention occurs of Bangued or any other part of the Abra valley area in the rather voluminous records of the time (Perez, 1904). The implication seems to be that it was not possible to advance the mission front here at that time. A record of Augustinian mission work in 1760, which was quoted earlier, does show in a list of "New Christians" and "Catechumens" a total number of "New Christians" and "Catechumens" in this zone of Ilocos a total of 17 "Igorots" in the "Territory of Narbacan" and 10 in that of "Magsingal"—but this shows anything but an active mission front (B&R, xlviii, 57). Mozo, writing in 1763, says of the Tinguian character that "although sufficiently obstinate," they are "more tractable" than the "Igolotes."

They are more gentle and industrious, and maintain a much more civilized condition, because they have much intercourse with the Christians in whose vicinity they live; and for the same reason they are more open to the teachings of the religious. And although so far as concerns the acceptance of baptism they have continued very obstinate, for many years refusing to allow a religious to live among them, yet it has always been a very satisfactory harvest which annually has been gathered and united with the Christians, as may be seen by the certificate of the father provincial which is presented above. . . . With such a drop of comfort as this, the ministers were consoled—who, not finding any hindrance in going from time to time to visit these savages, went in and out, carried away by their holy zeal. (B&R, xlviii, 68, 83, 86.)

Vigan appears in the records of this time as a particularly vigorous and busy capital town. In 1756, "on account of the multitude of Chinese mestizos" living there, its resident population was divided into two "guilds" (*gremios*): indigenous people (*naturales*) and mestizos (de los Reyes, ii, 167). The residence of the Bishopric had been shifted to here from Cagayan in the previous year. When in 1762 the British occupied Manila, it became the center of the "Silang rebellion."

The principal course of this outbreak was traced in the general chapter. Somewhat more detail can be added here, however, regarding its final episodes in which the murdered Silang's wife, the mestiza Gabriela, fled with her husband's followers into the Abra valley. We are told by de los Reyes that she was able to build up there an "army of cannibals and Ilocanos." This "brave spouse" then set out to "avenge the treason committed against her dear husband." Arriving back at the Abra mouth like a "horde of avid lions," her troops prepared to march against Vigan. But a miraculous mirage, attributed to the Virgin as protector of Bantay, appeared ahead of them, giving an impression that "thousands of soldiers" were in their path. At this, the "Igorrotes were intimidated," and "left for their rancherias." Gabriela's remaining forces were then scattered by the Spaniards. Gabriela, as told earlier, was hanged along with other rebels. But some of the "other chiefs" were able to escape by taking refuge in Abra (de los Reyes, ii, 171–90). This account seems to imply that active ties existed between the interior Tinguians and the coastal Ilocanos, doubtless rooted in trade, and it is also indicative of their hostility to the Spaniards.

A reference was made earlier to a list compiled by Pizarro in 1827 of towns in the Philippines which were "overgrown," and so particularly open to revolts by commoners. Vigan was included in this tabulation. By then it had a population of 17,320, which made it the second largest in Ilocos: the largest being Laoag, further north, with 25,242. In 1818 Ilocos was cut into two provinces, on Pizarro's recommendation to the Spanish government, and Vigan continued as the capital of Ilocos Sur (B&R, li, 199).

Nineteenth-century writers were led to comment on the secular and cosmopolitan character of the Vigan people. Three additional towns took separate form in its vicinity: Santa Catalina de Baba (1795), San Vicente (1795), and Caoayan (1825).

ABRA IN THE EARLY NINETEENTH CENTURY

In 1802, the Augustinian chronicler Martinez de Zuñiga wrote of the Tinguians that they were "unhappy Indios who live miserably in huts which are mere hovels," and sustain themselves with "roots of trees, hunting, and sweet potatoes and other roots which they cultivate." Some, he says, "have come down from the mountains, and have formed rancherias near the Christian pueblos." He estimates that such rancherias contained some 4,000 people. Though they developed such dependence on the Christian communities, and paid tribute, they "firmly resisted" being baptized; indeed, the fathers considered that the Tinguians still in the mountains "accepted baptism more readily" than those who were "subjects of the King."

The "Igorrotes," this observer continues, "are very different from the Tinguians." They "live in good houses; grow fields of maize, sweet potatoes and other roots; extract much gold from the mines and washings, and use it to obtain . . . cattle, carabao, and pigs." They were "heavy eaters," and physically robust. Some of the Igorrotes, too, had descended to the coast and formed rancherias near the Christian pueblos, like the Tinguians, "but with the difference that they have all become converted to the new religion." The Igorrotes, Martinez de Zuñiga says, also sell in the Christian pueblos the children they capture in their wars, and these are reared as servants (Maver's translation, II, 12–17).

Another interesting account of the Tinguians is given by a French surgeon, Paul P. de la Gironière, who settled in the Philippines in 1818. Somewhat more than a year after he had built his home near Manila, or around 1820, he visited the Ilocos coast with a Tagalog servant. A guide took them from Vigan to the Abra gorge, and helped make a bamboo "raft" in which the two of them worked their way upriver into the inner valley.

[We] perceived, in a small plain, the first Tinguian village. When we reached there we got out, and went toward the huts. . . . I allow it was acting rather foolishly to go and thus expose ourselves, in the midst of a colony of ferocious and cruel men. . . . Frightened at seeing us approach, they advanced towards us, armed with hatchets and spears. . . . I spoke to them by signs, and showed them some necklaces of glass beads. . . . They led us to their chief, who was an old man . . . and he took us under his special protection.

He describes the clothing, consisting for men of a "sash [clout], and a sort of turban," made out of "bark," and for women a "sash" and a "small nar-

row apron," together with sleeve-like bracelets of beads, and head ornaments of "pearls, coral beads, and pieces of gold." Each family had a day
"cabin" of "bamboos and straw" raised on supports about eight to ten feet
above the ground, and a smaller night one "perched upon great posts, or on
the top of a tree, about sixty or eighty feet above the ground." In the center
of each "village" there was a "large shed, in which are held the assemblies,
festivities, and public ceremonies."

From this first settlement, called "Palan" (clearly the present Palang
adjacent to San Quintin), they accompanied a group to the "small town of
Laganguilan y Madalag," evidently the later Lagangilang. The occasion
was to celebrate a victory in a fight with the "Guinanes," who were enemies
of the Tinguians deeper in the Cordillera, in which four heads had been
taken. The men had their "customary arms," a long spear, small hatchet,
and shield, while the women were decked out in cotton garments "of showy
colors." Large "vessels" full of *basi* (sugar-cane wine) were laid out, and
the heads were then chopped up and the brains mixed in with the *basi*.
The brew was then passed around as the group sang loudly "to the noise of
the tom-tom and gong," and then spirited dancing followed. With the
coming of night "each inhabitant retired with his family and some few
guests to his aerial abode."

The two travelers chose to stay in one of the ground cabins, keeping
alternate watches. La Gironière tells how he explored a "rather deep well"
under the cabin, with a removable cover over it, where he found a mum-
mified corpse. Next morning they went on to "Manabo," a still existing
center, southward up the Abra, accompanied by a Tinguian who knew a
little Tagalog. From him various customs were ascertained: "patriarchal"
leadership by the "oldest man"; marriage to "one legitimate wife, and many
mistresses"; "sacrifice" performed by "roasting hogs." At Manabo, their
meal consisted of "sweet potatoes, palms [*palmiers*] and dried venison."
Here the corpse of a man was seated "upon a stool" being slowly dried out
with fires burning in "enormous chafing dishes."

By then, la Gironière had "seen enough of the Tinguians." Taking
leave of the elders, he proceeded with his companion by a new route "inhabited by a few Igorrots"—apparently they traveled southwest into the
Tiagan area. At one point they encountered a small plain on which there
was a hamlet with "three cabins," indicative of the fact that the population
in the area was "far from being large." These people were smaller, darker
skinned, and more thickset than the Tinguians. The houses here had a
ground floor only, with walls of "thick piles, covered with a roof in the
form of a bee-hive."

As they proceeded, fields of sweet potatoes and sugar cane were seen,
"which of course must have been the only husbandry of those miserable

savages." For self-protection they had to fire at one point over the heads of a group of twenty men advancing against them from one "village." On another occasion, they met an Igorot leading a carabao on which were loaded jars of cooked meat, including a "human hand." After two nights camping out on the trail, they reached "rice-fields, cultivated after the Tagal manner," so that the servant cried out "Master, we are now in Christian ground." The implication here, as with the record to this point, is that they had not encountered wet rice cultivation in the country until then among either the Tinguians or the Igorots. Evidently they had reached the fringe of Ilocano colonization, possibly in the San Emilio area of Tiagan, though it took them another night and day to reach the coast. La Gironière speculates in a footnote that the Tinguians are "most likely" the descendants of shipwrecked Japanese sailors, while the Igorrotes could be descendants of the Chinese pirates led by Limahon (1854, pp. 107–37).

The fact that both Martinez de Zuñiga and la Gironière describe the Abra populations as still having at this time a root-crop economy rather than either a dry or a wet rice economy seems vital to the ethnohistorical record, and will be taken into account later.

From 1823, a new effort was launched to convert the "Tinguians and Igorrotes in the province of Abra." This was headed by Fray Bernardo Lago, working with two other fathers, and was called the "mission of Pidigan," a settlement just upstream from the Abra gorge, before Bangued is reached. By 1829, the fathers had "succeeded in reducing to village life and converting more than eight thousand" people from among these groups (B&R, LI, 49). Most of the modern towns date their founding from this period on, e.g., Pidigan, 1823; La Paz, 1832; San Gregorio, 1832; San Jose, 1840. On the heels of the mission workers, too, came the vanguard of Ilocano colonists.

By 1846, the pacification of Abra had advanced to a point where the region was made a province separate from Ilocos Sur, with a military administration initially, and with its capital at Bangued. Its inland boundary at the time was placed well east of the modern border, as it extended across the north-central part of the Cordillera to the borders of Cagayan Province, taking in most of what is now Kalinga subprovince of Mountain Province. Buzeta, in his encyclopedic survey of 1850, says that Abra was made a separate administration primarily because of the "difficult communication and transportation problems brought on by the terrain" which made its control of Vigan cumbersome. Moreover, the development of its potentially rich resources, such as lumber, wax, and minerals, and the full pacification of its various ethnic groups—"Tinguians, Apayaos, Guianaanes, Igorrotes, Besaos, and Ibilaos"—could be facilitated by putting it in charge of a "special authority" (Buzeta, I, 263–66).

LATER PERSPECTIVES

As in previous chapters, a description may be given of the principal settlements, from Buzeta's materials, including his population statistics for 1818 and 1847. The coastal districts will be covered first.

Southern Coastal Area. Narvacan was the largest settlement, with totals for the given years of 10,460 and 16,350, respectively. This was a major communication and market center. Population totals in 1847 for the other main settlements (with 1818 totals in parentheses) were: Santiago 2,842 (2,026); San Esteban 2,772 (1,768); Santa Maria 11,900 (7,455); Santa 10,810 (3,580).

Vigan Area. Vigan population totals for the given years were 17,059 and 16,680, a slight decrease. Buzeta describes it as having "more than a hundred houses of masonry construction," and "spacious plazas." Local industries included salt-making, fishing, and weaving. Populations in 1847 for the adjacent settlements (1818 totals in parentheses) were: Caoayan 5,757 (formed in 1825); Bantay 5,587 and San Ildefonso 4,365 (combined total 8,455); Santa Catalina 6,090 (10,730); Santo Domingo 8,467 (6,629).

Northern Coastal Area. Sinait was the largest settlement, with totals in the given years of 4,984 and 12,095. Others were Masingal 6,992 (1818, 6,850); Lapog 4,937 (3,929); Cabugao 9,627 (6,983).

By these figures, the coastal zones had a combined population in 1818 of 90,908, and in 1847 of 125,271, the latter paying 26,332 tributes, or one to every five persons.

Back of these coastal communities were settlements of the non-Christians. Of San Esteban in the south, Buzeta writes: "This pueblo has had a considerable population increment as a result of the incessant reduction of infidels who have settled in it and in neighboring areas" (II, 34).

Santa Maria had off to the southeast the "mission of Coveta," near which there were "three rancherias of infidels"; this in modern times has become the municipal district of Burgos. "Many rancherias" to the east also adhered to it, Buzeta says, before the province of Abra was created. The local people mined some gold in the Mt. Pingsal area. Narvacan had in the mountains between it and Abra "various rancherias of Tinguian infidels." Bantay is also noted as having "a rancheria of Tinguian infidels called Osboy" in the mountains to the east. Further north, Lapog had "a barrio of new Christians," and also a "rancheria of Tinguians" called Asilang, the latter still a settlement area today. Cabugao also had a new Christian barrio called Santa Barbara, and two settlements of infidels "which pay tribute."

Buzeta's information on Abra was inevitably fragmentary. In his 1818 census he shows the old center of Bangued as having 3,962 people, and Tayum 2,705 people. For 1847 he has statistics for six settlement areas as follows: Bangued 8,296; Bucay 6,728; Tayum 4,928; Pidigan 2,680; La Paz 2,604; San Gregorio 651. Buzeta notes that San Gregorio was a visita of La Paz, while Bucay had as visitas Manobo, southward up the Abra river, and Ba-ay, in eastern Abra. He says of Ba-ay that it was still an "embryonic" settlement, being "swelled every day by new conversions of infidels" from the adjacent mountains. Subject to the fact that this compiler sometimes has markedly different population totals in his place descriptions from those given in population tables for the period, his count for Abra shows approximately 30,000 people, paying 3,763½ tributes.

Buzeta includes in his survey of the ethnic groups of the area a general description of the "Tinguianes" or, as they were alternatively called, "Itanegs":

[Their] physical character, their virtues, a small amount of industry, some commerce, and their manufacturing establish a very marked difference between them and their mountain neighbors so that they are no longer considered savages. Therefore we must confine ourselves to the appellation of infidels, which is generally done, because they have not yet embraced the Catholic religion. Because of their frugal and isolated life they . . . submit to idleness rather than developing the characteristics [of civilized Filipinos].

The Tinguians, Buzeta believes, following speculations current in his time, are "descendants of the Chinese," and this origin has "imprinted in them their interest in agriculture and commerce." Their skin color is "so light" as to be only "slightly different" from the Chinese, and their dress, particularly the "type of turban which they wear," corresponds to that of the "fishermen of Fukien province," the nearest zone of China.

This turban is composed of a single piece of cloth the ends of which hang gracefully down the back. The men dress in long pants with a jacket buttoning down the front. The women's dress is similar to that of the *Igorrotes,* except that they wear white. Sometimes they wear fine clothes with sashes that are embroidered with red and white; and on their arms, from wrist to elbow, they wear glass beads of various colors which they obtain through trade. . . . In a similar manner they also adorn their legs from knee to ankle. . . . The men and women are clean, and observe a certain etiquette between themselves.

Of their settlement patterns and other customs, Buzeta says:

Gathered into tribes, they live happily in small, separate villages, and [are of] . . . peaceful character. . . . Banguet and Tayum, two villages which belong to these people, have long been converted to Christianity and the missionaries are working toward the conversion of the rest of the villages. These people also dedicate themselves to commerce, taking rice, wax, gold, and lumber to the [Ilocos] provinces and trading for merchandise which they need. They possess vast and rich rice fields which they plow and cultivate with intelligence; they also have numerous herds of carabao, horses, and oxen.

Back of the Tinguians, Buzeta continues, are the really "savage" peoples. Their immediate neighbors are the "Guinaanes," that is, members of the Kalinga ethnic group in what was then eastern Abra, of which Guina-ang was one of the nearest settlements.

[They inhabit] the eastern part of the same cordillera; but the Tinguianes have never had anything to do with the *Guinaanes,* because they are as cruel and fearless as the Tinguianes are human and peaceful. The former are continually waging war and whenever they come down from their mountain tops they lay waste the latter's possessions and residences. They are distinguished from the Tinguianes by marked physical and moral traits. (Buzeta, I, 54–55.)

Cavada, in his 1876 survey of Abra, shows the province as having a total population of 35,140 residents. The "Indios" comprised 24,183 Christians and 10,365 "infidels," and in addition there were 9 Spaniards, 6 Chinese, 10 "Filipinos" from other areas, and 567 mestizos (Cavada, p. 109). Malumbres, listing the "approximate number of infidels" in different jurisdictions of Luzon as of 1898, shows for Abra a total of 27,498 (1919, II, 403). Perez, in his "ethnographic dictionary," presents the usual Spanish classification of the Abra people in terms of three groupings. First are the "infidel" Tinguians, occupying 37 rancherias, in which the "sitios" have been organized into "pueblos." Second are the "semi-savages," or those who are "moved back to the mountains where they resist tribute payments." Third are the "savages," comprising the "Guinaanes," the "sanguinary infidels" of the eastern sections of Abra, that is, the Kalingas of the Saltan river and adjacent areas now in Kalinga subprovince (1904, p. 348–50).

A German scientist, Hans Meyer, writing in 1883,* has recorded some interesting glimpses of travel in the Abra area. He notes that peaceful Tinguian settlers had been pushing southward "as a wedge" between the Igorots in the east and the Ilocanos in the west, so that one of their southernmost rancherias was at Bila in the vicinity of Candon, seen in the last chapter. When visiting Bila, he was able to confirm the fact, "doubted" by Blumentritt, that there were some Negritos still surviving in this zone:

Chance would have it that a family of five men and two wives of this dying race had come to Bila in order to purchase tobacco and provisions. They are wretched creatures, completely of the type of Negritos from Mariveles [northwest of Manila], but weaker and more timorous. They dwell here in the foothills of the Cordillera Tovalina, from which woods they venture forth solely when hunger compels them. Down to the Ilocano they never come. . . . Women and men wear only aprons out of trade cotton stuff; two younger men were armed with bow and arrows. The number of all the scattered groups does not exceed a hundred by their own estimate. They speak among themselves an Ilocano dialect like their neighbors, the Tinguian, but with peculiar stress and mixture of idioms [presumably their own] which were strange to me.

Meyer then proceeded into Abra, where he gives a description of Bangued: "Bangued up to now has pleased me the most of all the provincial capitals. To be sure, it is in total character only a large village. . . . [The]

* *Globus,* XLIII, 11, 203–5; translation supplied by the Philippine Studies Program, University of Chicago.

little Spanish colony did every thing it could to make the stay comfortable." After busy "festivities and invitations," in which "the *copa* and *copita* drinking" became "distressing," he proceeded by the military "road" eastward into the inner zone of the Cordillera. His journey was undertaken in spite of "suspicious headshaking and much shoulder shrugging" by the local Europeans:

[The] mountain groups were visited, it is true, by an expedition of Spanish troops in 1879 and were presumably pacified. They have, however, actually so far remained unsubjugated, so much so that they have paid no tribute for ten years, have not one single military or guard post in their district [beyond Balbalasang], and have remained true to their old bloody customs of headhunting and feuding. Any subjugation extends only to the fact that they fight no more with the Spaniards, but confine themselves to feuds among themselves. . . . [Up] to Balbalasang [through Tinguian country] one scarcely needs a military escort, but from there on [one] . . . is indispensable.

This traveler reports a telegraph wire strung "from tree to tree" by way of intermediate civil guard posts to Balbalasang. He also noted the "many bleached horse and carabao bones" giving testimony of the difficulties of travel in the dry summer months. The rancheria of Balbalasang, near the military post in the Saltan river headwaters, consisted of two barrios. Their inhabitants "are nominally Tinguian in body-build, speech, and clothing," but their customs clearly had elements from the Cagayan-side ethnic traditions of the Kalingas, and they traded into Cagayan as well as Abra. Meyer, with a military escort, made a two-day journey to the Kalinga rancheria of "Guinaan," traditional enemies of the Tinguian.

MODERN CENSUS DATA

A review of the modern census data provides further demographic perspective; the statistics here will be concerned with the central and northern sections of Ilocos Sur Province and with Abra Province. As of 1903 the total population in these zones of Ilocos Sur was 127,191, and by 1948 it had risen to 179,694. Correspondingly, Abra had 51,860 people in 1903 and 86,600 by 1948.* The coastal flats are shown to be almost solidly Ilocano. Of the

* The following were the populations of the municipal units of northern Ilocos Sur in 1948:

Lowland

Santiago 6,610	Santa 8,917	Santa Catalina. 7,125	Masingal 11,697
San Esteban .. 3,617	Caoayan 9,064	San Vicente... 6,151	Lapog 9,777
Santa Maria ..13,637	Vigan 21,067	San Ildefonso . 2,034	Cabugao 14,823
Narvacan 22,237	Bantay 12,714	S'to Domingo 11,082	Sinait 12,015

Mountain

Burgos 4,783   Nagbuquel ... 2,345

For Abra, see bottom of p. 142.

Abra population, too, approximately 76.7 per cent of the 1948 total, or 66,422 persons, returned Iloko as their mother tongue. Those still identifying themselves as Tinguians have therefore become a minority group in their home area.

The 1903 census of Ilocos Sur, as noted in the previous chapter, showed it as having 13,576 "Igorots," of whom 2 were "civilized" and the rest "wild." The bulk of these people were in the southern mountain districts discussed in that chapter, but some were the Tinguians scattered along the mountain fringes from Santiago northward to Sinait. In 1903, Ilocos Sur also had 35 "wild" Negritos. The corresponding census figures for Abra show 14,019 "Igorots" (predominantly the counted Tinguians), of whom 52 were "civilized," and also 70 "wild" Negritos.

By the time of the 1939 census, the mountain districts back of Narvacan and other southern coastal communities contained 1,413 persons classed as "Igorot" speakers, but only a handful of "Tinggian" speakers. Apparently the old Tinguian settlements along this part of the coast had become fully Ilocanized. North of Vigan, the mountain peoples were classed by the census takers variously as "Igorot" or "Tinggian." The only groups of significant size were Masingal, 218 Igorot; Lapog, 126 Tinggian; and Cabugao, 202 Igorot and 34 Tinggian.

The 1948 figures identifying people by their mother tongues show for Ilocos Sur as a whole 4,208 speakers of "Igorot," but these would nearly all have been in the southern Ilocos districts. Only 476 acknowledged "Tinggian" to be their ancestral speech. There were also 8 Negritos left, of whom 5 were male and 3 female. In Abra, 22,348 returned Tinggian as their mother tongue, while other mountain groups with significant numbers comprised 155 Kalinga and 35 with Igorot dialects for the mother tongue. Only one Negrito, a female, was left.

Compared with the coastal zones, Abra in 1948 was still sparsely inhabited. The principal town districts were by then occupied by Ilocano majorities. Those returning themselves as Tinguian by mother tongue had their two largest concentrations in southern Abra: the Luba district with

---

The population of Abra in 1948 by municipal units was as follows:

Valley

San Quintin ..	1,518	La Paz	5,444	Bucay	6,215	Sallapadan ...	2,313
Langiden	1,297	Dolores	4,065	Peñarrubia ...	2,262	Pilar	5,944
Pidigan	3,473	San Juan	4,603	Manabo	3,658	Luba	2,276
Bangued	14,793	Langangilang .	5,450	Villaviciosa ..	2,474	Tubo	1,214
Tayum	6,281						

Mountain

Danglas	1,738	Anayan	100	Licuan	703	Bucloc	827
Langayan	2,222	Naglibacan ..	102	Matarangan ..	454	Daguioman ..	666
Caganayan ...	270	Tineg	587	Bangilo	536	Boliney	830
Alaoa	253	Lacub	771	Malibcong ...	686	Danac	749
Lanec	113	Buneg	173	Ba-ay	772	Tiempo	767

1,966, and the Sallapadan district with 1,716. Other principal groups of Tinguian were recorded as follows: Langangilang 1,616; Langayan 1,264; Peñarrubia 1,258, Villaviciosa 1,247; Tubo 1,211; and Danglas 1,078. Bangued, the capital, had only 702 in its total of 14,792 people. That is, even the valley Tinguian group appeared content to remain somewhat marginal in residence, and mostly in areas suited to wet rice terracing.

On the higher slopes of the valley, the scattered mountain jurisdictions showed very sparse populations except as Ilocano settlers have found workable areas for colonization. The Tinguian groups here are still mostly of the "mountain" dry cultivating type, living in hamlets. Along the northern mountains the districts have tended to lose population between the 1939 and 1948 censuses, some quite drastically: e.g., Buneg dropped by 191 to 173, Lanec by 158 to 113, Alaoa by 80 to 253. In the mountain districts to the east and south, where wet rice terracing is practiced to a greater extent, and settlements tend to be somewhat larger, the opposite is true; that is, they have tended to gain rather than lose population in the period. Of the ethnic minorities, the 155 Kalingas all live in Boliney district adjoining Kalinga subprovince, while the 31 "Igorots" are in the extreme southern district of Tiempo adjacent to Lepanto. Progress in the conversion of Abra non-Christians is indicated by the fact that the category "pagans or not belonging to any religious group" showed in 1948 only 4,496 persons.

REVIEW

The modern Ilocano identity in ethnic and linguistic terms seems to derive particularly from this central Ilocos zone through the consolidating influence of the capital, Vigan. Furthermore, Cole's hypothesis that the Tinguian people and customs derive from coastal groups who moved back into Abra in comparatively late times appears thoroughly plausible. Some of them, at least, were refugees of the Spanish period.

As with the Ibaloi in Benguet, the early nineteenth century was marked by a major reformulation in the earlier way of life. Adoption of irrigated terracing appears to date from this period. Tinguians also moved out to the coast, becoming Ilocanized in the process. A major question is whether the "wild" or "mountain" Tinguian are refugees in turn from the valley groups, continuing older dry cropping traditions, or trace back in part at least to an older stratum of mountain settlers. This problem, raised in the previous chapter, cannot be seen fully until additional zones east of the Cordillera ridge (Kalinga and Apayao) are examined, so that it will be discussed in the final chapter. The Negritos, here as in other areas, were an evidently old and minor population element, keeping to the more forested foothill country, and doomed to extinction in modern times.

VI. The Northern Ilocos Area

PLACE AND PEOPLE

This zone corresponds essentially to the modern province of Ilocos Norte, centered on its capital, Laoag. At Cape Bojeador, the northward stretching coast turns eastward to Pasaleng Bay where the provincial boundary adjoins a narrow strip or panhandle of Cagayan Province. Inland, Ilocos Norte adjoins the Apayao subprovince of Mountain Province. The Cordillera here is lower in elevation, and is often called the Caraballo Norte range. Its western spurs and foothills spread over the whole northern third of Ilocos Norte.

Most of the area is drained by the extensive Laoag river system. Its headwaters gather in five principal rivers which come together in the inland amphitheater of the Laoag valley, from which the main river runs some 12 miles to the sea. Lesser rivers are the Quiaoit and Badoc to the south, and the Bacarra and Bulu rivers to the north, the latter debouching into Bangui Bay. The coastal and valley flats have many small lakes and swamps.

The lowland districts are settled almost exclusively by Ilocanos. Some Spanish writers judged that the northern Ilocano show more Negritoid characteristics than their fellows to the south, and also that they have preserved a more "pure" Iloko speech. The mountain zones, except as land-hungry colonists from this group have recently moved in, are very sparsely utilized by non-Christian dry cultivators. No ethnographic or linguistic studies are available dealing with these mountain groups. Those on the southern and central heights are classed in the historical records and censuses as Tinguian, and appear to be northern elements of the mountain Tinguian noted in the preceding chapter. In the extreme east and in the north they are classed as Apayao, and are western extensions of the Isneg. Because this latter group is centered in Apayao subprovince, it can best be characterized in the chapter on the northwest Cagayan area (see Chapter VII). The historical records distinguish a separate small ethnic group called the Adan or Adang living in the upper Bulu river area inland from Bangui. This group no longer has a separate entity, but early ethnologists judged them to have strong Negritoid affiliations. Negrito bands at one time ranged some of the forested and swampy areas, but by the time of the 1948 census only one Negrito was recorded in all of Ilocos Norte.

The lowland communities grow their wet rice crop Ilocano-style in the rainy summer season. As Christie shows (1914), "irrigation societies" in which a group of household heads unite under a "chief" to distribute land and water represent a special development in northern Ilocos. Members must be present around the July period each year to work on the water-control system, and indigenous feasts and animal sacrifices were part of the annual cycle. Tobacco is the principal dry season crop, second cropping of wet rice being minor. Dry rice is grown in small quantity in the hilly central parts of Ilocos Norte (the Vintar and Dingras districts), but otherwise is negligible. Maize, sugar cane, vegetables, fruits, and cultivated and wild roots are important in the diet. The wild root *tugue* is marketed extensively, and helps to carry over the poorer households to the rice harvest. In the mountain districts, sweet potatoes and other root crops seem to have been the historic staples (Philippine agricultural censuses, and other sources).

Old trails cross the mountains from Ilocos Norte into Abra and Apayao. A major trade trail, now a road, also runs along the north coast between Ilocos and the Cagayan region. It has carried not only commerce but also numerous migrating Ilocanos to the north Luzon coast and the Cagayan valley. The main travel route, however, along this rugged and often stormy northern coastline has been by sea, with sheltering points in the bays and river mouths.

EARLY PERSPECTIVES

The record begins with the movement northward, in June 1572, of Salcedo's exploring party from the Vigan area to the landing at the mouth of the Laoag. As told by de los Reyes, the purpose was to continue on around northwestern Luzon. But both the Spaniards and the indigenous members of the party showed "little disposition to proceed," because of the "roughness of the seas at that time of the year." Instead, Salcedo moved upriver toward the pueblo of Laoag.

The inhabitants, rejecting the peaceful overtures of the Spaniards, received them with a "cloud of spears." A volley of arquebus shots opened the way for a party of thirty soldiers to land, and after further resistance with their arrows the people fell back. De los Reyes says that the Laoag area had, as today, "many people and settlements."

Salcedo postponed attempts to establish peace and returned down river in the face of stormy weather. Eight days were spent sheltering in the small

NORTHERN ILOCOS AREA

harbor of Currimao, south of the Laoag river mouth. Here Salcedo with twelve soldiers disembarked to explore a pueblo which was "three kilometers" from the sea, probably the later Paoay. They were met by a party of the local people who attacked them, but again the arquebuses drove them off to "seek refuge in the thickets." After Salcedo returned to the boats, a large party of people appeared on the shore, challenging the Spaniards.

A chief stood apart from the others brandishing a lance, and issued a challenge for a "personal duel." Salcedo, his *amor proprio* at stake, went ashore alone armed with his sword, forbidding others in his company to intervene. The chief drew him back to a hill where an "ambush was laid," and the youthful leader found himself set upon by some three hundred attackers. The Spaniards by this time had started to his rescue, and with their guns they were able to disperse the force. Salcedo next moved inland to explore the locality of the "pueblo of Barol," which was "two leagues" from Currimao. This could have been either the later Batac, to the east, or else Badoc southward along the coast. Here, again, the people were at first hostile, and the "women and children went into hiding." The Spaniards and the indigenous members of the party sacked the houses, obtaining plentiful foodstuffs. They were about to start back when a leader appeared and "asked that peace be made and the past forgotten." Salcedo received him in friendly fashion, so presents were exchanged and the headmen in the community subsequently made a "treaty of alliance." The people had explained to them the political and religious objectives of the Spaniards. Pleased with the arrangement, they brought to Salcedo on another day "120 onzas of gold."

Salcedo stationed a sergeant, Francisco de Saavedra, with a company of soldiers in the Laoag area. He also directed his lieutenant, Don Antonio Hurtado, to return to Vigan to establish a fort, as seen in the previous chapter. Salcedo, staying for some days, "reduced many pueblos" in the area. He then followed on down to Vigan, where he worked out his plan to circle Luzon island by proceeding north again around Cape Bojeador to Cagayan (de los Reyes, II, 15–20).

The establishment of encomiendas in this zone, following the disturbed period of initial contacts, provides here as in districts further south the first systematic information on places and population elements. A distinctive feature in the Laoag area was that the early Spanish parties were able to strike inland by way of its river system, so that, in addition to the usual chain of coastal encomienda centers, one was established some 14 miles from the sea at the present Dingras.

Loarco's survey of 1582 placed as the first settled locality northward of Sinait the "Valley of Vavo," with "about 1,000 Indians" and an encomienda. Described as "two leagues beyond Sinay," this was clearly the Badoc area. Next came the "Province of Cacaguayan," with a population of "about

4,000," and an encomienda with tribute assigned half "to the King" and half to a private encomendero. This was evidently the Paoay-Batac area. "Three leagues" further on was the "Province of Ylagua," this being one of the alternative early names for Laoag. It had a population of "about 5,000," described as "not all peaceful." No mention is made of an encomienda here, but inland a distance of three leagues was the "Valley of Dynglas," the later Dingras, with "about 2,000 Indians" and an encomienda. Finally, the "Valley of Vicagua," further "along the coast," had "2,000 Indians" and two encomiendas: the Bacarra-Vintar area. Loarca adds here: "This valley is twenty leagues from the Cagayan river. There are to be found some rivers and settlements, but the inhabitants are not pacified or even known." For what these early figures are worth, they show a total known population estimate for the region of about 14,000.

The 1591 "Account of Encomiendas" fills out this sketchy information somewhat. The listed holdings from south to north, all spoken of as having "peace" and "justice," are as follows:

Barao (Vavo, Badoc): private holding; 700 tributes from 2,800 people; "no instruction," i.e., ecclesiastical supervision.

Cacabayan (Paoay-Batac): private holding; 2,100 tributes from 8,400 people; "monastery," with 3 "ministers."

Bonsan: visited from "Ylagua" (Laoag), and probably at or near the later San Nicolas; 350 tributes from 1,400 people.

Ylagua (Laoag): Royal holding; 1,500 tributes from 6,000 people; mission center with 3 "ministers."

Dinglas (Dingras): shared between the King and a private encomendero; 600 tributes from 2,400 people; "no instruction."

Bacarra: private holding, 1,000 tributes from 4,000 people; 2 "ministers."

Balleçillo: locality uncertain, but possibly at Bangui in the north; 150 tributes from 600 people; "no instruction."

In all, therefore, this encomienda survey gives a population total of 25,600, based on the collection of 6,400 tributes.

To round out this first report, the 1612 "Status of Missions" survey may be added, showing four "convent" centers as follows:

Batac: the "Cacabayan" of the previous survey, served with its visitas by 3 ministers; 1,500 tributes, and 4,500 Indians "in confession."

Dinglas (Dingras): served with its visitas by 3 ministers; 1,500 tributes, and 4,500 "in confession."

Ylavan (Laoag): served with its visitas by 3 ministers; 1,400 tributes, and 4,200 "in confession."

Bacarra: served with its visitas by 2 ministers; 800 tributes, and 2,400 "in confession."

The sum of those "in confession" was therefore 15,600, and the total population when calculated at the conventional four-to-one ratio in relation to the 5,200 tributes, was 20,800.

With due caution, some comments may be ventured on the basis of these early demographic materials. First, a great contrast is obvious in this zone between the south and the north: the former well settled and under strong Spanish influence, but the latter sparsely penetrated and little known. In the mountainous northern zone, the one point of Spanish penetration by the early seventeenth century was Bangui, in the bay of that name. This settlement and port evidently developed as one of the landing points for the increasingly busy coastal traffic of the time. Vessels from the Laoag-Bacarra could put in here after rounding Cape Bojeador on their way to Cagayan as an alternative to going on along this often stormy coast to Pata in Cagayan. Or returning vessels from Cagayan could wait out rough seas here before attempting to pass around that cape.

Cavada (1876) lists 1625 as the founding date of Bangui. But this appears to mark its establishment as a separate civil and ecclesiastical center. De los Reyes records it as an encomienda, probably the one called "Balleçillo" in the survey above, and notes that in 1607 the encomendero, Captain Rivero, asked that a mission be placed there. This historian adds, though without identifying any contemporary record to support the statement, that "the people of this district were barbarous and obstinate, and were unwilling to receive baptism" (de los Reyes, ii, 73, 80).

Apart from Bangui, the only early record of this northern Ilocos area is Loarca's 1582 statement that it had "some rivers and settlements," the inhabitants of which were "not pacified or even known." The Cagayan records will show, however, that the trade trail mentioned earlier as passing through the area variously along or near the coast carried a busy foot traffic, and that in 1619 the Dominicans established a mission with a chapel-fort at Cabicungan on the Cagayan side of the border with Ilocos. It will be seen shortly that a mission father was to make the first recorded penetration of the interior mountains in this region in 1668, that is, nearly a century after the initial Spanish explorations. The first northern settlements other than Bangui also date from this time. For comparative numerical reference, it can be noted that this northern zone had as of 1845 a total population reckoned at 13,209, while the 1903 census yielded a figure of 17,142.

By contrast, the more benign southern coast and the great inland amphitheater of the Laoag river system were, by the standards of the time, heavily settled and quickly became known. The relatively narrow coastal strip of the Badoc and Paoay-Batac districts, about 15 miles in extent, had according to the statistics above some 6,000 and 11,000 people. Even with the enormous population growth and pressure among Ilocanos in later times, and the building up of Badoc, Paoay, and Batac as urban centers, this area held by 1845 a total of only 42,214 people and by 1903 only 44,831 people. The Laoag river areas correspondingly had in the period of the surveys somewhere between 9,000 and 12,000. In later times they were to become much more intensively utilized, so that with the rise of Laoag and other urban centers the totals of 1845 and 1903 became 77,616 and 90,761, respectively. The Bacarra river area had between 3,000 and 4,500, whereas it had 24,520 in 1845 and 24,051 in 1903. On the basis of the three sets of early figures, it seems a fair assumption that at the time the Spaniards arrived the peoples living on the coastal and river flats were wet rice cultivators.

CONTINUING RECORDS TO 1660

The Ilocos Norte area is all too rarely distinguished by special reference in the historical records, though of course much of the material on Ilocos given in the general chapter applies to it. As the geographically remotest section of the Ilocos coast, it was less drawn into commerce and other affairs centered on Manila. The area became something of a self-contained unit, focused upon Laoag, which in turn was overshadowed as a town center by Vigan. No such challenge existed in its mountain hinterlands for the early Spaniards as existed for them in the gold-rich southern areas of the Cordillera, with their more densely settled "infidel" populations representing large potential sources of tributes and conversions. Evidently the accessible populations were readily won to Christianity and accepted Spanish civil control, which in this remoter area may have been minimally demanding.

In 1574, as quoted in the general chapter, an official, who was listing the gold sources of Ilocos for the King, includes as one of the mining areas the neighborhood of "Dinglas." Though this northern zone has no large gold deposits comparable with those further south, alluvial gold does occur in its streams. In the mid-nineteenth century, Buzeta reported some washing of this metal in the mountains.

Soon after Salcedo's conquest of the coastal settlements, he had to send a punitive expedition to "Bacal," referred to above as either Badoc or Batac. In 1589, too, resistance developed at "Dinglas" and "Cacabayan" as a result of "illegal exactions and other abuses by the encomenderos." Six of the latter visiting from Fernandina (Vigan) to collect tributes were killed (de los Reyes, 11, 59; Philippine Census, 1918, 1,157). De los Reyes quotes the earlier chronicler San Agustin to the effect that "no little difficulty" attended the ecclesiastical enterprise here because of the abuses practiced by the encomenderos in Dinglas and elsewhere in Ilocos.

Besides, the Igorrotes of Dinglas were opposed to living in villages, and fled to the mountains, because the Spaniards were—so they said, terrible people, who ate fire [a cigar], whose feet were without toes [covered with shoes], and whose horses ate iron [a bit]. Moreover—they added—they had some balls [bullets] which searched out the person whom the Spaniards wanted to die.

This glimpse suggests that the "Igorrotes" of the region were really refugees from the Spanish concentration policy of the time rather than mountain peoples as such. The account adds that "these infidels . . . have a taste for dog meat, which they set out like exquisite dishes in their banquets" (de los Reyes, 11, 60). The Isneg people in Apayao still kill dogs in ceremonial feasts.

Medina (1630) tells how the people of "Ilaoag" (Laoag), taught by a mission father, were beginning to use tile instead of wood in house construction. Medina also notes that its church center had become a "priorate," and that the settlement "has more than 1,500 Indians," indicating its emerging role as the principal administrative and mission center of the north (B&R, XXIII, 279). By that time "Dinglao" (Dingras) had a "resident religious" and was an "excellent" center. Medina also classes Batac as "excellent," indicating that church work was flourishing in this northern region. Most seventeenth-century records, however, consist merely of recitals of names and dates relating to Augustinian fathers who served in the various centers.

REBELLION: 1660–61

Nearly a century after the initial Spanish penetration, the region became newsworthy in the wake of the Malong "rebellion" in Pangasinan. The attempt of a large force of Pangasinan and Zambal troops to move through Ilocos into Cagayan was seen to have been stopped in the Badoc region, after which it moved south again, to be defeated by loyal forces. As the record puts it: "The Zambals came, plundering and killing, as far as the slope of Baduc, but they could not pass from that place to the province of Cagayan, on account of the resistance made by Alferez Lorenzo Arqueros with a troop of Ilocans and Cagayans."

This quotation indicates that Argueros, the Spanish commander of military operations in Ilocos, had been able to rally local Ilocanos from northern areas to resist the rebel incursion. The Cagayan section of the force could have been brought in via land or sea. This northern area, therefore, escaped the destruction experienced by the rest of Ilocos.

Having suppressed the resistance in Pangasinan and punished the rebel leaders, the Spanish emergency forces were preparing to leave Ilocos when news reached them of a related outbreak in this northern zone. This collateral "revolt" is the more noteworthy in view of the long-standing pacification and seeming loyalty of the northern Ilocos population. As told by Díaz, it was set in motion by some of the "multitude of letters and documents which the usurping King Malong wrote" to leaders throughout the region advocating resistance to Spanish authority. Such communications were sent "more especially" to two influential chiefs in the north, Don Pedro Almazan, a "native of the village of San Nicolas," which was a visita of Laoag, and Don Juan Magsanop, "a native of Bangi" (that is, Bangui), north of Bacarra of which it was a visita.

[Almazan] was a very rich chief . . . and so bitterly hostile to the Spaniards that he kept in his house as many pairs of fetters as there were fathers and Spaniards in the entire province, in order to fasten these on them when he should have opportunity. . . . [He] formed an alliance with Don Juan Magsanop . . . and with Don Gaspar Cristobal, headman of Ilauag [Laoag], and a native of that village. The former, in order to make sure of Don Gaspar Cristobal, asked him for his daughter, to marry her to his own eldest son; and these three Indians, as being so influential, continually stirred up others to join their conspiracy."

The picture here is of major discontent, generated at the top level of local leadership. It also shows an old custom of such aristocratic families using marriage to cement alliances.

These lowland chiefs reinforced their strength by calling in the "Calanasa tribe" to help them. "[These] were heathen barbarians who lived in the clefts of the mountains and in other rocky places, and their only occupation was the killing of men and animals." The killing of men here refers to headtaking, as was to be shown in the account of their participation in subsequent events. The killing of animals is evidently a reference to animal sacrifices in the widely practiced manner of the time. The name "Calanasa" applies here and in later references to western Isneg groups on the Ilocos side of the Cordillera and in the Bayag district of Apayao immediately east of the main Cordillera ridge. The trading relations already spoken of as existing between them and the lowland communities evidently provided a bond which made such a war alliance possible.

Feeling safe with such aid as this, the leaders of the conspiracy undertook to make Don Pedro Almazan king of the province of Ilocos, and they swore allegiance to his son as prince; the latter celebrated his wedding with the daughter of Don Gaspar Cristobal, as they had agreed. In order that the function might be celebrated with all solemnity and not lack what was requisite, they plundered the church in the village of Ilauag, and with the crown which they took from the head of the Queen of Angels they crowned Don Pedro Almazan as king and the married pair as princes. All these proceedings were carried on so secretly that they could never be traced.

According to the Díaz account, these events had already taken place by the time the Pangasinan and Zambal forces moved northward into Ilocos. Another letter then arrived from Malong notifying the leaders that he had "conquered the Spaniards" in Pangasinan. In early 1661, on almost the same day the invaders were being defeated in the course of their southward retreat, Don Gaspar Cristobal brought the northern movement into the open. Magsanop had written to Cristobal from Bacarra, asking his opinion on what action should be taken:

[His reply] was to take a fagot of reeds in his hand, and himself set fire to the church in Ilauag; and he ordered the bearer of the letter to carry back the reply. When this was known to Magsanop, he made himself known, with banners displayed, at Bacarra . . . and sent word to the Calanasas to come down with all speed to his aid.

Two communities across the border in Cagayan were enlisted in the "rebel league," Pata and Cabicungan. The story of their part in the revolt will be told in the appropriate Cagayan context. These communities had close relations with the Bacarra-Bangui people as being the westernmost Cagayan groups on the busy coastal trade trail. In the course of "rebel" operations there, the resident Dominican father was killed and his head "cut off."

The rejoicing of the Augustinian fathers who were gathered in Vigan at the end of the Pangasinan invasion turned to "sadness and perplexity" at the news from the north. Fray José Arias, prior of the village of Bacarra, immediately returned to that center. Some adherents welcomed him back, but they "fled" when news came of the approach of some "Calanasas." After "carrying the friar with them" for some distance, they left him in the house of a "native helper."

The streets were full of rebels and Calanasas, who with loud shouts and yells acclaimed Don Pedro Almazan as king, and threatened all Spaniards with death. [Friendly Indians engineered his escape to Laoag, but en route a rebel band intercepted the part and, killing the father, dispatched his head to Magsanop.] . . . Magsanop and the other tyrants celebrated this victory, all drinking from the skull of the venerable father, which served in their barbarous proceedings as a previous vase. . . . After several days his head was ransomed, and interred with his body.

It is not made clear in this account whether the Christian Magsanop was participating in this ritual use of the skull as an act to please Calanasa leaders for whom it represented the appropriate custom, or whether this was a deliberate revival on his part of the old usages of the Bacarra-Bangui peoples prior to their conversion. As with many parallel reversionary movements elsewhere in the Philippines and in other parts of the world, it might well have been the latter.

The Spanish commanders quickly organized their forces to deal with this new threat. The army of General Francisco de Esteybar, which had been completing the subjection of Pangasinan, marched north to Bacarra. Meantime Arqueros, the local Spanish commander, had arrived there from his victorious field of battle further down the Ilocos coast with a "detachment of more than a thousand men, Ilocans and Cagayans." "[The] rebels and the Calanasas, not daring to face these, retreated with all speed to the woods, but Lorenzo Arqueros did not fail to search for them, in whatever places they had concealed themselves."

Magsanop, when seized, killed himself with a dagger. "King" Almazan is said in one account to have "died raging" while fleeing on a horse, but in another to have been hanged at Vigan. By the time Esteybar arrived with his army, he had "nothing to do, except to order that a fort be built in Bacarra" and garrisoned with soldiers, so as to "secure the province from other disturbances." Díaz, reviewing these events of 1660–61, says that such rebel outbreaks, aimed at gaining "liberty," could not have achieved such a result even if successful; on the contrary, he asserts, it would have been "their entire perdition." He bases this view on an account by an old northern Ilocos chief of the time, Don Pedro Anas, of the "confusion," "lawlessness," and "tyrannical" acts of the leaders (B&R, xxxviii, 197, 205–12). The arguments that Díaz uses to support this view have already been quoted in the general chapter.

THE MOUNTAIN POPULATIONS

In 1668, according to the continuing record of this Augustinian historian, conversion was begun of mountain groups living in the area between Bacarra, with its "last visita" at Bangui, and the Cagayan border, where the Dominican sphere commenced. The account speaks of them as "Payaos," or "Apayaos" in the later form of the name. It is generally thought that the term comes from the name given by the Isneg ethnic group to the principal river draining their territory, the Apayao; this later became likewise the name of the subprovince east of Ilocos Norte.

[They] are a barbarous and spirited nation, and for that reason are feared by the Indians round about. . . . Living in the darkness of their wild paganism, they are exempt from the yoke of subjection—the only means by which one is able to introduce the evangelical preaching among barbarous nations.

The account gives a glimpse of their customs, and at the same time indicates the persistence of "pagan" usages among the Christianized groups:

[They] practiced various superstitions, auguries, and a servile worship to the souls of their first progenitors—whom they reverenced not as gods, but like the Indigetes [patron deities of the country] of the Romans, to whom the people offered sacrifices to keep them propitious. This method of worshipping deceased ancestors is very common in these Filipinas, and very difficult to stamp out in those who are to all appearances faithful Christians. For in this regard fear has a great influence over them; and most of them believe that it is not opposed to the Christian faith to place on one and the same altar the ark of the testament and the idol Dagon.

Conversion of these mountain peoples "belonging to the mission of the convent of Bacarra" was initiated by Fray Benito de Mena Salazar, described by de los Reyes as "a *natural* of Vigan" (1890, ii, 127). First, Díaz says, he established a "military base" (*plaza de armas*) at Bangui for "that spiritual conquest." Then gradually through repeated visits into the interior by way of the Bangui river system he was "accepted and heard." In 1668, after much difficulty because of the "steepness of the mountains" and the resistance of the "minister of Satan," the initial baptisms were achieved. Many "miracles and prodigies" occurred to incline the people to Christianity, including the "resurrection" of a dead child who died again after baptism, and the healing of a leper. A chief also sought "salvation" before his death. The new converts were "especially clever in learning the prayers and Christian doctrine, a night or a day often sufficing."

Once the impetus to be baptized took hold, hundreds of conversions were made. Fray Benito was able to "found three villages," Aclan, Vera, and Bangbanglo. These became part of the Bangui ministry, and were administered from the Aclan church. Because of their usefulness as "frontiers opposed to the Calanasas," they were exempted from tribute: the name "Calanasa" has been seen above as another label for interior mountain groups (B&R, xxxviii, 239–42). Bangbanglo is the later town of Nagpartian, renamed in the twentieth century Burgos, near the coast somewhat east of Cape Bojeador. Aclan and Vera do not appear as settlements on later maps or in gazeteers. Díaz, however, at one point in his record, counts Vera and Bangbanglo as one place, so that the Vera people may have been absorbed into that settlement. But there is also a mountain peak named Vira northeast of Bangui, and this could provide an identification of its original placement. As regards "Aclan," Fray Benito is said in another reference to have founded before his death in 1676 a mission at "Adan" (B&R, xxxvii, 224). This will be seen below as a locality and an ethnic group name referring to the region and people of the upper Bulu river east of Bangui, in the vicinity of the present mountain administrative center called Adam or Adams. Probably, therefore, "Aclan" and "Adan" are the same name, and the historian de los Reyes assumes this to be so. Fuller accounts of the "Adan" or "Adang" people will also appear in later documents.

An extraordinary aspect of the records for this northern area is the lack of reference to "infidel" mountain populations until decades after the initial Spanish contact and pacification. Furthermore, though Bangui was founded as a coastal center, no efforts appear to have been made by officials or missionaries to penetrate the inner mountains north of the Laoag-Bacarra valleys—such as might have occurred if they were permanently inhabited. The account of the initial mission work by Fray Benito, moreover, makes no mention of the usual runaways who fled to such inner fastnesses in so many other zones, either prior to conversion or else apostatizing later. In terms of distance, it is notable that the Díaz account of Fray Benito's mission places the "first settlement" of the mountain pagans "four long leagues" from Bangui, which if correct would actually place it east of the Cordillera ridge in the present Apayao subprovince.

In the much fuller records of the adjacent Cagayan coastal strip it will be seen that under the first Spanish pressures there refugee groups did move inland. Moreover, it will be found that the documents make quite plausible a hypothesis that the later mountain populations of the Apayao river region who were to be called "Apayao," and in modern ethnographic terms "Isneg," did not permanently live in these inner fastnesses until after the Spanish conquest of the north coast areas. If this really were so, then it could be understood why this northwest mountain zone of Ilocos might not have had a permanent inland population at the time the encomiendas were being formed in the Laoag-Bacarra area, or at least was merely peopled by roving Negrito bands. In this case, the westward drift of these hamlet-living dry cultivators, called by the upper Apayao river names "Calanasa" and "Payao," would have brought them into contact considerably later with the coastal Ilocos settlements.

An impression is gained from further documents that many of Fray Benito's converts abandoned the newly formed settlements and returned to the mountains. This applies particularly to the "Aclan" and Vera converts, since these centers drop out of the records. De los Reyes, however, says that "Adan" converts moved in to Bangui (1890, ii, 122). Díaz states of the period which follows that "when there are plenty of religious in this province for such [mission] work," it went ahead; but otherwise it was "put in charge of the prior of the village of Bacarra" (B&R, xxxvii, 242).

A Dominican sketch map of the Cagayan missions, undated but apparently drawn between 1688 and 1692 according to evidence that will be cited in the Cagayan study, extends westward far enough to show Augustinian mission centers in this northern area as well. Those marked upon it are Bangui, Bangbanglo, Pasuquin, which is a center north of Bacarra, and Bacarra itself (B&R, xxxi, 298). Conspicuously absent are the Aclan or Adan and Vera mission settlements, which evidently had been abandoned by then. The northern mountain populations are shown as "Apayaos," except for an area east of Bangui, which is marked "Adan." Further south, in the mountains ringing the Laoag valley, the map shows the people to be "Tinguianes." The Murillo map of 1744 shows for this area only Bangui, "Babanglo," and a center called "Bangban," which does not appear in other records, but was by the mouth of the Banbang river about three miles west of Bangui.

The later Augustinian historian Mozo (1763) gives a general survey of what was known at the time of these northern Cordillera zones. After discussing the "Igolot" and "Tinggian" tribes, as seen in the previous chapters, he places north of them a third tribe, the "Apayao," with territory extending for "about thirty leagues," and comprising "many thousands of souls." Finally, at "one side," that is, to the west in northern Ilocos, "dwell another tribe, called Adang, which has fewer people, but, for the very reason they find themselves less powerful, they have their dwellings in places almost inaccessible—maintaining their own different dialect."

Mozo describes the Apayao as "not remaining behind the Igolot in cruelty, bloodthirstiness, and barbarism, but in a great degree surpassing it." His further description of this group will be set out in the northwest Cagayan section (Chapter VIII). Their headhunting forays, vividly pictured, were particularly feared by the settled Christian communities on both the Ilocos and Cagayan sides of the Cordillera.

Mozo goes on to describe a vigorous, though again brief, resumption of mission work in the early eighteenth century among the Apayao and Adan groups in the north, and also the development of missions at this time among the Tinguian mountaineers around the Laoag valley. Among the former groups, the brunt of this effort was carried by Fray José Herice. This father came to the area in 1720, and became known as "the hunter of souls" during his twenty-two years of work in mountain and lowland communities there. Mozo credits him with having formed the first "village of converts" among the "Adang" tribe, though it has been noted above that Fray Benito de Mena had done work among this group a half century earlier. This seems to confirm the view that whatever converts had been made at the earlier date had either been absorbed into coastal communities or else had returned to the mountains and apostatized. Herice is also noted as having established another village of Apayao converts, "which was called Vera." Here, too, is an implication that the older Vera founded by Mena had vanished, since the same name is used for a new settlement. This "Vera" may be a small settlement called today Vira near the headwaters of the Bacarra river. Herice was followed by Fray Jacinto Rivera, who "gained considerable extension for this mission."

Further south, Mozo says, corresponding mission work was developed among the Tinguians. Hitherto, he states, here as in other mountain zones, any fathers who had made an "entrance" had been forced out by threats of being killed. At most, therefore, a "few" persons had been converted "by missionaries in villages near them." In 1713, Fray Nicolás Fabro was sent to the Dingras area, and soon he had enough converts from the mountains to found a village "which he called San Juan," east of that center. By 1750, Mozo says, this settlement "contained more than a thousand souls." Fabro was followed by Fray Manuel Madriaga, who "accomplished wonders." In 1736, the latter formed another village near Dingras, "naming it Santiago." These two settlements of San Juan and Santiago are on the flats, so that in these instances the converts were evidently brought down from the mountains (B&R, xlviii, 81–87).

The ecclesiastical survey of 1738, used in previous chapters, speaks of "an extensive mission of heathen Tinguians in those mountains, from which little fruit was obtained until the year 1730." It also refers to a "curacy" of "San Diego" which was the "center of a mission to the Tinguians"; this seems to be Santiago, spoken of above. Fray Francisco de San Antonio, the author of this ecclesiastical survey, says that in 1735 the Tinguians begged "very urgently" for some fathers to "live in their villages." He states, however, that he was "unable to determine" the number of Tinguians in this mission, though he "made extraordinary efforts to do so" (B&R, xxviii, 158–59). The further ecclesiastical survey of 1754 also speaks of "San Diego, among the Tinguians, with some separate visitas." It strikes an optimistic note: "[There are] various missions of Tingianes and heathen in those mountains, where the same reverend fathers are commencing to form villages to the great advantage of those souls" (B&R, xxviii, 167).

In 1740–41, a Dominican father, Fray Tomás Marin, performed the feat of crossing the Cordillera twice from the Cagayan side through Apayao into Ilocos. This journey was made to test whether a "road" could be built through the mountains to facilitate mission communications. He found a route from Malaueg in Cagayan by way of "Apinan" and "Lacu" to Dingras in Ilocos to be "least difficult." In a letter to his provincial he states that besides having easier terrain, the "Calingas" of the area had been won over, and both the chiefs and people were friendly (Malumbres, 1919, 11, 376; Ayer Collection, Document 74).

In 1753, "two other Tingguian villages were newly formed," one "three leguas" from Santiago, "further within the mountains," and the other "four leguas from this" (B&R, xlviii, 87). This was evidently the beginning of the "mission of San Agustin de Banna," or Banna mission, in the mountains between Batac on the coast and Santiago and Dingras in the Laoag valley. Perez, in his collection of Augustinian documents (1904), includes several which refer to the early history of this mission.

One is a *Brief Relation* by Manuel Carillo, dated 1756. The author speaks of the "reduction" by which two Christian pueblos, Banna and Parras, had been formed. He describes Banna as having "at least a hundred houses," and as being well ordered, with "good fields of rice, cotton, and other products." He also speaks of "many Apayaos" as having been baptized in the northern areas of "Bangui, Pasuquing, and Bamban." The "Adanes," however, had dwindled, so that they were "reduced to one pueblo of approximately sixty houses." Carillo, following up with another report two years later, lists an additional 62 Tinguians baptized at Banna, Parras, and Santiago, 11 Apayaos at Bacarra and Bangui, and 41 Adanes at Bangui (Perez, 1904, pp. 114–16, 120).

A longer report on the Banna mission is given by Manuel Alvarez, who served there for several years from 1760 on. Banna, he says, had "thirty houses," and an adjacent rancheria called Paor was the only other Christian settlement. Parras, mentioned above, was an "infidel" settlement of "forty houses," and the other settlements in the region were Uguis to the south and Matangen and Buanga to the west, the last named having "twelve houses."

The Silang rebellion of 1762–63, which will be discussed further below, had repercussions in the Banna area. According to Alvarez, the representatives of the "Vigan insurgents" who came north to "seize the northern pueblos" found allies in these mountain settlements. Led by their "captains," Tagabuen, Pasuda, and Balastay, the "infidels" attacked the adjacent Christian lowland pueblos. In some of the churches the images were overturned and the "silver" raided. The mission of Santiago was among the points occupied, and church fathers, a special target of attack, were taken prisoner. This account differs from the general record, which shows the lowland communities taking Silang's side, yet the disturbed conditions evidently opened the way for reversion by the mountaineers to their older raiding habits.

The death of Silang brought a halt to this anti-Spanish movement, and Spanish troops under Arza y Urrutia occupied Banna. The rebels, Alvarez says, were then "pardoned," but the "new Christians" were removed to Santiago. Within the year, the latter "fled" back to Banna. With some difficulty, the mission was reestablished in Banna in 1764. Alvarez follows up his account of these events with a description of the "superstitions" associated with death ceremonies in the area (Perez, 1904, pp. 211–17). The mission zeal, however, both here and further north, seems to have dwindled away in the succeeding decades. Up to modern times, the mountain groups generally continued as "infidels," and any converts shifted out to settle in the coast and valley zones.

CONTINUING RECORDS

During this period, the lowland settlements were expanding and prospering. De los Reyes, in assessing conditions at the end of the seventeenth century, refers to an author (unspecified) who describes Laoag as having "many and very good people, fine Christians, and peaceful." Its church and convent were the most "beautiful and sumptuous" in Ilocos. Batac, too, was a "fine pueblo" with "very good people, quiet and good Christians." Bacarra was another center having "very good Christians," but "disdainful," which the cited author considers to be a northern Ilocano characteristic deriving from contacts and influences with Cagayan, where the people are more "belligerent" (de los Reyes, II, 145).

The 1738 survey of ecclesiastical establishments lists the old Augustinian centers at Badoc, "Panay" (Paoay), and Batac along the southern coast; "Ilduag" (Laoag), San Nicolas, "Leyrat," Dingras, and "Piric" in the central districts; and Bacarra, Vera, and Bangui with "other small mission villages" in the north. "Leyrat" and "Piric," the only two new names to appear here, were communities in the upper Laoag river valley. Leyrat is the later Sarrat and Piric is Piddig. No significant modifications of this list are made in the 1754 survey (B&R, XXVIII, 158, 167).

The coast and valley settlements were ravaged in 1754 by a particularly bad epidemic of smallpox in which 14,000 Ilocanos died. They also had an active role in the Silang rebellion of 1762–63. After Silang's successful investment of the Vigan area, according to Martinez de Zuñiga's account quoted in the general chapter, he "despatched emissaries toward the north." "All the native towns" then rose, and "robberies and atrocities" were committed. Hostilities were directed in particular against "some of the chiefs and Augustine friars," who were blamed for the fact that "the tribute had not been abolished." Anti-Spanish feeling showed "especially" in these northern towns, this author says, and in consequence many of the clergy were taken as prisoners to Vigan. This statement accords with the account by Alvarez referred to above. With his "authority acknowledged" in the north, Silang then directed his independence movement southward. With the killing of Silang, however, resistance evidently collapsed everywhere. The fathers returned, and a Spanish force "tranquillized" the discontented.

Further anti-Spanish outbreaks occurred during the early eighteenth century. In 1788, the Laoag area was one of the centers of opposition to the imposition of the tobacco monopoly. It is reported that "about a thousand persons" rose up in arms as a protest, and major hostilities were barely averted through the intervention of a trusted Bishop (de los Reyes, II, 199–200). In 1807–8 another "revolt" occurred in the face of "injustices" of the wine monopoly, that is, the control on the manufacture of palm and sugar-cane wines, which constituted one of the significant industries of the area. The centers of the latter outbreak, sometimes called the "Amparisto rebellion," were Laoag, Paoay, Batac, Sarrat, and Piddig (de los Reyes, II, 213–17; Philippine Census, 1918, 2, 157).

In 1811, a religious "conspiracy" broke out, attempting to replace Spanish Catholicism with a local cult centered upon a "god called Lungao." According to de los Reyes, its leaders attempted to gain converts among the mountain peoples of the Cordillera. The movement, however, was suppressed by the authorities (de los Reyes, II, 228–29). The Ilocos Norte people were later to espouse vigorously the anti-Spanish independence movement, and Batac was the home of Gregorio Aglipay, the founder of the Philippine Independence Church, often called the Aglipayan faith. In 1813–14, discontent with tribute arrangements following the promulgation of the Constitution of 1812 brought fresh outbreaks by the *kailianes,* or commoners. The government office at Sarrat was demolished, and troops had to be sent to Batac, San Nicolas, and other points (de los Reyes, II, 229–35).

An unsigned document in the Ayer Collection, dated around 1794, speaks of the growth of Laoag, and the potentialities of northern Luzon for further development. The writer proposed making this area a separate province, with Laoag as capital. The Laoag river could be a port "if the river bar is cleared." Dingras had already become a "garden spot." Space was available for breaking in more land and placing "ranchers" out from the settled communities. Moreover, moving their *estancias* further into the mountain country would serve to "force back the infidels." Payment of tribute by such colonists should be remitted for four years at least, since the people must establish new communities. *Principales* should be encouraged to migrate by offering "promotions." The government, the writer says, will eventually get "everything back with interest" (Ayer Collection, Document 251).

The late eighteenth century was a period of marked population expansion, presaging the virtual explosion of Ilocano numbers that was to mark the nineteenth century. Vintar, inland from Bacarra, became a separate community and district in 1774, and the same happened to Piddig and Pasuquin in 1775 and 1784, respectively. Laoag had become the largest town in Ilocos. Other zones were being colonized which were later to become independent communities.

As shown in Chapter II, Pizarro, who was responsible for separating Ilocos into its two provinces in 1818, wrote early in the nineteenth century of northern Ilocos as one of the zones having notable urban crowding and mass discontent. In a list of fifteen "most notable" Philippine towns marked by such conditions, he cites Laoag with 25,242 people, Pavay (Paoay) with 14,840, and Bacarra with 13,064 (B&R, LI, 199). This marked urban development helped to meet the problem of population increase in such a zone of limited rural space, and was to continue. Away from the towns, correspondingly, the Ilocanos here tended to spread out in small barrios and rancherias to an unusual degree, in order to utilize the cultivable areas most effectively. This rural distribution, too, may reflect persistence of a pre-Spanish pattern of scattered small settlements preceding the establishment of the early mission communities from which the towns took form.

LATER PERSPECTIVES

As in previous chapters, a brief description may be given of the principal settlements as described by Buzeta, based on his 1818 and 1845 population figures:

Southern Coast Area. In 1818, Paoay and Batac had populations, respectively, of 18,615 and 17,575; by 1845 the corresponding totals were 15,587 and 17,850. This falling off in numbers presumably resulted from out-migration. Together they had in the latter year "more than 5,500 houses." Badoc further south had totals for the given years of 8,390 and 8,777.

Laoag Valley Area. Laoag had population totals in these years of 30,135 and 34,560. Buzeta describes it as a thriving city of "some 4,000 houses." Other 1845 population figures (with those for 1818 in parentheses) were: San Nicolas 11,717 (8,745); Sarrat 7,650 (6,885); Dingras 11,672 (11,395); Piddig 8,780, and Solsona or Santiago 3,237 (the last two having a combined 1818 total of 10,035).

Bacarra Area. The Bacarra population totals for the given years were 12,250 and 16,690, the settlement in the latter year having "some 2,000 houses." For Vintar the figures were 5,160 and 7,830; for Pasuquin, 3,130 and 5,195.

Bangui Area. Bangui had an 1818 population of 2,641, and in 1845 had 475 houses and, with six small adjacent bariros, 4,007 people. Nagpartian had respective figures of 802 and 840.

These statistics yield population totals for northern Ilocos of 135,758 in 1818, and 154,392 in 1845. Buzeta speaks of the urbanized Laoag people as "restless."

Since old times of the conquest they have shown a propensity for uprisings, and even in later days, not so many years ago, they had a revolt promoted by *cailyanismo* [Indians who do not pertain to the *principalia*], and to calm them was needed the presence of . . . Bishop . . . Barriero, and . . . rectitude of the authorities in dealing with abuses. (Buzeta, ii, 153.)

This author makes clear in his accounts the economic basis for the unusual degree of urban development in Ilocos Norte. A network of roads and trails threaded particularly its south and central sections. The rural zones traded rice, maize, sugar cane, tobacco, and other crops into the towns, and sustained large horse and cattle ranches: seventeen ranches are cited by name in the Dingras area alone. The town households, too, notably swelled commerce by manufacturing cotton, fiber, and silk goods often of "magnificent quality," which were much in demand through the Philippines and even overseas. The ocean, together with plentiful lakes and waterways, supplied fish foods; salt was extracted along the shores; palm and sugar-cane wines were manufactured; and the usually accessible mountains had buffaloes, deer, and other wild game. Some gold and other precious metals were also washed from streams in "those mountains," and they were a source for valuable woods, resins, wax, and honey. Currimao, southwest of Paoay, served as the principal port from which the goods of the area were traded extensively by sea. Not least among exports, as noted already, were surplus people. In all, 32,197 tributes were collected annually, or roughly one to every five persons.

In the "steep mountains" east of Badoc on the southern coast, Buzeta says, there were "rancherias of Tinguian infidels," and some had settled in a "small pueblo" which was dependent on that town. Batac also had a "barrio of new Christians" called San Jose a short distance from it. An important commercial trail crossed the mountains to "Bana" (Banna), which was an "annex" of Dingras in the inner Laoag valley, and a trading center for the mountain groups.

The heights ringing the Laoag river system are spoken of by Buzeta as the "mountains of the infidels," the latter being "Tinguians." Their rancherias were variously counted as within the spheres of Dingras, Piddig, and Santiago. The mountainous one between the Laoag valley and the Bacarra river flats also had Tinguian settlements, which were dependent on Bacarra and Vintar. Buzeta's description of Vintar speaks not only of Tinguians but also of some "Negritos" as being located southward from it.

In general, the mountain groups further north were classed as of "Apayao" ethnic affiliation. Buzeta speaks of Apayao "infidels" living in the mountain country east of Pasuquin, and also notes an old "dependent rancheria" of these people at Pancian, in the Bay of that name near the Cagayan border. Buzeta's general description of the "Apayaos," whom he speaks of as "occupying the mountains which divide the provinces of Cagayan and Ilocos," may be given here because of its reference to Ilocos contacts:

They eat maize and roots primarily. They are particularly distinguished from the other mountain tribes by their finely constructed houses. . . . [These] are square, and each corner is built with extremely strong and durable wood. The floor, instead of being made with bamboo . . . is made of highly polished planks of a wood which is . . . a species of cedar. The walls which divide the rooms are made of palm leaves. The fireplace is located in one of the corners in the main house.

These people go to great lengths to have their homes well furnished and they obtain furniture by trading wax, which is very good; cacao, which is excellent; and tobacco, which approximates that of the lower Chico river area in Cagayan [counted the best in the Philippines]. . . . Their houses are adorned with vases and jars from China.

Because of their location, it is easy for them to smuggle tobacco into the neighboring provinces. They go down through the mountains . . . [to] the beaches of *Ilocos* where they expect to meet trading parties. They sell their merchandise on land as well as at sea. In the case of smuggling tobacco, they go to the lowlands of *Dingras* and *Nagpartian*.

The description given here of the substantial Isneg or Apayao house and its furnishings is a fair one.* The reference, however, to "maize and roots" as the principal foods is surprising, as in modern times their predominant crop is dry rice, with maize and roots as lesser crops. More will be said of this in the northwest Cagayan section.

Buzeta carefully distinguishes the "Adangs" from the Apayaos, and his descriptions give a series of alternative names for this smaller group: Adangtas, Andanginos, Adanes, Adamitas. The Adang territory is placed in the vicinity of Mt. Adang or Adam in the headwater area of the Bulu river, and he notes the existence of the small center called Adam or Adams where "converts were settled" in 1720 by Fray José Herice (Buzeta, p. 88). Buzeta judges the Adang to represent a "secondary stock derived from crossing with Negrito women." He speaks of them as

having in their isolation a distinctive language, which they retain, and special usages and customs, which show a unique and distinctive origin from their neighbors. The blind love of all Filipinos for their savage independence, supported by the difficulties of taming the soil in which [the Adang] have their miserable habitation, has blocked the penetration of religion and civilization.

Buzeta says that, after Herice died of his "heavy labors and infirmities," his successors carried forward the work in the region, though without much success.

* See Morice Vanoverbergh, "Isneg Constructions," *Philippine Journal of Science,* Vol. 81, No. 1, pp. 77–107.

A survey of Ilocos Norte by Cavada in 1876 shows that province as having a population of 150,947, of whom 23 were Spaniards, 56 Chinese, 7 Filipinos from other areas, 102 "mestizos," and one from an unidentified country overseas. Cavada notes that among the "mountain or independent tribes" were some Negritos.

Perez, in his collection of Augustinian documents (1904), includes a *Memorial* by an unidentified Augustinian on the mountain peoples of the northern Cordillera. First he traces three trails from Ilocos Norte into Apayao: one from Vintar northeast via the Adang area; a second from Solsona eastward; and a third from Dingras southeast to Anayan in northern Abra, then over the Cordillera. In 1872, he notes, a military expedition from Laoag crossed by the third route to Malaueg in the Cagayan valley. The mountain peoples are described as trading with both the Ilocanos and the Cagayan peoples, selling tobacco, cacao, wax, honey, ginger, and other products: "Like all the savage pueblos, they produce only what is necessary for life, a little rice, cacao, ginger, and some vegetables—the tubers tugui, camote, and camangeng." The author says that gold exists in some of the waterways, and there is a "copper mine" located in the vicinity of "Mt. Balbalitoc." Four mountain settlements, including Paor, were under the jurisdiction of Dingras, with a total population of 400, and five were under that of Badoc, with 800. The Apayao population was delineated with surprising accuracy, as will be seen in the northwest Cagayan chapter (Perez, 1904, pp. 222–31).

An illuminating account of relations between the Spanish authorities and lowland Ilocanos on the one hand, and the mountain peoples on the other, is afforded by the German scientist Schadenberg.* In 1888, this scholar traveled from Ilocos Norte into northwest Apayao. He notes that detached rancherias of "Apoyaos" extended westward into the vicinity of Angui and to the north coast. They were "passionate headhunters," and had been "extending the sport" into the Piddig, Solsona, and Banna areas. Shortly before his visit, the Provincial Governor had sent a large expedition against them, comprising civil guardsmen with lowland auxiliaries under command of a Lieutenant Medina.

On arrival at the first rancherias in the "Cabugaoan" area east of Solsona, this Spanish party had stopped to negotiate with Isneg leaders. The outstanding one was Onsi, who had had much Christian contact, and even wore the Spanish "Medal of Civil Merit." Forty "heads of rancherias" then assembled "without their arms." Medina, however, shot Onsi who was kneeling in obeisance before him, and as the rest fled sixteen more of them were killed. Medina was suspended for this act, and was awaiting trial

* A. Schadenberg, *Zeitschrift für Ethnologie,* Vol. 21, pp. 674–82, trans. by A. L. McPherron, Chicago Philippine Studies Program.

at the time of Schadenberg's visit. In retaliation, a party of twenty-four Ilocano traders, working their way through the mountain communities in pursuit of customary trade, were intercepted and killed. Headhunting expeditions also struck "even as far as Dingras"; more heads were being taken by the Isnegs "than ever"; and "the Christians dared to go into the nearest woods only in large bands."

Schadenberg himself, against the advice of the authorities, proceeded on his expedition with fifteen carriers and a personal servant only. He was able to penetrate through the northern section of the Cordillera into the Bayag district of Apayao (the territory of the "Calanasas" noted earlier). He states that many of the mountain people had received baptism "long ago," but by the time of his trip "no one bothers himself about them from the religious viewpoint." He speaks of the excellent tobacco grown there and traded illicitly in the face of the Spanish monopoly to the lowlands, sometimes by silent barter:

For the purpose of exchange there are neutral places at various points. Christians desirous of trade are informed by means of signs and calls. The Apoyaos lay down the tobacco which they wish to trade on the neutral place and retire; the Christians lay down next to it their objects of exchange . . . and retire likewise, whereupon the Apoyaos return and appraise the exchange articles. Should they find them suitable, they take them and leave the tobacco; if they find the offering too small, they remove a portion of the tobacco and leave as much as seems to them sufficient for the articles to be exchanged, retire once more, and wait to see whether the Christian Indian will show his satisfaction.

Schadenberg speaks of the "rancherias" as "uncommonly difficult of access," and as having from two to eight substantially built houses each. Little associated groups of such settlements, he says, are like "provinces in a western land," except that they form "completely independent units."

A description of Ilocos Norte by Camilo Millan y Villanueva, published in 1891, gives the names of 11 "rancherias" recorded in an 1887 census of the province, with a total population of 1,985. Nine of them had from 75 to 160 people each, and the other three had 245, 430, and 436. A list of "infidels in Luzon" as of 1898, cited by Malumbres, however, shows Ilocos Norte as supposedly having 12,880 non-Christians (1919, II, 403).

In 1890–91, as part of an acceleration of Spanish attempts to control and pacify the northern Luzon mountain peoples, three politico-military Comandancias were formed in the Cagayan–Ilocos Norte area. One, called the Comandancia de Cabagaoan, was organized in this western region, with its headquarters in Laoag. The other two, called the Comandancias of Apayaos and Itaves, covered the northeast and east sections of the mountains, respectively, and will be dealt with in the appropriate Cagayan chapters. This final period of Spanish rule was marked by persistent movements of Ilocano farmers, lumbermen, and fishermen up the river valley along the rugged northern Luzon coast, both in Ilocos Norte and Cagayan, as the Cagayan records will notably show. In turn the Isnegs stepped up hostilities in the face of such encroachments, so that the situation called for frequent military measures. Final pacification did not come until the period of 1908–13, when Philippine Constabulary forces based in Cagayan Province brought the inner fastnesses of Apayao under government control. Even then, official reports of the time show, many Isneg "runaways" moved westward across into the Ilocos Norte and Abra mountains in the hope of escaping the new supervision (Keesing and Keesing, 1934, p. 87). Of the "Adangs," Sawyer wrote in 1900 that they were "civilized," and had long been Christians (1900, p. 280). Cole in 1909, on his map of northern Luzon, shows them as "extinct," and Adam as "abandoned."

MODERN CENSUS DATA

The first American census of 1903 gave a total count for Ilocos Norte of 176,785 "civilized" people and 2,210 "wild" people. In ethnic terms the "wild" group were broken down into 2,198 "Igorots" and 12 Negritos. By 1918, the total population of the province had increased to 219,129, while the subsequent censuses of 1939 and 1948 showed further rises to 237,586 and 251,455, respectively.*

The 1939 census showed 552 Tinggian speakers in a new municipal unit called Nueva Era, along the mountainous southern boundary of Ilocos Norte. The only other municipal units in the south and central zones of the province with significant numbers of speakers of the mountain languages were Dingras with 151 Tinggian speakers, Solsona with 295 Apayao (Isneg) speakers, and another new mountain jurisdiction called Carasi, east of Piddig, with 248 Tinggian speakers. The mountainous parts of Vintar had 402 Tinggian speakers. Further north, Bangui had 131 speakers of Tinggian and 41 of Apayao, and Dumalneg and Adam had 239 and 209 Tinggian speakers, respectively. It is not clear whether the census takers, in classifying most of the northern mountain populations as Tinggian speakers, were here confusing this language and Apayao. But it could well

---

* The following were the populations in 1948 by municipal units:

Lowland

Badoc 13,573	Batac 22,577	Dingras 24,481	Vintar 14,882
Panili 8,318	Laoag 44,406	Solsona 10,423	Burgos 3,003
Currimao 4,296	San Nicolas .. 15,567	Piddig 10,496	Pasuquin 12,407
Paoay 11,257	Sarrat 14,345	Bacarra 15,851	Bangui 14,126

Mountain

Nueva Era ... 2,059	Dumalneg ... 454
Banna 8,611	Adam 170
Carasi 1,231	

represent a northward drift of Tinggian speakers. Correspondingly, Apayao speakers could have been moving eastward into Apayao subprovince. No separate identification is made of any Adang.

The 1948 census divided the Ilocos Norte population in terms of mother tongues as follows: Iloko 246,459; Tinggian 1,437; Apayao 26; Negrito 1; and others 3,532. A breakdown of these statistics by jurisdictions was not available at the time of writing. In religious terms the province is shown to be the stronghold of the Aglipayan faith, which had 150,204 adherents as compared with 93,217 Roman Catholics and 5,814 Protestants. The census category of "pagans and not belonging to any religious group" totaled only 912.

REVIEW

In this northern Ilocos region, the sparse mountain people seem to offer fewer problems for interpretation than do those calling themselves Ilocano. The southern mountaineers seem to be northern offshoots of the dry cultivating "mountain Tinguian," and their story matches with the previous discussion of the Abra people. Those to the north are western groups of the Isneg who have crossed the Cordillera from Apayao. What Negritos formerly lived in the region have virtually gone. Only the shadowy Adang or Adan challenge interpretation, and this has no significance today.

More open is the question of how far, prior to Spanish times, the population of the Laoag valley and adjacent coast were a northward continuity of the middle Ilocos people, or had a more or less separate ethnic and linguistic identity. This problem will become more meaningful as the study moves on to examine data on the populations of northwest Cagayan, the Cagayan valley, and the offshore Babuyan and Batan islands. Here, diversity seems to be the rule. As noted already, the matter of historic Ilocano identity will need to be covered in the final chapter.

VII. The Cagayan Region: General Perspectives

PLACE AND PEOPLE

The eastern or Cagayan side of northern Luzon presents some of the most dramatic and important material for ethnohistorical analysis in the entire study. This is not least of all because of the diversity of peoples occupying the valley, and their different responses to Spanish penetration. As with the Pangasinan-Ilocos study, general records dealing with the Cagayan region as a whole will be placed in this initial chapter. It will also present a geographic, ethnic, historical, and political description, which will prepare the way for the five specific area studies to follow.

The eastern slopes of the Cordillera Central descend to the long floor of the Cagayan valley, stretching north to south for approximately 150 miles. Eastward the terrain rises again to the heights of the Sierra Madre range, beyond which the rugged coastline falls away steeply into the Pacific deeps. The region is mainly drained by the great river system of the Rio Grande de Cagayan, or Cagayan river. Its southern headwaters arise partly in the two mountain systems flanking the valley and partly in the rugged cross-range of the Caraballo Sur mountains. Southward across this last range, as already seen, lie the plains of old Pangasinan and Pampanga. The Cordillera heights on the west side lie for the most part within Mountain Province. For the rest, the Cagayan side of northern Luzon comprises three provinces: from north to south, Cagayan, Isabela, and Nueva Vizcaya.

The northern shores around the Cagayan mouth are flat, with sand beaches and extensive swamps. Inland, the valley alternates between open stretches of flat land, often swampy, and undulating foothills. Secondary valleys finger into the mountains where the tributary rivers descend more or less turbulently from the heights. About two-thirds of the way up the Cagayan (i.e., southward), the river forks into two great valley systems, an eastern one traversed by the upper Cagayan river and a western one by the principal tributary, the Magat river.

The Cagayan valley lies in a different climatic belt from Ilocos, being between two great mountain systems over which the alternating monsoon winds blow. Rainfall is distributed throughout the year, with a short drier season in the late winter from January to April, and the wettest months usually in late summer from September to November. The annual precipitation diminishes southward up the valley where the bordering mountains are generally higher. The Bayombong weather station in the upper Magat valley shows even in the wetter summer season the fourth lowest precipitation for that period among fifty weather stations through the Philippines. This is the period when Baguio, on the adjacent southern Cordillera heights, is having the highest rainfall for that season in the Philippines, and the Ilocos coast its rainy extreme. In the winter season, however, Bayombong does not have the great dryness characteristic of the Ilocos side: it stands thirteenth from the bottom among the weather stations, and receives some five or six times the winter precipitation usual in Ilocos. Rainfall rises with elevation from the coast and valley floor. The Sierra Madre heights have a heavy rainfall, particularly during the northeast monsoon (winter) season (Philippine Census, 1918, and other sources).

Correlated with this precipitation pattern, the most heavily forested areas are in the mountains back of the northwest Cagayan Coast (Apayao subprovince), and on the heights of the Sierra Madres to the east and the Caraballos Sur to the south. The lack of seasonal extremes in precipitation gives a widened timetable for cropping throughout most of the Cagayan area. But in the high valley zone of the upper Magat river, which is about 1,500 feet in elevation, winters are cool and cloudy, so that tropical crops do not mature well at that time. Little published information exists on agricultural calendars in the different zones of the Cagayan region. Furthermore, as will be seen, cropping patterns were affected in most parts of the valley by the institution in Spanish times of a forced production system of growing tobacco (1781–1882), so that reconstruction of older usages is not clear cut.

The 1903 census states of the Cagayan valley: "Corn [i.e., maize] . . . constitutes practically the only food of the natives" ("Agriculture," IV, 52). The commercial tobacco crop dominates the agricultural cycle, with the seedbeds planted in the higher lands in July-August, transplanting done in September-October, and the harvest coming in January-February; in the lower lands, the cycle starts in October-November and harvest comes in March-April. Maize is still produced in large quantity, often with two or even three crops. Wet rice growing, prohibited during the tobacco monopoly period in areas where it would compete for labor, has burgeoned in recent decades, with planting after the brief dry season when the tobacco is harvested. Considerable dry rice is also grown on the hills to both the west and the east of the valley floor, and this will be seen as the older rainy-season crop featured in the Cagayan. Vegetables and root crops, the latter including the American root cassava (tapioca) as well as the sweet potato are grown in considerable amounts. But only on the southern Cordillera slopes near Benguet are sweet potatoes greatly emphasized.

In ethnic and linguistic terms the Cagayan region presents complicated and in some respects obscure patterns. In advance of more detailed analysis, a brief history can be given. The easiest way of classification, often used by Spanish writers, has been to speak of the Christianized valley population as the "Cagayan," and then to throw them into contrast with the "infidels" or non-Christians.

More specifically, the bulk of the lowland people are of "Ibanag" culture and language. With their homeland around the Cagayan river mouth, they have moved widely up the valley in historic times, and as the highest prestige group, they have tended to assimilate the older ethnic elements. Four such elements, however, still retain their identity: "Itavi" in the north, "Yogad" and "Isinai" in the south, and groups subsumed under the general name "Gaddang" between. In turn, all these indigenous lowland groups have been increasingly interpenetrated by vigorous Ilocano colonists, so that by the 1948 census approximately 425,000 persons, or two-thirds of the population of 638,301 in the provinces of Cagayan, Isabela, and Nueva Vizcaya taken together, counted Iloko as their mother tongue.

On the west or Cordillera side, the mountain populations comprise from north to south the Isneg or Apayao, the Kalinga, a few non-Christian Gaddang, the Ifugao, and the eastern Ibaloi. There are also Negrito remnants in the northern foothills. On the east or Sierra Madre side, the northern areas likewise have Negrito groups, the Cagayan river tributaries have pockets of non-Christian Gaddang, and the southern zones have scattered groups usually called collectively, together with some Negritos, Ilongot. On the Pacific side from Palanan southward, there are Tagalog-speaking Christian groups who have migrated up the east coast of Luzon.

INITIAL SPANISH CONTACTS

Relations between the Spaniards and the Cagayan people appear to have been marked by immediate clashes. In 1572, seven years after Legaspi's initial occupation of the Manila region, his grandson, Juan de Salcedo, encircling Luzon, traversed the coastal zone by sea with a party of soldiers, and apparently collected some "tribute" (Montero y Vidal, 1, 41–42). To follow up this contact, he then sent a party led by Don Luis de Sahajossa. A small ship of "galliot" type was next dispatched to "explore the province," but it was waylaid by the Chinese pirate Limahon and destroyed, as seen in the Ilocos study.

No detailed reports seem to be available either of these or of one or two further expeditions to Cagayan. But their consequences are indicated by

Bishop Salazar in his *Affairs in the Philippine Islands* (1581), where he quotes a clause in one of the instructions given by the Governor to Captain Juan Pablo de Carrion, sent in that year to found a settlement in Cagayan: "Tribute shall not be demanded from them for one year." Salazar then says of this clause: "I hope to God that it is to be one of much importance, in order that these Indians, who three or four times have been so wronged and scandalized, may now have peace" (B&R, v, 235).

The Cagayan groups living near the coast were already accustomed to dealings with outsiders. The river mouth had apparently long served as a sheltering and trading port for both Chinese and Japanese vessels, and in 1581 Carrion had to fight off a Japanese "fleet" in order to establish entry, as will be seen in Chapter IX, which discusses the lower Cagayan. In turn, the Spaniards were to use Cagayan as a northern base for both peaceful and hostile contacts with Japan, China, "Hermosa" (Formosa), "Camboja" (Cambodia), and nearer at hand the Babuyan and Batan islands off the Cagayan shore, which became part of the Philippines. Hostilities between the Spaniards and the Islamic peoples of the southern Philippines and islands further south sometimes had an impact on Cagayan in the form of "Joloano" and other raiders who pillaged coastal communities.

Carrion succeeded in establishing a settlement and fort some eight miles inland from the mouth of the Cagayan river. Called Nueva Segovia, and later by the local name of Lal-lo or Lalloc, it became the administrative and ecclesiastical capital. The name Nueva Segovia was also applied as an early provincial name to the valley, and to the Bishopric. Spanish historians state that the lower Cagayan was called "Segovia" because of climatic and other resemblances shown by this cooler and drier part of the northern Philippines to the Spanish district with that name. The Cagayan river was also called initially the "Tajo," after the Tagus in Spain. Loarca's *Relation* of 1582 speaks of it as being

a river of great volume, although its bar forms shallows. . . . On its banks are large settlements with a population of more than thirty thousand. The people gather a great quantity of rice, and keep many swine. They have also some gold, although there are no gold mines. Their trade is carried on with the men of Ylocos. (B&R, v, 101.)

This first enthusiastic estimate of the population and resources of the coastal and lower river sections of Cagayan will have to be reviewed in the light of further, more specific records.

The encomienda system was extended immediately to the Cagayan valley. A series of Royal and private encomiendas, which will be listed specifically in later chapters, was marked off along the settled coast and around the town of Nueva Segovia, and tribute collections began, backed by military force. By 1591, when an encomienda list for the whole of the Philippines was published, even the middle and upper parts of the valley along the river banks, where military parties had passed by boat, had been given encomienda names. Figures were also included for their tribute populations, even though for most places they were still vague estimates and there was a monotonous recital of two appended formulas: either "in rebellion" or "all hostile." This list shows a total of fifty encomiendas in the Cagayan, of which ten were wholly or partly "pacified" and paying tribute by that date (B&R, VIII, 108-10). It will be seen on later analysis that the tribute figures tend to run much higher than seems to be warranted by the other data bearing on demography. A possible explanation is that, with an officially fixed tribute maximum, a higher population estimate would enable an encomendero to collect a larger amount in his holding without running afoul of the authorities. Disturbances such as occurred in the Ilocos area over encomienda affairs became repeated in Cagayan, as will be seen in the chapters that follow.

In 1586, as part of the complicated power struggles in southeast and east Asia between Spain and the other interested countries, the Philippine governmental authorities proposed to the King that China be invaded, using the Cagayan port as the departure point for Spanish forces. Among eighteen reasons given in favor of making it the base are that "there is in the land great store of swine and fowl, and excellent hunting of buffalo and deer" (for the meat supply), and also "a great abundance of fish," "palm wine" in "great plenty," "kidney beans" which are "common," jars, sandals, a "great deal of cotton," linen cloth, and iron from China. The valley also has "an abundance of wood for vessels," and the "Indians . . . are already very skillful" in making boats. With the "assistance and labor of a few Spanish carpenters, to furnish them with plans and a model," an invasion fleet could be constructed—this perhaps indicative of a Spanish origin for the flat-bottomed *banquillo* made of planks that is used today in the valley and in the mountain streams of Apayao. One item states that "considerable rice" exists in the Babuyan Islands off the coast, but otherwise the reference to this food consists of a general statement that "warehouses" could be built to hold stores of rice "which is the staple food of this country"—presumably meaning the Cagayan area (B&R, VI, 204-6).

By 1588, according to a *Relation* by Salazar, the new town of Nueva Segovia had an alcalde-mayor and other officials, a fort manned by 40 soldiers, a "royal hospital," an Augustinian "monastery" with 2 priests, and 40 Spanish "citizens" who were encomenderos (B&R, VII, 37). Apportioned to 33 of the encomenderos were 26,000 Indians of whom 7,000 were "pacified and paying tribute," while another 1,700 were assigned to the King, with 1,000 of them tribute payers. The known populated groups of Cagayan from this count therefore were estimated to number 27,700 in all. Of the resources of the valley and method of tribute payment, Salazar says:

The whole [valley] is quite fertile and healthful, and abounds in rice, swine, fowls, and palm-wine; and there is much hunting of buffaloes, deer, wild hogs, and birds. A great amount of wax, cotton, and gold is collected in this district, in which articles the natives pay their tribute. (B&R, vii, 38.)

Still another *Relation,* unsigned and dated about 1586, says:

[The valley] is very densely populated and exceedingly well supplied with rice, cotton, very large fowls, deer, buffaloes, and a great quantity of wax. . . . Inasmuch as it is so near [China], and because it contains so many people and is so rich and well supplied with food, the effort has been made often to completely subdue and settle it, but that effort has not as yet been successful. . . . The people of the province of Cagayan resemble those of Ylocos. They are very vile, and poorly dressed, but are fine husbandmen. (B&R, vi, 383–86.)

PROBLEMS OF CONSOLIDATING SPANISH CONTROL

Almost from the start of the Spanish occupation of Cagayan, resistance developed among segments of the population. In 1589, the province was "all in rebellion," and "many Spaniards" were killed. Attacks were even made on Nueva Segovia, and "the natives were so bold and daring that they entered into the city to murder and rob." One of the encomenderos was killed while "collecting his tribute" in his holding, and it becomes clear from statements of the time that the arbitrary and sometimes extortionate demands made under the encomienda system supplied the main grievances. Certain "chiefs," evidently in the lower Cagayan, were reported as having "arranged with a Japanese captain to aid them," promising to give land to him in return, and also as sending "messengers to the king of Borney and other principal Indians of other provinces to ask assistance."

When word of this uprising reached Manila, the Governor dispatched an expedition of ships and soldiers, "over eight hundred with friendly Indians." The local leaders "refused to render obedience," as the Governor subsequently explained in a letter to the King, so that "it was necessary to open war." By that means, "all the inhabitants of that province were reduced in the space of six months, and came to pay the tribute," including not only the rebels but "others who had never been discovered until then." As resistance lapsed, so various contemporary records of this initial major outbreak tell, the principal chiefs were arrested. "Seven or eight" were "hanged and beheaded," and their property confiscated. "Many others were exiled, some from their villages, others to New Spain." One commentator, more skeptical than the Governor about the results achieved by this expedition, speaks of the people as "becoming somewhat cowed" by these punitive actions (B&R, vi, 185; vii, 123; x, 208; xxxiv, 409).

In a report on affairs of the Spanish Embassy in Japan, dated 1593, the Spanish Ambassador comments on a discussion he had with Japanese officials relating to the Cagayan, where relations of the resident Spaniards and visiting Japanese vessels had been veering between friendly and hostile: "The Japanese laughed. . . . They declared that the natives of Cagayan were ill-disposed to us; and that the Japanese would no sooner land in Cagayan, than the natives would deliver the Spaniards to them" (B&R, IX, 39–40).

The Japanese were perhaps judging the situation correctly as to what would happen if they chose to move into northern Luzon with an invasion force at the time. In that year the King gave authority for the tribute to be increased, though with instructions that the adjustment be made "with the mildest possible means." In 1594, an official report on Cagayan says that "there has been no lack of disturbances among the natives, with no little tumult and danger to the [church] fathers and to us also." Requests were made in this period for more troops, and "another fort as a protection against Indian, Japanese, and Chinese robbers." Whereas in 1591 the encomienda list for the Cagayan, mentioned above, hopefully showed an estimated total of 22,600 actual and potential tributes and over 90,000 people in the fifty encomiendas, a report of 1594 says that by then the encomenderos were only "twelve in number," and the figures had been revised downward to 10,400 tributes and somewhat more than 40,000 (B&R, VIII, 35; IX, 101, 194, 243, *passim*).

Another theme of Cagayan records at this time was the need for more religious personnel. "These priests," one says, "are very important for the pacification and permanent settlement of the natives. . . . [Seventy] are necessary, who, with the help and protection of the soldiers, will gather the inhabitants together and pacify them all, and seek out the rest of the people" not yet "apportioned in encomiendas" (B&R, VII, 39). The links between civil administration, military control, the collection of encomienda tributes, and mission work, are seen here, with concentration of the local peoples into larger, more permanent settlements as also a frequent accompaniment of the pacification process. The initial religious personnel had been supplied by the Augustinians, but they limited their work to the town of Nueva Segovia only. In 1595, when the Bishopric was established, the Dominican Order took over the Cagayan field, and so assumed responsibility for conversion of the "Indian" peoples. By 1598, the Dominicans had 71 "religious" located in twelve "houses" (mission centers). As of 1612, there were eleven such centers, some consolidated from older ones and some new. The mission count of the number of Indians being served at that date, 10,500, is much lower than the encomienda figures above (B&R, X, 181; XVII, 211).

The initial mission establishments in indigenous communities were developed along the northwest Cagayan coast and around the town of Nueva Segovia. The first Bishop, Diego de Soria, sent a group of newly arrived Dominicans to key encomienda centers there in 1596. In its next phase, between 1598 and 1618, the missionizing impulse carried Christianity well up the Cagayan river, and along one of its tributaries, the Chico. But the disturbed conditions described above brought setbacks, and except at a few key centers converts tended to "apostatize" and take to the fastnesses away from the river.

Aduarte's Dominican *History* (1640) is a major source for materials not only on these early missions but also on the backgrounds of local custom and the results of Spanish contacts more generally. It will be used extensively in the regional chapters that follow. Here his general remarks on the Cagayan may be noted:

The climate is one of the best in the islands, being refreshing, mild, and not . . . excessively hot. . . . It is for this reason that [the Province] was called Nueva Segovia, after Segovia in Espana, which is a cool region. . . . [It] resembles China in its good qualities—the abundance of fish in its rivers, of rice and other produce of the soil, of animals of the chase, and of wild boars and buffaloes in the mountains; while of Spanish plants which have been introduced here the crops obtained have been very large. In the colder [mountain] regions pines and live-oaks grow naturally. (B&R, xxx, 272–73.)

A report on *Military Affairs* in the Philippines dated 1599 speaks of another major "rising of the Indians" in Cagayan during the previous year. This is attributed first to "oppression" of the Indians, and second to the latter's warlike propensities (B&R, x, 215–16). Aduarte speaks of the conduct of the Spaniards in Nueva Segovia prior to the coming of the Dominicans as "so little Christian" that the Augustinian fathers who had pioneered ecclesiastical work in the capital felt it wise to leave them and the Indians "in their dissensions." In a quotation to be given more fully in the chapter dealing with the lower Cagayan, he speaks of "the excitement of the Indians resulting from the many homicides committed among them by the Spaniards," so that the latter could not leave the town or collect tribute without military escort. The local soldiers, an official record of the time notes, were paid and maintained by the encomenderos instead of by the government. Morga, in his *Events* (1609), speaks of the 1598 uprising as one of "various recent attempts" to be "rid of the burden" put upon the Indian people (B&R, x, 109).

Again a military expedition was sent from Manila, led by Captain Pedro de Chaves. The military report referred to above says that after suppressing the revolt, he "executed twelve of the headmen." Morga and other recorders of the time show that punitive action was taken also against the head official in Nueva Segovia, Don Ronquillo, for "the harm done" to the Indians: he was imprisoned in Manila. Morga notes that the rebellion came partly as a result of an official raise in the tribute rate, by one-third, so that the order for this was suspended for the time being as regards Cagayan. The leader of the outbreak, Magalat, was killed during the action—

Morga says he was slain by some of his followers to get the ransom on his head, but another record speaks of him as being ambushed by a party of soldiers. By the following year, the military report states, "all was quiet, peaceful, and tractable by land and sea." Over against this, one assessment of the time of the results achieved by Chaves states: "[He] did nothing except cut down their palm-trees and destroy their crops. . . . [The] Indians themselves burned their villages and went to the mountains. . . . [He] left the province in a worse state of war than before." Here we see happenings that probably occurred as well in Ilocos, though little recorded there: the killing or banishment of leaders by Spanish forces; the destruction of resources as a punitive measure; and the retreat of population groups into the mountainous hinterlands (B&R, VII, 123; X, 109, 169–70, 215–16).

Seventeenth-century records have frequent references to the continuing unsettled state of the Cagayan region. In 1618, for example, it was spoken of as having "much incompletely pacified country . . . [with] villages inhabited by very strong and warlike people who have given us much trouble." This account also speaks of the "natural restlessness of the Cagayan people," calling for regular garrisoning (B&R, XVIII, 100–101). In 1625, an official letter to the King says that "the province of Cagayan continues to revolt," so that a new policy was being introduced of ordering troops to "hold" zones they had entered instead of leaving: "for by their leaving the natives their fields and palm plantations, two consecutive years are necessary to reduce them." That is, food shortage could be used as a weapon for pacification (B&R, XXII, 69). A *Relation* of 1627–28 says:

A great proportion of the province of Cagayan . . . has been in revolt for some years. An extensive raid was made this year by our Spaniards and two thousand friendly Indians. Some of the enemy were killed, and eight villages were burned. The country was laid waste, with the fields that the enemy had there; and thus were they punished for the insolent acts . . . they had committed. (B&R, XXII, 211.)

It will be noted here how the Spanish uthorities usead the technique, familiar on so many frontiers, of employing friendly groups in campaigns to subdue hostile ones who in some instances were their traditional enemies. By this time, too, Indians were also being recruited in the friendly Cagayan districts for military service further afield, as where "bowmen" from the area participated in an expedition to Borneo (B&R, XV, 54). Medina's *History* of 1630, speaking of the "warlike" Cagayan people, says that "daily they rise and burn convents and churches and kill some of the religious" (B&R, XXIII, 233).

In the lower parts of the valley, events continued pendulum-like between order and revolt, with some of the disturbances being reflections of uprisings already seen taking place in Pampanga, Pangasinan, and Ilocos. By the mid-seventeenth century, Nueva Segovia, or Lal-lo (alternatively Lalloc) as it came to be called, had a population of some 200 Spaniards and mestizos, who appear to have considered it a place of exile because of its remoteness from Manila. Its fort was described by an Italian voyager, Dr. G. F. Gemelli Careri, who visited the town in 1697, as "needed for defence against revolted Indians."* A port, Aparri, had been developed by this time at the Cagayan river entrance for piloting and sentinel activities.

CONTINUING PENETRATION

Between 1591 and 1594, four Spanish expeditions explored the headwaters of the Cagayan by crossing over the mountains from the Pangasinan plains to the south. They gave the upper valley the name "Tuy" or "Ituy." Occasionally, too, an armed party ventured from Nueva Segovia by boat high upriver—not always returning, as the records will show.

In 1610, Dominican fathers moved up the Abulug or the Apayao river from the northwest coast to work among the "infidels" and "runaways" along the mountain margins of Apayao. In the subsequent decades sporadic attempts were made to establish missions and military posts in the deeper interior. But in the end such converts who continued loyal were resettled in the lower country. This already familiar pattern will be seen repeated in the mountain districts both east and west of the Cagayan all the way to its headwaters. Not until the later decades of the nineteenth century, and in some places (including Apayao) the early twentieth century, was effective penetration started. Alternations between mission benevolence and the punitive military expedition punctuated the long intervening period, and conversions were counterbalanced by fresh defections of valley people who took to the mountains. By the time of the first American census in 1903, nearly three-quarters of the known population of Nueva Vizcaya, the upper valley province, were still classed as "wild."

The mission and encomienda centers dotted along the middle reaches of the Cagayan river will be seen as having a complicated history of initial conversions and consolidations, followed by uprisings, dispersals, and then establishment of new settlements as Spanish control could be renewed. The modern residential patterns commenced to take form during the last quarter of the seventeenth century. The chief factor here was the stabilization of the principal town centers, including Tuguegerao, which was later to become the capital of the modern province of Cagayan, and Ilagan, the future Isabela Province capital.

Up to the Cagayan-Magat junction area, the valley was under Dominican ecclesiastical control. In the upper Magat river area, or "Ituy," where valley flats open out, a succession of mission workers crossed the mountains during the seventeenth century in sporadic attempts to convert the local peoples:

* *A Voyage Round the World*, Napoli, 1699, pp. 433–34.

first Franciscans from Baler and Casiguran on the east or Pacific side of Luzon, and then Dominicans from Pangasinan. Early in the eighteenth century, Augustinians in turn struck into this zone from their mission centers of Pantabangan and Carranglan described in the Pangasinan chapter. They succeeded in converting and resettling several thousand people on the upper Magat flats. Among these communities was Bayombong, which was to become the capital of Nueva Vizcaya.

In 1740, the Augustinians transferred this mission field to the Cagayan Dominicans. In the years immediately following, the districts between the middle Cagayan and this upper Cagayan area were brought under military and ecclesiastical control: until then they had been largely terra incognita. Old district names applied by the Spaniards to the valleys and mountains here will be clarified in the appropriate chapters: "Yogad," "Paniquy," and "Difun."

The ecclesiastical survey of 1738 shows the Dominicans just prior to their entry into the upper Cagayan as having 22 principal centers in the valley, together with 8 visitas and missions. Surprisingly, in view of the earlier population estimates, the religious count for the lower and middle valley districts, together with the offshore Babuyan and Batan islands, totaled only "about 25,752 souls." A secular census conducted in 1746 by a military officer, Varona y Velázquez, and used extensively for reference in later chapters, yielded a count for the lower and middle Cagayan communities of 36,646, which was somewhat higher.

The mention here of the offshore islands leads to a special feature of Cagayan history between the 1680's and 1760's: the resettlement of Babuyan and Batan population groups at different points in the lower valley and along the coast. These shifts occurred variously under mission and civil sponsorship, and were designed to bring these isolated peoples more fully within the Spanish sphere. As will be shown, the transplanting process proved a failure, and the islanders were allowed to return to their homes.

In 1718, a major "rebellion" occurred in the lower-middle Cagayan around Tuguegarao. A local leader will be seen as declaring himself "Pope and King"—one of a number of "nativistic" movements in Cagayan paralleling those already noted in the Pangasinan-Ilocos region. In this uprising, even Lal-lo, the earlier Nueva Segovia, was invested, and some of the Spaniards killed. Another major outbreak occurred in 1763 in the middle Cagayan around Ilagan, coincident with the British occupation of Manila and the "Silang rebellion" in Ilocos. In each instance, Spanish punitive measures caused even many townsmen to take refuge in the mountains.

Various observers will be noted later as speaking of the agricultural and other resources of the valley, and of products that filtered down by trade from the mountain peoples. In addition to the older crops, plants from Europe and America were found to thrive, including in some places wheat, flax, cacao, and tobacco. The Italian visitor Careri (1697) speaks of beeswax being traded in abundance from the mountain areas, and being "burnt instead of oil by poor people." He also notes that deerskins and carabao (water-buffalo) horns were being sold to Chinese merchants.

In the period 1780–84, as already noted, the Philippine Government by Royal order established a tobacco monopoly. This action generated resistance in Cagayan as also in Ilocos and the other tobacco-growing areas. Cagayan tobacco, being of extra fine quality, was in special demand, so that in 1781 the peoples of the lower-middle Cagayan and the lower Chico river zones were put under a forced labor system of growing the product. Among its consequences were considerable redistributions of population, as well as changes in the traditional cropping patterns.

Frederic Sawyer, who spent fourteen years in the Philippines during the late nineteenth century, describes this "horrible slavery" through which the "Cagayanes" were compelled to grow tobacco during the century to 1882:

In the villages of that province the people were called out by the beat of the drum and marched to the fields under the gobernadorcillo and principales, who were responsible for the careful plowing, planting, weeding, and tending, the work being overlooked by Spanish officials. Premiums were paid to these and to the gobernadorcillos, and fines or floggings were administered in default. The native officials carried canes, which they freely applied to those who shirked their work.

In order to avoid diversion of labor, Sawyer says, the Cagayanes "were prohibited from growing rice," being at most "allowed as an indulgence to plant a row or two of maize around their carefully tended tobacco." The latter crop was harvested for transport down river in December and January, when the wet season had declined and the leaves could mature without spoilage from rain. This forced cultivation, the writer goes on, was subject to abuses by "rascally agents," and involved "dreadful conditions." In 1882, a proposal to "sell" this Royal monopoly was sidetracked, and Governor General Moriones ended the system. From then on, a private Spanish-French company, the Compañía General de Tabacos de Filipinas, serviced the industry (Sawyer, 1900, pp. 131–32, 193, 252, 253).

Here, as in other parts of the Cordillera, the mountain peoples found illegal tobacco-growing a profitable occupation. Being outside the control of the government inspectors and collectors, they could produce as much as they wished within the limits of their terrain and then smuggle it down to Cagayan or Ilocano buyers. Spanish expeditions frequently struck into the mountains as the tobacco crop ripened, in attempts to locate and destroy the fields.

LATER PERSPECTIVES

In 1839–41, the Cagayan region was divided into two provinces, the northern part remaining as Cagayan, and the southern or upper part becoming Nueva Vizcaya. In 1856, the boundaries of each were cut back to form the third province, Isabela, between them. By that time, Spanish control of sorts was becoming extended to some of the adjacent mountain regions in the wake of "exploring" expeditions, and mission workers were beginning to take hold in more accessible localities.

Census figures for 1818 given in Buzeta's mid-century encyclopedic study show the old Cagayan Province (covering the whole area) as having 61,322 counted persons of indigenous background. There were also 336 Spaniards and mestizos, these latter being nearly all in Lal-lo. In 1846, the reduced Cagayan had a total population of 59,800, paying 14,449 tributes, while Neuva Vizcaya had 22,236, paying 5,410 tributes in 1847. That is, the total counted population was somewhat over 80,000. In 1876, Cavada gives the following population figures:

Province	Total population	Indios	Spanish	Mestizos	Chinese	Filipinos from other districts
Cagayan	71,657	71,082	38	189	278	70
Isabela	36,219	36,087	20	67	45	—
Nueva Vizcaya ..	32,209	32,184	13	9	—	3
Total	140,085	139,353	71	265	323	73

The formation along the Cordillera heights to the west of Abra Province and the Comandancias of Benguet, Lepanto, and Bontoc, as described in the previous chapters, meant that at least vague boundaries were established for such jurisdictions on the Cagayan side. In 1859, a Comandancia of Saltan was established as an adjunct of Isabela Province for the politico-military administration of what was roughly the present Ifugao subprovince. Around 1890, a further series of mountain jurisdictions was formed in a major effort to control the non-Christian groups: Comandancias of Apayaos and Itaves in the north, and of Quiangan, Kayapa, and Binalatongan in the south. The notably marked facets of policy in all such jurisdictions were the establishment of garrisoned forts, the cutting of trails to inter-connect the scattered settlements, and, in the case of missions, the building of chapels that could be used as fortified refuges from aggression. The par-ticulars of these jurisdictions, the boundaries of which were changed from time to time, will appear in the later chapters.

The Filipino revolution of 1896–98 brought to an abrupt end these Spanish efforts. Even in the more pacified mountain areas the old conditions of feuding, raiding, and headtaking, were generally resumed until Ameri-can occupation of the Cagayan region was made effective from 1898 on. With the establishment of Mountain Province in 1908, the Cordillera bound-aries of the Cagayan provinces became established, subject to subsequent minor revisions.

Ahead of the regional studies, note may be taken of two major ethnic trends that have affected the valley populations. First, the Ibanag ethnic group, and especially the Ibanag language, limited in early times to the lower part of the Cagayan valley, spread southward to predominate as far as its upper-middle sections. The speech of this strategically placed group became widely used as a lingua franca for trade, and for governmental and mission affairs. Among many local groups to the south, and perhaps along the northwest Cagayan coast toward Ilocos, the original speech became entirely replaced by the Ibanag, with its written documentation. Malumbres, in his *Historia de Cagayan* (1918a), places the main period of Ibanagization, as it might be cumbersomely called, between 1750 and 1800.

The second major ethnic trend was the movement of Ilocano colonists into the valley. From 1850 to 1897, Ilocanos were given free passages, advances of money, and other inducements to settle as tobacco growers, augmenting the local poulation (Sawyer, 1900, p. 253, and other sources). The first American census in 1903 showed 50,401 Ilocanos. These were living, together with 171,694 "civilized" descendants of the old populations, along the valley floor, and to a very minor extent in the mountainous areas of the three provinces in which 67,567 "wild" people had been accounted for by that time. By 1948, Ilocanization of the Cagayan provinces had progressed to a point where 435,519 persons counted Iloko as their mother tongue, or approximately two-thirds of their total population of 638,301.

REVIEW

This general description of the Cagayan region parallels the opening chapter on the Pangasinan-Ilocos region in giving a frame of reference within which local areas can be viewed. Because of much more varying geographic and human conditions on the Cagayan side of northern Luzon and the segmental way that the region was penetrated over a period of more than two centuries, most records could be put into the area chapters, so that this general presentation could be relatively brief. The opening presentation will deal with the northwest Cagayan area, adjacent to northern Ilocos.

VIII. The Northwest Cagayan Area

PLACE AND PEOPLE

The Cagayan Province today includes a coastal strip extending from the Ilocos Norte boundary for about 50 miles to the Cagayan valley mouth. At its west end, the Cordillera (Caraballo Norte) spurs come right down to the sea, but otherwise there are swampy flats bordering the shore. Back about eight miles, where the forested slopes reach mountain height, is Apayao subprovince.

The northern and central districts of Apayao are drained by a large river system, called in its lower reaches the Abulug, and in its main upper course the Apayao. This waterway debouches on the north coast about 10 miles west of the Cagayan river mouth. Of other rivers draining northward, the most important are the Pamplona and the Cabicungan. Southern Apayao discharges its runoff eastward by way of the Matalag river system into the lower Chico, and so into the Cagayan. In contrast to the Cordillera heights further south, with their grasslands and pine forests, the terrain here falls away into a maze of ridges and peaks rarely higher than 4,000 feet, with the main watercourses at about 1,500 feet. They are rain-drenched and malarial, with dense growths of tropical forest and rank savanna grasses.

Along the coast today, Ilocano settlers are in the great majority. But an older population, also Christian, is concentrated around the Abulug and Pamplona river mouths. At least in modern times it is Ibanag speaking, and it comprises about 6,000 people. In the foothills back of the coast are surviving Negrito bands. Higher in the mountains are the Isneg, numbering about 11,500. Roughly nine-tenths of them live along the main watercourses of the Abulug-Apayao river system. Approximately a thousand are on northern streams of the Matalag system in south Apayao, and will come particularly into the records of the lower Chico river area. Small numbers were seen to have crossed the Cordillera into Abra and Ilocos Norte, and a few are across the border in Cagayan.

Physically the Isneg are slender and gracile, with piercing dark eyes; Cole (1922) places them as most like the mountain Tinguian. They use rafts and flat-bottomed boats for water transport. Hamlets usually have from 3 to 8 houses, and the largest as of 1932 had 24 houses. Several hamlets may be placed a few miles apart along a section of waterway to form a settlement area. Their people in such an area intermarry, and, prior to modern pacification, were likely to be war allies. Leadership is in the hands of influential men who traditionally rose in status through success in war and headtaking, accumulation of ceremonial wealth, especially jars and beads, sponsorship of major festivals and rituals, and polygynous marriages which bring extra women as workers into their house groups. The dog is the key ritual animal; sugar-cane wine is the ceremonial drink; and women shamans provide religious expertness. Magic and medicine are absorbing concerns in the face of war uncertainties and the unhealthy conditions of these malarial forests (see the works of Vanoverbergh and others, summarized in Keesing, 1962).

In discussing recent glottochronological studies of the Tinguian language, it was said that Fox with others (1953) had classed it tentatively in a "Northern Division" with Isneg and Ibanag. The Pittman group (1953) found southern Isneg to be moderately close to an eastern Tinguian dialect, and also to the Batan islands dialect to the north. Marked differences showed, however, between southern Isneg and Ibanag, and also Iloko, northern Kalinga, and Itavi, the speech of the adjacent lower Chico people in the Cagayan valley. Anderson (1960), by contrast, found Ibanag to be moderately close to the southern Isneg, though it was considerably more differentiated from northern and western Isneg dialects. In all instances, however, much could have depended on the localities from which the word samples were taken, e.g., the two Ibanag samples were from informants located in the Itavi-speaking lower Chico and in Ilagan high up the Cagayan valley, neither of them in the basic Ibanag speaking area around the Cagayan river mouth. Vanoverbergh distinguished five Isneg dialects, and Anderson records the same number, the greatest variation being between the southern group and the others.

Along the coast, the principal wet rice crop appears to follow the Ilocano summer-to-winter cycle. A second crop of considerable proportions is also produced around the Abulug-Pamplona river mouths occupied by the older Ibanag speakers, but little double cropping is done by the Ilocanos. Dry rice, too, is grown in appreciable amounts only in the Abulug-Pamplona area. Sweet potatoes and cassava (tapioca) are cropped along the coast, but almost no maize or tobacco.

The Isneg are dry rice cultivators par excellence. Gardens are cleared and burned during a brief drier season around March-April, and the cropping season follows along, after which maize or tobacco is usually planted.

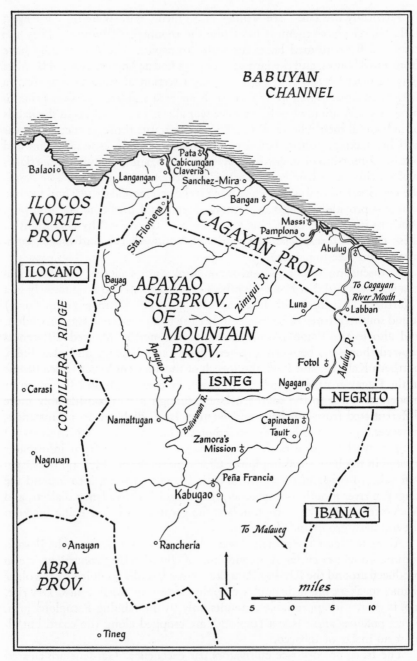

NORTHWEST CAGAYAN AREA

Building and maintenance of terraces would here be ecologically disadvantageous, and government attempts to introduce sedentary wet cultivation have consistently failed. For the Isneg, root crops are of low prestige, with taro preferred over sweet potatoes or yams. Only in the higher, more open country of the Bayag district adjacent to the Ilocos Norte border (the "Calanasa" territory of Spanish records) are sweet potatoes grown in quantity. Dry rice, it was seen, is notably absent in the adjacent mountain districts of northern Ilocos, where the population has been counted "Apayao" (Philippine agricultural censuses, and other sources).

EARLY PERSPECTIVES

The Spaniards coming by sea, and then traversing the coast constantly, were able to "reduce" the coastal settlements more rapidly than happened elsewhere in Cagayan. Their populations were allotted into encomiendas, and the encomenderos resident either locally or more usually at Nueva Segovia ranged out with armed forces as necessary to collect tributes. The 1591 survey of encomiendas, in its "Cagaian" section, lists five holdings here (B&R, VIII, 108):

Cabicunga (the Cabicungan river area): 500 tributes, and 2,000 "souls"; the district "pacified."
Pata (the Pata river area): 200 tributes, and 800 souls; "pacified."
Bangal (the Bangan river area): 300 tributes, and 1,200 souls; "pacified."
Massi (west of the Pamplona river mouth): 500 tributes, and 2,000 souls; "pacified."
Tulaque (the lower Abulug river area, called alternatively in early records Tular, Afulu, Affulug, Abulug): 1,500 tributes, and 6,000 souls; the "greater portion pacified."

According to these figures, the region had 3,000 actual or potential tribute payers, and an estimated total population of 12,000 persons. To the extent that such rough statistics corresponded to the demographic situation —and tribute records of 1588 indicate that the encomenderos of this area must have collected a considerable proportion of the approximately 2,000 tributes actually paid at that time in all of Cagayan (B&R, VIII, 37)—they indicate a moderately dense coastal population, especially in the Abulug district. Such groups would have access to sea foods as well as to garden and forest resources, hence a diversified economic base.

The 1612 ecclesiastical survey, used in previous chapters, shows the Dominicans as having three mission centers in this zone. Two were on the coast: Pata, to the west, needing 2 missionaries for 800 Indians, and Tular (Abulug), needing 2 missionaries for 1,100 Indians "or a trifle more." Additionally a mission had been established at "Potol" about 17 miles inland, up the Abulug river in the Apayao foothills, needing 2 missionaries for 300 or more "new Mandaya converts"—Mandaya, from an Isneg root word meaning "upstream," being the name given by the missionaries to the Isneg people of the Abulug river area. It will be seen below that the Pata and Abulug missions had by that date been in existence for seventeen years, and so were well established and the people Christianized (B&R, XVII, 211).

The striking discrepancy between the total of 12,000 "souls" supposedly in this zone at the time of the encomienda count and this religious census of approximately 1,900 coastal "Indians" two decades later seems more than an error in reckoning, a result of decimation by disease, or a failure on the part of the mission to count hostile or unconverted people. It strongly suggests that under Spanish pressures many of these people had meantime fled into the mountains, as the formula of the time had it. The question is whether the present Isneg people in the Apayao fastnesses, with their firm attachment to waterways as settlement areas, may have lived along this coast and in the adjacent river valleys at the time the Spaniards struck in, so that their occupation of the deep interior occurred only as a rejection of Spanish control. This will be one of the key problems to be tested through further evidence. To give perspective, it can be noted that in 1846 the total population of this coastal area was 8,194. By 1948 it had 43,871, but of this number 37,292 were immigrant Ilocanos.

THE PEOPLE THROUGH MISSIONARY EYES

The records indicate that travelers by sea between Manila and Cagayan frequently used Pata and Abulug as stopover points. These landing places became the first centers of civil administration and mission work. Abulug subsequently was to grow into a port town, with a population that included a small Chinese community, and a busy trade by way of the Abulug river with the Isneg people of the interior and with Negrito bands of the foothill and swamp country.

Aduarte (1640) devotes considerable space to the initial establishment of the missions here. In 1595, after developing centers around Manila and in Pangasinan, the Dominicans sent two fathers to Nueva Segovia, and shortly after that six more were dispatched to start missions in the rural areas. In 1596, under the leadership of Fray Diego de Soria, who was the first Bishop of Nueva Segovia, this group opened their initial station in Pata, and their second in Abulug. From Pata the fathers branched out to establish churches in the other encomiendas of the region, in their most usual spellings Massi, Cabicungan, and Bangan. Abulug correspondingly served as the base for the development of the inland mission work at Potol, or Fotol, mentioned above. Subsequent ecclesiastical surveys of the Dominican establishments in 1738 and 1754 list these same mission centers for the region, though without statistical counts of their adherents (B&R, XXVIII, 159, 174).

Aduarte's account of the start of this mission work opens with the statement that "[this] land was ruined not only by the continuous wars which the villages all wage with one another, but still more by the settled peace which they had all made with the devil."

[His] demands were so great and so grievous that they could not put their hands upon anything from which he did not take tribute, and with which he had not commanded them that they should do him honor by means of some superstition, threatening them with death if they failed therein. They were accustomed to call whomsoever they adored *anito* [i.e., spirit]; and they said that they had a good *anito* to whom they attributed all the good fortune that happened to them, and a bad *anito,* who caused all their hardships, poverty, temporary evils, maladies, and deaths.

Some thirteen pages follow in the Blair and Robertson translation (xxx, 286–98) describing the "wretched state" of these "Indians," delineating particularly religious and social customs. Aduarte describes their religious practitioners in terms meaningful to the modern ethnologist:

[They] employed more priestesses, or *aniteras,* than priests, though they had some of the latter. . . . The devil entered these *aniteras* or sorceresses, and through them, and by their agency, he gave his answers. By these priestesses the Indians performed their superstitious rites and sacrifices, when they wished to placate their *anitos* or obtain anything from them. If anyone fell sick, the *aniteras* immediately came, and with oils and a thousand performances they [sought to cure the patient]. . . . [At] times [the devil] made the people believe that the soul had left the body, and that the *anitera* had restored it by the power of her prayers and her medicines.

This could represent an amateur's description of the ideology and practice of a female shaman among the Isneg today. While they do not have corresponding male practitioners, men may perform sacrifices and read omens in the course of ritual activities. The account goes on:

Before sowing their fields they used to celebrate three solemn feast-days, during which all the men gave themselves up to dancing, eating, and drinking until they were unable to stand; and after this came that which commonly follows— namely, giving loose rein to the flesh. The women did not drink, for this was very contrary to their customs as they are very laborious; but they made up for it as well as they could, and in the dances and all the rest they did as well as the men.

Here, once more, is a fair description, this time of a ceremonial festival as an accompaniment to major work effort and to other high points in the life around such as is still practiced in many forms among the mountain peoples, including the Isneg, and was a forerunner of the *fiesta* of modern lowlanders. Isneg women, too, do not drink on such occasions. The account then describes omen-reading from sneezes and the flight of birds; offerings of food prior to undertaking a journey; sacrifices connected with house-building; and regular feast-days, "like our great ecclesiastical feasts." "Receptacles like charity-boxes" were set out in dark places, as in ravines or cane-brakes, to receive offerings for the *anito*.

Even when they were in plain and open places, and even . . . when things of great value were placed in them, no one dared to take anything out of them, even gold, or stones regarded by them as precious. They also had some places of devotion where the sick went to pray for health, and ate food. When they went home again they were obliged to cast into these places the jars and other utensils . . . [as] a kind of sacrifice. There were different places for different infirmities, while for the chiefs only there were separate places.

At a later point in Aduarte's account another reference is made to these sacrificial places, which were also found by the mission fathers in their work in the Cagayan valley flats, as will be seen in further chapters.

In the province of Nueva Segovia the religious labored hard in the search through mountains and valleys, and other secret places, for the huts where the devil had been adored, to which those people used to make pilgrimages in search of health or other favors, giving offerings of bits of gold, or of stones regarded by them as precious. The natives dared not take anything from those places, or cut a reed or a tree from the natural growth of the earth in them for fear of death. . . . In the villages on the coast many such little huts were found, with many little figures and idols in them. The religious burnt and broke the boxes with the offerings; took the gold and the stones, and all the other offerings; and burnt and ground to dust everything, and cast it into the sea. (B&R, xxxi, 155.)

Later, Ilocano settlers along the coast were to turn up many whole and broken Chinese jars in zones without indigenous settlements, such as the Allacapan area west of Abulug, which may indicate such sacred places as well as former house sites where jars were buried with the dead (Vanoverbergh, 1932, p. 57). The Isneg do not have in their modern religious system such "huts" or "idols," though they do have sacred trees and other places where sacrifices are made, and food and other offerings are left. Jars and other ceramic wares have to be obtained from the coastal peoples, and they tend to be held as valuable heirlooms. A precious jar, however, may sometimes be buried alongside the grave of an important person.

Back to Aduarte's initial materials, "certain trees, flowers, and mountains" were also "dedicated to the devil" (i.e., sacred); these are familiar elements in the beliefs of the mountain peoples today. An account follows of an *anitera* whose master, the devil, had put on her wrists in a dream gold bracelets and "many strings of precious stones." The people are also spoken of as wearing on their wrists "blessed beads," much as do the Isneg and Tinguian peoples in modern times. The mention of beads and "stones," together with gold ornaments, is significant because of the great importance of such items as ceremonial wealth among the Isneg and other mountain groups today.

That this discussion applies to the northwest Cagayan coast is indicated by the fact that the account is interspersed with reference to specific communities. In mentioning "their sort of holy water," Aduarte refers to the village of Massi as using "a certain water" with which they washed the limbs and foreheads of children, especially those of the chiefs. This is reminiscent of Isneg use of coconut oil and under some circumstances water for ritual application and massage, and also in various magical practices. In 1592, before the establishment of the mission, the son of the Spanish Governor of the Philippines stayed overnight in Pata on a voyage along the coast, so that the alcalde-mayor, Captain Mercado, ordered building materials to be cut from a "little hill" nearby to construct huts for the soldiers in the party. This hill was "dedicated to the devil" as being the site for "sacrifices and celebrated festivals," and therefore the Indians offered to bring all the materials needed from other places. But the Spaniards "would not wait so long, and compelled them by force to cut what they needed" from the hill. That night "a frightful wind arose," driving waves up to the camp, so that the official party was "obliged to flee," and valuable equipment was washed out to sea.

Ideas regarding death are described at some length. The soul has to cross a river, transported by a boatman to whom a toll is paid—this is a belief persisting among the modern Isneg. A woman could not pass across unless her hands were "tattooed with black." Food, clothing, oil, and some gold were buried with the dead, and in the case of a chief "one or two slaves to serve him." There was also a belief that "their deceased fathers and ancestors must return to life in this world": apparently referring to the wandering and visitations of ghosts of the dead, familiar among mountain and lowland peoples alike, rather than to any idea of reincarnation. A chief in mourning fasted, "not even eating rice, which is the ordinary bread of that country, or drinking wine—a deprivation which, for a race so fond of wine as this is, must have been a great hardship." When the "people of the village" felt that the mourning had gone on long enough, and it might have lasted "for years" in the case of a loved and esteemed person, they all "contributed to buy a slave," and "before them all the chief cut off the slave's head." This was evidently a commercial alternative to a headhunting expedition, as the account continues:

This, however, was not the most honorable manner of bringing the mourning to an end; for those who could slay anyone belonging to their enemies did so, even though it was a woman, a child, or an old person whom they killed. This was the best way of concluding the mourning, and was accordingly followed most by those who were in mourning.

In the Apayao of later times, the end of mourning could also come when a headhunting expedition honors the dead with a trophy.

Villages, the account continues, waged war among one another "on the slightest occasion." Where arbitration was substituted in the case of a wrong, the offending party might buy a slave and deliver him to the injured group. The latter would then kill him, "not one failing to give him a wound even if he were already dead." In general they "took their enemies by surprise"; to slay anyone "was a great honor among them; and it sufficed to give the slayer the name of a valiant man, and to grant him the privilege of using certain marks of honor reserved for the valiant." The Isneg, up until modern pacification, counted war bravery as the highest value, and successful killing and taking of heads provided the key rungs on the ladder of social status for males.

"Above all," Aduarte says, "they were drunkards, from the greatest to the least, and each of their drunken feasts surpassed all the others."

From this vice all the other vices followed in a troop, as if they were leagued with it; and this drunkenness was continuous, and excessive. . . . [They] regarded that person as happiest who could indulge the most in these vices. . . . [They] envied him who had gone furthest in them, for they regarded him as the most powerful—as indeed it was generally true that the man who had the greatest power was the most vicious.

The generous use of sugar-cane wine (*basi*) especially in ceremonial feasts is again a characteristic feature of the northern mountain peoples. As already noted, an Isneg leader builds up his status through giving such feasts.

Equally worrying to the mission fathers, from the viewpoint of gaining conversions, were the marriage and family usages.

As for their marriages, they came to an end as soon as the husband was vexed with his wife, or the wife with her husband. This was all that was needed on either side, to cause them to separate and to make a new marriage, unless they had children; for they loved their children so much that this tie was sufficient to keep them from separating. . . . The men were allowed to have as wives those to whom they could give a dowry, for it is the husband that gives the dowry. . . . To their equals in rank the husbands gave large dowries, which were practically in the power of the fathers and kinsfolk of the woman. . . . So common was a separation that there was almost no man or woman who had not been divorced from a legitimate wife or husband. This was a thing which caused much trouble when they were to be baptized, since they were living in improper relations of marriage.

This picture, sketchy as it is, hits on several points important in Isneg marriage customs: the paying of a bride-price appropriate to the status of the marrying pair, the ceremonial wealth concerned going not to the bride but to her kin group; the commonness of divorce; the stabilizing influence of children upon the marriage relation. A reference is also made by Aduarte to a powerful leader in the region with two wives.

The behavioral patterns described here deviate most notably from those of the Isneg of modern Apayao in their reference to "slaves." The Isneg social structure does not include slaves or even an institutionalized servant category. It will be seen, however, that the records for other sections of the Cagayan valley give some prominence to possessing slaves, apparently persons captured in war or purchased through regular trade channels. The records also suggest a certain commercial sophistication in matters of intergroup relations, including war, beyond what the Isneg of later times would admit. There is nothing in this sketch of custom, however, that would rule out at least a close ethnic relation between these lowland groups and the mountain Isneg of later times.

THE COASTAL SETTLEMENTS

Aduarte tells of the faith needed by the fathers at this time in venturing unarmed beyond the guarded gates of Nueva Segovia, and so opening themselves to the attacks of this "barbarous and bloodthirsty race"—and through them of the devil. Yet the erection of churches in Pata, Abulug, and then in the Cagayan river mouth area, was "easily done," because they were "very small and poor." Two fathers were placed in residence at each center, while the group leader, Bishop Soria, "went out to visit all the villages, to the great spiritual and temporal profit of the Indians."

The mission in Pata village had the advantage of support from the local Spanish encomendero, Juan Fernandez de Najara, who had taken up residence there, and from the local chief named Yringan who was "devoted to the Spaniards." A cross, indeed, had already been set up by the Spaniards in an attempt to grapple, through prayer preceded by the shooting of arquebuses, with a contagious disease which had caused "many deaths." When, however, the fathers entered this village and others, they had "absolutely no knowledge of the language" (being fresh from Spain), and "not a single person . . . desired to receive the faith."

[The devil] had kept them prejudiced against it—by the threats which he uttered, and by telling them that their ancestors would return and would be greatly grieved to find them under a different law from that which they had followed. Moreover, the works which they saw done by the Christian Spaniards whom they knew there were not such as to cause them to be converted. . . . They had heard of [the fathers], but very confusedly and uncertainly, by reports brought from Pangasinan.

Some villages, such as Massi at first, "refused to admit them" at all. At Pata, though kindly enough received, the fathers "labored much with very small results." Beset by food shortages, they nevertheless worked hard on mastering the language, and in due course were able to "translate the Christian doctrine" into it. At last the "devil's oracles" in Pata, which had been delivered through a sorceress named Fulangan, ceased, as first the children and then the adults finally submitted to baptism, and the chief as a good Christian transmuted into Don Francisco Yringan.

At the village of Cabicungan further to the west, a famous priestess voiced the devil's opposition to the fathers. Unable to "frighten her" by threatening to have her taken to Nueva Segovia or Manila, they sent Yringan to "bring her over." With a headcloth on which one of the fathers painted a cross, this chief was able to terrify the devil so that he "caught up his priestess, and she disappeared." Following this "miracle," the Indians "began to feel respect for the law that the religious preached to them," and a mission center was opened in 1619 at this village.

Pata, Massi, and other settlements of the region were, prior to the coming of the missionaries, under the influence of a "lord," a "very noble and valiant Indian" named Siriban. His rivals told the Spanish alcalde-mayor that he had "many wives," though in reality he had "no more than two." That official had the two women arrested and flogged, though one was pregnant. Siriban then "withdrew to the mountains." Because he was much beloved, his subjects "accompanied and guarded him with great fidelity." This type of withdrawal, it was suggested earlier, could have occurred widely in the face of the encomienda system and other Spanish pressures. In this case, however, Bishop Soria was able to arrange a meeting with Siriban. As a result of the father's assurances, he "came down with his followers to the village of Pata." He and seven other chiefs were later baptized in a ceremony at Nueva Segovia. Don Diego Siriban, as he was subsequently called, "became very friendly to the Spaniards." The mission "harvest of souls" was also enlarged through a "great plague of epidemic smallpox . . . so malignant that it did not leave a child alive," but added greatly to the number of child baptisms. Doubtless such epidemics were a factor in reducing the Indian populations throughout the Cagayan as in other zones of early contact with Europeans.

Further to the east, at Abulug, "a more populous town, the people of which were very proud and esteemed themselves highly," the Indians had given help in building the first church. But this, Aduarte reports, was because the Spanish alcalde-mayor had ordered them to do so. At the same time the chiefs held a council in which it was "agreed to do what they could to interfere with it," and so oust the fathers. The highest ranking chief, Cafugao, with his nephew Tuliau, undertook to voyage to Manila as "ambassadors" to request that the missionaries be compelled to leave. With a "great quantity of gold," which they knew the Spaniards coveted, they set sail. In a miraculous way, storms and calms held back their boat, though not other craft. Furthermore, the chiefs in "Ylocos" told them they were making a mistake, since to "oppose having priests there was to strive in vain." After four months of effort to reach Manila, and in the light of knowledge gained of the Dominican mission work in Pangasinan, they returned home and became converts. Additionally, several miraculous healings occurred which accelerated the turn of the Abulug people to

Christianity. The first rough church, having burned down, was replaced by one of stone and brick. The "village" before long had "more than a thousand inhabitants," and became the most important center in the region (B&R, xxx, 298–315; xxxi, 27).

THE APAYAO MISSION

The ecclesiastical survey of 1612 lists a mission at Potol, or Fotol, serving some 300 "new Mandaya converts." It was called by its full name Nuestra Señora del Rosario de Fotol, and was located about 17 miles up the Abulug river, where swampy flats extend inland along its banks. Malumbres says that the ecclesiastical permit to build a mission here was granted in 1604, and it was founded in 1610. Nine years later, another mission and village of converts was established some 8 miles further up the river, San Lorenço de Capinatan. As described by Aduarte, this second center was near the "remote and craggy mountains" where the Abulug debouched by way of a series of rapids, dangerous in places to the raft and boat navigation used by the Isneg communities. Vague reference is also made to a third mission center called San Cecelia de los Mandayas opened in 1623 (Malumbres, 1918a, pp. 244–45; Vanoverbergh, 1932, p. 28).

Aduarte gives an account of the founding of the Fotol mission, "one day's journey up the river from Abulug." Fotol was a "village . . . in the midst of a number of other smaller villages, as is customary among the mountains." This is a fair description of a series of hamlets in a settlement area, with the mission-concentrated village comprising a larger center.

When these villages were visited [by an encomendero with an armed party] for the purpose of collecting tribute, the religious was accustomed to go along that he might be there conveniently to give them some knowledge of the law of God. . . . This diligence, although it was exercised so seldom—only once a year— was yet not in vain; for the words of the gospel sown in the hearts of these heathen took root and caused them to go down [the river], voluntarily, for the purpose of seeking a preacher to live among them. . . . [The] vicar of Abulug sent there father Fray Diego Carlos.

Because the Spaniards had not dared to visit the village, "except in numbers and with arms" when they collected the tribute, and because Fotol was surrounded by "mountaineers who were heathen, untamed, and ferocious," it seemed to the "Christian Indians of Abulug" that the father ought to have a guard to protect his life. But Fray Diego went with his associate unarmed. "All the Indians, great and small, came out to receive them with great joy. . . . In a short time they did a great work, and baptized not only those of this village, but also those who dwelt near there. They left their old sites and, gathering in this one, formed a new settlement." Capinatan was then established further up the river. The Christian faith "went on flourishing" until the devil, "hating so much good, disturbed them and caused them to fall away for a time" (B&R, xxxi, 285–86).

Aduarte takes up the story of this falling away at another point in his account. After the fathers had "taught and baptized many people," and settled them in the new mission communities, their "affection for their ancient places of abode so attracted them" that they "endeavored to escape to the mountains." Though they were "prevented twice and their efforts came to nothing," they so planned a third attempt, and "kept it so secret," that they "carried out their evil purpose." They even "stirred up the old inhabitants of Capinatan, and persuaded those of Fotol, bringing them to join them by means of threats and prayers." The crisis came in 1625, when three chiefs of the Capinatan area asked the father and lay brother there for "permission to go to some villages on their ancient lands." On being told that the matter would be referred to the "regular minister when he comes," one of the chiefs "cut off the head" of the brother and badly wounded the father. Some Indians, "ignorant of the conspiracy," proposed to take the latter down to Abulug, but the chiefs entered the "house of the chieftainess," where he was lodged, and killed him. The Capinatan people then moved in a body to Fotol, where they set fire to the churches and defiled them. As a result of this "revolt," the converted Mandayas willingly or through force of their fellows, "turned their backs on the faith, fleeing to the mountains" (B&R, xxxii, 147–50; see also a brief reference in Malumbres, 1918a, p. 245).

In the following year a Spanish force was sent to quell this "uprising of the Mandayas." "In order to reduce them, a great number of palms were cut down, that they might the more easily be brought to subjection for lack of food" (B&R, xxxii, 157). Such punitive action, apparently the most that the troops could do without essaying to penetrate the inner mountains, was hardly likely to make friends. It remained again for the missionaries to try to re-establish confidence.

PENETRATION OF INTERIOR APAYAO

In 1631, Fray Geronimo de Zamora was sent to be superior of the Fotol mission. This father made the first venture up the Abulug rapids into the main Apayao settlement area. "[When he] saw that these heathens sometimes came down for trade with the villages, he began to show them some kindness, and to give them some trifles that they thought much of, until at last he secured their goodwill." At first they were "not inclined to the faith or to accept ministers." But in the following year he thought that he could trust them enough to "go up to their villages."

Hereupon he most courageously went up into the mountains . . . taking with him some Indians . . . [who were] acquaintances and friends of the Mandayas. It took him a day and a half of most laborious traveling to reach their first village, for they had to row upstream against the current, which is always strong and in some places terrible. The river runs between great mountains. . . . They received him with great pleasure, and lodged him in one of their best houses, though it was built of thatch after the custom of the country.

Zamora had a building erected next to the house, where he could conduct services, and sent around to the chiefs of other villages to ask them to attend. "They did so readily because of their good will toward him," listening with attention. All said that they "wished to receive him and be taught." He asked "in joy" to be allowed to baptize "their infant sons," and on the following day ten were brought and baptized.

When Zamora proposed to leave, the Indians were "greatly grieved," but he promised that he would return. They "asked for a minister," so that the church authorities assigned him with two helpers to this inland post. Again he had great difficulty in getting up through the rapids, taking "three days." Greeted with "great demonstrations," he soon had baptized over three hundred infants. A chief and his wife and brother were also baptized. "It was marvelous how quickly they learnt so many prayers— not in their own language but in that of more highly civilized Indians. Although they usually all understand this latter, they never speak it among themselves." This statement on the language is a significant one, but it still leaves important questions unanswered. The language of the prayers was presumably the Ibanag speech of the northern Cagayan lowlands, which will be seen in later chapters to have become a lingua franca for much of the Cagayan region. It could hardly have been Iloko (Ilocano), because the missions on the Ilocos coast side were run by Augustinians, not Dominicans. The statement particularly leaves unresolved the vital question whether the coastal groups at the time of Spanish penetration were ethnically of Ibanag stock, or whether they were of Isneg affiliation and so directly related to the inland groups.

The mission fathers went to two villages higher up the river, approaching the locality of the present capital of Apayao subprovince, Kabugao. After welcomes and baptisms, they decided to go back to their first headquarters. Unhappy about this, "the council [of Mandayas] resolved to keep the fathers by force" if they tried to leave. As a compromise, one father, Fray Luis, stayed behind. He reported "great eagerness": they "learned Christianity with ease." "Indians who in heathen days spent a week weaping and mourning dead children, with a thousand superstitions and extravagances before burying them, now accepted readily taking the bodies to be buried in the church."

Within the year more than 500 persons were reported as baptized, and Apayao seemed on the way to Christianization and pacification. The mission father then "left the Mandayas to help workers in the lower villages." To counter the "grief" of the people, he left behind "an Indian, Don Francisco Tuliao, master of camp of Nueva Segovia," possibly the Tuliau of Abulug mentioned earlier.

[He] accompanied the Indians in good work, being also directed to lead a war for the reduction of some Indians near the Mandayas in villages called Ysson [not identified]. They had risen and, being in the midst of mountains, had refused obedience and tributes to the encomendero. This was happily settled, and Fray Geronimo had summoned the chiefs of Ysson with the rest and they yielded. As a token of their fidelity they cut off their hair which is much cherished."

Fathers Geronimo and Luis returned, after furlough periods for their "confessions," and resumed their work. Included in further baptisms were 40 "elderly men." Some missionaries, however, felt that it was unwise for the mission work to "spread so fast," since opinion in Nueva Segovia held that these Indians were "fickle and inconstant, and of small capacity." In rebuttal, the fathers reported that "they have given up killing and wronging their neighbors . . . [and are] so friendly and peaceful that they visit and entertain each other without suspicion." Aduarte's historical account ends on this happy note. (The materials to here are from B&R, xxxii, 226–39).

A Dominican *History* of the next decade by Baltazar de Santa Cruz resumes the "Mandaya" story as of 1639, telling of another insurrection which was "so disastrous that it cost considerable blood and not a few scandals" which are "yet bewailed." The account first belabors the inefficiency of the alcalde-mayor of the province, for having permitted these mountain villagers to be abused:

Although by order of the government [he] had made a fort, with a new sentry-post, in the said Mandaya villages, and had a suitable garrison of soldiers, yet so many were the burdens that they put upon the shoulders of the wearied Indians for their support that the latter considered themselves as conquered. . . . The mine of anger [against ill treatment by the commandant] exploded, because [he] punished one of the principal women, because she had displeased him, by forcing her to pound rice for a whole day; she and her husband were so angry that they became the principal promoters of the insurrection. The nearby villages were invited [to join in the movement]. . . . They entered the sentry-post . . . and killed the sentinel and others who offered them some resistance. They went thence to the fort . . . [and killed] about . . . twenty soldiers who formed the garrison. Five who escaped [were burned to death when hiding].

The attackers killed a Chinese in the convent, but spared the mission father. With his religious and other effects they "embarked him" so that he could proceed down river. They then "burned the church and the convent." No mention is made of the locality of this incident, but it was probably Capinatan (B&R, xxxv, 35, 47; see also a brief reference in Malumbres, 1918a, p. 245).

The record of this mission effort resumes in still another account of the Dominican work, by Salazar, covering the period from 1670 to 1700, that is, several decades later. Fray Pedro Ximinez, another very active worker, was sent in 1684 to the "village of Fotol on the border of Mandaya country." He found the people "in the midst of famine, for the fierce Mandayas of the uplands will not allow them to cultivate their fields." By that time the interior mission had been abandoned, and the converts had apostatized.

Ximinez began a new effort for "a reduction of the Mandayas" by "writing letters to an influential apostate who is living in the mountain regions." This man became so stirred that he "resumes the faith" and aided in restoration of the mission. The devil then set to work by causing an "inhabitant of the village of Nabayugan to murder another heathen whereupon all is confusion and the breathing of threats." Nagbayugan is a name still used today for one of the Abulug tributaries south of Kabugao. The father, "learning that murder may be atoned for by two ways, namely, by fighting or by a fine, promises to pay it himself." Through "ambassadors" he sent a present of shirts, salt, needles, combs, and *tibores* to the aggrieved faction. The latter agreed to accept them, and to descend to Capinatan to meet the father. The "devil upsets the boat" carrying the presents, but Ximinez went upriver to meet them all the same.

After parleying, a party of six, including two chiefs, agreed to accompany the father to Capinatan and then to Abulug on the coast, "a not slight undertaking on the part of these timid people, as they are in constant fear of treachery." They were well received by the commandant of the Abulug "fort." Once more the devil got busy.

One of three heathens who go down to the village of Malaueg [a mission and trading center in the Cagayan to the southeast of Apayao] is killed by the inhabitants of that place, and the other two are seized and sent to the commandant of Nueva Segovia. But the commandant frees the captives and seizes the captors. The former were sent to the father and returned to their people [which thwarted the devil's designs].

A party of 22 of the "heathens" then accompanied Fray Pedro to Aparri at the Cagayan mouth, where the alcalde-mayor "confers on them titles and honors, thus increasing favorable opinion." A village called "Calatug," however, proved "an obstacle to the general peace." Calatug could refer to a settlement of southern Isnegs called today Talifugo on the northern branch of the Matalag river in southern Apayao, or alternatively to a settlement of northern Kalinga called Calafug or Calapug on one of its southern branches. They "are hostile to the Mandayas" (an enmity that has persisted in the case of both groups to the present), having declared that if the latter "become civilized . . . and reduced," they "will attack and kill them." "The Mandayas who wish to become civilized, after holding a council, resolve to ask aid of the alcalde-mayor [of Aparri] against the village of

Calatug, and that aid is promptly promised them." Later, as recounted below, the Calatug people did play a role in destroying this new mission activity.

Reports then came down river of a plot to kill Ximinez. Amid protests from "all sides, including the commandant of the fort at Capinatan" (this is the first mention of its being a military post), he "ascends to the mountains," where he was met with a "joyful reception." Later he went again, and "at that time a church is built which is dedicated to Nuestra Señora de la Peña de Francis." Vanoverbergh places the site of this church in the settlement of Nagsimbanan, just west or upriver from Kabugao, the name meaning "place where the church stood" (from *simban,* "church"), though no trace remains of it today (Vanoverbergh, 1932, pp. 29, 33). Salazar says of Peña Francia: "In 1686 that church numbers more than one thousand three hundred converts and apostates who have come back to the faith. The number of converts in that mission is opportunely increased by an epidemic of smallpox [which led to many baptisms]."

The growth of this work led to the dispatch of two associates to aid Ximinez, and in 1688 he was made an "independent missionary." Then, however, the standard technique of resettlement was initiated: "That increase enabled him to found another village in a district less mountainous and hence less difficult to administer, and soon there is a Christian population of over five hundred people there." The location of this new village is not indicated by Salazar, but records in Malumbres' *Historia de Cagayan* indicate that it was at Ngagan, or Nagan, near Tauit and between Capinatan and Fotol on the Abulug river (1918a, pp. 247, 488). Ximinez took ill, according to Salazar, and found it necessary to retire. "The people of Calatug, still hostile to the Mandayas, assault the village, and all but one hundred and forty of [its people] are either killed or flee to the mountains. Then the alcalde-mayor of the province removes to the village of Camalayugan." Camalayugan is presumably a mission center of that name near the mouth of the Cagayan river, to be discussed in the next chapter. The account then concludes with the added words "and that mission comes to an end" (B&R, XLIII, 72–75).

The record to here covers the early materials on the Isneg as seen from the Cagayan side. They supplement the information given in the northern Ilocos chapter on the more marginal Isneg population west of the main Cordillera ridge. To reiterate briefly: it was seen how "Apayao" groups were first mentioned in documents of that region, when in 1665 Augustinian missionaries began work among them. Converts of the time were settled in mission villages near the coast, but apparently many of them returned to the mountains.

In 1763, the Augustinian, Mozo, described the "Apayao" tribe as occupying the northern part of the Cordillera through an area extending about

"30 leagues." Consisting of "many thousands of souls," they were "cruel and barbarous."

For not only are its men continually going about, placing a thousand ambushes in the roads, in order to exercise their rage on the wretches who have the misfortune to fall into their hands, without sparing any person, no matter of what rank or condition he may be; but they have, besides, a specially barbaric custom and cruel superstition at the funerals and obsequies of their chiefs and other persons whom they respect.

After a long digression showing similarities to Greek and Roman funerary customs, Mozo goes on:

[Because] they believe that the shades of the deceased take delight in human blood, they endeavor to give them this pleasure by killing people—a greater or less number, according to the station of the dead man. To do so, they avail themselves only of those whom they capture for this purpose . . . as soon as the dying man has ceased to breathe. . . . They assemble a considerable number of men, and, some taking one road and some another, they go down from the mountains well armed, and hiding in the brushwood near the roads, they wait . . . for some passers-by. . . . [They then] attack them with great fury, and kill them with their javelins. . . . This done, the assailants cut off their heads, and . . . carry them to their own dead, and place the heads about him. After this they celebrate their sort of banquet, at which they eat and drink like beasts; and when this is finished they complete the burial. Placing in the tomb some portion of food and drink, they bury the corpse with those heads, being greatly . . . satisfied at having pleased the shades of their dead, and believing that through this whatever they undertake will have a prosperous issue.

This is a reasonably accurate account of the Isneg usage of conducting a headhunt as part of the ritual connected with the important dead. Mozo goes on to tell of the reopening of mission work among the western Apayao in 1720, as recounted in the northern Ilocos section, though its vigorous prosecution again lasted for a brief period only and converts were settled outside the mountains (B&R, xlviii, 81–87).

Apparently few further efforts were made during the Spanish period to Christianize the inner settlements of Apayao. Church centers were continued into the eighteenth century at Capinatan and Fotol, and their names appear in several religious surveys of 1738–54 (B&R, xxviii, 160, 174; xlviii, 131). A survey of Cagayan made by Varona y Velazquez in 1746, quoted by Malumbres (1918a, p. 310), shows Fotol in 1746 as having 320 people, and Capinatan 178. The latter center also had 7 Spanish soldiers and a corporal, together with some lowland soldiers and a chaplain. Both had fortress-like stone churches, the ruins of which still exist overgrown with forest today. As seen in the Ilocos study, a Dominican father, Fray José Tomás Marin, traversed Apayao on two trips in 1740–41, one from Fotol to Dingras in Ilocos Norte via the upper Abulug, and the other into south Apayao and on to Anayan in what is now Abra Province.

Fotol, Capinatan, and Ngagan were finally abandoned in 1769. The Christians were transferred down river, first to Simayung nearer the coast, and then in 1818 to Abulug, Camalaniugan near the Cagayan river mouth, and other lowland areas. Even an attempt to reopen the Fotol mission in 1890 proved unsuccessful, and not until 1925 did the inland Isneg have direct mission work resumed among them (Vanoverbergh, 1932, pp. 31–35).

CONTINUING RECORDS

Once Christianized, the coastal settlements of the area receive passing mention only in the documents. Fathers came and went, and occasional "miracles" or other notable events were recorded. The "devout" Don Francisco Yringan, spoken of earlier, was made "governor" of the Pata area. Some Indian women in confessions accused themselves of having "eaten *buyos*" on fast days, the *buyo* being a betel quid, indicative of the fact that betel chewing was then customary as it is in Apayao and other northern mountain areas today. When about 1623 one of the pioneer fathers, Fray Miguel de San Jacinto, died at Massi, "the Indians of the villages of Abulug, Massi, Pata, and Cabacungan gave him the most costly funeral honors within their power, and made up a subscription for more than five hundred masses, which at four reals apiece came to more than two thousand." Here the coastal communities are seen as meeting peaceably in a common enterprise. In Massi, a communicant, Sebastian Calelao, received divine aid: "His sown rice had not sprouted on account of the drought; but, in response to his prayers, God sent rain so that his crop was saved." This is the nearest hint in all these records to the type of cropping practiced along this coast. The references would appear to be to a natural rainfall, or dry rice crop rather than to an irrigated crop (B&R, xxxi, 33; xxxii, 147).

The Pata-Cabicungan area in the extreme northwest corner of the province adjoining Ilocos Norte was important for communication by both land and sea. Malumbres (1918a, pp. 274–75, *passim*) refers to a Dominican record of 1633 that speaks of the extraordinary number of Indians passing back and forth along a trail through this area with loads of goods. At Cabicungan a "chapel" was built in fortress style as a "bulwark against invasions": these could come from the sea, as with Japanese, Chinese, and Moro attackers, or by land from the interior, or in the course of disturbances among the coastal populations.

In 1661, as seen in the northern Ilocos chapter, an anti-Spanish movement flared up in the Laoag area under leaders headed by "King" Almazan. As told by Díaz, they gained the support of the Cabicungan and Pata people, and also called upon the "Calanasa tribe" to help them: "heathen barbarians who lived in the clefts of the mountains and other rocky places

... their only occupation [being] the killing of men and animals." A record is given of happenings at Pata:

The Dominican . . . Fray José Santa Maria, hearing the tumults and shouts of the rebels . . . went out of the convent, against the advice of a Spaniard who had taken refuge in it. . . . [But] as soon as the rebels saw him many attacked him; and, piercing him with many javelins, they cut off his head, and with great delight went to sack the convent. . . . [The Spaniard, with mission servants loading guns for him] accomplished so much that the rebels, persuaded that some company of soldiers were inside the church, retreated.

It is not clear whether this headcutting represented a revival of venerable custom among the coastal people, as happened in some comparable movements, or was done by "Calanasas" from the interior. In the face of Spanish punitive forces, the disaffected communities submitted, and the Calanasas "retreated with all speed to the woods" (B&R, xxxviii, 205–10).

By this time, something of a balance of relations appears to have been established between the coastal and interior peoples. Isneg and Negrito parties came down to trade, though doubtless hostilities occurred at times. Murillo's 1744 map shows the settlements at Cabicungan, Pata, Bangan, Massi, Abulug, Fotol, and Capinatan. In 1743, some Babuyan islanders were settled at Tagga and several other points a short way up the Abulug river. The 1744 Varona survey of the Cagayan population shows them as numbering 349. But in 1769 this population group was transferred to the northeast Cagayan coast, as will be seen in the next chapter.

In the nineteenth century, affairs became dynamic once more with the progressive settlement of Ilocanos along the coast. By the last decades of the century, Ilocano settlers were pressing up the river valleys as fishermen, lumbermen, and homesteaders. Records of the time show determined efforts by the mountain groups to halt such encroachments, and some major raids were even made upon the coastal settlements, so that the Christians did not venture far from them except in armed parties. In 1890–91, two politico-military jurisdictions were formed in the region to advance security and pacification: a Comandancia of Apayaos on the Cagayan side, with headquarters at the old Capinatan; and a Comandancia of Cabagaoan on the Ilocos side, as already seen, with headquarters at Laoag.

LATER PERSPECTIVES

A brief survey can now be given of further statistical and other information available on the various zones of northwest Cagayan, not least of all because changes were to occur in settlement patterns and place names which had obscured in some respects the early history as traced here.

First, the coastal centers may be reviewed in briefly tabulated form, the population figures for 1746 being from the survey by Varona y Velazquez, and those for 1818 and 1846 from Buzeta's survey.

Abulug. This is the only community that has continuity up to the present. Population: 1746, 1,113; 1818, 2,243; 1846, 2,994. Buzeta's description emphasizes its significance as a port and trading center.

Massi–Pamplona. Massi had a recorded population in 1746 of 666. Several other settlements grew up around it, notably San Juan somewhat inland on less swampy terrain. In 1818 the latter was the principal center, and Massi one of its visitas: the area population was 1,927. In the early nineteenth century, manufacture of palm wine made it a thriving center. In 1841 the communities were consolidated further inland under a new name, Pamplona, and joined by groups from Pata and other old settlements to the west. Malumbres quotes an 1877 document describing the Pamplona people as sparing in food and drink, but showy in clothing, miserly in the necessities and prodigal in the luxuries, ceremonious in religion yet in life dissolute (1918a, pp. 410–11).

Bangan–Sanchez-Mira. The old Bangan mission never became a large center. In 1746 it had 499 people, but the 1818 census omits mention of it. By the mid-nineteenth century the principal pueblo was called Nalaqui, which had Bangan as one of its barrios, and was a minor trading point for ceramic wares and other goods. As Ilocanos moved in, some at least of its population shifted to Pamplona. In 1894 the settlement was reorganized and named Sanchez-Mira, after a Cagayan Province governor.

Pata–Cabicungan. In 1746 these old trade route centers had populations of 374 and 302, respectively. By the early nineteenth century the area began to fill up with Ilocano migrants, particularly under a scheme promoted by Governor Claveria. The 1818 and 1846 counts do not list either settlement, and Buzeta notes that the newly formed Pamplona included "descendants" of the Pata people. Malumbres says, however, that they moved first to the Bangan area (1918a, pp. 274–75, *passim*). In 1865 the old Cabicungan was reorganized as an Ilocano settlement under the name Claveria. Other Ilocano settlements in the area include Cadcadir and Langangan; there is also one of Isneg converts, Santa Filomena.

The later history of Fotol, Capinatan, and the other interior missions has been discussed already. Malumbres describes a map of the Apayao area prepared in 1778 by Fray Antonio Feijas. It showed 57 settlements then situated along the waterways of central and southern Apayao. Many of these had names corresponding to existing Isneg hamlets, indicating the considerable permanence of the Isneg residential pattern. For some settlements, Feijas recorded the number of houses, the totals running from as low as 6 to as high as 66, with most of them having from 15 to 30. Isneg hamlets of later times were noted as being considerably smaller. This suggests either that the population total has diminished in the last two centuries, or that it has become more spread out (1919, II, 390–92).

Accounts of the Apayao or Isneg way of life given by Buzeta and Schadenberg during the nineteenth century have already been quoted in the northern Ilocos chapter. Reference was also made to one of the Augustinian documents assembled by Perez (1904) in which an unidentified writer described the mountain populations of the north as of 1890. He speaks of three principal trails connecting Ilocos Norte with Apayao. A surprisingly accurate survey is given of the names and localities of Isneg settlements. They are listed in four regional categories: the "Apayaos," in the lower Abulug river area, with 24 rancherias and 2,540 people; the "Calanasanes," in the western or Bayag district, with 13 rancherias and 1,516 people; the "Balioananes," on the Baliwanon tributary, with 6 rancherias and 748 people; and the "Cabugaoanes," in central and south Apayao with 57 rancherias and 6,872 people—a close approximation to the statistical picture shown in the initial American census of 1918.

The full pacification of Apayao had to await the opening of the twentieth century. After preliminary explorations by Worcester and other Americans, a Philippine Constabulary port was established at Tauit in the lower Abulug. When Mountain Province was established in 1908, the region was constituted as Apayao subprovince, with Tauit as its first capital. Various conflicts occurred, and numbers of the Isneg became runaways, some crossing into the Ilocos Norte and Abra mountains. In 1912–13, Tauit was attacked by Isnegs of the lower Apayao settlements, after which they fled inland. The major source of grievance was the migration of Ilocanos into the lower Abulug river in the wake of the new government authority. After a decisive defeat by the Constabulary at Waga, a truce was negotiated; but the Isnegs have never returned in any numbers to the lower Abulug districts. In 1916, the capital of the subprovince was moved upriver to Kabugao.

Almost nothing is recorded of the Negrito along the mountain fringes of Apayao until the twentieth century. Their unobtrusive bands ranged from the swamps of the Cagayan valley east of Apayao to the Claveria area. They also worked occasionally for Ilocano colonists, especially in lumbering operations. Isnegs expressed astonishment when Worcester told them that they should refrain from fighting the Negritos (1914, p. 436).

MODERN CENSUS DATA

It was noted earlier that the encomienda estimate of 1591 added up to 12,000, whereas the 1612 mission survey yielded a figure of 1,900. Varona's record of 1746, excluding the Babuyan islanders, shows a coastal population of 3,522. The 1818 census published in Buzeta indicates a rise to 4,170, and his figures for 1846 yield a total of 8,194, paying at the time 1,301 tributes. For the interior mountains of Apayao, prior to its complete exploration and pacification, guesses as to total population numbers ran as high as 25,000.

In recent times the Cagayan Province strip became divided into five municipal units, comprising from west to east Langangan, Claveria, San-

chez-Mira (the old Massi and Bangan areas), Pamplona, Abulug, and Ballesteros. The 1903 Philippine census showed a total population for the
area of 21,219, and by 1918, the figure had risen to 24,509. Subsequent totals
are 40,446 for 1939 and 56,156 for 1948.

The 1948 census distinguished the principal language groupings by
"mother tongues" as follows:

Municipal unit	Total population	Ibanag	Iloko
Langangan	1,095	—	1,094
Claveria	12,703	155	12,519
Sanchez-Mira	10,611	26	10,505
Pamplona	8,029	3,282	4,503
Abulug	11,433	2,714	8,671
Ballesteros	12,285	33	12,121
Total	56,156	6,210	49,413

It can be seen that the overwhelming majority of the modern coastal
people are of Iloko-speaking origin, and they now form almost the only
population element in the three western districts. In Ballesteros, which is
a new municipal unit formed in the ten-mile stretch of swampy coast between the Abulug and Cagayan river mouths, the population is likewise
almost exclusively Ilocano. It might be expected that, if the Ibanag speakers
of today were an ethnic extension of the Ibanag of the Cagayan valley lowlands, there would have been a continuous settlement of Ibanag along this
intermediate coastal strip. But, as the figures show, the only concentrations
of Ibanag speakers are in the Abulug-Pamplona area. That is, Ballesteros
has been opened up by Ilocanos in modern times.

The 1948 census does not distinguish speakers of the Isneg and Negrito
languages by districts, putting them in an "Other" category. In the 1939
census, however, totals were given for the number of "speakers" of these
languages, though in some instances they could have been Ibanags or Ilocanos who made bilingual returns. The 1939 figures showed 202 Isneg
speakers, of whom 176 were in the Claveria municipal unit, 16 in Sanchez-
Mira, and 10 in Abulug. The Negritos numbered 1,266, of whom 977 were
in Abulug, 261 in Pamplona, and 8 in Claveria. In the religious category
of "pagans or not belonging to any religious group," the coastal districts
had a total by that census of 1,625 persons.

The 1918 census, the first to be taken after Mountain Province was
formed, showed 9,330 Isnegs and 774 Negritos in Apayao subprovince. The
1948 census showed Apayao as having a total population of 19,357, of whom
10,207 were in the predominantly Isneg districts of Kabugao, Bayag, and
Conner; Luna, comprising the old lower Abulug settlement areas, with
9,150, was rather solidly Ilocano. In terms of language, Mountain Province in 1948 had 11,135 "Apayao" or "Isneg" speakers and 305 "Negrito"

speakers, in both cases nearly all in Apayao. If those outside Mountain Province are counted, the Isneg appear to be holding their own in population numbers at about 11,500 during recent decades, but the Negrito groups in this northwest Cagayan zone are dwindling.

REVIEW

The ready hypothesis here is to consider the Isneg people as offshoots of the northwest Cagayan coastal population. Moving particularly up the Abulug-Apayao river system, they would have adjusted their culture to the specialized mountain habitat. Certainly no close historic relation seems to exist with the Ilocos peoples further west, while likenesses in custom to the mountain Tinguians could be interpreted partly as old shared elements and partly as adaptations to generally similar ecological conditions.

Interesting questions arise, however, regarding the ethnic background of the coastal population, now so confined and Ibanagized. The records suggest that the people here were not originally Ibanag. What was said in the northern Ilocos summary about the possibility of northern Luzon having in earlier times a variety of small linguistic and ethnic groups applies to this area as to others. Yet the picture is still incomplete. Besides the need for materials to be filled in on the Ibanag, there is another valley group called Itavi adjoining Apayao on the southeast side (the lower Chico river area of the Cagayan), which must be taken into account. The Isneg, indeed, will be seen as having important dealings with this group as well as with the northwest Cagayan coastal settlements. South of the Isneg, too, are dry cultivating "northern Kalinga" peoples who are relevant to the picture. Again the ethnohistoric survey must await its full analysis in the final chapter.

IX. The Lower Cagayan Area

PLACE AND PEOPLE

This zone comprises roughly the northern half of Cagayan Province, that is, the valley floor from the Cagayan river mouth to the junction of the Chico river some 30 miles inland, together with the northern sections of the Sierra Madres that extend along its east side. On the west side, across an almost impenetrable terrain of swamps and foothills, lies Apayao sub-province. The Cagayan-Apayao border runs some 10 miles west of the course of the Cagayan river.

The northern Cagayan shore line has, back of a sandy beach, a tangle of estuaries and swamps, usually densely grown with *nipa* palm. To the east in the Cape Engaño region, the coastal flats give way to rugged mountain spurs that come down to the sea. On the Pacific side, the Sierra Madre drop particularly steeply into the ocean. The Cagayan river flows in its lower reaches through low hills, opening out in places into flat lands. It carries a tremendous volume of water, and has a bar that is dangerous to navigation at its mouth. Tributaries join it from east and west, notably the Dummon and Paret-Paranan on the Sierra Madre side, and the Sicalao and Sinundungan draining the Apayao margins. The 1932 Coast and Geodetic Survey map shows a large part of this latter area "Unexplored."

The ethnohistory of the lower Cagayan is primarily concerned with the Ibanag ethnic group, for which it appears to have been the main homeland. No detailed studies are available of their physique and customs, but they share the general patterns of Christian lowlanders. Approximately 18,000 Ibanag live in this area today, but they are now outnumbered about five to one by Ilocanos. Negrito bands rove west of the Cagayan river around the Apayao border, and also in the Sierra Madre fastnesses. These districts away from the main river course will also be seen in the records as being retreats for runaway groups, so that they became targets of mission effort. Like the offshore islanders who were brought temporarily to the mainland, they either have moved back to their homes or else have become assimilated into the modern Ibanag milieu.

As was seen in Chapter VIII, the glottochronological relations of Ibanag with adjacent languages are imperfectly defined for want of good word samples. Comparisons to date suggest that Ibanag is moderately close to Isneg, Itavi, the local Negrito speech, and the offshore Batan islands language, called Itbayat. The limited Pittman group studies suggest that the differences increase considerably when Ibanag is compared with Gaddang and Yogad, and become much greater in the cases of Kalinga and Ifugao. Anderson (1960) also shows very marked contrast between Ibanag and the latter two languages. No material seems to be available on dialect variation within Ibanag. Malumbres states that it exists in "purest" or most basic form in the area from the Cagayan coast to Gattaran, north of the Cagayan-Chico junction (1918a, pp. 13–14).

The Ilocano-Ibanag communities in the flat swampy districts around the Cagayan river mouth produce two wet rice crops yearly, and this double cropping is also done on flats around Gattaran further upriver. Considerable quantities of dry rice are grown in the hilly Calayan district along the coast toward Cape Engaño, and also in the Dummun and Paret-Paranan river areas east of the Cagayan. Maize is grown in fair amounts, the climate making possible two or even three crops annually. Sweet potatoes are produced in quantity, especially in the hilly areas east of the Cagayan, and the same is true of cassava (tapioca). Although the districts near the coast produce little tobacco, this crop is grown extensively in the Gattaran area, and the river valleys further east (Philippine agricultural censuses, and other sources).

EARLY PERSPECTIVES

The 1591 survey of encomiendas shows the general pattern of settlement found by the Spaniards in the lower Cagayan (B&R, viii, 108). From the coast to the Cagayan-Chico junction they were listed as follows:

Camalayuga (the present Camalaniugan area near the Cagayan mouth): 500 tributes, and an estimated total population of 2,000 "souls"; "pacified and paying tribute."

Camanaguan (the Camannauan area, along the coast east of the Cagayan mouth): 300 tributes, and 1,200 "souls"; "pacified."

Tocol (the area of the later Tocolana mission somewhat upriver from Nueva Segovia): 100 tributes, and 400 "souls"; "pacified."

Gotot (apparently the Gangoc area north of Nueva Segovia): 600 tributes, and 2,400 "souls"; "one or two settlements pacified."

Maguin and Taviran (probably the coastal area around Buguey east of the Cagayan mouth): 500 tributes, and 2,000 "souls"; "unpacified and hostile."

Manacu ("adjacent" to Sinavanga and probably on the Cagayan bank): 100 tributes, and 400 "souls"; "friendly persons."

Dumon (Dummun river, flowing east from the Cagayan about 24 miles from the coast): 800 tributes, and 3,200 "souls"; "hostile."

LOWER CAGAYAN AREA

Talapa and Gatara (the present Gattaran area on the Cagayan): 500 tributes, and 2,000 "souls"; "hostile."
Talanauga (possibly the present Agganatan, below the junction of the Cagayan and Chico): 50 tributes, and 200 "souls"; "hostile."
Nasipin and Buto (the Nassiping area at the Cagayan-Chico junction): 600 tributes, and 2,400 "souls"; "all in rebellion."

Subject to the uncertainty of such estimates, presumably made by the encomenderos who had taken up residence at Nueva Segovia and were eager to get tribute paying under way, these figures show a total of 5,050 actual or potential tributes and 20,200 people.

In 1612, the Dominican ecclesiastical survey showed the following mission centers: Camaluyuga (Camalaniugan), 3 ministers for 600 Indians, or "a few more or less"; Bagunbaya (the present Bagumbayan) just south of Nueva Segovia, 2 ministers for 100 Indians; Tocolana, somewhat further up the Cagayan, 3 ministers for 1,000 Indians; and Asiping (Nassiping above, at the Chico junction), 2 ministers for 700 Indians, or "a few more." The total Indian population, therefore, after about a decade and one-half of reportedly successful mission work, was placed at about 2,400 (B&R, xvii, 211).

This early period, as has been indicated already, was a very disturbed one, with great hostility to the Spaniards, and much "apostatization." The discrepancy between the total of 20,200 in the encomienda estimate and this figure of 2,400 suggests, therefore, that many of the lower valley people, among whom the administrative and military center of Nueva Segovia was established, moved away in the face of Spanish controls, exactions, and punitive measures. The report, for example, of the De Chaves expedition quoted in the general chapter spoke of villagers in this region as going "to the mountains." For perspective, it may be noted that in 1846, prior to the coming of Ilocanos in force, the lower Cagayan had a population of slightly less than 14,000, whereas in 1948 the total of those counting Ibanag as their mother tongue was 17,547.

The early descriptions of settlements, foodstuffs, and other facets of culture in the general survey of the Cagayan undoubtedly apply primarily to the Ibanag as being the group immediately accessible to observation from the Spanish townsmen getting established in Nueva Segovia. Once more, Aduarte (1640) is a source for greater detail on local communities and their early contacts with the Spaniards. His record starts with an account of the defeat of a Japanese "fleet" in 1581 by the Spanish colonizing expedition under Captain Carrion, with whom a Dominican father was serving as chaplain. The Japanese were "desiring to have control of this region because of the abundance of products which it yields that are lacking in Japan." After an inconclusive encounter with a Japanese vessel that was "prowling along the coast and pillaging it," the Spaniards entered the Cagayan river mouth and, passing by the main Japanese fleet, "went up the river and intrenched themselves on land"—the site of the later capital. Their fort withstood Japanese attacks, and then subsequent attacks by the local Indians after the Japanese left.

The Spaniards accordingly suffered much hardship, want, and hunger, because supplies from Manila came very slowly, while they had in that country nothing but cruel war. At the same time, they were much aided in their purpose to remain in it by the many factions and wars among the Indians, who could not live in peace and were constantly slaying one another.

At Camalaniugan, on this "large river," a "valorous Indian by the name of Guiab" had "raised himself above the others" and at the head of three hundred followers was in "a fair way to make himself lord of the province" —a hint of the possibly small and scattered character of settlements. Admiring the power of the Spaniards, he "strove to procure their friendship by sending them a great present of rice, chickens, large fat hogs, and other products of the land."

But as Guiab had oppressed many of the people . . . and had frightened all, they went to the Spaniards, begging them not to ally themselves with Guiab. . . . [On] this account the Spaniards, proposing to gain the good will of so many, caught Guiab and hanged him on a tree. The event was altogether the opposite to what they had expected; for all the Indians retreated from the Spaniards and began to make open war upon them, often challenging them to lay aside their arquebuses and to come out into the field, man to man.

This description of a strong warrior leader, patterns of intergroup hostility, and misunderstandings of the acculturation frontier, appears to ring particularly true. A story follows of bitter enmity in this same locality between two brothers, one of whom, Tuliao, captured the other and held him for a long time in a "cage": "brother was unable to trust brother, and no man left his house unarmed."

He who had the greatest power made as many slaves as possible on any ground, no matter how slight—even for taking a single stalk of sugar-cane, when the poor people were dying of hunger because they could not cultivate their fields on account of the wars. Many of them went, of their own will, to eat in the houses of the chiefs, in order to save their lives, and in this way became their slaves.

Aduarte goes on to say that the Spaniards, by "the aid of some of the Indians against the others, conquered many of their villages, though at the cost of many deaths."

The Dominican father who accompanied Carrion returned to Manila soon after the founding of Nueva Segovia, and was succeeded by Augustinian fathers. These built up a "monastery" in the capital, but "undertook no ministry to the Indians."

They even felt that a mission to them was impossible because of the excitement of the Indians resulting from the many homicides committed among them by the Spaniards. . . . Besides this these Indians were so warlike that not even a religious [i.e., a father] went out of the town except in a company of soldiers and with arms; nor did the encomenderos go to collect their tributes without an escort of many soldiers, coming back immediately with anything that the Indians were pleased to give them.

The conduct of the secular Spaniards, Aduarte relates, was "so little Christian" that the Augustinian fathers felt it wise to leave them and the Indians "in their dissensions." The church buildings were neglected and misused. In 1955, however, with the establishment of the Bishopric of Nueva Segovia, the Governor of the Philippines requested the Dominicans to re-establish religious work in the town, and their first two fathers were sent there (B&R, xxx, 272–85).

Aduarte describes in a later section a meeting of the mission group under Fray Diego de Soria, the first Bishop, to plan the opening of their work among the local communities. Essentially they saw it as a campaign against "the devil."

[They] perceived that he was very active among his Indians; for the religious frequently heard them (sometimes by day but ordinarily by night) in the villages about the city, named Daludu and Tocolana, and in the houses in the fields in that vicinity, making a great noise with their voices and their *gasas*—which are their bells, though they are not formed like our bells. . . . [They were] making sacrifices to the demons; for, induced by their diabolical industry, they . . . [were] offering special services to the devil, and . . . striving to appease him by feasts, that he may keep and preserve them in their ancient rites and customs. (B&R, xxx, 300.)

The reference to *"gasas"* is to brass gongs, still used among the mountain peoples of northern Luzon in rituals and festivals. There is also a glimpse here of the presumably characteristic residential pattern, namely, of having a centralized "village" for permanent residence and houses adjacent to the fields for occupation during work periods. Unfortunately, the records never make clear whether wet rice cropping was practiced in this lower valley area when the Spaniards arrived, but this was probably the case. The general tenor of early descriptions already quoted, including the fact that a *Relation* of about 1586 speaks of the people as "fine husbandmen," suggests that they used irrigation techniques on the flats.

Following the initial establishment of mission centers on the northwest coast, as reviewed in the previous chapters, two fathers were sent to found the mission at Camalanuigan, about three miles north of Nueva Segovia on the Cagayan river bank.

The Indians there are among the most intelligent in those provinces. They were very friendly with the Spaniards, and gave them great help in pacifying the whole country, by their great fidelity and continued assistance in the wars which took place. . . . The chief and lord of this village was so rich that, if we were to believe his vassals, or even some of the old soldiers who were there at the time, he weighed the gold he had with a steelyard, as iron is commonly weighed. Afterward, however, he suffered from the vicissitudes of fortune, and lost the greater part of his property.

The leader pictured here suggests the status pattern, noted as still characteristic of the Isneg, by which a man could rise to the top through war prowess and wealth manipulation, yet dwindle again in authority, rather than the more or less hereditary aristocrat of the wet rice mountain areas or the modern cacique of the lowlands.

In spite of their general friendliness to the Spaniards, the Camalaniugan people "showed so little pleasure at having [the fathers] in their village that no one visited them or spoke to them, except to ask when they were going to depart." But they were not forcibly opposed, so that it was possible to build a house and then a church: "like the rest, poor and small, and with a roof of thatch." Malumbres gives a date of 1596 for the ecclesiastical foundation of this church, dedicated to San Jacinto. The plans of the fathers were a matter of much speculation; women looked at them by stealth only, and "ran away like so many fallow-deer" if one was encountered; and their heavy robes caused the "most wonderment of all." However, as the story of the mission happenings in Pata and Abulug had reached this area, "the Indians did not find the missionaries quite so strange, or treat them quite so badly, as they did at those places."

Almost immediately, Aduarte continues, the fathers branched out to form a second mission at Buguey, along the coast eastward from the Cagayan mouth. For a time both these missions were annexed to the Dominican convent in Nueva Segovia; but as new centers were formed at Tocolana and other points further up the valley, Camalaniugan and Buguey became separate mission establishments. Progress in making conversions was slow at first, since "their evil ways of living had been sucked in by them with their mothers' milk, and, having been continued by them all their lives, they had become second nature." But "within a few years" the fathers were fully accepted, and districts without them were asking to have them sent. The case is cited of a "great Indian chief named Bacani," evidently in a district inland from Nueva Segovia, but not identified by name:

This man . . . offered in his own name, and in that of the other chiefs of his tribe, to gather in one village more than a thousand inhabitants, and for this purpose to leave his own villages and estates. The reason for this was that the villages were so small and scattered that it was difficult to give instruction among them; and hence the offer was made that many of them would assemble together in a new village, in some cases one or two days' travel distant from where they had been living.

Here is a clear picture of a scattered hamlet settlement pattern, possibly a concomitant of a dry cultivation system in some hilly zone. The leader had evidently become familiar with the mission-supported policy of concentration, which will be specifically described in some of the records that follow. Whether this group lived on the Cagayan valley flats or in the foothills along its flanks is not made clear, so that the quotation does not help clarify the problem of whether wet rice cultivation was present in the area prior to Spanish times (B&R, xxx, 316–20).

Nassiping, or Nasiping, founded as a mission in 1604 at the junction of the Cagayan and Chico, is a particularly interesting center because it provides some rough clues to population numbers. As noted above, the area had an encomienda population in 1591 estimated at 2,400, and a mission population in 1612 of 700 or a "few more." By 1625, according to Aduarte, the mission registers showed that in the first twenty-one years more than 3,400 persons were baptized (B&R, xxxi, 203). If the above mission figure of somewhat more than 700, say 750, were to be taken as the population baptized or available for baptism as of 1604, and the birth rate for the group is set at the reasonable figure of about 40 per thousand per year, the number of additional births over twenty-one years would total around 950. The baptismal total would then have become some 1,700 persons. But the baptismal register had more than 3,400 names. This suggests, therefore, that the population of the Nassiping area as of 1604 was nearer 1,500 persons. Such calculation, however, is complicated by the fact that the mission geography of the time is quite uncertain. Dominican records cited by Malumbres indicate, for one thing, that as early as 1598 a mission center called "Dummung" had been established somewhat northward of Nassiping: presumably on the "Dumon" encomienda and near where the Dummun river joins the Cagayan. This mission appears to have been in existence for a brief time only. In 1623, too, a separate mission center was established at Gattaran, somewhat further north still. The encomienda list shows estimated populations in these two places as 3,200 and 2,000, respectively.

In the general chapter, a variety of references built up a picture of the capital, Nueva Segovia, and its surrounding communities, together with the often disturbed conditions pertaining to their early history. Morga (1609) said of the "city": "It has two hundred Spanish inhabitants who live in wooden houses . . . [and] is two leguas from the sea and port. . . . There is a stone fort near the city for the defence of it and the river. . . . The city abounds in all kinds of food and refreshment at very cheap prices" (B&R, xvi, 147).

The distance of Nueva Segovia upriver, while providing security from water-borne attack, called for the development of a port at the Cagayan mouth. This settlement, named Aparri, was for most of the seventeenth century an extension and visita of Nueva Segovia. Malumbres notes that in 1604 the port was given a "licence to build public edifices," and in 1625 a vessel was supplied by the Governor to the "sentinels of Aparri." Duties here evidently comprised not only watching for Spanish ships and piloting them across the rather treacherous bar, but also keeping a lookout for Japanese and Chinese vessels, friendly or otherwise, and for pillaging Islamic raiders. In 1680, Aparri's growing importance justified a separate civil and ecclesiastical establishment.

The valley settlements of the lower Cagayan are referred to occasionally in Aduarte's further materials: the tenure of various fathers; miracles and other evidences of progress in the faith; and changes in the organization of the religious establishment. In Camalaniugan a father "drove a demon out of a woman who was possessed"—this is a not infrequently reported happening, in some instances the women being "aniteras." In Aparri an image turns away a threatening fire. In Nassiping a woman of faith had her "field of maize protected by the Lord" during a bad locust infestation—indicative of the establishment of that crop in the valley. By about 1637 Aduarte could write of the region:

The Indians . . . have not only become very devout toward God, but very friendly to the Spaniards; thus the religious have put peace and security where they were not before. As a result, in regions where soldiers and garrisons used to be necessary, there are now none, and the country is very peaceful. (B&R, XXXI, 25, 141, 203; XXXII, 145.)

THE SIERRA MADRE MISSION

As the valley flats came more or less fully under civil and mission control, attention was turned not only to the Apayao mountain fastnesses (as seen in the previous chapter) but also to the Cape Engaño and Sierra Madre districts to the east. The Dominican fathers approached this area by working along the coast from Buguey, establishing a mission variously called Vangag, Vuangac, Ibangac, or Palavig. Its initial base appears to have been located in the Wangag, or Wangan, river area near the present town of Gonzaga. Here the flats between the beach and the Sierra Madre foothills narrow toward Cape Engaño. Salazar's *History* dealing with missions of the 1670–1700 period says:

That mission is composed of . . . Indians of the opposite coast of [Cagayan] province, who fleeing from the village of Paranan [Palanan] and from other villages, inhabit those mountains, where they are safe because of the inaccessibility of those ridges. Among them are some Christian apostates and many heathen who were born in the mountains.

The Palanan people referred to here fell within the sphere of Franciscans working up the Pacific coast, and will be discussed in Chapter XI. Salazar's information, however, seems incomplete, as many of these mountaineers evidently were runaways from Cagayan valley communities and some possibly from other northern Luzon provinces. Mora, for example, in a quite detailed report on a visit to Cagayan in 1805, speaks of the Engaño area as "home for many fugitive people from Cagayan and other Provinces and many Negritos, who occupy themselves in a search for wax and betel-nut [for trade]" (Malumbres, 1918a, p. 343). Doubtless new refugees from the various "rebellions" fed this pool of people from time to time.

The founding date of the mission at Vangag must have been somewhat before 1653, as in that year, according to Salazar, Fray Juan Uguet established a new center further inland at Palavig, "on the brow of those [Sierra Madre] mountains"—that is, evidently in the Palawig river headwaters near the northeast cape of Luzon. Many people were then baptized, and "others reconciled from their apostasy," so that they settled at the new center. "They were then frightened by the Indians of the village of Buguey, and they consequently returned immediately to the mountain, and the mission was abandoned and destroyed, and all the toil of the father came to naught through the persuasion of those bad citizens." Possibly here a pattern, which will be seen later in the upper Cagayan, was involved, namely, that of a Christian lowland community opposing Christianization of mountain groups to whom they supplied trade goods, through the fear that their profitable commerce would be destroyed. Some "new" mission fathers then persuaded the people to return to Palavig, but they "afterward left it again because of the annoyances which they suffered annually from a commandant who goes to that district to watch for the ship from Acapulco." This is a reference to a "centinela" or lookout point maintained near Cape Engaño from which the arrival of the Spanish galleons was watched for.

In 1718, the fathers transferred the mission center back to the coast, settling at Bauag, or Bavag, apparently the present Bawa area. From there they moved back to the original mission center at Vangag in order to "draw those people from the mountain whence they had gone." For the same reason, they shifted once more to a coastal site several miles east of Buguey, called Dao, which at the time of Salazar's record, shortly before 1742, was the mission headquarters, though still referred to as Vangag. Finally, according to Malumbres' later account, these people were shifted to Buguey itself (1918a, p. 408). Dao was also for a time a settlement point for Babuyan and Batan islanders: the Varona survey shows 993 settlers in the area as of 1746.

Salazar's record tells of two fathers who, traveling in the mountains, were transported across a river by Negritos:

Those blacks of the mountains are very barbarous and ferocious, above all the other inhabitants of Cagayan. . . . [They] flee from the water even more than from fire; for every night in order to go to sleep, they make a fire in the open, and sleep on the cinders or hot ashes; but they will never bathe or wash, in order not to get wet.

As noted earlier, these northern sections of the Sierra Madres had been inhabited in modern times only by Negritos. Evidently any Malayan-type refugee groups who did not choose to settle in the Buguey area returned in due course to their homes, or else moved southward further from the coast into the inner valleys east of the Nassiping-Gattaran area which, as will be seen, have had "infidel" populations into modern times.

CONTINUING RECORDS

Ecclesiastical surveys of 1738 and 1754 (B&R, xxviii, 159, 174) list the Bishopric headquarters at "Lalo" (Nueva Segovia), and also the old church centers of "Camalayugan" (Camalaniugan), Tocolana, and Nassiping; additionally, there were centers at Aparri at the Cagayan mouth, Gattaran, and Buguey, with its associated mission of "Ibangac" or "Vuangac," just discussed. The 1738 survey gives a total population count of 25,752 "souls" for the whole Dominican establishment through the lower and middle Cagayan and in the Babuyan and Batan islands off the Cagayan mouth, a figure underlining the continuing sparseness of population in the pacified and Christianized regions. An indication of what proportion of this total number were in the lower Cagayan may be gained from the Varona survey of 1746, which shows for this zone a total population of 8,791, paying 1,932½ tributes. The Murillo map of 1744 shows Aparri, Buguey, and "Guanguan" (Vangag) on the coast, Lal-lo, Camalaniugan, Gattaran, and Nassiping upriver, and "Palagut" (Palavig) in the Sierra Madres.

In 1738, a new mission was opened in an area west of the Cagayan-Chico junction, and near the present Apayao subprovince border. It was directed at a group called "Aripas," occupying fastnesses of the upper Sinundungan river area. This locality has virtually no population today. The site of the principal administrative and mission settlement of the time, called Aripa, was about 6 miles northwest of Tabang on the lower Chico river, and the mission was opened by following a trade trail through the foothills from that center.

The "Aripas" do not appear to have been described specifically in the records. They might have been Negritos, or else outposts of the southern Isneg, provided some of this group were living considerably further east than has been the case in modern times. Almost surely, however, they were runaways who had fled from the valley settlements into the rugged country west of the Cagayan. In 1739, just after the mission was founded, a number of Christianized Kalingas were transferred into the Aripas area from a settlement called Orag, south of Tuao, also to be seen in the next chapter. They were part of a group of converts brought down to Orag from the mountains, part of which is now Kalinga subprovince. These resettled Kalingas broke into factions, and the group spoken of here received civil and ecclesiastical permission to move to the Aripa country "under the leadership of Bitagun and Anog" (Malumbres, 1919, ii, 389-90).

Though various records mention the founding of this mission, its continuing work is vaguely reported. Varona in his 1746 survey speaks of Aripa as having a population of 91 persons, this presumably the total who had settled in the mission center. A hundred years later, Buzeta speaks of the Aripas as "peaceful infidels," suggesting that the mission had made at most limited headway by that time. Malumbres, writing in the twentieth century, says that the people of the district had by then "scattered among the pueblos of Itaves," that is, the Chico river settlements to be seen in the next chapter, and presumably this meant that their conversion had been completed. He also notes that the bell of the abandoned Aripa church was still preserved in Nassiping (1918a, p. 344).

LATER PERSPECTIVES

As in previous chapters, a brief summary can be given of later statistical and other information by localities. First, the lowland centers may be reviewed, the statistics being from the Varona survey of 1746 and Buzeta's 1818 and 1846 figures.

Aparri. This port center tended to wax at the expense of the upriver capital, and was at its heyday around the 1860's before sea traffic gave place increasingly to roading. Population: 1746, 1,988; 1818, 3,871; 1846, 5,905. This is the one lower Cagayan district where the Ibanag group has not become greatly outnumbered by Ilocanos.

Buguey. This old center, together with Vangag, and the coastal strip east to Cape Engaño, remained outside the mainstream of Cagayan affairs. Buzeta describes Buguey in 1846 as having "45 to 50 miserable houses." Population: 1746, 530 (Buguey 322, Vangag 208); 1818, 644; 1846, 421. In modern times Ilocanos have virtually taken over this coastal area.

Camalaniugan. This farming area shows population count as follows: 1746, 1,814; 1818, 2,388; 1846, 2,178.

Nueva Segovia. Called in later times Lal-lo or Lalloc, it was described in 1746 as having 43 Spanish residents, together with a cadre of Spanish officials and military officers, with Filipino army and navy personnel mostly recruited from Pampanga Province; there were also 823 *naturales*. Nearby were the old Tocolana and Bagumbayan, with 557 and 435, respectively, and a new settlement, Siguiran, with 807. Mora, visiting the capital in 1805, records it as having 349 Europeans and *mestizos*. Buzeta's description at the mid-century speaks of the town as made up of 362 houses, together with the old government and mission buildings. The district population in 1818 was 2,523 and in 1846, 3,343.

Gattaran–Nassiping. The weight of importance swung back and forth between these two communities. In 1746, Gattaran had 399 people and Nassiping 346. The 1818 count speaks of the former as a visita of the latter, their combined population being 1,188. Buzeta by mid-century records Gattaran as ascendant, with 1,160 people, and the Nassiping community down to "about 500" people. The more favorable terrain around Gattaran fostered this trend, and Nassiping lapsed to the position of a visita. By 1897 a census cited by Malumbres shows only the name Gattaran, with a population of 2,148. In that year, however, Nassiping was reconstituted ecclesiastically. It showed a count of 875 in the 1903 census; Gattaran by then had 2,152.

The picture that emerges over the period for the "infidel" populations to west and east of the lower Cagayan is surprisingly vague, considering the extent of traffic up and down the river. Varona's 1746 count, besides showing 91 persons in Aripa west of the Cagayan, as noted above, recorded 914 persons in the "Paranan" area east of Gattaran. In Buzeta's mid-nineteenth-century survey of this section of the Cagayan, the significance of these outlying populations is underscored by the fact that he gives a total figure for the Gattaran area, counting both Christians and "infidels," of 11,180, and for the Nassiping area, with both groups counted, of 10,493: or a combined figure of 21,673. The figures Buzeta gives for the two pueblos as quoted above (Gattaran 1,138 and Nassiping about 500) appear to represent at least the bulk of the settled Christian population. The rest, not far short of 20,000 in number, therefore, must have represented the estimates of the time for the more or less uncontrolled "infidel" groups in the wild country to the east and west.

Buzeta's reckoning here, so far as it concerned peoples west of the Cagayan river, could have included not only the "Aripas" but also the Isneg people of the central Apayao fastnesses. Population estimates for the latter would have been a matter of guesswork at the time. On the east side, he was evidently recording estimates of infidel populations occupying the Dummun and Paret-Paranan river systems back into the Sierra Madre fastnesses. (The Paret was at that time called the "Fulay.") These groups, like the ones to the north of them which were targets for the Vangag mission, appear to have been predominantly refugee populations from the Spanish-controlled areas. Malumbres tells of their intergroup hostilities and incursions against the settled communities (1918a, pp. 370–76).

In 1787 a Christian settlement called Fulay was established as a southern outpost at Nassiping at the junction of the Paret (Fulay) river and the Cagayan. This became the present town of Alcala (which will be discussed in Chapter XI). Its prime purpose was to provide a communication link with the settlements further south, but it also served as a center of attraction for the infidel groups up that tributary. It will be seen that Alcala, and especially a town called Amulung, a short distance further up the Cagayan, subsequently became organizing centers for mission work along the Paret-Paranan river system. In 1896 the establishment of a civil and ecclesiastical center called Baggao some distance up the Paret marked important progress in the conversion of these peoples. By the time of the 1939 census, the Gattaran-Nassiping districts showed the only non-Christians left to be about 200 Negritos back in the Sierra Madre foothills. The Alcala-Amulung-Baggao districts together had slightly less than 200 non-Christians, these also Negritos. By then, the rest of these eastern "infidel" populations had evidently settled in local Christian communities or had scattered elsewhere in the valley.

MODERN CENSUS DATA

For the lower Cagayan zone as a whole the 1818 census figures yield a total of 10,614, compared with Varona's 1746 total of 8,791. Buzeta's 1846 record shows somewhat less than 14,000 people in the controlled settlements, plus numerous non-Christians. By 1903, when the first American census was taken, the indigenous groups had added to them the growing number of migrant Ilocanos. This census showed a total population in the lower Cagayan region (exclusive of Apayao, which was still part of Cagayan at the time) of 44,876, and this number had risen by the 1918 census to 55,262. Subsequent census totals rose to 97,718 in 1939, and 102,707 in 1948.

In modern times the region has been organized into eight municipal units: Aparri, Buguey, Gonzaga, and Calayan along the coast, and from north to south along the Cagayan river Camalaniugan, Lal-lo, Allacapan (near the Apayao border to the west of the Cagayan), and Gattaran. The 1948 census distinguished the principal language groups by "mother tongue" as follows:

Municipal unit	Total population	Ibanag	Iloko
Aparri	24,974	9,531	14,880
Buguey	14,530	744	13,765
Gonzaga	10,811	90	10,659
Calayan	3,501	33	3,448
Camalaniugan	7,708	2,282	5,419
Lal-lo	10,703	2,462	8,223
Allacapan	4,638	72	4,417
Gattaran	25,815	2,333	23,085
Total	102,707	17,547	83,896

Here, too, it is seen that the Iloko speakers had become easily the majority group by this time. Ilocano immigrants, moreover, comprised almost the whole population of formerly little-inhabited areas along the east coast toward Cape Engaño and westward of the Cagayan in the Allacapan area. The Ibanag speakers were concentrated in the old residential areas along the Cagayan river. The low Ibanag total, not much greater than Buzeta's count of approximately 14,000 persons in the region, seems surprising in view of the rapid rate of over-all increase of lowland groups during the last century in the Philippines as a whole. It evidently relates primarily to the southward movement of the Ibanag population, to be seen more fully in later chapters. Only in the port area of Aparri have Ibanags gained substantially.

The 1948 census does not give separate figures by districts for the smaller language groups, putting them in the general category of "Other." The 1939 census, however, did list "speakers" of these languages, though in some cases Ibanags or Ilocanos might have claimed competence in them, making bilingual returns. That census showed 1,351 in the Negrito group, distributed as follows: Allacapan municipal unit 414, Lal-lo 303, Buguey 272, Gattaran 208, Gonzaga 124, Aparri 24, Camalaniugan 6. An impression is gained from these figures that the remaining Negritos have moved in modern times from the remoter fastnesses of foothill and swamp areas nearer to the larger settlements with which they trade, and where lumbering and other jobs may be open for casual money earning.

REVIEW

This chapter has shown the Ibanag in what seems to have been their homeland prior to their great expansion up the valley, to be seen in subsequent chapters. In the foothill margins, Negrito groups attest to the older history of the area. The story of runaway populations, and of the resettlement of offshore islanders, adds dynamic threads to the record of Spanish times.

In the final chapter the possible ties between the Ibanag and the Isneg will be discussed. In the next two chapters the relation of the Ibanag to the Itavi and other groups adjoining them to the south will also be described.

X. The Chico River Area

PLACE AND PEOPLE

The Rio Chico de Cagayan, or "little Cagayan," has its sources in the high axial center of the Cordillera, and as such it vies in importance with the Agno and Abra in shaping the ethnohistory of the mountain peoples. In its headwaters are Lepanto settlements, with those of the Bontok somewhat down river. Entering Kalinga subprovince it continues northwest through mountains gouged deeply by its swift waters and by those of its tributaries. In northeast Kalinga it levels out in a maze of foothills and swamps. In Cagayan Province it continues through flats and foothills, joining the Cagayan river in the Nassiping area.

In its higher reaches within Kalinga, the most important tributary is the Tanudan, which drains rugged country along the Ifugao subprovincial border. On the west side, the Saltan river rises along the Abra border, cutting a long valley that joins the Chico near the Cagayan border. Along this valley ran an old trail connecting Cagayan with Abra, and so with Ilocos. Northward is the Mabaca river, and betwen the Saltan and Chico the Bananid river. Lower down, the Chico receives the runoff of southern Apayao by way of the Matalag river system referred to in the northwest Cagayan chapter.

The lower Chico flats are homes of the Christian ethnic and linguistic group called so far Itavi, but also referred to as the Itaves, Ytabes, Itawis, or Tawish. No ethnographic study of them is extant. Numbering nearly 12,000, they have been joined by many Ibanag speakers, and are outnumbered today by Ilocanos. The lower Chico settlements concentrate on growing tobacco as a commercial crop, since the local soil and climate produces perhaps the best tobacco in the Philippines. They also produce a wet rice crop, and also a fair amount of dry rice on hilly slopes. Maize is the food crop second to rice, with two or even three cropping cycles. Little double cropping of wet rice is done, and root crops are minimized.

The name "Kalinga" is an Ibanag word meaning "enemy," and was

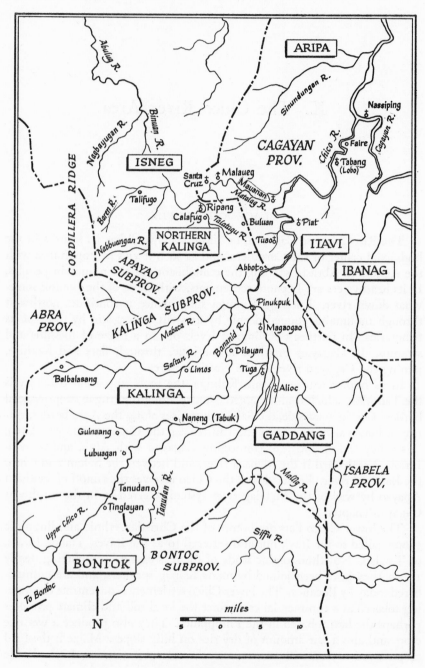

CHICO RIVER AREA

widely used in Spanish times for mountain peoples adjacent to the lower and middle Cagayan valley. In American times it was applied particularly to the subprovince and people in this eastern part of the Cordillera. Barton has provided detailed ethnographic information on the Lubuagan district of central Kalinga, and Dozier has recently studied the Saltan and Mabaca groups. It is also known that the upper Saltan communities adjacent to Abra show strong marks of Tinguian infiltration, and the Tinglayan communities adjoining the Bontok higher up the Chico are transitional to that ethnic type. Yet there is still much to be learned about the congeries of people classed under the Kalinga rubric. In Apayao, for example, on the southern streams of the Matalag river system, there are several hundred people who for want of better classification are called "Northern Kalinga." Spanish writers, it will be seen, used a variety of district and ethnic names in characterizing the Kalinga groups. Beyer, in his 1917 survey of the Philippine population, was led to say: "[They consist] of several distinct peoples who are now so exceedingly mixed in physical type, language, and culture that it is difficult if not impossible in the state of our present knowledge to separate the constituent groups and define their distinguishing characteristics" (1917, pp. 49–50).

In the higher southern areas such as the Lubuagan district, the people live in rather large villages and have extensive wet terracing systems. Their house styles, clothing, social structure, and other usages differ markedly from those of the Bontok and Ifugao further south. They grow dry rice on the slopes as well as great amounts of wet rice, the latter now under a double cropping system, so that this upper region is often called the "granary of Mountain Province." The Kalinga walling techniques represent another distinctive version of terracing. Though courses of stone are placed at the base of the wall, as in Bontok, they are topped with an inward sloping earth wall, which is less economical of space than the Bontok construction method. Like the Bontok, the Kalinga use carabao for trampling the soil.

Further north, where the elevation falls away, dry cultivation of rice and root crops becomes the rule. Though this seems the ecologically suitable adjustment in these northern Kalinga districts, and correlates with sparse populations and hamlet-sized settlements, wet terracing has been spreading into the area in modern times. Scott (1958) gives a vivid account of this new terracing, which is often poor except where expert Bontok workmen are being employed. Among variants of the pattern is an area of wet terracing in the upper Saltan, which may have spread from the Abra Tinguians, and the use of the banana as a staple among Pinukpuk people near the Saltan-Chico junction. The Kalinga peoples generally use high color in woven materials, and with their often elaborate traditional ornaments have been called the "peacocks" of the Philippines (see Worcester, 1912, 1913, for illustrations).

Glottochronological studies, as already noted, appear to indicate a moderately close relation between Itavi, Ibanag, and Isneg. Surprisingly, both the Pittman group and Anderson found a very marked difference between Itavi and the immediately adjacent Kalinga dialects of the Pinukpuk and Tabuk districts. This contrast increases in word lists for Kalinga districts more or less according to their distances upriver. Each of the five Kalinga groups analyzed by Anderson (1960) had a different dialect, and the degrees of variation corresponded closely to their distances apart. The differences between the Kalinga dialects and the Bontok speech, higher up the Chico, are very marked, but less than those distinguishing them from Itavi. Tinguian-Kalinga linguistic relations are not yet well defined; as seen earlier, Ifugao shows somewhat greater contrast to Kalinga than does Bontok. The Fox group tentatively classed Kalinga in the "Central Division" of mountain languages.

EARLY PERSPECTIVES

The first records speak of the Chico, before it was known in its higher zones, as the "estuary of Lobo," a name still used for a village on its banks. The peoples on its lower reaches call it the Bangag or Vangag. The country around became known as "Ytabes" or "Itaves."

The encomienda survey of 1591 lists only one holding, "Lobo," with 4,000 tributes, and 16,000 "souls," described as "all hostile." The Dominican mission census of 1612 lists the local mission under the title of "Pia on Lobo creek," requiring 3 ministers for 2,000 Indians—again a great numerical discrepancy. Aduarte, writing in 1640, describes the Christianized villages as constituting more than 2,500 "tributes." If he meant that this number of payments was collected, rather than being the tribute-paying group, it gives at the four-to-one rate a population total of over 10,000. For perspective it may be noted that in 1846 the lower Chico districts had a total population of 7,622, while the 1948 census shows 11,488 persons counting Itavi as their mother tongue.

In 1604, according to Aduarte, three "religious" were sent to the "estuary of Lobo and the country of the Ytabes," and established two initial church centers, Lobo, called later Taban or Tabang, and Pia, at the present town of Piat. A third was added in 1612 at Tuao, further up the Chico (B&R, XXXI, 204). In a document published about 1594, the names of Taban and Tuao also appear in a list of villages "subdued" by Spanish troops, suggesting that military force had been used in the area more than a decade earlier (B&R, IX, 82). By 1604, conditions had evidently become very disturbed, for reasons which Aduarte shows:

All these Indians are heathen, and though by nature they are very tractable . . . and concerned with nothing but their agriculture, still the outrages of those who took tribute from them [i.e., the initial expeditions and the encomenderos] were so great that they enraged the natives and obliged them to take up arms, to the great loss of the Spaniards.

The record speaks of "the courage and valor of this tribe," as a result of which the Spaniards were "very fearful of them." But soon, through the mission efforts, they were changed from "bloodthirsty wolves to gentle sheep." One of the three fathers is quoted by Aduarte as saying that "their reformation has been great and marvelous," as they "have gone from one extreme to the other, almost without any intermediate state." Before that,

they were so free, so completely without God or law, without king or any person to respect, that they gave themselves up freely to their desires and their passions. Evidence of this is found in those wars which they were constantly waging among themselves, without plan or order; and in the drunkenness and the outrages of which they are guilty. . . . He who was most esteemed among them was the greatest drunkard, because, as he was the richest, he could obtain the most liquor. He who slew the greatest number of men was regarded as superior to all the rest. They married or unmarried daily, with one or many wives.

The value system, summarized here, it may be noted, could again, as with the northwest Cagayan coast peoples, be a superficial characterization of modern Isneg behavior. Aduarte's account continues:

[The] religious instantly laid a general interdict upon all their ancient vices; obliged them to consort solely with their lawful wives; even forced many to abandon their land and their old villages, that they might come where teaching was given them; and, in a word, compelled them to enter all at once, and in a body, into ordered ways of living. . . .

After the religious went among them, they were gathered into large villages that they might be more easily instructed in the faith, having been previously scattered among many small ones, like so many farmsteads. There were three villages thus formed: one of about five hundred tributes, named Taban . . . and the other two of more than a thousand tributes each . . . Pia [Piat] . . . [and] Tuao. . . . Thus all the people were brought together and united, to reduce them to settlements, and to a civilized mode of life and government; and to the church . . . [with] all the fields around [the villages].

This account contains the tribute figures discussed above. It gives every indication of a shift, under mission auspices, from a dry cultivation way of life in small hamlets, such as is found among the Isneg and the northern Kalinga groups of today, to the wet cultivation village economy and society characteristic of the lowlands in later times.

Aduarte's account goes on to tell of the reduction of sicknesses and deaths as a result of medical aid given by the fathers. In this context, he speaks of the "ancient days of superstition" as follows:

[When] a man fell sick he generally died, because he was treated only by the witchcraft of the aniteras, whose sole purpose was to get gold from the sick person by false promises. The sorcerers did them no good and indeed rather harmed them, since cures came from our worst enemy, the devil.

Here, too, the female medium or shaman appears as in modern Apayao and other adjacent mountain zones.

In 1623 a shrine was set up on "the road between Pia and Tuao" to contain an image that had originally been at Pia but had been sent to Tuguegerao in the central valley further east, and was now being returned at the request of the Pia people. On the day it was consecrated, "more than ten thousand persons were gathered together" from the now peaceable villages. Various subsequent miracles are reported, including heavy rains coming to needy areas as a result of prayer (B&R, xxxi, 204–12). Salazar's later history of the Dominican missions (1742) tells how a mission father, Fray Juan Yniguez, who was sent in 1688 to Tuao to develop work among the mountain peoples (see below), was also "charged to learn the language peculiar to . . . the Ytabes," "which he did" in "the short space of six months, and reduced it to a very detailed grammar" (B&R, xliii, 78). Here the fact is made explicit that the area had a distinctive speech.

Following the establishment of the three principal mission centers, a fourth was opened in 1617 at Malaueg, a settlement that in modern times has had its name changed to Rizal. This center is located in foothill country about 10 miles westward from Piat on the Matalag river, and some 2 miles from the southeast border of the present Apayao subprovince. It is a fair assumption that the mission fathers, in establishing Malaueg as a base, were following in the wake of refugees who had fled up the river in the face of the initial Spanish pressure and control. It quickly became a well-established Christian community, and as records assembled by Malumbres in his *Historia de Cagayan* show, it served as an important point of contact and trading center for the non-Christian peoples in the mountain fastnesses further west.

SOUTHERN APAYAO: THE SANTA CRUZ MISSION

Salazar speaks of how crucial it was in dealing with the "heathens" of the mountain areas, whether the Spanish "forts" had good or bad commandants. His record tells of three persons who visited Malaueg from the Apayao fastnesses, one of whom was killed in the settlement, and the other two seized and sent to the commandant at Nueva Segovia. To the surprise of their captors, the commandant seized them instead and freed the captives to be returned by the mission fathers to the home area. Salazar also speaks of the warlike people of "Calatug," to whom reference was made in the chapter on the northwest Cagayan coast. They were seen as either southern Isnegs of the Talifugo district or northern Kalingas of Calafug or Calapug, both settlements on Matalag tributaries west of Malaueg. The record as of 1670 rather prematurely claims that "the fierce dwellers of the village of Calatug are reduced to the faith" (B&R, xliii, 74, 92).

In 1693, according to Salazar, the front of mission work was shifted somewhat further up the Matalag river to "a place called Gumpat near a visita of Malaveg [i.e., Malaueg], called "Santa Cruz." This center became known as Santa Cruz de Gumpat, and its sphere of work as the Santa Cruz mission. Salazar describes the founding of this enterprise by Fray Joseph Galfaroso as follows:

While vicar of Malaveg, he, not being satisfied with the administration of the said village, made various entrances through the neighboring mountains in search of the heathens who lived in them, in order to lure them to the bosom of our holy faith. These mountains are rough and broken, and the heathen who inhabit them are very brave, and give the Christian villages much to do with their continual raids and assaults with which they keep them terrified.

Note must be taken here of a variation from this account, set out in 1932 by the pioneer mission father in the Apayao of modern times, Father Morice Vanoverbergh, as a result of using Malumbres' historical volumes and some other Dominican records. Vanoverbergh dates the founding of the Santa Cruz mission as 1614. He also places the location of Gumpat at the modern settlement of Ripang, or Conner, on the Matalag river inside the Apayao border and nearly 4 miles southwest of Malaueg. Here, he states, traces of old mission walls are still visible (1932, p. 28). It was noted above, however, that Malaueg itself was not even founded until 1617, some three years after the date mentioned.

Vanoverbergh's reconstruction suffered from the fact that Malumbres' records of the Santa Cruz mission as given at different points in his three histories are not consistent. Malumbres apparently gathered more information during the period of his inquiries and revised his materials accordingly. In an appendix to his first volume dealing with Cagayan as a whole, he gives 1614 as the date of the "ecclesiastical foundation" of "Santa Cruz de Gumpat." But in a fuller description of the mission center he speaks of Gumpat or Lingay merely as "mentioned" in "acts of capitulation" at that time. Only in 1692, he says, when Galfaroso brought together there various Christian refugees along with infidels from mountain areas did it become important (1918a, pp. 393, 446). In his third volume, which includes the special study of Mountain Province, Malumbres speaks of Santa Cruz as having been established "toward the beginning of the seventeenth century" (1919, ii, 390–92). Salazar's account, noted above, states that a Santa Cruz had been in existence as a visita of Malaueg, but that the Santa Cruz mission was established by Galfaroso in 1693 at Gumpat near this settlement.

An additional check on the founding date of this mission is provided by a highly useful Dominican map reproduced by Blair and Robertson and already referred to in Chapter VII (B&R, xxxi, 289). These authors date this map at "circa 1641," but since several Cagayan ecclesiastical centers, which will be seen as not established until the period 1678–88, are shown by name, it must have been drawn after the second of these two dates. For the locality being discussed, however, it shows Malaueg as the only mission center, and Santa Cruz is not indicated as being in existence. The inference is that the map was really drawn between 1688 and 1692–93, the latter being the time of the move to Gumpat. The chronological placement of this map is important for dating other mission areas elsewhere in the Cagayan area.

The locality of Santa Cruz de Gumpat also has a somewhat elusive character in the records. Vanoverbergh's statement that its ruins still exist at Ripang would place it nearly 4 miles southwest of Malaueg. But Malumbres' first volume places Gumpat "northwest" of Malaueg. He also quotes the Varona survey of 1746 as locating it "half a league" or less than 2 miles beyond Malaueg. After the founding of Santa Cruz, he says, "construction was begun at different places in this mission of stone buildings of which the remains still exist, but which were never finished" (1918a, pp. 310, 393–94). This last statement might then account for the Ripang ruins. In his subsequent history of Mountain Province, however, Malumbres states that the mission center itself was shifted at various times. He describes it as "flourishing" at first, but does not place its original locality. Then it "declines."

[It] was [then] shifted to the proximity of the [junction of the Matalag with the] Bay river, then next to Quinalian, and later on to Buluan, a sitio near to Dapmui to which came down over 3,000 infidels. . . . After the death of father Sampso they returned to the mountains, having previously killed some Christians, and the remainder moved back to Quinalian, which is situated about two miles from Malaueg. (1919, pp. 390–92.)

Though the river name "Bay," described here as the second site of the mission, does not appear on modern maps, a Dominican map of the Apayao area drawn by Feijas in 1778 shows it as a tributary of the Matalag which branches southward and then divides into the Nabuangan and Talitugu. Ripang is at the junction of these two streams, so that it could well have been the second locality in which Santa Cruz was placed. A settlement point a little further south up the Talitugu still bears the name "Santa Cruz." The "Buluan" referred to in the Malumbres' account is evidently the settlement of that name on an important trail, now the government "road" from Tuao through the foothills to Ripang. "Quinalian" is not identified on modern maps, but was apparently the Santa Cruz described by Varona as near Malaueg.

The impression gained by reviewing these varied statements on time and place is that shortly after the founding of Tuao and Malaueg early in the seventeenth century, attempts were made from both these points to penetrate the interior in order to convert runaways and mountaineers.

Then Galfaroso, late in the century, developed the area as an active mission, working out of Malaueg. The principal mission center was apparently shifted several times, and for one period it apparently operated out of Ripang as Vanoverbergh claims, though whether this was before Galfaroso's time is not clear. The Santa Cruz of later times is about 2 miles northwest of Malaueg.

Salazar's account says that Galfaroso gathered fugitive Christians and new converts from the rancherias of Turicat, Tumutud, Nabbuangan, Binnuan, and Nabbayugan. Turicat is the old name for the north fork of the upper Matalag river, now called the Baren, and has a settlement the name of which is usually spelled Puhicud, spoken of by the southern Isneg of modern times as their oldest home place. Tumutud, or by its modern name Talitugu, and Nabbuangan, with the same name today, are southern tributaries of the Matalag, occupied by the so-called Northern Kalinga. The Binuan and Nagbayugan rivers are the southernmost tributaries of the Abulug river, discussed in the Northwest Cagayan coast chapter, and lie north of the Matalag; both still have Isneg hamlets along their banks today. The Nagbayugan people have already been mentioned in connection with the lower Abulug mission work.

Both Salazar and Malumbres speak of the support given to Galfaroso by an outstanding local leader, called by his Christian name Don Joseph Bucayu. Son of a "no less famous" leader named Carag, he had been "the terror of all these mountains and of the neighboring villages," and "prominent for his valor and courage." Bucayu had his heart "softened" and "embraced the faith," so that he became the sponsor of the Santa Cruz mission and many were drawn into its sphere because of his influence (B&R, XLIII, 83; Malumbres, 1918a, pp. 393–94). The description given here of Bucayu, it may be noted, could fit equally well a great Isneg leader of this southeast Apayao area of the early twentieth century, Diego Kinegoran, who likewise had gained a Spanish name, and was not only a warrior scourge but also a mediator with the lowland Christian officials when occasion required.

By 1710, according to Salazar, the Santa Cruz mission was "on the decline" (B&R, XLIII, 78). In 1718, as noted in the general chapter, the "whole Cagayan province rose in revolt" against the Spanish authorities, with the disturbance starting around Tuao and Malaueg, under two leaders, Sinaguingan and Matatanga, of these respective communities. Santa Cruz became deserted and "its inhabitants took to the mountains." This outbreak was put down by a punitive expedition by de Orduña (Montero y Vidal, 1, 44, referred to in the above source).

After this abortive uprising, the Santa Cruz work was resumed, presumably at the site nearer Malaueg. The mission is mentioned by name in various ecclesiastical surveys of 1738–54 (B&R, XXVIII, 160, 174; XLVIII, 131). For 1746, two counts are available for the population at Santa Cruz de

Gumpat; one gives a total of 331 inhabitants, and the other, which is more specific, lists 62 "old Christians," 266 "recently baptized persons," and 4 men who were migrants from the Babuyan Islands north of the Cagayan coast (Malumbres, 1918a, 310–11). Vanoverbergh, who had access to various unpublished Dominican records at Tuguegarao as well as to the publications of Malumbres and others, judges that the mission "must have been abandoned early in the XIXth century at the latest" (1932, pp. 28–31). Buzeta does not list it as a center in the 1818 census, but in 1851 he shows Santa Cruz as a visita of Malaueg, with 35 houses and a population of 223 (Buzeta, 1, 562). The town of Malaueg doubtless continued to serve as an important trading point between the mountain and lowland groups, just as it has done in modern times.

The Feijas map of 1778 offers some interesting perspectives regarding changing settlement patterns in this southern Apayao area. For the Matalag river system it shows 7 settlements on the upper Matalag or Baren river, 5 on the Nabbuangan, and 6 on the "Tumtut," or Talatugu. The Binuan and Nalbayugan rivers somewhat further north had 6 and 11 settlements, respectively. In all, therefore, there were 35 settlements. Today these river systems have some 43 settlements. But as was shown in the corresponding discussion for northern Apayao, the size of such communities judged from the number of houses was considerably larger at the earlier date: on the Baren, for example, one is shown by Feijas as having 66 houses, where the largest as of 1932, and perhaps the largest in modern Apayao, had 25 houses.

Also this map appears to show that the population of southern Apayao has experienced more shifting since 1778 than that of northern Apayao. Less of the settlement names on these rivers are still recognizable today than is the case regarding those listed for the Abulug-Apayao river to the north. The Talatugu tributary, particularly, which runs eastward toward Tuao and so was the district most accessible to Spanish penetration, has lost most of its population subsequent to the Feijas survey. An impression builds up that the people of southern Apayao have both moved back and scattered out in the course of continuing Christian-infidel conflicts. Both the southern Isneg and the northern Kalinga still have vivid memories of such conflicts today. An added dynamic also came from traditional struggles between the northern Apayao communities and these southern groups.

KALINGA: THE TUGA MISSION

The Santa Cruz mission was part of a larger Dominican mission effort that operated out of Tuao; it also conducted work further up the Chico river within the present boundaries of Kalinga subprovince of Mountain Province. The general name given to this latter sphere of activity was the Tuga mission. Its first site, San José de Tuga, appears to have been at the present small settlement area of Tuga, some 16 miles up the Chico from Tuao. This is in the foothills where the Chico debouches from higher zones by way of the Gobgob area, where in recent times the government has been establishing agricultural settlements of the mountain peoples.

The Dominican mission map discussed above shows Tuga as established by the time it was drawn, and Salazar's Dominican *Historia* of 1742, which is the main source for a record of the initial work at Tuga, gives its founding date as 1688. The latter source tells how Fray Juan Yniguez was entrusted at that time with the "conversion of the Indians of Mananig and the other neighboring nations which inhabited the rough mountains near Tuao . . . on the western side . . . and extend north and south for many leagues." "[He] founded a new village . . . in the very lands of the heathens about six leagues south of the village of Tuao, on a plateau below the creek of Tuga, whence the mission took its name."

The term "Mananig" that appears in this record is also written on the Dominican map referred to above in the form "Manani." From its placement it evidently referred to the people of what is now called the Bananid river valley in the higher country immediately to the west and southwest of Tuga. This map likewise gives a number of other names for the mountain peoples, though the lettering in some instances is hard to decipher in the photograph available in the Blair and Robertson volume. Further west of the Tuga mission, in what seems to be the Saltan river valley, it has a name which is apparently "Remus." This is almost certainly the present Limos, or Limus, settlement area in the central Saltan directly west of Tuga. In the Chico headwaters there is a name which is apparently "Sabangas," seemingly the Sabangan area near Bontoc, the present capital of Bontoc subprovince, known by then through Spanish expeditions from Ilocos. On the Ilocos slopes of the Cordillera, too, in roughly their correct place to the west of these peoples, are put the "Tinguianes," and beyond to the south are the "Ygolotes." In the general area of Lubuagan, straddling the middle-upper Chico and Tanudan rivers, is written what looks like "Tabucan Tobu Pueblos," this apparently referring to Tabuk, alternatively called Naneng, the first major community up the Chico. The use of the term "Pueblos" in this one section on the Cagayan side of the mountains seems to indicate that it was the only zone in which large compact communities were being encountered. This fits in with the distribution in later times of wet rice "pueblos," by contrast with the more scattered-out settlement patterns of all the other mountain groups on the Cagayan side. It may be noted that Murillo's 1744 map shows the Chico river penetrating deeply into the Cordillera, but no settlement names are given.

The further record of the Tuga mission, as summarized from Salazar's history by Blair and Robertson, tells how the church was dedicated to St. Joseph (San José) and "notwithstanding the many oppositions offered to the new mission, it grows and prospers." In 1696, however, following the familiar mission resettlement patterns, the Tuga center underwent a series of shifts to lower and more accessible localities. "[It] is moved to a more pleasant site two leagues nearer Tuao, and though named Tuga, it is sometimes called St. Joseph de Bambang, from a mountain named Bambang. In 1710, [the] lack of friars causes its abandonment as an active mission, and it becomes a visita of Tuao." This new locality, according to Malumbres, was at Magogao, or Magaogao, near the junction of the Chico and Saltan rivers.

Malumbres fills out Salazar's record here from other Dominican documents. In 1704, he says, there is mention of "acts of capitulation" by the "pueblos of Mananig, Dilayan, and Tabucan" so that they became visitas of San José de Tuga. Mananig and Tabucan were places spoken of above, and Dilayan is a name still used for a settlement in the Bananid valley back of the old Tuga site. Another group becoming subject at this time to mission influence, Malumbres continues, were the "Abbagaos," the name of whose pueblo was "Catabangan." Abbagao is still a settlement area name in the lower Saltan, while a settlement called Catabogan still exists just below the junction of the Chico and Saltan-Mabaca river systems. "Catabangan," he says, became a visita of Tuao. In 1706 there is cited a place called "Calauan" which became a visita of Tuga. This settlement, probably the present Calanan, somewhat up the Chico from the old Tuga site, was to give a later general name, "Calauas," for infidel peoples of the lower-middle Chico, as will be seen below.

Salazar speaks of a "decline" occurring in the Tuga mission, so that by 1715 many had fled to the mountains and "resumed their pagan life." Shortly after this, he says, with the great Cagayan revolt of 1718, the "new Christians" of Tuga, like those of Santa Cruz, "returned to their former sites and mountains and apostatized from the faith which they had received." Malumbres covers this period by stating that in 1709 the Christians of Tuga were deprived of a missionary because of scarcity of personnel. Some neophytes revolted and, after burning the Tuga church, fled to the mountains. Nevertheless, many held firm in the faith, and these people came down to Tuao, where some stayed while others migrated to lowland pueblos elsewhere.

In 1722, Malumbres continues, the Vicar Father of Tuao made a trip to the mountains and succeeded in reducing once more many of the "apostate remontados." He also had new mission buildings constructed "in the margins of Alioc," some four and a half leagues, or four hours' journey, upriver from Tuao. Alioc seems to have been the settlement area later called Laya, a little east of Gobgob, and in the swampy country where the Chico spreads out after debouching from the higher mountains. Alioc was later considered as a capital site for the Comandancia of Itaves, but was judged to be too unhealthy. Two fathers were stationed there in this earlier period, and succeeded during the next three years in reviving the Tuga work.

Before long, however, the adherents of the mission were moved down river to a new site at Orag, or Orac, about five miles south of Tuao. This was done, Salazar says, "because of the greater conveniences." This writer places the date of the shift as 1731, and notes that the new community was still called the Tuga mission. Malumbres says that the church and mission house were built at Orag in 1729, under the patronage of San Luis Beltram.

In 1738, Malumbres' account continues, the "Calauas" requested that a mission center be established in their territory. In this they were influenced by a leader named Datul, or Otul, working with Fray Bernabé de la Magdalena. The mission, called the Minanga mission, was created along with a civil establishment in 1739 at a new pueblo called "Cayagan," or "Cayang." Minanga is today a settlement area in the lower-middle Chico adjacent to Tabuk, or Naneng, discussed above, and the ruins of the old mission still exist there.

The Tuga mission center at Orag had a troubled history at this period. It has been seen already that in 1739 a discontented group, headed by Bitagun and Anog, received permission from the civil and religious authorities to shift to the Aripa area further down the Chico. In 1741, a revolt occurred among the people remaining at Orag. After killing ten persons, at least many of them fled to the mountains. They took with them the image of the Virgin, 77 prisoners, and all the loot they could carry. A month later, they attacked the settlement of Alioc which had evidently been reoccupied. Most of the people at the time were attending a Mass in Tuao. They attacked that settlement, and a number of the stay-at-homes were killed. The Alioc people experienced other attacks, which they met "with valor."

The Tuga mission continued to operate, though at a low level of activity, in Orag and Alioc. In 1752, Malumbres says, another center was established for mountain converts in "Pata," apparently a settlement area with that name southeast of Tuao. Four years later, the "few Christians who had stayed on in Orag and Alioc" moved to an area less than a mile south of Tuao, where a community also called Orag was established. After another three years, that is in 1768, still another mission center was founded some six miles upriver from Tuao at a locality called "Bubug," possibly the present settlement called Abbot. From this time until around the middle of the nineteenth century, Malumbres says, Dominican fathers made visits to the mountain communities, but then they were "abandoned" because of the "continuous outbreaks, monstrosities, and insurrections of the Kalingas." Mission work, as will be seen, was not resumed until 1891. The records here are taken variously from Salazar (B&R, XLIII, 78–80) and from Malumbres, especially his *Historia de . . . Provincia Montañosa* (1919, II, 358–61, 388–90).

LATER PERSPECTIVES

As in previous chapters, a brief résumé may be given of the statistical and other materials relating to the Chico river region from the eighteenth century on. First, information on the lowland zones may be summarized, the 1746 population count being from Varona, and the 1818 and 1846 counts from Buzeta.

Tabang. Scene of the initial mission work, the area had in general less favorable terrain for economic development than the other lower Chico zones. Tabang became at different periods an adherent community and visita of Galtaran to the northeast and of Piat to the southwest. It served, however, as the entry point and trade center for the old settlement area of Aripa. Population: 1746, 447; 1818, 367; 1846, 422. In 1894, by then largely colonized by Ilocanos, it was reorganized at a new center, Santo Nino, somewhat nearer the Chico-Cagayan junction. In turn, this became Faire.

Piat. This town, though always overshadowed by Tuao, has had a continuous civil and ecclesiastical history, and has been a communications and agricultural center. Population: 1746, 1,697; 1818, 1,770; 1846, 1,480.

Tuao. Strategically located in relation to the central Cagayan valley districts and to the mountain river systems, this town has been the principal town of the lower Chico. The Spanish authorities maintained a fort and garrison there. Population: 1746, 2,156; 1818, 2,976; 1846, 3,617. The Tuao area, with neighboring Malaueg, gained the reputation of producing the finest tobacco in the Philippines. Buzeta, and later Malumbres, gave particularly full materials on Tuao.

Malaueg. This old settlement, important as a mission base, became an important tobacco-producing center. Mora speaks of it in 1805 as an administration point for "many infidels." In 1725 a new community, Mauanan, was established between Malaueg and the Piat-Tuao area in order to safeguard travelers from hostile attacks by the interior people. Population: 1746, Malaueg 1,133, Mauanan 414; 1818, the two communities 1,550; 1846, Malaueg 1,614, Mauanan 266. The name "Malaueg" was changed in the twentieth century to Rizal.

In the generally scanty materials on the mountain groups over the period, an interesting reference was made by Mora in 1805 to peoples living up the Chico river from Tuao. In this area, he says, "there are many infidels of various nations: Calauas, Rimus, and Pinapo." Pinapo, or Pinukpuk in its contemporary spelling, had at the time a market "frequented by Christians and infidels." This is a settlement at the junction of the Chico and Saltan rivers where the mountainous terrain begins. Mora also notes that the non-Christian peoples of Itaves greatly enjoy beating "ganzas," or brass gongs (Malumbres, 1918a, pp. 346–47).

Buzeta's encyclopedic survey provides a key source for appreciating what at this date the Spaniards knew, and did not know, about the mountain zones of southern Apayao and the middle Chico—the latter the Kalinga subprovince of Mountain Province today. He discusses the now depopulated "Aripa" area northwest of Tabang, and also the southern "Apayao" and "Calinga" groups westward up the Matalag river from Malaueg. Southward of these groups, and extending "as far as the territory of the Gad-danes," were the "Calauas" or "Calaguas," that is, in the lower-middle Chico region.

They have a peaceful nature and live as tranquil and harmonious families. They cultivate rice and other vegetables. They have large tobacco plantations which they cultivate by means of a simple and natural system inherited from their forebears. The tobacco . . . is considered as the best of the Cagayan province. . . . [Some is] taken in canoes on the Abra river to the province of Ilocos Sur.

The "natural" system referred to here was evidently the application of their dry cultivation method of rice and root-crop production to this newer prod-uct. So far as the tobacco was traded to the Ilocos side, the trail used was presumably that up the Saltan valley and over into the Abra river head-waters. This was later the military "road" from Abra into the upper Saltan, with its guard post at the settlement of Balbalasang. Deeper in the moun-tains were the "Guinaanes," with their name derived from the settlement of Guinnang—"as cruel and fearless" as the Calauas were peaceful. Buzeta mentions several place names in his references to Kalinga, including Limos on the Saltan, and "Labuagan," or Lubuagan, the present capital of Kalinga subprovince. Other Spanish writers give additional names for groups in the area, e.g., Bayabones and Gamunanes for peoples south and east of Tuao; Banaaos for the Saltan river people.

Most of the present Kalinga subprovince, as already noted, had been incorporated into Abra Province, which at the time of its formation in 1846 had a politico-military character. Between the upper Chico river and the Cagayan valley floor to the east, too, a Comandancia of Saltan was formed in 1859 by the newly established province of Isabela to control and admin-ister its mountainous sections. In 1889, as part of the general policy of stepping up efforts to control and assimilate the mountain populations, the Cagayan Province authorities created a "Partido" or Comandancia of Itaves to administer the mountain areas west and south of the Chico flats. Alioc, the settlement noted earlier, was considered for its headquarters, but in-stead a more healthy location at Magogao, or Magaogao, one of the old Tuga mission sites, was chosen. In 1890–91 the Dominicans reactivated their mission work by opening a center in Magaogao. From there they spread out to various other northern Kalinga communities. Malumbres, in addi-tion to telling of these events, gives a list of the settlements in the area at the end of the nineteenth century, together with their population and house numbers (Malumbres, 1918*a*, pp. 211–23; 1919, 11, 356, 361–62, 393).

MODERN CENSUS DATA

The Varona survey of 1746 showed a total counted population in the whole lower Chico zone of 6,819 paying 1,831 tributes. This is a surprisingly low figure considering that the early-seventeenth-century data shown at the beginning of the chapter suggest a considerably larger population at that time. Disease, defections to the mountains, and apparently some forced or voluntary out-migration to the Iguig area along the Cagayan river to the east, as will be seen in the next chapter, appear to have been factors cutting back the counted population. The 1818 census indicated a further drop in numbers to 6,673, and then Buzeta's 1846 figures showed a rise to 7,622, paying 2,015 tributes. The 1903 census showed 18,047 people in the lower Chico, and by 1918 the number had risen to 24,084. Subsequent totals are 35,042 in 1939, and 39,160 in 1948.

The modern municipal units are Faire (the old Tabang area), Piat, Tuao, and Rizal (the old Malaueg area). The 1948 census distinguished the principal language groupings by "mother tongues" as follows:

	Total population	Itawis (Itavi)	Ibanag	Kalinga	Iloko
Faire	9,947	762	272	151	8,705
Piat	7,099	3,667	57	35	3,307
Tuao	16,365	6,762	3,273	92	6,035
Rizal	5,749	297	4,844	—	577
Total	39,160	11,488	8,446	278	18,624

These figures show the immigrant Ilocano as the largest ethnic group. The descendants of the original Itavi-speaking inhabitants are seen to number about 11,500; some 24,400 more Itavi-speaking people will also be noted in the next chapter as living further east in municipalities adjacent to the Cagayan river and in the provincial capital, Tuguegarao. The principal Ibanag-speaking concentrations are in the Tuao and Rizal districts, and apparently many are settlers from crowded communities further east in the Solana-Tuguegarao; others could have been brought in to work the tobacco fields in Spanish times. The Kalinga speakers appear to represent two groupings: those in Faire and Piat are probably descendants of the Orag Kalingas who moved to Aripas, while the Tuao group would be predominantly migrants down the Chico.

No statistics were given in the 1948 census for Isneg speakers or Negritos; they were included under "Others." But in the 1939 census Isneg speakers numbered 46 and Negritos 178. The Isneg, as would be expected, were nearly all in Rizal. Of the Negritos, 115 were in Rizal, 54 in Faire, 5 in Tuao, and 4 in Piat. The presence of this number of Negritos in the Chico region, where they had not been recorded previously, indicates that their bands had been drifting south through the foothills, perhaps as a result of colonization pressures by Ilocanos along the north coast. The 1939 census also showed 644 persons in the category of "pagans or not belonging to any religious group": 392 in Faire, 226 in Tuao, and 26 in Piat.

Statistical perspectives for the neighboring zones of Mountain Province may also be noted. The 1918 census showed Apayao subprovince as having a total population of 10,978, of whom 9,330 were Isnegs, 347 Northern Kalingas, 774 Negritos, and 427 lowland Christians, nearly all Ilocanos. Of this number the southern Apayao population comprised somewhat over a thousand Isnegs, all the northern Kalingas, and perhaps 150 of the lowlanders. By the 1948 census, the southern Apayao municipal district, Conner, had a total population of 2,112, of whom the southern Isneg probably numbered about 1,100, the northern Kalingas about 600, and the rest were lowlanders.

The 1918 census showed 20,588 Kalingas in the subprovince of that name. In 1948, the four municipal districts in Kalinga subprovince had a combined population of 25,993. Mountain Province as a whole had at that time 33,725 speakers of Kalinga dialects.

REVIEW

In general, it would appear that the mountain peoples of the extreme southern parts of Apayao subprovince and of Kalinga subprovince derive from the lower Chico region. The obvious hypothesis is that they share a common ancestry with the now Christianized Itavi. The marked differences found among the modern groups subsumed under the name Kalinga could then be interpreted in terms of local habitat conditions, contacts with peoples deeper in the mountains, and other dynamic factors. Account needs to be taken, however, of the possibility that movements of people into the inner valleys may have occurred over a long period, including in later times refugees from Spanish control.

The question arises once more here whether the Bontok and even the Lepanto who live in the Chico headwaters may have had their origins on this Cagayan side rather than on the Ilocos side. The matter will need to be taken up in the final chapter, when materials on the Gaddang and Ifugao peoples further south will also have been covered.

XI. The Middle Cagayan Area

PLACE AND PEOPLE

This zone comprises the valley floor from the Cagayan-Chico junction to the Cagayan-Magat junction, together with the mountain hinterlands to the east and west. It corresponds roughly to the southern half of Cagayan Province and the northern half of Isabela Province, and is centered today upon their respective capitals, Tuguegarao and Ilagan. The distance from north to south is about 80 miles. The Cagayan banks alternate between open plains and foothills, and the rainfall diminishes progressively up the valley.

The Spaniards often called this middle part of the valley "Irraya," or "La Yrraya," which comes from an Ibanag root word meaning "upriver." For districts in its higher reaches, other names will also appear, notably "Zimbuey," "Siffun," and "Yogad." Of the many tributaries that join the main river course, the Pangul, Mallig, and Siffu on the west side drain extensive zones along the Cagayan slopes of the Cordillera (eastern Kalinga and Bontoc subprovinces), while the Tuguegarao, Cabagan, Tamauini, and Ilagan gather the main runoff from the Sierra Madre heights. The Pacific slope of the Sierra Madres is rugged except in Palanan Bay, where there are coastal flats. Large sections of this eastern mountain area are marked "Unexplored" on the Coast and Geodetic Survey sheets of 1935.

This section of the valley shows a southward continuity of the Ibanag ethnic group, and of the Ibanag speech as a lingua franca. At the time of the 1948 census there were approximately 113,000 Ibanag speakers, and they were slightly outnumbered by Ilocanos. The northern districts also hold nearly 25,000 Itavi speakers, representing an eastward continuity of that ethnic group from the lower Chico flats. The early records will also show that the populations along the valley were often called at the time Irraya. Some were also called Gaddang or Gaddan. Today there are fairly numerous "Christian Gaddangs" south of the Cagayan-Magat fork, and in the Cauayan district they outnumber the Ibanag. But otherwise the Gaddang speakers comprise scattered groups of non-Christians, or recently converted Christians, occupying the higher reaches of the tributary rivers.

THE MIDDLE CAGAYAN AREA

On the Cordillera side, several hundred non-Christian Gaddang live in the high west country of Cagayan and Isabela, and in the Natonin district of eastern Bontoc subprovince. They are scattered out as dry cultivators, and into modern times some have lived in tree houses. On the Sierra Madre side, the Gaddang speakers are sometimes called Kalingas, in the general sense of "enemy" mountaineers, or else have local river names such as "Kata-langan" and "Kalibugan." But one group east of Ilagan is still called Irraya. Their numbers are small, and they are dry cultivators except as they have adopted lowland wet cropping in comparatively modern times. Except for a recent paper by Father Godfrey Lambrecht on the western and southern Gaddangs, these groups are known in general terms only. Scattered Negrito groups also live along the Sierra Madre slopes. In Palanan Bay, on the Pacific side, a small Christian population called "Palanan" is the northernmost extension of Tagalog groups who settled along the east coast of Luzon.

As indicated earlier, glottochronological studies comparing the valley languages are so far inadequate. Marked differences show, however, in the Pittman group studies between Ibanag and Gaddang. The same is true of Yogad, spoken further up the valley, and fairly closely related to Gaddang. Ibanag and Gaddang are both very markedly different from Ifugao. No dialect geography is available for the Gaddang except in very general terms (Beyer, 1917).

The agricultural economy of the valley floor has been changed in modern times, as noted already, through the forced labor system of growing tobacco. Tobacco cropping is still a major feature, the southern districts having a particularly large output. The wet rice crop is also heavily productive, and large amounts of maize are grown, usually with double, and in places triple, cropping. Second cropping of wet rice, however, is relatively rare. Dry rice is usually the principal crop of the Gaddang hill peoples, but otherwise it is grown in small amounts. The only zone in which root crops are produced in quantity is between the Cagayan-Magat junction and the upper Ilagan river (the Reina Mercedes district) and along the non-Christian Gaddang of east Bontoc (the Natonin district); in each instance, sweet potatoes predominate.

The Palanan people on the Pacific coast side grow a wet rice crop, but do almost no second cropping, and are uninterested in dry rice. They produce a fair amount of maize, and proportionately large quantities of sweet potatoes and cassava (Philippine agricultural censuses, and other sources).

EARLY PERSPECTIVES

Once the Spaniards became established at the Cagayan mouth, they sent armed parties by boat up the river. When in 1591 the first military expedition entered the Cagayan headwaters from Pangasinan, it found one of the

MIDDLE CAGAYAN AREA

settlements deserted because, as will be told in the next chapter, its people had killed "seven Spaniards" who were members of such a party. The 1591 encomienda list names a series of holdings at least tentatively carved out along the middle reaches of the Cagayan, as follows:

Caralanga, Yaguan, Ygui, Tagoran, and Pagamon (five holdings apparently from the Paret-Paranan river system to the present Iguig area): 600 tributes, and 2,400 "souls"; all "hostile."

Nabugan (perhaps the lower Pangul river near its junction with the Cagayan): 700 tributes, and 2,800 "souls"; "in rebellion."

Galalatan, Gat, Tapia, and Dudulique (four holdings, probably on the west bank of the Cagayan in the vicinity of the present Solana, Dudulique apparently being the modern settlement of Magurig): 600 tributes, and 2,400 "souls"; all "hostile."

Tubigarao, Tabagar, and Acuba (the Tuguegarao area on the east Cagayan bank): 700 tributes, and 2,800 "souls"; "in rebellion."

Batona, Sulu, Rot, and Lapugan (four holdings apparently from the Cagayan area south to Lapogan, on the east bank of the Cagayan north of Ilagan): 500 tributes, and 2,200 "souls"; "in rebellion."

Cimbus (called by the mission Zimbuey, apparently the Pilitan area on the west bank of the Cagayan): 1,200 tributes, and 4,800 "souls"; "all in rebellion."

Nalaguan (apparently the Ilagan area): 500 tributes, and 2,000 "souls"; "hostile."

Bololutan (presumably in the Cagayan-Magat junction area): 500 tributes, and 2,000 "souls"; "in rebellion."

Obviously this encomienda list, especially as it relates to the remoter zones to the south, is merely an expression of the Spanish hopes of collecting tribute in areas and from peoples sighted by their expeditions traversing the Cagayan river. For what the figures are worth, however, this gives a total estimated population along the river of 5,350 tributes, and hence 21,400 persons.

The Dominican mission tally of 1612 shows three mission centers: Malaguey, requiring 2 ministers for 1,000 Indians; Tugiguerao, requiring 3 ministers for 1,300 Indians; and Pilitan, requiring 4 ministers for 1,600 or more Indians. The last-named mission was also making "new conversions" at the time "among the tingues (hills) of Zinbuey." One of these centers is obviously Tuguegarao, and the others will be identified below. The mission count was therefore around 4,000 persons. As of the mid-nineteenth century the middle Cagayan had a population of approximately 41,000, and by 1948 the total had risen to nearly a quarter million, of whom somewhat more than half were Ilocanos.

THE NORTHERN SETTLEMENTS

Morga's *Events* of 1609 opens the specific record of happenings upriver from the Cagayan-Chico junction with an account of "rebellions." In the wake of a series of uprisings in the lower valley in 1598, referred to in the general chapter, two chiefs, of whom the most powerful was named Magalat, had been "detained" in Manila as exiles. Some Dominicans persuaded the authorities to release them in the interests of good relations. But on their return to Cagayan they again "incited the whole country to rebellion." With the help of "some other chiefs of Tubigurao [Tuguegarao] and other settlements" they "so stirred up things" that Spanish lives were rendered unsafe. An expedition headed by de Chaves suppressed this outbreak, and the leader Magalat was killed (B&R, x, 170; xv, 101-2).

The initial mission centers here were founded around 1604 to 1607, that is, shortly after those in the adjacent lower Chico area. Two churches, Aduarte says (1640), were located in "Malagueg" at Nalfotan and Yguig, and a third at Tuguegarao. The place name Malagueg does not appear on later maps, but Yguig is the modern Iguig, and Nalfotan may be the present Annafatan, near the town of Amulung. In this area a traveler passing up the Cagayan from the Nassiping mission finds the river banks opening out into flatlands after having passed for several miles through foothills. Aduarte speaks of Nalfotan as being at the time "the chief village among those which are called the villages of Malagueg." (As an aside, it may be noted that a confusion exists in the Blair and Robertson index and some of the other sources between Malagueg and the Malaueg mission that was seen to be in the lower Chico.)

As told by Aduarte, the "chief and lord" of Nalfotan at this time was an influential young leader named Pagulayan. Hearing that the "Ytabes Indians, his neighbors," had been taught "a sure and certain road to salvation," he journeyed down to the town of Nueva Segovia "many times" to request that fathers be sent to his people. At first no father could be spared, and Pagulayan therefore took home a Christian child so that the boy could instruct him so far as possible. He and his people then erected a church in their village to ensure that when a mission could be established in the district it would be in his community, and they even brought a boat to Nueva Segovia in which a father could travel. Finally in 1607, Fray Pedro de Sancto Tomás was dispatched, and "the whole village—men, women, and children—gathered . . . with much joy" (B&R, xxx, 320; xxxi, 264-66).

Aduarte's account, in referring here as among so many other groups to the local prevalence of war, includes the novel twist of speaking praisingly of the Pagulayan and the Malagueg people as "courageous" and imbued with the "military spirit":

[Before] the coming of the faith they were constantly at war among themselves and with their neighbors, being men of fierce mind and lofty courage, and highly prizing their valor, strength, and spirit, an inheritance left to them by their ancestors. Thus they and their neighbors of Gatarang and Talapa, with whom they were very closely related, gave the Spaniards a great deal of trouble, and were feared and still are feared by the other Indians of that large province.

The relationship indicated with the "Gatarang and Talapa" people considerably further down the river suggests that the Malagueg people were a southward extension of the Ibanag ethnic group.

The devil, "as he saw himself losing, all at once, villages which had been his for so many ages," took a hand almost immediately.

By means of a sorceress, a priestess of his, named Caquenga, [he] began to disturb the Indians, to whom this wicked woman said such things that many determined to follow the rites of their ancestors and not to receive the teachings of the divine law. So devilish was this cursed anitera that she kept stirring up some of them against the religious, while at the same time with those who wished to keep him she pretended to be on their side; thus she deceived them all, especially those who were influenced by their zeal for the ancient superstitions. Hence they themselves killed their fowls and the swine they had bred, tore down their houses, and cut down their palm groves . . . and, crying out, "Liberty!" they fled to the mountains. Here they joined forces with those who had hitherto been their enemies.

The reference here to mountains would seem to apply to the immediately accessible heights where the Paret-Paranan river drains the Sierra Madres rather than to the high Cordillera country nearly 20 miles away to the southwest. Their former "enemies" in this case could then have been other refugee groups who were apparently accumulating in the fastnesses here, as seen in Chapter IX.

In the face of this uprising, Pagulayan with some of his "vassals" remained loyal to Fray Pedro, and "strove to bring back those who had revolted." He arranged a conference between the father and the chief who had led the outbreak, Furaganan. The latter, "annoyed with Caquenga, who had caused the disturbance," asked that she be turned over to him as a slave: she, too, "as part of her deception," had stayed on in the village. Before the father took action, the insurgents made a midnight attack and "set fire to the church, thus alarming those who had stayed on in the village, and causing them to take flight." Pagulayan enabled the father to escape safely to Piat in the lower Chico, but the anti-mission group was able to seize the church valuables: "They cut the ornaments of the mass into pieces, to make head-cloths and ribbons. They tore the leaves out of the missal, and drank out of the chalice, like a godless race governed by the devil. Taking the image painted on the canvas, they set it up as a target for their lances."

Information of this outbreak, together with one that occurred at the same time in "Zimbuey" further up the valley, was sent to Manila. A military expedition was sent under de Azcueta, and some of the insurgents were captured and sent to the "wretched life of the galleys." The expedition reported that the Malagueg people had been roused by the "intrigues of Caquenga." The villagers then sent representatives to Nueva Segovia to ask that the mission be re-established, so Fray Pedro returned. "All this disturbance came to an end, and he built convents and churches and . . . in the course of time all those people were baptized."

In 1626, the records of baptisms in the Nalfotan church were "counted," and showed a total of 4,670 over the "eighteen"-year period, "in addition to those baptized in sickness, who were many." It is not made clear how many of these baptisms relate to Nalfotan itself, then the largest and most prosperous community in the area, and how many to other villages of Malagueg; but presumably it was the general register for the mission. As was done earlier for Nassiping, a rough demographic analysis can be made of this total. Assuming for statistical purposes that 750 persons were converted or available for conversion when the mission was founded, and that children were born and baptized at a guessed rate of 40 per thousand per year for the intervening eighteen years to 1626, the resulting accumulated total would be 750 plus approximately 800, or 1,550. As the 1626 figure was 4,670, the corresponding original total of the Malagueg population at the time of mission entry would therefore have been around 3,000.

The young chief Pagulayan adopted the name Don Luis. After his early death one of his sisters named Luysa appears to have been the key church leader. Aduarte tells how she supplied villagers beset by "famine," and also "reported truthfully" any "tumult or disturbance" which arose:

When some superstitious performances were carried on here by some of the chiefs, she immediately informed the religious. When he asked her if she dared to declare the matter before the guilty persons, . . . she replied that she would venture, even though they should give her poison; for they were unable to venge themselves in any other way, and she had reason to expect them to do this.

This record again shows reversionary tendencies at work in the Malagueg villages (B&R, xxxi, 266–73).

Iguig, the second mission center, lies several miles further upriver. The original site was called Nabunanga, which Aduarte says was "now in the village of Yguig," suggesting that the latter may have been consolidated as a mission settlement. His record implies that this church was founded after Nalfotan, but Malumbres later places its establishment in 1604, or three years prior to Aduarte's date for Nalfotan (1918a, p. 446). The encomendero of this locality, Aduarte says, had collected his tributes "with great care," but had "given no attention to providing the people with Christian instruction, as God and the king commanded him." As divine punishment, "this encomendero lost all" in a series of misfortunes, which came upon him "one after the other." Realizing that the cause was "his supporting [of] idolatry and the service of the devil in that village," he asked for a mission father to be assigned, and this was done.

Up to the time of Aduarte's writing, it had been necessary to build the Iguig church on "four separate sites." The first three selected had in turn been inundated, "although it did not appear possible that the river should reach land situated so high." The fourth site was upon "a very high hill. . . . The river . . . is very large; and its floods are . . . extreme. . . . Among all these changes and difficulties, this tribe would have been scattered and their village destroyed, if the religious had not sustained them with alms and charities."

Here, too, one chief, who took the name Don Ambrosio Luppo, stood out in terms of his assistance to the church and to the Spaniards. Aduarte tells a story of his faith as follows:

He went for many days under a temptation of the devil to kill another Indian chief, who had wrought him a great wrong; and could not rest by day or by night for thinking how he might obtain satisfaction against the guilty man . . . [he] was in such disquiet that he could not conceal the matter. The religious came to a knowledge of this . . . and rebuked him earnestly for . . . the great sin which he was designing. . . . [As a result he pardoned his enemy.] (B&R, XXXI, 273–76.)

Tuguegarao, the next mission center up the valley, lies approximately 10 miles south of Iguig. It seems to have been founded in 1604. Aduarte tells how in that year "an Indian" from that village made "the two days' journey by water" to the Nassiping mission and there "very earnestly desired the religious to give him the holy sacraments." Though seemingly well and strong, this visitor suddenly died, "at which the religious wondered," taking it as a sign to them (B&R, XXXI, 203).

The establishment of the Tuguegarao church was carried out by Fray Jacinto Pardo. Aduarte first tells of this father's earlier achievements:

[At] that time . . . the natives [of Nueva Segovia Province] were fierce, constantly causing alarm from warlike disturbances, and were very much given to idolatry and to the vices which accompany it. . . . [He] immediately learned the ordinary language of that province so perfectly that he was the first to compose a grammar of it.

This is evidently a reference to the Ibanag speech of the lower valley, as Aduarte's context here is Nueva Segovia Province in general, for which Ibanag was already serving as a lingua franca for trade and mission contacts. The account goes on to say:

Although the inhabitants [of Tuguegarao] understood the common and general language, [they had] another particular language of their own, in which it pleased them better to hear and answer. . . . [So the father] undertook the labor of learning that also . . . [though] this language could be of no use outside of this village.

This quotation indicates that Tuguegarao represented an old linguistic breakpoint, its language being probably at the time the most northerly of the "Irraya" or Gaddang dialects. The account proceeds:

They were a warlike, ferocious, and wrathful tribe; and being enraged against their Spanish encomendero, they killed him, and threatened the religious that they would take his life unless he left the village. Being enraged, and having declared war against the Spaniards, they did not wish to see him among them.

Fray Jacinto, desiring to "bring them to a reconciliation," was unwilling to leave. "Under these circumstances, he fell sick," and a few days later he died. The Spaniards, "knowing what the Indians had said," believed that they had "given him poison" (B&R, xxxi, 240–41). Nevertheless, work at Tuguegarao continued, and in due course this settlement became the main ecclesiastical and governmental center for the lower valley.

THE SOUTHERN SETTLEMENTS

At the time of the Malagueg uprising described above, Aduarte says, the "Indians of Zimbuey [the 'Cimbus' encomienda], in the level parts of La Yrraya . . . , rose and murdered their encomendero." This was because he had treated them "with more rigor than was proper" on his previous year's visit to collect tribute. "The Indians, in fear of like severity during the present year, had mutinied against [him] and thrust him through with a lance. Out of his shin-bones they made steps to go up to the house of their chief." As noted in connection with the Malagueg uprising, an expedition was sent from Manila under de Azcueta. He "ascertained the facts" and brought out that "the excesses of the dead encomendero had caused the Indians of his encomienda at Zimbuey to rise" (B&R, xxxi, 270–71).

The Zimbuey area also appears in Aduarte's record as the site of the Pilitan mission, "at the utmost borders of Yrraya province." This center was some 25 miles up the valley from Tuguegarao, and close to the later town of Tamauini. The circumstances of its founding are described by Aduarte as follows:

There lived in that city [of Nueva Segovia] Captain Alonzo de Carvajal, encomendero of Pilitan, which is distant from the city five or more days' journey. He collected his tribute from the natives, and desired to give them a minister, as he was obliged; but he was unable to find anyone who was willing to undertake the mission. He accordingly urged Fray Antonio de Soria [who had pioneered missions in the lower Cagayan] to go to visit these Indians and their country, called Yrraya. . . . The journey was long and hard, not only because it was up the river, but because there were enemies on the road. . . . He preached the holy gospel, and the Lord gave him such favor with the tribe that he led them by his command like tame sheep.

Malumbres gives the remarkably early date of 1598 for the founding of Pilitan (1918a, p. 24), and this appears to be confirmed by the fact that the

Fray Antonio de Soria mentioned here (not the Bishop, Diego de Soria) died about 1599. Aduarte writes of the marked differences between the Pilitan area and the lower Cagayan zones:

In this place it seemed that another climate had been found, different from the rest of the province, other fields and spacious meadows, another temperature, and another race of people. The country is very fertile, and abounds in game. It is very well watered, very pleasant, and very healthful, although at first it did not seem so for the religious [as the first vicar died, and his associates took sick].

It had seemed, indeed, to many of the fathers that the district was so unhealthy and so distant that the initial work undertaken there should be abandoned.

The devil, Aduarte indicates, "greatly resented" the encroachment of the mission on his spheres, and "complained and uttered frightful howlings through the mouths of his priestesses or aniteras." He "often appeared to . . . his deluded followers in dreams, bidding them resist and not become Christians." The devil called the missionaries "barbarians" because of their "little knowledge of the language at the beginning": presumably the people spoke another Gaddang dialect here. He also drew attention to "their white teeth because the Indians regard this as a blemish, and make their own teeth black"—the practice of tooth-blackening, which has been continued by some of the mountain peoples into modern times. The initial successes scored by the mission at Pilitan were "several baptisms" of children on the verge of death.

To build the church, the mission pioneer, Fray Antonio de Soria, "threw down the hut of an old woman, a noted anitera." The devil, Aduarte says, was later to express "on many occasions" his resentment for this act, and when in due course the father died "he sometimes claimed the credit." Fray Antonio served the Pilitan people with such success that "long after, when Christianity was more settled in Yrraya, and there was some difficulty in rooting out some superstition which had remained among them," the old people often remarked that if he had still been alive, he could have commanded them and it would have been abandoned. The account also notes that he founded a church at a village called Nalavangan, "a day and a half journey" upriver from Pilitan, and "baptized many people" (B&R, XXXI, 138–48). Nalavangan does not appear on modern maps, and furthermore it drops out of the mission records as such.

From this point on, the early history of this southern Yrraya zone will be drawn variously from Aduarte's account, Salazar's later Dominican *History,* and Malumbres' chronicles of the modern towns in the area. Salazar speaks of Pilitan as having been a "new village" formed by the mission, that is, presumably an existing small settlement in which previously scattered populations were concentrated. He also refers to the establishment around 1608 of three other new mission villages in this southern area:

Abuatan, Bolo, and Batavag. Abuatan, according to Malumbres, was at the present small settlement of Bangac some 10 miles upriver from Pilitan, and just north of the Isabela Province capital of Ilagan. Bolo was the site of the later San Fernando de Ilagan mission, that is, Ilagan itself. Batavag was in a locality today called Lullutan near the site of the later Santa Rosa mission, now Gamu, which is close to the junction of the Cagayan and Magat rivers. According to Salazar, the four villages of Pilitan, Abuatan, Bolo, and Batavag contained in all "two thousand houses," which could indicate a total population of perhaps around 15,000. Almost all these people, he says, "belonged to a tribe called Gadanes"—apparently the first use found of the ethnic name Gaddang in the Cagayan records. Aduarte also tells of the founding of Batavag, "in the high region at the head of the great river," six days' journey from Nueva Segovia: "Here, father Fray Luis Flores . . . gathered together seven little hamlets, making one very peaceful one" (B&R, xxxi, 287). Later he refers again to this concentration of the Batavag people:

They had been brought to the [dwelling place] they now had, that they might be more easily—and more to the profit of their souls—taught and baptized and given the sacraments, in sickness and in health; for so long as they were divided as they had been, into tiny hamlets at great distances from each other, it was impossible to do that. (B&R, xxxii, 57.)

Aduarte also shows one of the fathers, Fray Juan de Anaya, at work in Pilitan, prior to his death in 1609:

He learned the language very quickly, and so wrought with them that he not only taught them the gospel and the Christian life, but also civilization. He showed them how to build their houses, and how to work their fields; and taught them all other matters of human life, not only by instruction, but by example. He sought out the Indians, and brought them down from the mountains and the hiding-places where some, deluded by their sins, had gone to hide from grace. . . . [Trusting] in his natural strength, he went to look for them . . . among the thickets where they hid. He compelled them to enter upon the path of their welfare, not by the violence of a tyrant, but by the force of love and charity.

Aduarte tells of the circumstances of this father's death at Pilitan. Some of the Indians "lost all of their harvest from an overflow of the river." Not daring to wait for the encomendero who was expected to collect his tribute, and "indeed through fear of starvation," they "left their village, and many of them fled to the mountains." The grief and worry of these events led to the illness and death of the father (B&R, xxxi, 291). A general impression is gained from these records that the southern peoples had previously been hamlet-living dry cultivators and, from the Pilitan instance, that their inexperience with water control brought disaster on them.

Another of the early missionaries at Pilitan was Frey Francisco Minaio, who was stationed there with an associate. This father "learned the language well," and was assiduous in trying to root out the old customs.

[The two fathers] went about through all that region, searching for and burning the huts where superstitious sacrifices were offered to the devil, who was consulted as an oracle in these places. These huts were generally hidden among the mountains and crags in the midst of bushes. . . . The devils were greatly angered by these insults; and the Indians heard, in their fields, the complaints of the devil because they believed these men with white teeth. But they were obliged to confess their weakness to the Indians, who in this way were converted to the true faith.

Fray Francisco, "not contented with the work in this village," began the "conversion of the idolatrous tribes of the great and spacious plains in the neighborhood of Pilitan." "So diligent was he that churches were built on these plains and practically all were baptized and became good Christians."

Aduarte again tells about one of the outstanding converts of the region, a chief named Guab. This leader became severely ill, so that his adherents wanted to bathe him in blood from a sacrificed child. The father intervened, and by ransoming the child persuaded the chief to abandon the ritual. After baptism, the chief died, and by his request Fray Francisco "divided his gold among his relatives, and gave liberty to many slaves whom he wrongfully held" (B&R, xxxii, 42–44).

ANTI-SPANISH UPRISINGS

Both Aduarte and Salazar take up next the story of a series of "rebellions" in southern Irraya, marked by lapses from Christianity to elements of the old faith. To 1615, as the former puts it, the religious province of Nueva Segovia had "sailed with a fair wind" in its dealings with "heathen and new converts." But in that year it "began to feel a hurricane which caused much anxiety and pain."

The record starts with Batavag, the "furthest village in the province of Nueva Segovia."

Seven years had passed since the village named Batavag . . . had been formed by assembling a population of mountaineers. Many of these were still heathen; while the adult Christians . . . who were in the minority in the village . . . had been educated in their idolatries, and therefore had not completely rooted out from their hearts their ancient customs.

He goes on to describe how "in times of sickness," the "former priestesses of the devil" continued to offer their services, killing certain birds and anointing the sick with their blood, and practicing "other superstitious ceremonies."

If the evil had been confined to this village, it would not have been very great, because Batavag was small and had not a very large population, and a majority of the adults were not yet Christian; but the evil spread to other villages which were larger and older in the faith, such as Bolo, Pilitan, and Abuatan, each of which had two thousand inhabitants or more. . . . When [the fathers] received information as to what was occurring, they went with great secrecy to make an investigation into the evil; and they wrote down the names of the old aniteras or witches, in whom was the whole foundation of this sin.

One of the Indian participants in this secret investigation "warned the old women of Batavag." In turn, they "began to stir up the inhabitants of that village" in order to "escape the punishment which they feared."

When the religious went there . . . the people of Batavag were in tumult and alarm because of what the witches had said to them, and had determined to flee. . . . Being . . . desirous of abandoning their faith, they returned to their ancient sites, which more readily permitted each one to live in the law which he preferred.

In spite of this reversionary behavior, the Indians did not at this time attempt to destroy the church property or to harm the mission fathers. The latter were able to carry down to the "nearest Christian village" the "adornments of the church," at the same time "taking with them some Indians who feared God and did not wish to follow the pernicious behavior of those who fled from God to the devil." Such loyal converts were then resettled down river.

[The fathers] made continual efforts to bring back the rest, declining no labor, no journeys, and no discomforts, in order to gain some soul among these lost ones. . . . Since they had retired into the mountains, the Spaniards, as they were few, did not pursue them, deeming that on account of the roughness of the country where they were the pursuit would have little effect. . . . Hence many of them remained apostates from the faith and the baptism which they received. (B&R, xxxii, 55–58.)

Salazar, in his later Dominican *History,* gives a similar account of this 1615 outbreak. But he speaks of it as affecting all four mission villages, Batavag, Pilitan, Bolo, and Abuatan. Aduarte, who was nearer these events, describes the other three as staging a major revolt in 1621. Anti-Spanish action began in Abuatan, by then the largest village:

On the Friday before [the sixth of November] a very large and beautiful cross had been set up in the court or cemetery of the church. . . . At this time the Indians gave every evidence of joy . . . and even of devotion to the Lord. . . . [But] on the following Sunday, instigated by the devil, they burnt their churches and villages, and avowed themselves enemies of the Spaniards, and even of God, whom they left that they might return to their ancient sites to serve the devil in exchange for the enjoyments of the liberties and vices of their heathen state.

Aduarte then goes on to explain the genesis of the outbreak. "Practically all those in this village," he first notes, as well as "many of those in Pilitan," belonged to "a tribe called Gadanes."

This tribe was always . . . regarded as one on a lower plane of civilization than the others [in Nueva Segovia], and more devoted to freedom, and enemies to subjection; for they were a race bred in the most distant mountains and the wildernesses of the province, and they had less communication and commerce than did the other tribes—not only with the Spaniards, but even with the rest of the Indians.

"These Gadanes," Aduarte continues, "became restless, and disquieted the other inhabitants of the region." What is meant here by the "other inhabitants" is not clear, but it seems to indicate that the name "Gadanes" was being applied at the time to people drawn in from the mountain flanks and the upper reaches of the Cagayan to join the settlements along the middle valley floor. The "other inhabitants" are spoken of by Aduarte as "always having been very faithful to God and to the Spaniards." They had "even sustained many bloody wars with the neighbors by whom they were surrounded," in support of their pro-Spanish position.

But now these people revolted and joined the insurgents, partly as a result of force applied by the Gadanes—for the latter greatly excelled them in numbers, and caught them unprepared for defense—and partly also carried away by their own natural desire for liberty to which they were invited by the safety of the mountains to which they proposed to go. The mountains, being very rough, offered opportunities for easy defense; and, being very fertile, promised them an abundant living.

The Gadanes, according to Aduarte, had planned this revolt "far ahead," but had "appointed" a later date for its start. This was because they hoped to "get back first certain chiefs who were held as hostages in the city of the Spaniards," presumably Nueva Segovia. They had already sent their most influential elderly chief, Saquin, to try to secure their release. It happened, however, that "the father Vicar of Abuatan had grown weary of his work," and so went down the river at this time to arrange for a rest period.

The Gadanes, accused by their own bad consciences, supposed that he had detected their purpose of rising and had gone down to ask for soldiers. . . . In fear of interference, they hastened on their treacherous act; and, without waiting . . . for the return of him who had gone down for the hostages . . . they decided to rise at once.

Fray Alonzo Hernandez, the resident missionary at Abuatan, "heard the tumult" and "tried his best to quiet" the people. He pointed out not only their spiritual gains, but also their "many temporal advantages, which they possessed in their trade," both with the Spaniards and with the "rest of the Indians," which made them "the richest and most prosperous Indians in all that region." The chiefs replied that they were "weary of the oppressive acts of the Spaniards." The father was urged to leave, because they could not promise that "some drunken Indian may not try to take off your head."

Perceiving their "obstinacy," Fray Alonzo "went away to watch over the village of Pilitan," which he found to be quiet at first. "[Soon] he heard a very great noise and a loud Indian war-cry. They came in a crowd, after their ancient custom, naked, and thickly anointed with oil, and with weapons in their hands. It was the insurgents from Abuatan, coming to force the Indians of Pilitan to join the uprising."

One of the young chiefs leading this party, Don Phelippe Cutapay, had been "brought up from infancy in the church," and as a child had "aided in mass as sacristan and afterward as cantor"; moreover, he was at the time "governor of Abuatan." This chief went to the church and urged the fathers to go down river for safety. By then, "about eight hundred Indians armed and prepared for battle" were in the church courtyard. Fray Alonzo got them to sit down, and urged them again to desist. Once more the leaders responded by stating that they were "weary" of Spanish oppressions. Some of the people then "set fire to some houses, upon which a great outcry arose in the village." Cutapay managed, however, to restrain the people until the fathers could leave. They then provided boats and men to row the fathers and their goods down "to the friendly villages."

The insurgents immediately began to commit a thousand extravagances. They set fire to the houses, they drank and they annoyed the people in the village. If any were unwilling to join them, they threatened them with death by holding lances at their breasts. The result was that many joined them, being forced by the fear of instant death, and waiting for a better time when they could again have religious. A few of them succeeded in hiding and going down the river after the fathers. . . . The insurgents did not cease until they had aroused all the villages in their vicinity. As men abandoned of God, and directed by the devil, they were guilty of horrible sacrileges [slashing the church image and misusing other sacred objects] . . . as a barbarous tribe of apostates.

Here again is a vivid picture of such a reversionary movement. Shortly after these events, the Spanish collector of the encomienda tributes in the area made a visit in the hope that he could "bring them back by argument." But "they no sooner saw him than they killed him." It may be noted that although the fourth mission village, Bolo, is not mentioned by name in this account, it is indicated later by Aduarte that the Bolo people were included in the movement (B&R, xxxii, 112–21).

In 1626 a secret expedition was planned by the Spanish government against the Dutch in "Hermosa," that is, Formosa. This expedition, one of the many incidents in power struggles of the time involving the Philippines area, stayed over at Nueva Segovia, and the ostensible reason given for its organization was that "the troops were going to pacify the rebellious Indians of Yrraya, who had fled to the mountains" (B&R, xxxii, 156).

PACIFICATION AND RESETTLEMENT

Among those Dominicans "most grieved by this disastrous uprising," Aduarte says, was Fray Pedro de Sancto Tomás, who had been for a time vicar of the Zimbuey churches. He determined, therefore, to try to win the people back.

The places where the insurgents had betaken themselves had been selected as particularly strong and secure, and were in the midst of mountains so high and so craggy that they might be defended from the Spaniards, if the latter should try to bring them back or to punish them. Hence the journey to them was long and excessively difficult.

The father made his way to them alone, in spite of the "great danger which he ran by passing through villages of other Indians—with whom he was not acquainted, and who were generally looking out for an opportunity to cut off some head without running any risk." He was "admitted and entertained," though "no Spaniard dared appear among them"—an interesting distinction between the missionaries, who were of different nationalities, and the "Spaniards," which appears at a number of places in the mission records. Reaching "agreements with them" he was able in 1622 to bring back with him "in peace" some 300 households who had gone with the insurgents from the villages of Pilitan and Bolo. Most of these were people who "had been compelled" to participate in the evacuation of the mission centers.

Returning "to a pacified region," the account says, these households were "settled at the mouth of the river of Maquila." Malumbres places this settlement point near Labag at the junction of the Tuguegarao river with the Cagayan. Later, in 1646, the group moved southward to form the settlement and mission center of Cabagan. Its original site was at Cabagan Viejo, but in 1877 a new center was developed a little further south at the present town of Cabagan (Malumbres, 1918a, pp. 30–31).

Shortly after bringing out the first group of people from the mountains, Fray Pedro "went further up the river of Balisi" and made additional contacts with the insurgents. This is apparently a minor river system joining the Cagayan near Balasig, between Cabagan and Tumauini, and draining mountains on its east side. At this time "the alcalde-mayor and the troops" were "advancing against the rebels," in an apparently futile punitive expedition, and this made the enterprise "most difficult." The "leader of the revolted enemy," Don Gabriel Dayag, elder brother of Cutapay mentioned above, met the father and "kissed his scapular with great reverence." Though he did not agree to return, he "finally came down in peace later." He also "revealed to the father some ambuscades on the road in some dangerous passes where the Indians planned to kill the Spanish soldiers." Fray

Pedro died in 1622 from physical disabilities incurred in these travels (B&R, XXXII, 120–21).

Salazar's later Dominican *History* now takes up the record. In 1673, he states, the "religious of that province" of Cagayan petitioned their provincial head to resume active missionary work in southern Irraya. He sent two fathers there, Fray Pedro Sanchez and Fray Geronimo de Ulloa. They "played the part of explorers, in order that by talking and by treating with the apostates they might sound out their minds and good will."

The "apostates" received them well, yet they would not agree to "reduce themselves to their former villages." This refusal is attributed, in the account, to the influence of the villagers of Cabagan, the founding of which was discussed above, and by then the principal community in the adjacent lowlands. As it was put:

[Those] people . . . induced them, for their own private interests, not to return to their Christianity. . . . Just as in the wars with Portugal some did not wish that country to be conquered, so that they might have an easy refuge in time of any trouble, so also those Indians of Cabagan, although Christians, induced the heathens not to become Christians, and pointed out to them the burden of the tribute, the *polos* [labor services], the personal services, and other penalties and troubles which the Christians feel when they are settled.

Salazar notes that this was not the only instance where Christians wanted their "infidel" trading partners in the mountains to remain unconverted, so that their profitable commerce could be continued and they would have allies among whom they could find refuge in times of insurrection. In order, therefore, to "get them to reestablish the said villages," the Cagayan people were "prevented from trading with the heathen," presumably with Spanish troops backing up the order. But the fathers could not break the "obstinacy" of the mountaineers.

The problem of reducing the "infidels and apostates" of this area figured largely in the decision of the Philippine authorities, in consultation with the mission Orders, to develop "active missions." Baltazar de Santa Cruz (1676) says of the mountain populations of Irraya at this time:

Most of those people are heathen, although there are many Christians among them who have fled from their own villages. They have been subdued at times, but their misfortune has immediately aroused them to rebellion. Now we are considering how to attract them by love, and with security; and our religious are moving alone in this matter, with none of the horrors which soldiers bring. (B&R, XXXVII, 145–46.)

The authorities, in consultation with the Dominican leaders, resolved that a "venerable" father, Fray Pedro Ximinez, the vicar of Cabagan, should attempt the task of pacification. As told by Salazar, the father was directed to select "five Spaniards, five Pampangos, and sixteen Indians," this apparently a military force, and to "proceed to the reduction of those heathens," summoning them "in the name of the king," and informing them that they would be pardoned for all their "apostasies, murders and other crimes," and excused from paying tribute for three years, and the heathens for ten years if they were converted." The expedition was organized by the local officials, but Fray Pedro refused to take any soldiers with him, using "only the sixteen Indians for his protection and . . . as rowers in the boat."

The father ascended to those paramos [i.e., wildernesses] and desert places, and by treating those heathens with kindness and gentleness he reduced many of those of a district called Ziffun to descend and settle in a place called Santa Rosa, where the village of Batavag had formerly stood. They did that immediately without any delay. Besides them others offered themselves to the father, in number about three hundred, but since they lived farther inland, they needed escorts to accompany them and to take charge of their effects and household goods. The alcalde-mayor [of Cagayan Province] . . . was of great help with his measures. They were allowed to select a village where they wished to live. Some of them went to Cabagan, others to . . . Santa Rosa, and others to another new village called Ytugug. . . . Besides them a hundred persons descended and founded the village of San Fernando, where the ancient village of Bolo was established.

The names of Santa Rosa and San Fernando were referred to earlier as, respectively, the initial mission names for the later town of Gamu, close to the Cagayan-Magat junction, and Ilagan, or San Fernando de Ilagan to give its full name. The "new village of Ytugug," south of Gamu between the forking Cagayan and Magat rivers, and the site of a Spanish fort, will be seen later to have had a less continuous existence.

The devil once more stepped in, "envious of that reduction."

He suggested then to an Indian of Cabagan to stir up the Indians who had descended, but the latter not daring to do it himself made use of a heathen called Baladdon. The latter treacherously killed twelve persons of those who had recently become settled, and through that deed the reduction was on the point of being undone and the Indians of returning to the mountains, seeing how little security there was in the villages. In order to quiet and calm them the alcalde-mayor took a hand. By means of a troop of soldiers whom he sent, he avenged those treacherous murders by killing some of the accomplices and capturing others, in all seventy in numbers; and by looting their possessions and foods, which rightly went to the troops. . . . [Thus] the new villages were calmed and quieted, and the enemies were too fearful to attempt another such thing.

Fray Pedro worked in these new villages, instructing the "apostates" and "catechising" and baptizing "heathens."

As an additional measure to ensure the safety of the resettled groups, the Spanish authorities next sought to extend their control southward and westward into adjacent districts called "Ziffun" or "Difun," "Yogad" or "Yogat," and "Paniqui" or "Paniquy." These regions will be discussed mainly in the next chapter, but part of their story is relevant to the middle

Cagayan. Fray Pedro, according to Salazar, had "formerly treated with some heathens of a place called Ambayao to descend to the new villages." This place name could relate to Mt. Amuyao, a district landmark on the high mountain ridge separating the Gaddang ethnic area of today from that of the wet rice terracing Ifugao.

[With] the aid of the alcalde and his men Fray Pedro went down [i.e., probably southward along the Magat] to the said Indians, with their wives, families, and household goods, and reaching the village of Ytugug with them, they were allowed to choose a site in which to live. Some hundred of them remained there, while the others went down to Cabagan, Lalo, Yguig, Fotol, and to other villages.

When this "reduction" was at the "height of its success," the devil put forth all his efforts against it. He persuaded the Spanish civil authorities that the use of "troops and escorts" to "bring the heathens to settle" was not justified. The father was "ordered not to take troops."

The religious obeyed the new order and took care only to instruct those who had been reduced. . . . But alone, without troops or noise, people kept descending those mountains, and many of them summoned him to go to get them. . . . [With] only the Indians of the new villages, some of whom were neophytes and others catechumens, he went through those deserts and collected many apostates and heathens.

On one occasion, the account continues, the father led out 115 persons, and one week afterward another 35 followed from a place called Yobat. The latter group told him that if he would stay on in Yobat two days more, "a vast number of people will descend." The father, however, "did not understand it so," but "thought on the contrary that they were enemies" and could not be trusted. Yobat may be Yogad, or the Echague region, to be discussed in the next chapter. But it is also tempting to think of this name as applying to Hogad, the nearest of the Ifugao settlement areas to the Mt. Amuyao ridge and to the gorge of the middle Magat river, hence of some of these resettled people as Ifugao. Several Ifugao colonies were established in the Magat gorge country during the nineteenth century, though their populations later returned to the mountains. Small groups of Ifugao also settled in the lowland towns of the upper Magat.

Salazar goes on to say in his enthusiasm that Fray Pedro "reduced very many apostates, and baptized innumerable heathens" during the seven years of his work in the district. Finally the devil "laid such snares" and "so many witnesses rose up against the father," that he was transferred elsewhere. Later, being vindicated, he was permitted to return to work in the "Mandaya" mission in northwest Cagayan: "[After Fray Pedro's removal] that mission was taken charge of by other fathers . . . who made their raids into those mountains and the districts of the heathens from time to time, and led many of them by means of their inducements to descend to live [in the various lowland settlements]."

Of the later fathers working out of Ytugud, Salazar notes especially

Fray Vicente de le Riesgo, who "reduced again" the villages of "Ytugug, Santa Rosa, and San Fernando," apparently after some additional unrecorded disturbances. This father was also "charged with the reduction of Yogat and Paniqui," which he carried forward successfully. These latter zones are further up the Cagayan valley, and mission activities in them will be reviewed in the next chapter. Salazar also speaks of "another harvest field, no less abundant."

[This] had been discovered, in the very center of those mountains, on the side looking toward the east, in an extensive field called Zifun. There the venerable father, Fray Geronimo Ulloa, vicar of the village of Tuguegarao, filled with zeal for the reduction of those infidels, had made various raids. . . . He entered those mountains alone in search of those straying souls . . . without stopping to consider dangers or discomforts.

So great was Fray Geronimo's success that he was released from other duties to give full time to this work. "Zifun" as used here could refer again to the Siffu river. The phrase "on the side looking toward the east," would then refer to the eastern slope of the Cordiller. But this ambiguous phrase could alternatively mean the eastern or Sierra Madre side of the Cagayan rather than the Cordillera side. In this case the upper fork of the Cagayan and adjacent mountain areas to the east, also included within the old "Ziffun" or "Difun," could be meant (B&R, XLIII, 57–64, 92–93).

At the date of Salazar's writing, shortly before 1742, so he reports, the San Fernando (Ilagan), Santa Rosa (Gamu), and Ytugud missions were currently active. The 1738 survey of the Dominican establishments lists south of Tuguegarao the following centers: Cabagan, Ilagan, with its mission Tamavini or Tumauini, of which more shortly, and Ytugud, with a mission of Ziffun (B&R, XXVIII, 160, 174). Here, again, the term "Ziffun" might appear to refer either to the Siffu river area or to the upper Cagayan area. Fortunately, another mission survey for 1739 (B&R, XLVIII, 131) resolves this problem in still another way by referring to this Ytugud branch center as "Santa Rosa of Cifun," that is, the Santa Rosa mission. The survey notes in passing that the mission "was founded in Ziffun by Fray Pedro Ximinez, and afterward was transferred to the location which it now has, with the title of Santa Rosa." The name Ytugud passes from the mission records soon after this, and in a Dominican survey of 1752 a new mission center nearby, "Cauayan" appears instead as the area headquarters (B&R, XLVIII, 136).

Murillo's 1744 map shows for this zone of the Cagayan the valley settlements of Iguig, Tuguegarao, Cabagan, San Fernando, Santa Rosa, and Cauayan, also the district of "Sifun" near the last-named town. The Cagayan tributaries are lined in for short distances only, and the forking of the Cagayan and Magat is not shown; only one river course continues into the Cagayan headwaters, apparently the Magat.

The map has Palanan on the Pacific coast side marked as an anchorage, with "Dicalayo" and "Davilican" shown as neighboring localities. Apart from sea travel along this rugged shore, the settlements here were served by long-existing trails across the Sierra Madres from tributaries of the Ilagan river. The religious survey of 1738 speaks of Palanan as having "a very fine mission of several barbaric people called Irrayas, Negritos, and Aetas" (B&R, XXVIII, 160). As noted earlier, the speech of the Malayan-type people here is reported to be of Tagalog affiliation, and if so, they evidently came up the east coast rather than being linked to the Cagayan peoples.

The sparsely settled east coast area was first effectively penetrated by Franciscan mission fathers, who commenced their work in 1588. Starting in the more accessible bays of Dingalan, Baler, and Casiguran considerably south, they "extended their missions down the beach toward the province of Cagayan, and founded the village and district of Palanan."

They hoped that [although] there were few people and conveniences, as these mountains which were peopled by pagans were nearby, they could continue ever to increase their flock. . . . For besides the Christians already reduced, the fathers had to contend with an innumerable number of heathen who overran the neighboring mountains for a distance of more than thirty *leguas* from the point of San Ildephonso [in the south] to Cape Engaño [the northeast tip of Luzon]. (B&R, XLI, 94, 97.)

The Palanan mission has been noted already in a discussion of the lower Cagayan mission of Vangag, where refugees from this coastal area were seen in the lower Cagayan chapter to be living in the Sierra Madre fastnesses. A Franciscan mission history of the period from 1640 to 1649 speaks of Palanan as a "visita" of Casiguran, the nearest coastal settlement to the south, and as having 250 tributes, or 700 persons (B&R, xxxv, 282). The religious survey of 1738 says that the Franciscan workers "possess the administration of the village of Palanan with seven hundred souls," of whom those converted in the "various settlements" numbered by then "about six hundred" (B&R, xxviii, 160). A Franciscan historian Martinez, quoted by Malumbres, speaks of the work at Palanan as involving "a painful and difficult conversion" (1918a, pp. 175–76).

The Iguig area, Malagueg of the early records, was apparently the locale for the first resettlement of offshore islanders on the Luzon mainland. Shortly after 1680, as told by the Dominican historian Salazar, a father dispatched to the Babuyan islands, Fray Mateo Gonçalez, preached with such fervor that he "filled with terror" his hearers, so they consented to accompany him to Cagayan. The group included "both apostates, of whom many had gone to that island, and heathen." The wording here indicates that such offshore islands had been serving as one of the refuges for northern Luzon mainland people wanting to escape Spanish control. "Leaving *en masse*," the group was "settled in a new village between Yguig and Nassiping." This village was "suppressed later," and its inhabitants were shifted, probably to the Buguey coastal region, seen earlier. Salazar then states: "Another village called Amulung is stationed there in 1733 which is formed of Indians from other villages, and a church and convent established" (B&R, XLIII, 80).

It will be noted shortly that modern census figures show the population in this zone as largely Itavi speaking rather than Ibanag speaking, which suggests that this resettlement involved at least in part families from the lower Chico. The ecclesiastical survey of 1738 refers to Amulung as a visita of Iguig.

The valley towns were the locale for two major "rebellions" during the eighteenth century, in 1718 and 1763. The first of these has already been noted as starting in the Tuao-Malaueg area. In Tuguegarao, a visionary named Rivera took the opportunity to declare himself a local "Pope and King." He and his followers, according to Malumbres, "deprived all the townsmen and dependent communities of the Church," ruled in "irreligious and despotic fashion," and even carried their attacks upon the Spaniards into the capital at Lal-lo (1918a, pp. 56, 380). When this uprising was suppressed by Orduña, many people "left for the forests and mountains" from Tuguegarao, Cabagan, and the other population centers.

The "bellicose character" of the Tuguegarao people, Malumbres says, also found outlet in the 1763 rebellion. This outbreak occurred when the British had occupied Manila, and coincided with the "Silang rebellion" in Ilocos. The overt grievances were concerned with tribute exactions, demands for labor, and other Spanish pressures, but underlying these was the growing hope of throwing off alien control as in so many comparable "nativistic" movements. The leaders of the Cagayan revolt were Dabo and Juan Morayac, and it was particularly centered in Ilagan, Cabagan, and Tuguegarao. Martinez de Zuñiga gives an account of this outbreak as follows:

In the town of Yligan [Ilagan], the Indians, whom we call Timavas, had flogged the commandant of the place. They presented themselves to the chiefs, who were appointed receivers of the royal revenue, declaring themselves no longer tributary to the Spanish government: other towns followed their example, and the rebellion thus gained ground. The chiefs called in the aid of the infidel Indians, and some skirmishes took place; but not being able to succeed in reducing the insurgents to submission, they applied . . . [for] the assistance of the Spaniards. Don Manual de Arza . . . Captain-General of the three provinces of Cagayan, Ylocos, and Pangasinan . . . [collected] a number of loyal Indians and some Spaniards . . . [and] overpowered the rebels, hanged the ringleaders, and restored tranquillity. (Maver translation, 1814, pp. 211–12.)

Malumbres, in his account of this outbreak, says that some thirty-three leaders were also deported. This suppression probably led to the retreat of additional groups into the mountains, including the upper river valleys eastward of the Cabagan-Ilagan zone. The peoples of this latter area, spoken of at the beginning of this chapter as of Gaddang affiliation, and called collectively Kalinga or Irraya, will be discussed below. Still other outbreaks were to follow in the valley communities up to the close of the Spanish regime, but are beyond the time scope of this study.

LATER PERSPECTIVES

As in previous sections, later statistical and other information on the valley settlement zones can be presented in tabulated form. The sources for population figures are the Varona survey of 1746, Mora's record of 1805, and Buzeta's surveys of 1818 and 1846. First come the northern districts:

Amulung. The establishment of this center was described above. Population: 1746, 685; 1805, 748; 1846, 1,421. In 1818 its population was counted along with that of Iguig, of which it became a visita. In 1787 a settlement called Fulay was established as a stopover point between Amulung and Nassiping to the north, as seen in the lower Cagayan chapter. In 1843 it was reorganized as Alcala, and its population included converts from the non-Christian groups of the Paret-Paranan river system. In 1846 it had 608 people. In 1896 an additional center was established at Baggao on the Paret river, marking progress in the conversion or reconversion of the "infidel" populations to the east.

Iguig. This old town area lost population in the eighteenth century, but prospered again with the development of the tobacco monopoly. The following are recorded totals: 1746, 1,723; 1805, 851; 1818 (with Amulung), 1,318; 1846, 1,061. In 1896 a settlement, Cordoba, was established on the Pangul river west of Iguig, with Ilocano colonists apparently predominating.

Tuguegarao. The favorable terrain of this center and its strategic position in relation to valley communications were factors triggering off the growth which was to make it the capital of Cagayan Province in 1841. Population: 1746, 6,328; 1818, 11,699; 1846, 17,405. Migrants from outer communities such as those in swampy zones of the lower Cagayan were moving into it, while from it Ibanag speakers were moving into adjacent zones and southward up the Cagayan. Buzeta describes the town itself at mid-century as having a network of streets and many substantial homes as well as the usual *nipa* huts. Of satellite communities, Solana became separated in 1815, Enrile (first called Cabug) in 1849, and Peñablanca in 1896.

Southward of Tuguegarao, the Cagayan Province border is crossed into Isabela Province. Information on the Isabela districts is found particularly in Malumbres' second volume, *Historia de la Isabela* (1918b).

Cabagan. This trading and agricultural center shows the following population figures: 1746, 4,126; 1818, 6,863; 1846, 9,773. In 1877, Cabagan Nuevo was established, involving a shift to a better location a little south of the old settlement. Santa Maria was separated administratively in 1878, and San Pablo in the twentieth century.

Tumauini. According to Malumbres, this settlement was founded as a civil jurisdiction in 1704, reportedly with Gaddangs and "Calingas" from the older missions. Population: 1746, 879; 1818, 1,790; 1846, 2,996. It was a visita of

Ilagan during the eighteenth century. When Isabela Province was formed in 1856, it served for a brief period as its capital.

Ilagan. The chronicles of this important town place its establishment in ecclesiastical terms, according to Malumbres, in 1678. Population: 1746, 1,407; 1818, 2,422; 1850, 2,841. Shortly after the founding of Isabela Province in 1856 it became the capital, and, as will be seen, further population growth set in strongly.

Palanan. This isolated zone on the Pacific coast side of the Sierra Madres was linked by trail to Ilagan, and so had something of the character of a dependency in commercial terms. The 1738 ecclesiastical survey quoted above showed about 700 persons, of whom 600 were converts. The 1818 count, however, gives a figure of 467, and that of 1850, 800. A survey of ports along this coast in 1850 speaks of the settlement of Palanan as having two adherent "missions," Dicalayon and Divilican (B&R, xxviii, 288). The latter were small settlements perched on the rugged coast between Palanan and Casiguran.

The Cagayan-Magat junction area was notably important in the water communications system of the valley, and with roading, the wider river courses here presented problems of traffic crossings. Southward, old and new communities appear.

Gamu. This is the oldest settlement with a continuous history in the area. The locale of the Santa Rosa mission, it was seen as a resettlement center for reconverted refugees from the older mission. To the southwest, where the main north-south "road" crossed the Magat, a ferrying point called Furao developed, and was a visita of Gamu. Population: 1746, Gamu 1,145, Furao 349; 1818, Gamu with Furao 1,039; 1850, Gamu 1,277, Furao 490. Furao dwindled as new roading bypassed this ferry point. In 1896 Naguilian, on the east bank of the Cagayan, separated from Gamu.

Itugud. This mission center was situated on the west bank of the Magat river at a locality called "Calering." Spoken of by Mora as "three gunshots away" from the newer community Furao, it was still in his time (1805) the site of a garrisoned Spanish fort. According to Malumbres, the "Calering" people shifted to Ilagan in 1700. No population figures are recorded. In 1849 a settlement called Alamo was formed further up the Magat out of converts from among the "infidels." Population: 1850, 515.

Cauayan. In 1739 the community with this name was founded between the Cagayan and Magat forks. In 1766–69 this growing center was shifted to its present site further up the Cagayan fork. Population: 1746, 152; 1818, 1,386; 1850, 1,038.

Calaniugan–Reina Mercedes. By the eighteenth century a settlement called Calaniugan or Calanusian had developed as an annex of Cauayan on the east bank of the Magat ferry, opposite Furao. Population: 1818, 693; 1850, 1,210. In 1885 Calaniugan was reorganized to form Reina Mercedes, so named as being sponsored by Alonzo XII, and its people moved to the site north of Cauayan which is occupied today.

To the east and west of the Cabagan-Ilagan-Cauayan valley flats were mountain non-Christian groups, of whom at least the great majority other than the Negritos appear to have been runaways of earlier or later times. Malumbres cites documents which show that from 1739 on, Dominican fathers attempted to develop effective mission work among the "infidels" of the upper river systems to the east—the Tumauini, Ilagan, Catalangan, Casiguran, Disabungan, and others. In the years mentioned, some "Irrayas" were brought down to a mission settlement at Lapogan near Tumauini. In 1743 Fray José Martin opened mission work among the "Catalanganes," and a center was established there in 1756 by Fray Blas Berbera. The groups concerned, however, were also being visited by Franciscan fathers from Palanan. As a result, jurisdictional questions arose between the two mission bodies, and their efforts ultimately withered away (1918b, pp. 70–71, 113–15, 596).

From then on, sporadic references occur to these population groups. Buzeta in 1850 speaks of the regions east of Ilagan and Gamu as "inhabited by black savages" and by the "rancherias of the infidels of Catalangan." A German scientist, Karl Semper, who traveled in the area during the 1860's, gives a general account of these groups.* He distinguishes two types, both basically Malayan: the Catalangans on the "eastern arm" of the Ilagan river, and the "Irayas proper" in the mountains on the Ilaron river, not far from Palanan. The latter group, he says, are mixed in part with the Negritos, with whom they "live socially," and with so-called "Christian remontados" of the plains "who have fled before the arms of the authorities into the somewhat inaccessible mountains."

The Catalangans, Semper found, cultivated meticulously with hand tools, had houses with very thick high roofs, favored elaborate art decorations, and were inhospitable "egoists." The "Irayas" used the carabao and plow, but were careless agriculturalists. They had rough, flat-topped houses, employed simple geometric art motifs, and were friendly and hospitable. The implication here is that the first group were dry cultivators and the second group wet cultivators. Both were "peaceful," and appeared to have much the same clothing and ornament, religious beliefs, and feasting and other ceremonials. Cavada, writing in 1876, speaks of the Catalanganes as living peaceably in "little rancherias and poblaciones." Perez, by contrast, in his "ethnographic encyclopedia" (1904), classes these eastern Gaddang generally as "bellicose infidels." Beyer distinguished three groups on the basis of records in 1916, Kalibugan, Katalangan, and Iraya (1917, p. 24). In 1896 an administrative center called San Mariano was established in the upper Ilagan river, marking a turning point in control and Christianization of these peoples. Yet even by the 1939 census, 1,639 persons in the Tumauini-Ilagan-San Mariano districts were counted in the category of "pagans and persons not belonging to any religious group."

In 1859, according to Cavada's dates, the western part of Isabela Prov-

* *Die Philippinen und ihr Bewohner*, 1869; translated in *Journal of Anthropology*, London, 1871, pp. 298–300.

ince, comprising eastern slopes of the Cordillera Central, was made into a politico-military "comandancia of Saltan," and in 1876 he records it as having 4,480 inhabitants. Included was the high country of the "Gaddanes," some of whom, he rightly says, lived in tree houses. Other "savage infidels" of this Cordillera region were the "Bungananes and Majoyaos," that is, the northern sections of the Ifugao ethnic group: the first name possibly coming from the settlement of Bangao near Hogad, and the second referring to the well-known Mayayao area. Cavada describes all these mountain peoples as ferocious, superstitious, insolent, and cannibalistic, using their arms constantly. Semper, the German scholar referred to above, also speaks of the various "races" of "Ygorrotes" west of the Cagayan as being spirited warriors, defending themselves against one another and also against the Spaniards: "Whole districts have been laid waste . . . in the course of the last decades of years. . . . Villages have been burned down and their inhabitants chased away, because one of them has cut off the head of a Christian." A favorite time for Spanish raids, he notes, was when their tobacco fields were ripe, in the attempt to "extirpate smuggling." Semper (pp. 301–2) gives one of the earliest specific descriptions of terraced rice fields. A Governor of Isabela Province, writing in 1877, describes the mountain Gaddang on the Cordillera side as having "houses of bamboo," and as eating "dry rice, camote, and other plants" (Perez, 1904, p. 375).

MODERN CENSUS DATA

By the twentieth century the population of the middle Cagayan had expanded greatly. Varona's survey of this zone in 1746 yielded a counted total of 18,540, and if the figure of 700 for Palanan at approximately that date is added, the population rises to nearly 20,000. Buzeta's record of a century later yields a corresponding total of approximately 41,000 people. The 1903 Philippine census showed a population of 103,869. By the 1918 census, after some provincial boundary changes, it was 149,886, and by the 1939 census 246,452.

As noted in earlier sections, the 1948 census identified the principal ethnic groups in terms of those claiming the language concerned as their mother tongue. First, the figures for the four northernmost municipal units, Alcala, Baggao, Amulung, and Iguig, were as follows:

Municipal unit	Total population	Ibanag	Itawis	Iloko
Alcala	13,214	15	—	13,188
Baggao	11,232	586	70	10,534
Amulung	12,734	799	3,005	8,922
Iguig	8,115	127	5,579	2,393
Total	45,295	1,527	8,654	35,037

This tabulation reveals a great preponderance of the Ilocano element, except in Iguig. Surprisingly, in terms of an expected continuity of Ibanag speakers up the valley to the districts noted below, where they are numerous, they are represented here by not much over a thousand persons. The majority of the indigenous population, as noted earlier, is Itawis speaking. The 1939 census, which gives a more detailed breakdown of language speakers, showed 169 Negritos and one Kalinga in this zone, evidently making up the bulk of 188 persons returned as "pagan or not belonging to any religious group."

Next, in the general Tuguegarao area, there are four municipal units today, Solana, Enrile, Tuguegarao (including the city), and Peñablanca. The 1948 census shows the mother tongue of the principal population elements as follows:

Municipal unit	Total population	Ibanag	Itawis	Iloko
Solana	18,758	11,262	1,515	5,902
Enrile	11,130	418	10,371	312
Tuguegarao	29,083	22,815	2,016	3,686
Peñablanca	8,799	6,765	1,831	199
Total	67,770	41,260	15,733	10,099

Here, for the first time, a lowland zone is encountered with the Ilocanos still a minority group. The great majority are Ibanag speaking today, though some at least could originally have had a distinctive dialect, as suggested by the initial mission records. These people could later have adopted the Ibanag speech as being the lingua franca and the prestige language of the lower valley. The great number of Itawis (Itavi) speakers, particularly on the west side of the Cagayan, indicates an ethnohistorical continuity with the lower Chico "Itabes," as some of the early records had suggested. The 1939 census listed 47 Kalingas and 35 Negritos in this zone, and a total of 208 were returned as "pagan or not belonging to any religious group."

Next, in northern Isabela, the thirteen municipal units in this part of the valley today may be taken together, continuing from north to south. Unfortunately, the detailed 1948 census figures on the mother tongues were not included in the published reports that were available, so that the 1939 census figures on speakers of the various languages must be used. As noted earlier, these involve some multilingual duplication, particularly a tendency to show more speakers of the Ibanag lingua franca than there are persons of Ibanag ethnic affiliation. With this proviso, the totals in 1939 were as follows:

Municipal unit	Total population	Ibanag	Itavis	Gaddang	Kalinga	Yogad	Negrito	Ilongot	Iloko
Santa Maria	5,794	5,750	58	—	9	—	—	—	388
San Pablo	6,241	5,980	—	61	—	—	—	—	1,580
Cabagan	18,795	16,595	—	6	177	8	4	3	3,911
Tumauini	14,343	8,186	3	352	25	—	—	1	6,739
Ilagan	31,323	13,307	115	23	104	11	1	1	24,713
Gamu	18,201	4,239	117	225	66	—	—	30	16,275
Naguilian	6,871	4,316	—	4	—	—	—	—	6,443
Reina Mercedes	4,376	2,717	34	876	—	—	—	—	2,917
San Mariano	7,046	6,788	—	—	846	—	—	—	1,969
Cauayan	17,418	1,775	51	3,759	20	7	15	—	14,718
Dalig	3,185	120	—	292	477	—	—	—	2,832
Antatet	2,009	140	—	65	—	—	—	—	1,862
Total	135,602	69,903	438	5,663	1,724	26	20	35	84,347

In addition to these twelve units, Palanan on the east coast had 2,703 speakers of the local dialect and 365 Negrito.

These statistics on language speakers are somewhat formidable to interpret. The immigrant Ilocano are again in the majority, but they have settled principally in the outer, sparsely occupied districts. Many of them probably reported themselves also to be Ibanag speakers, and the Ibanag speech predominates in the old towns of southern "Irraya," Tumauini, Ilagan, and Naguilian, with their immediately surrounding districts. Again the question is raised of how far this language, carried by mission and government, was really indigenous to the area.

The Gaddang, who played a key role in the early history of the Irraya settlements, are represented today by only 5,663 speakers, particularly in the Cauayan ditsrict. The continuing self-identification of the Cauayan people as Gaddang may be better understood when it is noted in the next chapter that the populations of old Paniquy to the south, untouched by the Ibanag lingua franca, likewise identify themselves with pride as Gaddang. Probably, too, numbers of these Gaddang speakers in Isabela are recent migrants into the valley from the non-Christian Gaddang settlements of the high Cordillera. Where earlier counts in Mountain Province showed several thousand Gaddang (the number varying because of changing boundary adjustments with Isabela) the 1948 census placed the total number of Gaddang speakers in Mountain Province as only 466.

The "Kalinga" census category evidently combines two groups. First are people from the Kalinga districts of Mountain Province (the middle Chico area) who have migrated at least temporarily to Isabela for work. These would tend to be in the north districts around Cabagan. Second are the so-called Kalinga or Irraya of the mountain valleys eastward of the Cagayan, discussed above, most of whom are in the San Mariano district in the upper Ilagan river area toward Palanan Bay.

Of other groups, few Itawis speakers are found south of the Cagayan-

Isabela border, while few Yogad or Ilongot speakers are found this far north. Also, very few Negritos are in this zone of the Sierra Madres. For the Palanan group on the east coast, the 1948 census gives a later total of 3,351 Palanan dialect speakers. A few Ifugaos come down into this part of the valley from their densely settled mountain area south of the non-Christian Gaddang country; but their links are almost entirely with the upper Magat communities to be seen in the next chapter.

The religious statistics for 1939 show for the category of "pagans and not belonging to any religious group" a total of 1,015 persons in the districts south to Ilagan: 225 in the Cabagan area, 574 in Tumauini, and 216 in Ilagan. Further south their numbers total 1,852, with 849 in the San Mariano district, 673 in Dalig, 255 in Gamu, and minor numbers in other districts. A check with the language categories indicates that most of them are obviously in the Gaddang and Kalinga groups. Palanan had a total of 366 in this religious classification.

REVIEW

The dynamics of this section of the valley are dominated, prior to the mid-nineteenth century, by the southward movement of the Ibanag, and of Ibanag language and custom, southward. Only the small minority of older Christians identifying themselves as Gaddang, together with the non-Christian or recently Christianized Gaddang and Gaddang-like groups to the west and east of the valley attest to the apparent wide spread in earlier times of this older population element. Back in the eastern foothills, too, were Negritos, while along the Pacific side the Palanan group had worked their way up from the south.

The middle valley floor seems to have been a zone of dry cultivation prior to mission settlement and agricultural instruction. The chain of towns along the Cagayan, and the vigor of the townsmen, stand out in the ethnohistorical record. To complete the picture, the higher valley must be seen, especially the flats southward between the Cagayan and Magat forks, together with the upper Magat region of "Ituy," and also the heavily populated heights of Ifugao on the eastern slopes of the Cordillera.

XII. The Upper Cagayan Area

The upper part of the Cagayan valley, it has been seen, forks by way of two great river systems: the continuation of the Cagayan river on the east or Sierra Madre side, and the Magat river, or Rio Magat de Cagayan, on the west or Mountain Province side. Their headwaters drain in a complex fashion the adjacent sections of the Sierra Madres and Cordillera Central, together with the northern slopes of the Caraballo Sur mountains. Trails across this southern mountain system, and in Spanish times two roads of sorts, the principal one by way of the Balete Pass, gave land access to the south. The upper Cagayan area comprises the southern half of Isabela Province, together with the province of Nueva Vizcaya.

The Magat river passes in its lower-middle reaches by way of a gorge through rugged and mountainous country. Above this, two fertile valleys open out, the northern one being the old "Paniquy" and the southern one "Ituy." On the west side a series of rivers fall turbulently from the Cordillera heights. To the southwest, the Kayapa valley discharges its runoff southward into Pangasinan to form the Agno and its tributary the Ambayabang. The main road up the valley in Spanish times, as also the modern highway, passed from the middle Cagayan by way of the Ganano valley, over a range into the upper Magat in order to bypass the gorge country, then south across the Caraballo Sur range into Pangasinan.

Eastward, the Cagayan river fork passes for many miles through foothills interspersed with generally narrow valleys and flats. Higher up, its waters accumulate by way of numerous tributaries arising in the rugged fastnesses of the Sierra Madre and Caraballo Sur ranges. The 1935 Coast and Geodetic Survey sheet for this area marks as "unexplored" the large mountain sections to the east and south of the Cagayan's main course, and between its headwaters and those of the Magat.

The Spanish regional names here were unusually complex, and were

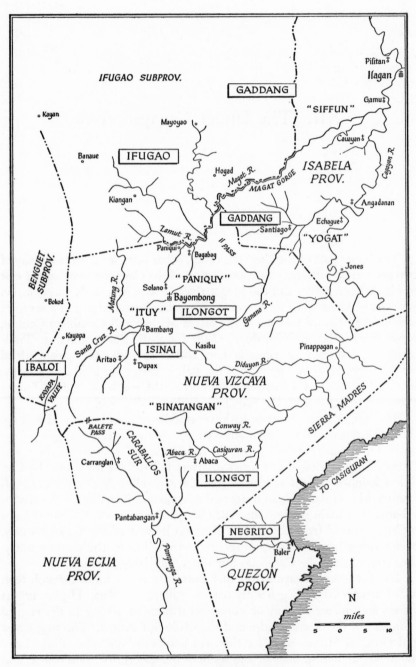

UPPER CAGAYAN AREA

not always used in the same way. It may be well, therefore, to tabulate them.

Paniquy (Paniqui). The middle Magat area around Bayombong; the name also was applied more widely to include the Ganano valley area. A small settlement called Paniqui still exists west of Bagabag.

Yogad (Yogat, Yoga). The region around the Cagayan-Ganano river junction, home of the linguistic and ethnic group also called Yogad, and centered on the town of Echague.

Ituy (Itui, Tuy, Tui, Ytui). The upper Magat area from Bambang to Aritao and Dupax. It was at times applied to the whole middle-upper Magat region.

Diffun (Difun). The mountainous zone between the upper Cagayan and Magat rivers. There are still a dominant mountain and small settlement of that name.

Sinay. Corresponding to the ethnic name "Isinai," this term was occasionally applied to the upper Magat area.

These areas have an almost bewildering array of ethnic names in Spanish documents, as can be seen notably in Perez' "ethnographic dictionary." Paniquy (here the modern nomenclature will be used) has as its predominant element the Gaddang, numbering nearly 20,000. The Yogad ethnic group, though not well reported, is closely related to the Gaddang and totals somewhat over 8,000. In Ituy the indigenous population, as indicated above, is called Isinai, now numbering less than 4,000, and known only through general descriptions. Today the Cagayan-Ganano valley peoples alternate cropping of wet rice and tobacco; considerable amounts of dry rice and maize are also grown, but root crops have a minor place. On the Magat flats, higher in elevation, wet rice, coffee, considerable amounts of maize and root crops (especially sweet potatoes) are grown, but little dry rice.

On the slopes of the Cordillera west of Paniquy are the Ifugao. The Ifugao are wet rice terracers who live typically in small local clusters of scattered homesteads (see, for example, photographs by Worcester in Villaverde), but sometimes grouped in hamlets of two dozen or so houses. Well known for the extensiveness and spectacular character of some of their terrace systems, they have been described by Beyer, Barton, Lambrecht, and others.*

Here, again, walling techniques differ, the Ifugao favoring more sloping walls of stone and earth which follow the hillside shapes in graceful contours, giving a sculptured appearance. They do not use work animals, but turn the soil by hand with wooden spades. Rather than let the fields dry out for alternating seasonal crops, they keep a constant flow of water, at

---

* Knowledge of Ifugao culture should be greatly increased by the work of Harold Conklin, an outstanding field worker, who is currently studying in Ifugao. It is hoped that his research will provide answers or further clues to a number of the problems raised in this book. R. M. K.

most heaping up the soil for growing vegetables. Enormous quantities of sweet potatoes are cultivated on the slopes; e.g., the Banaue district alone in 1948 produced 14,971,000 kilos, or much more than the total for any of the lowland provinces of northern Luzon (see Appendix on crops, p. 345). Very little dry rice is grown, and that traditionally never near to the wet rice. Double cropping of wet rice has been adopted extensively in recent times. The Ifugao house type, clothing, and many other cultural elements are distinctive. Included are elaborations of kinship, law, and ritual, which bind neighbors closely and regulate interaction short of more distant, formerly warring groups. Busy trade trails link Ifugao districts with the Magat valley communities.

South of the Ifugao, where the land rises toward the Kayapa valley and the Benguet heights, the non-Christian people are classed as "Igorot." They appear to be eastern groups of the Ibaloi, speaking dialects of Inibaloi. They stress production of root crops, particularly great quantities of sweet potatoes, and they appear to follow the scattered residential pattern seen as characteristic of the Ibaloi. More than 10,000 of them live within Nueva Vizcaya, and numerous settlement sites are shown on modern maps, along with a network of mountain trails; but they remain undocumented as regards custom and language.

East of the Magat, and through old "Difun" and the Caraballos Sur to the Sierra Madres, are the always sparse groups classed as Ilongot. These have continuity with the Italong Abaca, and other groups along the southern Caraballo slopes seen in the Pangasinan chapter. They are in general dry cultivators, growing rice and roots. Groups in the upper Cagayan fork have been described by William Jones (who was killed by them; see Rideout, 1912; Wilson, 1947, also gives a brief characterization). The Sierra Madres here also have a few surviving Negritos. On the Pacific coast in the Casiguran area there are also lowland settlers who are Tagalog speakers, like the Palanan people seen in the preceding chapter (Philippine agricultural censuses and other sources).

Linguistic studies of the area are not well advanced, but some early results can be reviewed to give a perspective on possible relationships between these ethnic groups. The Pittman group found the Gaddang speech of Bayombong and the Ganano valley to be closely alike, and Yogad to be moderately close to Gaddang. Isinai, by contrast, is very markedly different from the Gaddang-Yogad group and also from both Ifugao and Inibaloi in the mountains. Even more extreme are differences between Isinai and languages further south: Pangasinan, Pampanga, and Tagalog. Perez, in his "ethnographic dictionary" (1904, p. 368), speaks of dialect variations in Isinai, but these have not been studied.

The Ifugao and Inibaloi relationships have already been discussed in previous chapters. Anderson found considerable dialect variation in Ifugao word lists, especially between north and south. Two mountain groups, on the eastern and southern fringes of Ifugao, while rather close in speech, showed a very marked contrast from the rest, suggesting the presence of elements from an ethnically separate and older population; more will be said of this later. The Ilongot dialect groups have not been included so far in the published surveys.

Of all these ethnic groups, the people most interesting and challenging to the Spaniards, as might be expected, were the gold-rich Ibaloi or "Ygolotes" on the Benguet heights to the west. Early Spanish interest in the upper Cagayan, indeed, apart from missionary work, was based primarily on the hope of being able to penetrate Benguet from both sides and thus get control of the gold mines.

EARLY POPULATION PERSPECTIVES

The degree of early Spanish knowledge of the upper Cagayan region, and early population estimates, are shown by the remaining entries in the 1591 encomienda survey. Apparently all of those listed were south of the Cagayan-Magat junction.

Batuagan and Sugarro (probably the area around the present town of Cauayan and up the Cagayan to the village called Fugaru): 600 tributes, or 2,400 souls, "in rebellion."

Balissi, Moyot, and Camaguil (probably the area of the lower Magat): 550 tributes, or 2,200 souls, "in rebellion."

Purrao Culit (not identified, but probably in Paniquy around the present Bayombong): 500 tributes, or 2,000 souls, "in rebellion."

Taotao (possibly the Aritao area in the upper Magat): 500 tributes, or 2,000 souls, "in rebellion."

Yoguan and Togol (apparently the Yogad area around the Cagayan-Ganano junction): 400 tributes, or 1,600 souls, "in rebellion."

Pugao (spoken of as at the "headwaters of the Rio Grande" or Cagayan river, possibly Fugu near the present town of Jones, and described as "still unformed"): 2,000 tributes, or 8,000 souls, "in rebellion."

The totals estimated for this section of the encomienda list are thus 4,550 tributes, or 18,200 people. In 1592 the Governor of the Philippines wrote enthusiastically to the Spanish King: "fifteen thousand tributarios (in Tuy) are subject to your obedience" (B&R, VIII, 109–10; IX, 60).

SPANISH EXPLORING EXPEDITIONS: 1591

This last figure is based upon descriptions carried back to Manila by three Spanish expeditions dispatched in 1591 to explore the upper Cagayan by way of Pangasinan. It has been a subsequent matter of dispute whether they derived the name "Tuy" from the resemblance of the district to a locality called Tui in Galicia, Spain, or from the name of a local village, a leading chief of the area, or a tree found there. These first Spanish contacts are described in some detail in a notable compilation by Dr. Juan Manuel de la Vega called *Expeditions to the Province of Tuy* (Manila, 1609).

Two expeditions sent by the government prior to 1591 in an attempt to open overland communications with Cagayan had failed. The second had turned back because friendly Indians in Pangasinan advised the commander, who had no orders to fight, that "the people whom he was going to discover were numerous and warlike, and were hostile and would kill him" (B&R, xiv, 282). In July of that year, Governor Dasmarinas sent his son, Don Luis, with a party consisting of seventy Spanish soldiers, two Augustinian fathers, many armed Indian chiefs and men from Pampanga, and over 1,400 Indian bearers, to explore the region. Traversing the Balete Pass area, they reached the first "village," called Tuy, on the upper Magat river flats. There they erected a cross, and gave small presents to the people, who in taking an oath of allegiance to the King "swore peace in their own manner" by throwing eggs ceremonially to the ground.

Chiefs of the neighboring villages of Bantal, Bugay, and Burat were then summoned, and with similar ceremonies became "friends and vassals of his Majesty." Because the "wives" had been hidden in the mountains, the Spaniards ordered the chiefs to return them to the village, but they refused. A chief called Tuy, "after whom [this compiler says] the province was thus named," had refused to take part in this peacemaking, and Don Luis also "heard that a great number of armed Indians were in the mountains" to which they had apparently retreated. He therefore "attacked the trenches of the fort built by a troop of Indians, who declared with loud boasting that they desired no peace." The "natives then burned down the village of Tuy itself."

The expedition then visited three of the neighboring villages, which they found deserted, as their inhabitants had "gone to join" peoples further down the river who "before that time had been hostile to them." The chiefs of Tuy, Bantal, Bugay, Burat, and Sicat villages then "begged pardon," and promised to keep the peace and pay tribute. Tuy gave "seven little trinkets of gold in the shape of necklaces," and others also gave such gold necklaces together with some rice.

Proceeding down the Magat, the expedition entered "the province of Dangla" by way of a "passage" at Cayan. Here, too, the chiefs took the oath of allegiance and gave gold necklaces, beads, and "other trifles." Over a seven-day period ten villages were visited, the names of which will be discussed shortly in a geographic review. The people of one village, Boloc, "seized their weapons and fled to the open fields," but otherwise the villagers gave homage. Food shortages were plaguing the party, in spite of the fact that supplies had been "seized" at Tuy and other villages, sometimes without recompense. Proceeding still further down river, they encountered traces of Spaniards who had come up the Cagayan valley from Nueva Segovia. The "old village of Yugan" was deserted, since the people "did not dare" to live in it after having killed seven Spaniards who had come up the Cagayan. They had scattered instead into three hamlets, and the chief had "gone to make peace with the Spaniards who were coming up the river." Four chiefs of these communities rendered homage. They also "pardoned the damage committed by Don Luis in one of the hamlets," and "offered to ransom some women and children" whom the Spaniards had in their camp; after which Don Luis "gave these to the Indians freely." The expedition proceeded from this furthest point in what they called Tuy to Nueva Segovia at the Cagayan mouth (B&R, xiv, 282–87).

This record offers interesting glimpses of the initial contact situation. Alternatives of acceptance or rejection of new cultural elements are seen, and also attempts by the incoming group to force the issues at certain points, with resulting conflicts. The atmosphere of relationships left in the wake of this first expedition is discernible in the records of a military "troop" dispatched about a month later by the Governor to find out what had happened to his son, from whom he had not heard. This second expedition was given a "cordial reception" in Tuy village. But at Bantal the villagers were "drawn up . . . with lance and shield." At Bugay they were "stationed in the passes with the same preparation of arms," and when the commander tried to buy rice they tried to "fool him with some bundles of grass."

The Spaniards here responded by seizing two of the Bugay chiefs. In Dangla valley, again unable to get rice, they seized another chief. Escaping, he "had the village put under arms," and the expedition had to "fortify" themselves for the night, as the people "insolently molested the Spaniards." The two other chiefs then escaped, and the other villages visited were found to be either "under arms" or deserted. This expedition also went down the Cagayan to Nueva Segovia.

This quickly moving military party was followed in November by a third expedition, headed by Don Pedro de Sid, and sent by the Governor to make additional explorations. It found Tuy village deserted, but the people returned after getting assurance of peace. When asked about other settlements existing in the region, they told of "several thickly-settled valleys back of a mountain," presumably in what is now Benguet subprovince. The commander was given "two fowls and a small quantity of rice" as a sign of homage. He told the villagers that tribute would not be collected "for the present," but that "they should settle and cultivate their fields and grow their products, in order to have the wherewithal to pay their tribute when it should be asked. They answered that they would do so." When queried about the source of the gold they possessed, they said that it was received from the villages of "Yguat, Panuypui, and Bila, which were located behind a range of mountains opposite them." Their inhabitants, in turn, received it from the village of Bayaban, located near the "town of Yguat, close to the Ygolotes, where the gold mines were situated, and where the gold was traded." The extent to which such early place names can be located today will be discussed below. Chiefs of three other villages in the Tuy area also gave homage, and small ceremonial gifts were exchanged. In Bugay, Don Pedro was "bled with them" and each drank the other's blood "in order to make the peace sure."

In the valley of Dangla, the same pattern of "friendship" was repeated, with "hens, chickens, swine, and rice," and sometimes a little gold, given in recognition of homage. In return, the commander gave "some bits of cloth, bells, rings, needles, small strings of beads, and combs." This expedition reached the Cagayan river to the northeast, and then moved up southward into its headwaters. At one village, Pintian, the people gave as recognition "venison and sweet potatoes," indicative of the entry of the sweet potato into the upper Cagayan by that date. After a four-day march over "very rough roads," the expedition worked back to Ayubon, through which it had "passed on the way up," and so returned to Pangasinan. Ayubon is possibly the present Imugan, close to the Balete Pass (B&R, xiv, 287-92).

On the basis of information furnished by these first three expeditions, the authorities in Manila debated whether a permanent settlement should be made in the upper Cagayan; but no action was taken. A 1592 account of the first Don Luis expedition says: "The land is very fertile. . . . All the houses are quite large and well constructed. . . . [The] villages have about five hundred or more inhabitants. . . . Two crops of rice are gathered yearly, one being irrigated and the other allowed to grow by itself." This statement is a particularly vital one for ethnohistorical reconstruction, since it indicates the existence of large communities supported by irrigated cropping along with the dry cultivation that probably provided the economic base in most parts of the Cagayan valley at the time of the Spanish arrival. Unfortunately it is not made clear whether the houses were clustered, or scattered out in hamlets such as were seen to be characteristic of the settlement patterns throughout so much of the Cagayan valley. Presumably the irrigation techniques had spread to the upper Cagayan from Pangasinan and the other great flat zones to the south. The records suggest that the overland trails used by the Spaniards to cross the Caraballos were old trading routes, and later records show the existence of linguistic and other contacts between the "Tuy" peoples and those of Pangasinan. This 1592 account of Tuy lists as among its resources deer, buffaloes, swine, goats, poultry, anise, ginger, cotton, and "many wild fruits." Places were set apart where "public matters" were dealt with, because they could not be discussed "in the houses with women." Each village had its chief, but there was no overarching authority among villages (B&R, VIII, 251).

CONTINUING CONTACTS: 1594–1609

In 1594 Captain Toribio de Miranda, with four Franciscan fathers, eighty soldiers, and a group of bearers, undertook a new expedition to "pacify and complete the exploration of the province of Tuy." Its report refers to the vicinity of Tuy village as "the valley of Dumagui"; the fathers gave to it the name Todos Santos (All Saints). At Guilaylay village, "which lies in front of Tuy," the expedition was courteously received. At Anit village, they found that "From the houses were hanging the heads of people and animals. On being asked why they did that, the people answered that it was their custom."

The expedition built a fort which they named St. Joseph. The chiefs of other villages visited them, and one, Ybarat, promised them rice, but failed to bring it. Later he came wtih "a suckling pig and four jars of rice." The Spaniards, suspecting treachery, seized him. He continued to be "insolent," refusing to bring "provisions either by requests or by threats." The commander also heard that the "chiefs were waiting in the village of Buguey [Bugay] to kill the Spaniards." To meet the need for food, the soldiers took rice, "by orderly means," from the granaries of Bantal village, which was deserted. One of the principal women, however, the "mother of Chief Tuy," proved friendly, and visited the fathers in the fort. The chief, Ybarat, was freed, but his children were held as hostages, and the same was done with another chief who had been "arrested."

Leaving for the valley of Dangla, this expedition was generally received in more friendly fashion. In the first village, Agulan, many children were wearing gold necklaces of "good quality," which were said to come from Balagbac. In another, Yrao, "a quarter-legua's distance" away, that is, about three-quarters of a mile, they saw "chased gold necklaces, and armlets reaching to the elbow, and anklets," together with earrings of "fine gold." In Palan village the chief was Ybarat's brother-in-law, indicative of marriage between high-born families of this upper Magat area; here the Spaniards had to seize rice, which they paid for in cloth.

From Dangla, the expedition crossed "a lofty mountain to which the Spaniards gave the name Altos de Santa Zicilia" (St. Cecelia's Peaks). On the other side, in what was evidently the Ganano river valley, the villages continued to be large. The Spaniards had to force their way into the first two villages, Tuguey and Giarin, in the face of "stout resistance" with bows and arrows. The people ceased to resist, however, at the "discharge of the arquebuses." As the expedition was passing another village, arrows were shot from a thicket and killed a guide. The expedition entered several other villages, including Balagbac, telling the people of their purpose, and having the fathers "instruct them in the faith"; presents were also exchanged. Some villages were deserted. "The Indians seemed to be much disturbed, and with threats warned the Spaniards to depart from their country, since all the valley was uniting in order to kill them. . . . [Even] the Pogetes, who are Indians of the more rugged parts of the mountain, had joined the others." An "extensive ambuscade" was discovered, but at a volley from the arquebuses the people fled.

The expedition then returned to its fort in Tuy. In passing back through Balagbac and other villages, it found them abandoned, and the fort was in a state of semi-siege on its arrival. The commander made two further journeys, and "discovered certain very small villages among the mountains," possibly hamlets of dry cultivators, but failed to locate some supposed gold mines. In a further sally, the chief Ybarat was captured. He was later sent to Manila, where he was well treated by Don Luis, who had become Governor in place of his father, and in due course returned home "well satisfied." The commander also returned to Manila because of sickness.

In his place, the Governor sent Captain Clavijo, "with orders to penetrate the mountains further in order to discover the mines of the Ygolotes." But his party was turned back by an assault from what he reported to be "more than one thousand Indians," in the course of which his guide was wounded. The fort was then abandoned, and the whole expedition returned to Manila (B&R, xiv, 292–99).

In 1606 an encomendero and two other Spaniards tried to enter Tuy, with a considerable party including twenty chiefs presumably from the lower Cagayan. The Tuy people attacked them and killed "more than a hundred," including the Spaniards and chiefs. A year later, two leaders from the region traveled to Manila to offer their homage, and they were well treated, though the matter was "regarded lightly." Nevertheless, a certain Don Dionisio, who had been on all the Tuy expeditions, was given permission to go back with them. He then brought seventeen chiefs to Manila, but they were treated "coldly" in view of the killing of the encomendero. Don Dionisio reported that the people wanted to receive the Christian faith. Already they had learned "the prayers and Christian instruction" in the "Tagal language" (i.e., Tagalog) from a servant of the chief Ybarat, and "went to pray before a cross raised by the same chief."

Don Dionisio reported that the region "contains many settlements and many level plains, while its rice is the best that is grown in the Yndias." Sugar cane was produced in abundance. In addition to forest, there was much grassy land and many bare mountains, the highest of which were very rugged (B&R, xiv, 299–301).

Manuel de la Vega's *Expeditions to the Province of Tuy* (1609), from which most of these materials are taken, has a special section on "what has been known from old times, in these districts, of the rich mines of the Ygolotes." Already, however, the relevant materials from this account have been summarized in the Pangasinan chapter, so they need not be repeated here. This compiler's work concludes that even apart from the gold, Tuy province offers as "wealth" the prospect of reducing to the faith a total population "said to number more than 100,000 souls" (B&R, xiv, 301-6, 315).

THE EARLY GEOGRAPHY OF THE UPPER CAGAYAN

At this point the geography of the upper Cagayan may be reviewed in the light of the place names appearing in these initial Spanish accounts. Already, as shown, the encomienda names of 1591 for the upper Cagayan valley mostly appear to be identifiable in terms of general localities. Expeditions coming overland appear to have used the Balete Pass area to cross the Caraballos, taking what was presumably a pre-Spanish trade trail through "Ayubon," suggested to be the present Imugan. They would then descend into the upper Magat valley in the vicinity of the present town of Aritao.

The flats here, with their large communities and irrigated agriculture, evidently comprised the valley of "Dumagui," or Todos Santos. Stretching down the Magat for some 15 miles, it had as named settlements the following: Tuy: 60 houses; Bantal: 30 houses; Barat and Bugay or Bugney: 500 houses; Guilaylay: 40 houses; Anit: 70 houses; Sicat and Marangui: house numbers not recorded.

Of these names, none show as such on modern maps or in the Philippine *Gazeteer*. But Bugay, important in mission records to follow, will be seen as the modern Aritao, while Sicat could be the present small settlement of Ducait.

The Magat passes down for about three miles through foothills and then opens out again through some seventeen miles of open flats before it enters the rugged gorge country spoken of earlier. This appears to have been the valley or province of "Dangla," later to be counted a part of Paniquy. The settlement names given in the various expedition records vary considerably. They are Dangla or Agulan: 80 houses; Yrao: 60 houses; Palan or Japalan: 80 houses; Bayaban, Balayan, Chicanen, Yabios, Bugai, Bayocos, Banete, Lamut or Pamut, Palilamot, Bolo or Bolos, Balabad or Balabat, Nacalan, and Paita or Paitan: none with house numbers recorded.

Of these, Bayaban could have been ancestral to the present capital of Nueva Vizcaya Province, Bayombong, and Balabad to the town of Bagabag. Lamut and Paitan are presumably the settlements with the same names today, and Bugai possibly the present Bangar; otherwise the names are not identifiable.

From the Dangla area, travelers of the time could proceed down river through the Magat gorge country, and this may have been the route taken by the first two 1591 expeditions. Alternatively, they could cross by trail some 10 miles eastward over the mountains, apparently past "St. Cecelia's Peaks." This would bring them over into the headwaters of the Ganano river, anticipating the modern highway route. Then by going down the Ganano valley they would join the upper Cagayan river near the present town of Echague, in the province of "Yogad" or Yogat." From there they could continue by water direct to Nueva Segovia near the Cagayan mouth. Alternatively, they could head up the Cagayan river, as the third 1591 expedition did, going south and then west via one of the Cagayan headwater streams such as the Conwap or Casecnan and over arduous mountain trails to the Tuy area. Or they could cross southward over other difficult trails from the Cagayan headwaters into the headwaters of the Pampanga river in what is now Nueva Ecija Province. This is Ilongot country, to be described later.

The record of the third 1591 expedition says that it "shifted its course" at the village of Balabad, and "went up the river." This suggests that it left the Magat at the present Bagabag, as the modern highway does in crossing eastward to the Ganano valley, and so proceeded up the Cagayan river. Only four settlements are named as having been encountered: Yanil, Sanguli, Pintian, and Purao. The 1594 expedition also tells of crossing from Dangla past "St. Cecelia's Peaks" into what was evidently the Ganano-Cagayan valley area. The following settlements were reported: Yanil: house numbers not recorded; Tuguey: 112 houses; Giarin: 40 houses; Pao: 40 houses: Bizinan: 12 houses; Balagbac: 120 houses; Buya: 30 houses; Apio: 180 houses; Paytan, Palali, and Batobalos: house numbers not recorded.

A guide also informed the commander about "certain villages located in the mountain to the south" called Piat, Pulinguri, Malias, Ybana, and Aplad. A few of these names bear a vague resemblance to those on modern maps: Tuguey to Diadi, the first settlement at the head of the Ganano valley; Paytan to Patul; Buya to Bayug; Apio to Ipil; and Piat to Payac. But such identifications are tenuous indeed. The river name "Ganano," which appears on contemporary maps, has an alternative form "Gaddano," found for instance on Algue's 1899 map of the area, and so may be derived from the ethnic name Gaddang or Gaddan.

Certain villages were named as the sources of gold from the mountains: Yguat, Panuypui, and Bila, with Yguat as the "town" receiving the gold from Bayaban. The name Panuypui will be seen later in a more general form as used for some of the peoples living in the Caraballo Sur mountains south of Aritao. Yguat could conceivably have been the present Ibaloi (Benguet Igorot) settlement of Bokod in the nearest gold-producing area, located close to the headwaters of the Santa Cruz river, which is one of the principal waterways of the upper Magat, or else may relate to the name of the adjacent Mt. Agat; just west of this area are the gold deposits of the upper Agno river region. The name "Bayaban" does not appear on modern maps of Mountain Province; presumably, therefore, the lowland settlement of that name was a trading and distribution point for the metal. It must be emphasized that all this early geography and nomenclature, mainly worked out by Manuel de la Vega in the light of the expedition reports, has a margin of vagueness which makes its modern reconstruction largely a hypothetical exercise.

RECORDS OF THE EARLY ITUY MISSIONS

One of the Augustinian fathers who was a member of the first 1591 expedition estimated that the conversion of Tuy would require "at least forty" missionaries (B&R, IX, 102). According to Aduarte's *Historia* of 1640, a Dominican father, Fray Juan de San Jacinto, visited the area early in the seventeenth century from the Pangasinan mission run by that Order. He was accompanied by "only two Indians."

Here he taught, settled their disputes, and brought them to the faith. These people were a race of mountaineers, among whom other religious had not been safe even with an escort of many soldiers; but [the father] . . . caused them to become calm, and many of them came sometimes to Pangasinan to ask that religious be given to them.

When, however, the Dominicans proposed to the Governor that they establish a mission in Tuy, the Franciscans "came and said that this conversion belonged to them because it was very near to the ministry and convent they had in Baler." Aduarte states that the Dominicans "instantly yielded" (B&R, XXXI, 287–88). The Ayer Collection includes a document, dated 1609, which actually granted the Dominicans the right to evangelize Ituy, prior to the Franciscan move (Document 18).

The Franciscans assigned this new mission to fathers working out of Casiguran. An unsigned history of their Order written in 1649 gives an account of their efforts:

[Tuy] province has some valleys enclosed by rough mountains, which are bounded on the north by the province of Cagayan and on the east by the village of Casiguran, the last of our missions. [The provincial father] heard of these people . . . and in order to reduce them to civilization and to obedience to our God and our King, sent fathers Fray Pedro de la Concepción and Fray Joseph Fonte to them, as well as . . . [two brothers] to act as nurses. These religious lived in the province for two years, and the Indians furnished them with what was necessary, with all respect and kindness.

The account tells of small children being baptized "when in danger of death," together with an aged sick man.

Considering how poor were the facilities for that conversion—for the people were scattered in groups of huts, and had no villages or government—and that between the said village of Casiguran and the said valleys of Tuy intervene thickets and mountains inhabited by savage Cimarrones [i.e., Negritos or Ilongots—or both]; and that these mountains in themselves are very rough, so that no one could go to and return from Tuy without undergoing the worst kind of trouble and danger; therefore the father provincial returned to his mission at Casiguran with all the religious. (B&R, xxxv, 317–18.)

The reference to the Tuy people as scattered in "groups of huts," even if it plays down the population picture, may indicate that some at least of the so-called "villages" really consisted of separate clusters of hamlets. A *Relation* by Coronel in 1621 describes the people as "peaceable" and offering "no opposition" (B&R, xix, 287; xxxv, 317–19).

Aduarte's *Historia* (1640) next takes up the activities of the Dominicans in the region. He notes that the Franciscans achieved "little result," because of "death and sickness." By the 1620's the Dominican fathers working in adjacent Pangasinan were receiving repeated requests from Ituy for missionaries to be sent. These culminated when a delegation of some thirty chiefs came to meet the father provincial of the Order during his visit to Calasiao, in Pangasinan. Again the Ayer Collection has a document, dated 1625, in which the Dominicans were authorized to take over the mission (Document 27). Two fathers, Aduarte says, were then dispatched on an exploratory visit, with orders to return and report on their impressions.

They went about through the villages of the province, setting up in the public squares large crosses. . . . That the devil might begin to give up his ancient possession of the natives, the fathers taught them the worship they should perform, and some prayers of the "Christian doctrine" translated into the language of Pangasinan. That language they half understood, though it was different from their own. They understood it all so well that they immediately began to say the prayers they knew, around the crosses, seated on cane benches which they made for the purpose—two of them intoning the prayer, and the rest repeating it.

This brief glimpse into the acceptance of the symbols of a new religion is a significant instance of acculturative response of a voluntary nature, and seems to repeat an earlier self-motivated adaptation to Christianity reported by Manuel de la Vega.

The fathers left, and circumstances were such that they could not be sent back immediately. Several years later a group of chiefs called once more on the Dominican father provincial when he was visiting Pangasinan. On December 6, 1632, therefore, Fray Tomás Gutiérrez, one of the two fathers who had made the exploratory trip, was sent with Fray Juan de Arjona to open a permanent mission. They were received with "great demonstrations of joy" at the village of Ituy, where "ambassadors" from all the villages of the province visited them. They then made a round of the "eleven" villages, "great and small." In a letter written by them three months later they sent back a report which Aduarte summarizes. Of agricultural methods, they noted that

the country was so fertile that when the Indians desired to plant their rice they only burn over a part of the mountain and, without any further plowing or digging, they made holes with a stick in the soil, and dropped some grains of rice in them. This was their manner of sowing; and after covering the rice with the same earth, they obtained very heavy crops. . . . They leave the rice which they gather, each one in his own field, heaped high in the spike and covered with straw. They go there and carry what they want to their houses, to grind and eat, without fearing that anyone will take what is not his.

This precise account of a dry cultivation system is of key importance as it appears to belie the earlier reference to wet rice cropping, along with dry rice, and with storage in granaries. The months from December to February, when the fathers were making these observations, should have had plentiful evidence of wet rice fields along the valley floor. If the usual June to November-January growing cycle of the lowlands prevailed, they should have seen the harvest in progress as in their familiar Pangasinan settings. Or if, in this high and cool zone, rice varieties suited to the December-January to midsummer cycle that marked the Cordillera wet rice terracers prevailed, they would have seen the transplanting in full swing. More will be said later of these alternative possibilities, and of their significance for reconstructing lowland-mountain relationships. The implication for the record at this point would seem to be that either wet cropping had been abandoned or the valley groups concerned had moved back into the mountains. Correlated with this apparent drastic change in the economic base was a sharp shrinkage in population numbers. Early-eighteenth-century mission counts will show that the hundreds of houses and thousands of people had vanished. An inventory of baptized persons throughout the upper Magat valley in 1740, when supposedly everyone was converted, was to show a total of 2,755, and the Isinai ethnic group of today numbers less than 4,000.

There were, the fathers recorded, "pleasant valleys with quiet rivers and streams in them from which the natives obtain some gold." The fathers noted the use of gold earrings. "They have no sort of money, so that all their sales and purchases are carried on by barter." Fish caught in the rivers were an important item of diet. The villages were kept "very clear and in good condition"—a "new thing among the Indians." Also unusual was the "great fraternity between different villages," rather than "the law of 'might makes right' . . . at the expense of their heads." Apparently a voluntary self-pacification had occurred, judging by their earlier warlike tendencies. The people readily offered their "infants" to the fathers for baptism, so that within about three months they had baptized "some four hundred." They moved more slowly with adults, however, because preparing them for the catechism called for translating the materials into the local language, which the fathers were still in the process of learning. They also introduced the standard mission concentration policy:

In order that so few ministers may be able to teach the Indians, it is necessary to bring them together into a smaller number of villages, conveniently arranged so that the people may be visited and helped in their necessities. Since the country is very mountainous, the fathers have determined to bring and gather them in large settlements, at sites convenient for their fields, near a river which rises in this country. . . . This is the only point as to which they are somewhat obstinate, because they are greatly grieved to leave their ancient abode. However, most of them have accepted it, and it is hoped that the rest will come. (B&R, xxxii, 192–201.)

The river referred to here is of course the Magat, of which the fathers had only limited knowledge at the time, since they had come from Pangasinan. Malumbres, in his tabulation of missions founded in Cagayan, names four mission communities established in the area at this time: San Miguel near the present Dupax (1633), Dongla in the same area (1637), Tuhay which is presumably Bugay (1637) and Baxabax which could be either Bagabag or Bayombong (1637).

Shortly after this work was started, Fray Tomás, then seventy-three years old, died after a fall from a precipice in the course of his travels (B&R, xxxii, 215). Ituy drops out of the records, so that it may be assumed that the Dominicans could not continue to staff the area. The anonymous Franciscan *History* of 1649 quoted above refers to this Dominican withdrawal by saying tersely, after telling of the earlier abandonment of its own mission activities: "The fathers of St. Dominic also . . . abandoned them for the same reasons as we" (B&R, xxxv, 318). A description of the Philippines by another Franciscan, Fray Bartolomé de Letona (1662), speaks of Ituy as "peopled by heathen Indians, not yet subdued" (B&R, xxxvi, 194).

A later Dominican *Historia* by Baltazar de Santa Cruz (1676) indicates some revival of the Dominican work, as the name of the mission of "San Miguel of Ituy, in the province of Nueva Segovia," occurs in a list of authorized "houses" of the Order. He says:

That is a great stretch consisting of heathen settlements for the greater part, although there are some Christians among them, some of whom are those who flee from other villages. It lies on the eastern border of the province of Cagayan, and extends from some high mountain chains to the coast; and, as it is so rough a land, it has not yet been possible to conquer it, although many attempts have been made, the religious going sometimes with and sometimes without soldiers. Missionaries have also been appointed on various occasions; but although they have baptized many persons, they have not been able to convert them all.

On one occasion, he reports, an appointed vicar, Fray Teodoro de la Madre de Dios, entered the province with "some priests as companions" and with a "presidio of Spanish soldiers at the command of the governor." But many soldiers and two of the fathers died, "because of the poor climate or poor food." The party continued in residence for two years, and "baptized many people there."

But either because of the sickness, which had developed into a plague, or because the Indians were at war continually with other people of the interior, more powerful, who greatly persecuted them, and the faith of Christians: for all these causes, and because they could not cope with so many dangers and troubles so long as the natives were not quiet, the presidio that was still left retired to Cagayan, and the fathers returned, as they had lost hope of obtaining more fruit.

The account adds, however, that "our religious are accustomed to return there every little while," and on such occasions some were baptized, and the faithful "do not fail to come." In another section this Dominican history speaks of various fathers of the Pangasinan mission knowing the language of Ituy, presumably the Isinai dialect (B&R, xxxvii, 98–99, 138).

THE MOUNTAIN MISSIONS

Shortly before his death, Fray Tomás had noted that in the mountains west of the area "there wander a tribe of Indians known as Alegueses, a vagabond people having no settled places of abode." Fray Tomás sent word to them by an Ituy chief that "if they wished to come and settle one of the new sites which he indicated, he would receive them there as sons." They agreed to come, but had delayed doing so up to the time the mission work lapsed (B&R, xxxii, 201).

These Alegueses, or Alaguetes as they were later called, were evidently a segment of the mountain populations living along the fringe of the present Mountain Province, apparently in the vicinity of the lower Kayapa valley (Pampang river). Their "vagabond" way of life was presumably a shifting dry cultivation system. They came again to the notice of Dominican missionaries penetrating from Pangasinan into the southern zones of Benguet subprovince. About 1685, according to Salazar's Dominican *Historia,* a "mission for the reduction of the Igorots and Alaguetes" was established at a center called San Bartolomé, and lasted for more than two decades. Its history was reviewed in the Pangasinan chapter, where it was seen that some of its converts became absorbed in lowland areas and some returned to the mountains. In 1732, a new mission village was opened on almost the same site as San Bartolomé, at a location called Maliongliong, for "the conversion of the Igorots," and this center was called San Joseph. It became one of the stopover points with a resthouse on a road built shortly afterward from Pangasinan to the upper Cagayan, as will be seen below.

Salazar says that one result of the work at San Joseph was to interest the Dominicans once more in the mission opportunities in Ituy and in Paniquy, where they resumed work in 1739 (B&R, XLIII, 76–77).

In the late seventeenth century, as was noted in the previous chapter, the government encouraged the spread of the Dominican work in the middle Cagayan southward toward Paniquy and Yogad. These "provinces" lying between Irraya and Ituy were still virtually unknown. The Dominican map of this period referred to previously as drawn between 1688 and 1693 shows Paniquy as corresponding roughly to the valley of Dangla, above the gorge area, with what seems to be "lomillas pequeñas" written across them, i.e., presumably little saddles or ridges. Yogad appears on the map as the "province of Yoga," and covers the Cagayan-Ganano valley area around the present towns of Echague and Santiago. The province of Ituy is indicated as comprising the Magat headwaters area, while the upper Cagayan river is labeled "province of Sifun." No mission stations are shown on this map for any of these zones, by contrast to those spotted through the lower and middle Cagayan as far as Itugud.

Before the Dominicans were able to move far south, however, the Augustinians took over Ituy as a mission field. Working up the Sierra Madres by way of the Pampanga river headwaters, in what is now Nueva Ecija Province, they had opened a mission in 1702 for the mountain peoples, variously of Ilongot and Negrito ethnic types, scattered through the rugged area from the Caraballo Sur mountains to Baler Bay on the east coast. From the Pampanga headwaters, the fathers of this Order carried their work in turn as a geographic continuity across into Ituy and the headwaters of the Cagayan to the east.

The bases used for this work were two settlements fairly high in the mountains, Pantabangan and Carranglan, both small towns of today. These two centers, and the mission activities in the area, were discussed in the Pangasinan chapter, where the work of Fray Antolin de Arzaga in these mountain areas and his descriptions of the "Italon" and "Abaca" were set out in detail. Also described were the activities of Fray Antolin's successor, Fray Alejandro Cacho, who in his "more than forty years" of work turned "what was . . . a gloomy and impenetrable forest" into "a fertile field and beautiful province" (B&R, XIV, 70, n. 18).

CONTINUING MISSION WORK: PANIQUY AND ITUY

Fray Alejandro, in the course of his work, moved across the Caraballos into Ituy, and so came to include the Isinai group within its scope. As seen above, the Dominicans had let this mission field lapse except for occasional visits from their Pangasinan centers. Despite the "stubbornness, violence, and cruelty" of the people of Ituy, which had hampered Dominican work,

Fray Alejandro, laboring there from 1715 to 1723, "softened their hard hearts." Fray Antonio Mozo, the principal chronicler of these Augustinian mission efforts (B&R, xlviii, 69–78), tells how, with his fellow workers, he was able to "found four new villages" of the Isinai people "not to mention many others besides, from other tribes," who "united themselves" with the five Italon mission villages previously established by the Augustinians in the mountains to the south. "[By] the year 1738 he had come to the end of baptizing and converting the entire Isinay tribe, with a large part of other tribes, whom he settled in different villages. All these [were] thoroughly subdued and tamed, baptized, and established in a well civilized mode of life."

In 1740, the Ituy mission was "surrendered" by the Augustinians to the Dominican Order. This was done voluntarily, in order to devote effort to other areas, and was approved by Royal decree. A laudatory inventory referred to by Mozo noted that at the time the number of baptized persons was 2,755, a very low figure in view of the claims made in the Augustinian records above, but it is consistent with the eighteenth-century population figures to be given shortly.

Dominican recorders now resume the story of the Ituy and Paniquy missions. A pamphlet by Fray Manuel del Rio (*circa* 1740) speaks of the district of Paniquy as having long been a target for Dominican mission work, based at the Itugud and Santa Rosa (Gamu) missions discussed in the previous chapter. According to Fray Manuel, seven attempts were made prior to 1736 to establish a mission in Paniquy, but these met with "only indifferent and occasional success" (B&R, xlviii, 131–32). Salazar's *Historia* also mentions such repeated attempts of the Dominicans in the Cagayan to work southward, especially into mountainous areas:

[Although] the attempt has been made several times to reduce all that paganism, it has been impossible to obtain it until now as the said heathens live in remote places and are separated from communication with other provinces. Therefore, they seem almost unconvertible, as the missionaries could not live among them without notable discomfort, lack of health, and even not without danger to their lives. For on the eight or more occasions that the religious have entered those mountains for the purpose of reducing the heathens who live in them, sometimes escorted by soldiers, and at other times without that aid, in all of them, they have experienced lack of health and death. . . . Hence, the reduction of all that paganism was deemed impracticable. (B&R, xliii, 65.)

In 1735, according to del Rio's continuing account, the Augustinians, who by then were planning the transfer of the Ituy missions to Dominican control, informed the latter that "those hearts were becoming softened." In 1736, therefore, Fray Diego de la Torre, who was based at the Ilagan mission in the middle Cagayan, made a "reconnaissance" among the heathen peoples. He first met with "rebuffs," but was later able to win the "confidence of some among them." They told him that the "only obstacle" to mission success was the "impassableness of the high-road from Cagayan to Pangasinan"; if this were open to travel, they said, "they would have no longer a barrier between themselves and Spanish influence." This interest in roads for trade and peaceful contact has its parallels in other acculturative situations, including the responses of the Mountain Province peoples to early American penetration.

In 1737 the Philippine Government "granted the establishment of a mission in Paniqui," composed of four Dominican fathers and "the guards necessary for their protection, at the expense of the King." They "encountered determined opposition from the natives, who, advised by the demon, would not admit them into their villages. The chiefs demanded, as the price of even allowing the missionaries to remain near the villages, gifts of beads, cattle and horses, and gold; and, finally, two men to slay as offerings to their demons." One of the fathers died, and it was suspected that he was poisoned. Then "an Indian woman of rank" placed the missionaries under her protection, and in due course some at least "consented to make a treaty of peace," a number of the chiefs "even going to Nueva Segovia to ratify it."

Even so, the fathers "still experienced much opposition." This came especially from the people of the mission village of Bayombong, referred to by Fray Manuel del Rio as "the most southern and the chief village of that heathen district," i.e., Paniquy. Here too, perhaps, there was a commercial reason for wanting to keep Christianity from the satellite infidels. The lives of the fathers were often in danger, "especially when their Indian guards became frightened and began to retreat to their homes." Two more of the fathers then died suddenly, again "probably from poison." The Government, at the appeal of Dominican authorities, then established military posts both to guard the missionaries and to "ensure the safety of the road which was to be built from Pangasinan to Cagayan." Meantime, however, one of the surviving fathers had secured the support of a powerful chief, Danao, and "toleration" from another, Ansimo, so that "almost nothing remained to be overcome" (B&R, xlviii, 131–33).

Del Rio, the chronicler of the above events, was sent to make the necessary explorations for the planning of the Pangasinan-Cagayan road. He gives useful descriptions of the region and people, which may be summarized here. The "province of Paniqui," he says, extended north to south from the last Christian village of Cagayan, which was Itugud, to the last infidel village, called "Bayongbong," the distance between being about a three-day journey. Its breadth, not by then ascertained, included "more than fifteen leagues of plains" from the mountains of the "Igorrots" to those of the "Ilongots." Two ranges of lofty peaks intersected the region, and "in these mountains dwell these two and other barbarous tribes, whom hitherto it has been impossible to conquer." The villages are "numerous, although not very large"—"on the shores of the Maga river alone, which flows through the length of that province from south to north, are counted eighteen villages, including both large and small ones." Of the unconverted people in Paniquy, presumably southern Gaddang groups, he says:

The people of that tribe are distinct from those adjacent to them, and have a different language from the others. The men are accustomed from childhood to file their upper teeth into points . . . and the teeth, after being dyed a sort of dark blue, are adorned—when the person of rank is a chief—with small golden pegs. For persons of rank, it is considered very unsightly to have white teeth. . . . [They] pay respect only to some chiefs who have acquired a reputation as such by their valorous deeds.

These people, del Rio continues, are not "given to religion or worship." They have

only some superstitions regarding the songs of birds, and similar things, founded on oracles which are given to them by the demon, through the agency of their aniteras, or priestesses. These women . . . after taking a certain potion are possessed by the same demon; and through their mouths this enemy is able to declare his will to those wretched people. . . . [Those] heathen are wont to buy Indians from other provinces, in order to offer them in sacrifice, by killing them, to the demon. (B&R, xlviii, 124–25.)

In reporting on his planning of the road, del Rio speaks also of the opposition of the "Igorrots" to the undertaking. The steps he took to get the assent of these "bloodthirsty and very treacherous people" have been described in the Pangasinan chapter. The road for the two days' journey was completed in 1739 under joint government and mission (both Augustinian and Dominican) auspices, by local Indian labor. It extended from Asingan in Pangasinan to the "village of Buxay [Bujay], among the Isinay people." This, as noted earlier, was not the route of the modern highway, through the Balete Pass, but was further to the west. Roadhouses for travelers were built at regular intervals "in the places called Colong, Malalapang, and Malionlion." At Malionlion, referred to as "the last town on the border of Pangasinan," a missionary was stationed to serve "some Igorrot Christians" living there, with others who were prospective converts. A reference is made in passing to an attempt by a Governor of the Philippines twenty years previously to open such a road, which had proved unsuccessful in spite of heavy expenditures. When this new road project was completed, del Rio was accompanied to Manila by Danao and other prominent chiefs, where they were "feasted and laden with presents" (B&R, xlviii, 134–36).

Another Dominican chronicler, Fray Bernardo Ustariz, wrote an account at this time (1745) of the Paniquy and Ituy missions. He tells how, until 1739, "the gospel had secured no stable footing" in Paniquy, which was "hiding among the provinces of Cagayan, Pangasinan, and Pampanga." In the four succeeding years, however, "encouraging progress" was made, with liberal aid from the government. "In those remote and wild regions, the missionaries suffered greatly from lack of suitable shelter and food, the inclemencies of the weather, and the hardships of traveling." Ustariz illustrates this by telling of a father who reached a village named Lacab at nightfall. On calling to its inhabitants, a "confused yelling from the women" indicated angrily that he should not enter. The villagers were at the time "offering a public supplication" in order to obtain rain, and were afraid that "the devil would not speak to them" if the father were to be lodged there. Only slowly was such opposition broken down, and even many who "desired baptism" were "lured away by the devil, speaking through the priestesses," or else intimidated by the "opposition of their friends." Some believed that to become a Christian would "render one a perpetual slave to the Spaniards."

By 1743, however, the fathers had succeeded in "erecting six churches, in the villages of Cauayan, Appiat, Bagabag, Lappau, Daruyag, and Carig." In addition, Bayombong had a church taken over from the Augustinians. Of Bayombong, which was to become the capital of Nueva Vizcaya Province, Ustariz says:

[Although] some Christians were there when it was received from the reverend Augustinian fathers, there were still many infidels, of whom some lived with the said Christians, and others had fled to a forest called Vacal—from which they have gradually come out by dint of the visits which the missionaries have frequently made them—and with the baptisms among them an increase has been made in the number of the Christians who were in Bayombong.

Vacal is probably the present-day settlement area of Wacal in the mountains some five miles northwest of Bayombong. In the seven churches listed above, there were reported to be 970 persons baptized in the six years to 1743, besides ten "apostates" who had returned "after many years" to the faith—again an extraordinarily low figure. It was also noted that special care had to be used in administering baptism, since many requests "were caused by the desire to escape from tyrannical lords, or from creditors, or from the penalty due to their crimes"; moreover, "not a few imagined that they could thus gain some more influential position among their people." This last-mentioned line of reasoning is also found in other acculturation situations: some persons may judge that an alternative socio-religious system will give them status and power not available to them in their traditional system.

By 1745, when Ustariz wrote his work, a "gratifying change" was taking place in the "feelings of those people, even among the infidels." They "even live more peaceably among themselves, committing fewer murders." The government had provided "extraordinary Indian guards" who were undertaking various "works" in all the villages. In Bayombong, Cauayan, and Lappau, these guards had built "substantial houses and churches of planks," and they had wooden houses and churches under construction in the other four villages. Previously the mission buildings had been "little more than hovels." The Indian workers employed for such construction, as also for road building and repair, were paid by the government. But the missionaries found it necessary, in order to "influence [the heathen] not only by fear but by love," to give them "gratuities and presents." They also had to support some of them, "even for several months," when they "came from a great distance to receive instruction and being in a strange land, had no means of support." The fathers also "furnished plows to all who asked for them."

PROBLEMS OF CONSOLIDATING SPANISH CONTROL

Ustariz next comments on mission work in the "district of Ytuy," including the "villages of Bujay and Dupay." There the Dominicans met "many obstacles and afflictions," as the people were not so "docile" as those in Paniquy. "Nevertheless, much fruit has been gathered, in baptizing many infidels of the neighboring tribes, Ygolot, Ylongot, and others; and in reclaiming some apostates who were hiding in the mountains."

The missionaries were troubled not only by the "obstinacy" of the Ituy people, but also by the hostilities committed on their converts by a "tribe close by," called "Panoypuyes," who made raids on the settled communities. The "Ysinays," he says, were by contrast "a timid people," and these marauders kept them in "abject submission"—killing them when found alone or unprotected, raiding their "cattle," and demanding "contributions of produce" and even human beings whom they "offered in sacrifice to their false gods." The name "Panoypuyes" apparently corresponds to the locality name "Panuypui," noted by the 1591 expedition as a "village" in the mountains which was one of the sources of gold.

Fearing that the Ituy mission would have to be abandoned because of these raids, Ustariz says, the Dominicans appealed to the government for aid. In 1745 an "armed body of men" was sent from Pangasinan, without much result. Three years later, 282 soldiers were sent from Cagayan, under a Spanish commander, Ibarra, including recruits from the Tuao-Malaueg area in the lower Chico further north, and they were joined by Indian guards and converts from Paniquy. This expedition captured and burned the "villages of the Panoypuyes," including "Ajanas," their principal center. They also killed Sapac, the leading chief. Ustariz quotes a report of the expedition as telling of a large "pavilion," in Ajanas, on higher ground than the rest, and surrounded by a wall of stones. "[It] was destined only for the residence of the unmarried men, who, according to the custom of that tribe, are not allowed to cover the more shameful part of their bodies, nor sleep where the married people live; and the said pavilion also served as a watchtower, the duty of sentinel service belonging to the unmarried men."

After this punitive expedition, "the missions and Christian Indians" enjoyed peace, and people "flocked for baptism." In "Bujay" alone, about 200 Ygolotes were baptized, and by the date that Ustariz wrote, 1745, "more than seven hundred souls" had been newly added in the Ituy mission. "[The] valor of the Cagayan Christians in this undertaking having spread abroad, it has penetrated into even the most remote part of the mountains, attracting even the most secluded of the Ylongots, a tribe who rival the Panoypuyes in valor and fierceness."

The Paniquy mission areas also felt the effects of the punitive action, for "at the report of such an achievement more than six hundred persons came to enroll themselves for the catechism from the Yogad and Gaddang tribes." Furthermore, "forty souls from the village of Ybana in the Ygolot tribe . . . united themselves to the village of Bayombong," these possibly Ifugao. On the south side of the Caraballos, "many families" came down to the mission center of Puncan from the "Gumangi" tribe, where Augustinians were at work (B&R, XLVIII, 124–30).

Malumbres fills out this account in a number of specific ways. He identifies "Ajanas," or as he spells it "Afanas," as in the mountainous country of the Dupax district. He speaks of the first expedition of Pangasinan soldiers as behaving timidly, and being dispersed: a "disgraceful" affair, he calls it. The later force entered the area "by a difficult route" so as not to "alarm with its march the numberous tribes of savages who populated the mountains and countrysides." The "Panuypuyes" were forced to abandon an apparently impregnable eminence at Afanas after a vain defense with machetes, lances, and rocks. The "desperate and miserable Sapac," who had "aspired to universal domination of the mountains and all the races populating them," was killed. The expedition then based itself upon Afanas, and in further sorties reduced to ashes the settlements of Masi, Taveng, Bangao, Balangan, Patar, and Ibila. The defeated Panuypuyes "dispersed into the mountains" (1919, II, 25–29).

The mountain settlement names here are not on modern maps. Dupax, however, lies at the northern edge of the Caraballo Sur heights, and a major peak south of it is called today Mt. Kanabuy, probably derived from Panupuy. Malumbres speaks of a "fort of Afanas or Aritao" as having been established, and places Afanas as one of the principal barrios of Aritao. This latter center, some five miles west of Dupax, was the old Bugay or Bujay, and was reconstructed as Aritao in 1765. Afanas became one of two main defensive posts in the upper Magat, the other being at Bagabag. In 1772, however, the Afanas garrison was transferred to Carig. Malumbres also speaks of Masi as having been a large pueblo of the "Jumanguies and Auas" not far from Aritao (1919, II, 52, 54, 172).

The use of ethnic names here such as Panuypuy, Jumangi, and Aua appears to indicate that these were segments of old Ilongot populations of the Caraballo Sur heights. Such labels, however, clearly included not only "infidels" but also runaways who had moved back to the fastnesses. Malumbres quotes in his discussion of this period a Franciscan father, Lobato, who describes Bujay or Aritao as a gathering place for people from the "various pueblos of infidels and apostates of the Jumanguies and Auas" (1919, II, 171–72). In another source, Martinez de Zuñiga's history of the Philippines (1803), a version is given of these events which also indicates that apostatizing Christians participated along with mountain groups in the disturbances. He starts with the transfer of the mission work in 1740:

[In that year] the Augustine friars had delivered over to the Dominicans the missions of Ytuy, or Ysinay, so that . . . the provinces of Pangasinan and Cagayan, by the south side, might be united. The Indians, Christians as well as Infidels, took umbrage at this alteration in the establishments and a kind of civil war among them was the consequence, so that . . . [the civil authorities] deemed it necessary . . . [to send] troops to quell these disturbances. But a few years afterwards fresh discontents on the same account arose; . . . many of the Christians became apostates, and uniting with the Infidels, were guilty of the greatest excesses.

Several churches were burned, this writer continues, and a great many who retained their attachment to Christianity were "murdered." The disaffected elements, "losing all respect" for the missionary fathers, "diligently sought their lives." "This induced Señor Arandia to despatch an expedition in aid of the missionaries, to the mountains of the Igorrotes, which proved of very little effect; for the only purpose it answered was to drive the Indians to the recesses from whence they again issued on the retreat of our forces."

Martinez de Zuñiga follows up this account with a plea for leaving the civilizing process to the mission fathers, while merely providing "military stations or escorts," for their basic protection; that is, taking "cautionary" rather than "splendid" and "noisy" measures. He points to the laborious travels which the fathers had to undertake in their ecclesiastical work, and the poverty of their "stipend": "[At times] they are compelled to subsist on what is allowed them for their escorts, and live without that protection, rather preferring to be exposed to the insults of those heathens, than to perish through hunger." This writer goes on to warn that conversion of the non-Christians could not be expected to occur as rapidly as at the time of the original "conquest":

Even the Christian converts persuaded them not to be baptized, that they may avoid the payment of tribute and other imposts. The custom, too, of one tribe revenging the murder of an individual of that tribe upon the tribe of the murderer, very much impeded conversion, and consequently civilization, for from hence results the necessity of the weakest tribes changing their residence, or forming a confederacy with others. In such case Christianity must suffer, for the baptized Indians must always follow the Infidels of their tribe and be alienated from the fathers, or be exposed to constant hostility. (Maver translation, 1814, pp. 125–30.)

Among the documents presented by Malumbres is a kind of census of decapitations for the Christian communities of the upper Cagayan for the years 1832 to 1845, the recorded total being 226 (1918b, p. 227).

CONTINUING RECORDS OF THE EIGHTEENTH CENTURY

In 1755, the Franciscan Lobato, mentioned above, led an expedition that attempted to find a better "road" from the upper Magat into Pangasinan. His party moved up the Caraballos Sur from the Afanas fort to a rancheria called "Dangatan," which looked out over both the upper Cagayan and Pangasinan. After eight days of travel through rough country, Lobato reached Asingan "in a direct line." Enroute they passed through country "known for the ferocity of its people," and seemingly "impossible to administer." Dangatan and other settlement names mentioned in the record of this journey do not appear on modern maps. Lobato judged that cutting a road through this terrain was impossible (Malumbres, 1919, I, pp. 52–54, 171–72).

In 1785, following the establishment of the tobacco monopoly by the Spanish government, resistance developed in the upper Cagayan as in some other parts of the Philippines. This new control inflamed already strong grievances generated by the collection of tributes. Two non-Christian chiefs, Labutao or Lagutao and Baladon, led an uprising. As told succinctly by Montero y Vidal, "there was a revolt of the heathen Indians in Ituy and Paniqui headed by a Calinga chief named Lagutao, who assembled over 1,200 men; but it was put down by a force of 300 musketeers sent from Cagayan, and Lagutao was killed in battle" (B&R, L, 57; see also Philippine Census 1903, I, 168). Martinez de Zuñiga, writing in 1801, speaks of the "Indios" of Ituy as restless and inconstant, favoring novelties and superstitions (1893, I, 27). In 1878 another major revolt occurred, foreshadowing the final uprising against Spain near the end of the nineteenth century.

LATER PERSPECTIVES

As in previous chapters, a brief summary may be given of statistical and other information on the various settlement areas. The Varona survey of 1746 used previously gives only fragmentary population figures, as the upper

Cagayan was still little opened up by then. Materials from Mora's 1805 visit are used, and also Buzeta's 1818 and 1850 descriptions. An important source for additional data is Malumbres' third volume, *Historia de Nueva Vizcaya* (1919,1).

The Cagayan-Ganano area, the old Yogad, may be dealt with first. The settlements here were built up notably by Gaddang populations around the middle of the eighteenth century, migrating under government and mission auspices from Magat river valley zones where cultivable land was limited. In 1754, a Dominican, Fray Andrés de Mendoza, wrote enthusiastically of the "success" of this "mass migration" (Ayer Collection, Document 85).

Angadanan. The baptismal register of this settlement, according to Malumbres, begins in 1765. Its people were migrants from the Bayombong area, notably from old communities called Angadanan, Daruyag, and Gapag or Abiang. Some also came from Diadi, probably the present mountain settlement of that name on the Magat-Ganano trail, because of the "unsuitability of their lands for cultivated fields." Population: 1805, 791; 1818, 773; 1850, 1,038.

Camarag (Echague). Lappau, which became one of its constituent settlements, had 97 people in 1746. In 1752 it conjoined with two other settlements to form Camarag. Settlers from the Magat and Diadi filled out the district population to 969 by 1805; later figures are: 1818, 1,129; 1850, 1,564. In 1841 Camarag was made the capital of the new province of Nueva Vizcaya, but in 1856 the government headquarters were shifted to Bayombong. In 1850 it had 264 houses. Around 1870 its name was changed to Echague.

Carig (Santiago). In 1746 it had only 30 persons. Here, too, settlers from the Magat and Diadi areas have filled out the population. It also drew in converts from non-Christian groups to the south. Carig was the site of a garrisoned fort called Santo Niño (Malumbres, *Historia de Cagayan,* pp. 323–27). Later population figures: 1805, 1,140; 1818, 862; 1850, 765. In 1881 an outer barrio of Carig, called Estella, was separated under the name of Cordon, and in the early twentieth century Carig had its name changed to Santiago.

Jones–Pinappagan. No named jurisdictions were formed in the upper reaches of the Cagayan river until the late nineteenth century (see below). The modern settlements of any size are almost exclusively Ilocano—i.e., Jones, named after the American Indian anthropologist who lost his life there while studying Ilongot groups, and Pinappagan.

The figures cited here show the Ganano-Cagayan zone as having population totals as follows: 1805, 2,900; 1818, 2,764; and 1850, 3,367. Cavada's 1876 count shows a growth to 6,434.

The Magat river section of old Paniquy, with its long and often obscure history of Spanish contacts, shows approximately its modern residential patterns by 1740, when the Dominicans took over. The following is a summary by settlement areas, from north to south:

Bagabag. In 1746 its population totaled 130. Later population figures: 1818, 1,277; 1850, 1,230. This was the site of a garrisoned fort. Mora in 1805 speaks of the Ilamut and other rivers descending from the Cordillera, but makes no mention of the Ifugao people living on their upper courses. Buzeta speaks in 1850 of Bagabag as "controlling many mountain settlements."

Lumabang (Solano). Formed in 1760, it was in 1805 a visita of Bayombong. Mora describes it in that year as "growing much irrigated rice." Population: 1818, 687; 1850, 873.

Bayombong. In 1746 its population was 329; later population figures were: 1818, 1,593; 1850, 1,776. Mora in 1805 speaks of the small settlement of Paitan to the south as "inhabited in early times by some Isinay." According to Malumbres, Bayombong absorbed converts from "Ilongot" mountain settlements to the east (1918a, pp. 320–23). In 1856 it became the capital of the reorganized Nueva Vizcaya Province. Cavada's 1876 survey shows 2,879 inhabitants.

By these counts, the Paniquy area had a total population of 724 in 1746, a figure consistent with the ecclesiastical count cited previously, and in later years the following numbers: 1818, 3,557; 1850, 3,899. In modern times Ilocano colonists found room within the confined space of this valley to outnumber the *naturales* several times over, and a trickle of Ifugaos also came from the mountains to live and work there.

In Ituy, the Magat headwaters area, continuous history also dates from the Dominican entry, though built upon the long previous record of Spanish contacts with its Isinai people:

Bambang. Varona's 1746 survey mentions only one center in the Ituy area, "Capag," with 105 people. Alternatively called Gapag or Abiang, it seems to be a small settlement north of the present Bambang today called Abian, and one of the localities from which migrants moved east into Yogad. According to Malumbres, Bambang was organized as a town in 1747. Mora speaks in 1805 of Bambang as having various "visitas and rancherias," including Abiang, Duhao, Mayon, Diangan, and a part of "Binatangan"—that is, the mountain area to the east—in which there were "many Igorrotes." Mora also notes the turbulence of the Matung river to the west, but makes no mention of the mountain peoples of the Cordillera. Later population figures are: 1818, 2,833; 1850, 3,451. The latter total shows it to be the largest settlement in the upper Magat, having at the time 566 houses.

Aritao. This was the old Bugay or Bujay, and the mission ruins caught Mora's attention when he visited it in 1805. This traveler reached it after a day's horseback ride from Carranglan. Malumbres dates its reconstitution as Aritao in 1765. Population: 1818, 1,146; 1850, 1,226. Buzeta speaks of the town as having the "adjacent mountains" under its jurisdiction.

Dupax. This old settlement was constituted in its present form in 1741. Population: 1818, 2,255; 1850, 2,553. Mora noted a "coffee plantation" there, pioneering later production of this crop.

The lack of information accessible to Varona at the time of his survey is understandable enough in view of the disturbed condition of the area in his time, as described earlier. For 1818 the population total was seen to be 6,234, and for 1850, 7,230. Here, too, the predominating resident group, in this case the Isinai, were to become well outnumbered by the Ilocanos on the limited, busily worked flats.

CONTACTS WITH THE IFUGAO

Buzeta speaks of the Christianized Isinai as "little different from the Igorrotes," even though converted (1850, 1, 58). His work contains interesting if all too brief descriptions of the "Igorrotes" of the high mountains, the Ifugao, and the Ilongot groups. As noted in the Pangasinan chapter, he speaks of the Igorot as wearing bark loincloths, and eating for food "forest fruits, sweet potatoes, *letaro* [taro] roots, rice, which they cultivate, and meat from the bufalo [carabao], bear, and deer which they hunt and whose meat they preserve. Also there are some cannibals."

Of the Ifugao he says:

In spite of the fact that they have been given the cultivation of rice which would suffice to feed them, their disposition for committing robbery does not permit them to limit themselves to such simple means of subsistence, and so they steal the possessions of their neighbors. . . . [They] lurk in ambush in order to kill passers-by, whose heads they carry to their huts where they keep them as . . . trophies. The more heads one has to show the greater is his prestige.

The Ifugao, he notes, "maintain an extreme hate" for the "Gaddanes" and "pursue them without cease" (Buzeta, 1850, 1, 52–56).

Malumbres, in his historical volumes, assembles extensive materials on the penetration of what is now Ifugao subprovince. In 1793, Fray P. Antolin made what seems to be the first recorded expedition into the high country around "Quiangan," northwest of Bagabag, and Fray Juan Molano followed in 1801. Among notable later explorers in Ifugao were Galvez, Oscariz, and Fray Juan Villaverde. One of the nineteenth-century surveys, in giving a list of the principal Ifugao settlements, shows many of them as having from 20 to 40 houses. If correct, it would mean that the characteristically smaller hamlets reported by later ethnographers represent a recent scattering out of the population, presumably under Spanish pressures. The extensive growing of rice in terraces was noted, along with cultivation of camotes, taro, and yams. What are now called the Ifugao were usually grouped under three district names: the "Quianganes" in the more accessible eastern districts, based on the settlement named Quiangan, or Kiangan; the "Mayoyaos" of the north, around Mayoyao; and the Silipans," in Banaue and other western districts, named after a settlement called Silipan (Malumbres, 1918a, especially pp. 182–210; 1919, 11, especially chapters 4, 6, and 7).

In 1852, according to Cavada's dates, a "pueblo" or district called "Lagaui" was established by the government of Nueva Vizcaya as a first step in bringing Ifugao groups under official and mission influence. A second "pueblo" called "Ibaay" was formed in 1865, apparently on the Santa Cruz river near the modern Pingkian, to advance similar work among the Igorot population west of the Bambang-Aritao area. Meantime, in the high Cordillera, boundaries of sorts had been established through the formation of the Comandancias of Benguet and Bontoc, as seen in earlier chapters. These boundaries still left the Ifugao and many eastern Igorot (Ibaloi) settlements within Nueva Vizcaya. By Cavada's figures of 1876, the counted population in the Lagaui district was 9,268 and in Ibaay 8,591.

Step by step, the Spanish authorities cut trails and established garrisoned posts through the Ifugao and eastern Ibaloi country, and mission chapels were built in fort style. Malumbres gives a series of dates for the start of mission centers in this mountain zone: Mayoyao 1851, Bungian 1851, Silipan 1851, Lagaui 1867, Ibaay 1867, Cayapa 1894, and Nangaua near Quiangan 1896. As part of the civilizing process, attempts were made to get some of the people to resettle in lower, more accessible zones: Ifugaos in the Magat gorge country at Diadi and other points, and Ibalois in the Santa Cruz and Kayapa valleys. Later, however, these communities were to be almost wholly abandoned (Malumbres, 1918a, 182–210; official reports and other sources on the American period).

LAST SPANISH ATTEMPTS AT CONSOLIDATION

In 1848 the provinces south of the Cagayan valley were reorganized, the new province of Nueva Ecija being formed in the upper Pampanga river area. In 1856 a politico-military district called Principe was formed as an adjunct of Nueva Ecija, comprising the mountainous Sierra Madre zone around Baler and Casiguran and adjacent to the upper Cagayan river headwaters.

Between this Cagayan river fork and the Magat fork, the complex tangle of rather dry and barren foothills and mountains appears to have been largely terra incognita to the Spaniards. The settled communities along the upper Magat flats from Bagabag to Dupax were indicated in various records as having adherent "infidels" on this eastern side. In modern censuses they are classed as Ilongot. Their greatest concentration is in the mountainous area now called Kasibu, which is really the headwaters of the Ganano river. It is a fair presumption that many of these people were runaways from either the Ganano river flats or the Magat river flats, and quite possibly both. Unfortunately, they have not been described in the ethnological literature, so that the problem of their origin and relationship must remain in abeyance. In general this wild zone of the upper Cagayan was called "Binatang" or "Binatangan."

The start of the last decade of the nineteenth century saw a determined effort by the Spanish authorities to bring the mountain zones of Nueva Vizcaya both west and east of the Magat under government control. The period also appears to have been marked by anti-Spanish counter-movements among the non-Christian populations as a response to these increasing pressures, so that military buffers were needed for the safety of the valley populations. In 1891, three politico-military "Comandancias" were set up: "Quiangan" as a jurisdiction for the Ifugao area, "Cayapa" or Kayapa in the Igorot area, and "Binatangan" for the area east of the Magat.

Malumbres, writing early in the twentieth century, says that the "Igorrotes" of Kayapa were "diligent" workers, growing "*camotes* [sweet potatoes], potatoes, beans and cabbages" upon the slopes. They were also "dedicated to the extraction of gold from the Anbayuan (Ambayabang) river." Their main commerce was with Nueva Vizcaya, but they also traded into Pangasinan. This writer fails to mention rice growing, even though deserted terraces were later seen in the valley by Barrows, as noted below. However, this fact must be treated with some caution, since, as Eggan has suggested, the terraces *could* have been used for cultivation of sweet potatoes (personal communication). In 1894, a mission center called Santa Cruz de Aua was established, apparently on the Santa Cruz river at the present Pingkian. A second followed at Bison, or Bisong, close to the Kayapa of today. In 1898 the Kayapa Comandancia was estimated to have an "infidel" population of 4,000. Binatangan is described by this same writer as stretching through rugged country to the east coast. Sparsely peopled by "rancherias of Ilongots and Ibilaos," it was estimated to have in 1898 a total population of 1,500, "more or less." In 1894 a mission was opened at "Mungia," apparently the modern settlement of Manga on the river of that name (Malumbres, 1919, I, 329–31, 400–403).

The last of the Kayapa population moved out when *insurrectos* from Pangasinan occupied the area in 1898, so that when Barrows went there shortly after the American occupation, he found the Kayapa valley deserted and the terraces overgrown (1903; Paper 12, Beyer Collection). Barrows also reports that when the Spanish military force had to move out of "Quiangan" in 1898 after various "massacres" of the Spanish garrisons, an "orgy" of headhunting ensued (Philippine Census, 1903, p. 870). The initial American information on Nueva Vizcaya notes that only a "very small part" of the mountain populations had by then been "subjugated" (*Report of the Philippine Commission*, 1900, III, 31).

MODERN CENSUS DATA

For the upper Cagayan as a whole, the 1818 census figures give a counted population of 12,555, of whom 9,791 lived along the Magat, and 2,764 in the upper Cagayan and Ganano rivers. In 1903, the valley districts of the upper Magat showed a total population of 16,026 and this figure rose by 1918 to 23,318. Because of boundary adjustments, a 1903 figure of 46,515 "wild" (i.e., mountain) people in this area had fallen by 1918 to 5,116. The upper Cagayan river districts (Echague, etc.) had totals in the two censuses of 17,389 and 31,922, respectively.

By the time of the 1939 census, to take the latter zone first, new settlements had spread higher up the Cagayan with the result that two new districts had been formed, Jones and Pinappagan. The name of the Carig district had also been changed to Santiago. The statistics on language speakers in this zone were as follows:

Municipal unit	Total population	Ibanag	Gaddang	Yogad	Negrito	Ilongot	Iloko
Angadanan	16,047	3,101	1,681	402	32	—	11,970
Echague	16,249	1,228	143	7,226	10	—	11,130
Santiago	34,154	1,516	937	47	—	10	32,550
Jones	14,703	296	30	343	—	4	14,364
Pinappagan	3,923	—	3	—	52	1,174	2,772
Total	85,076	6,141	2,794	8,018	94	1,188	72,786

It is obvious that the hitherto sparsely settled districts of the upper Cagayan have had in modern times a great influx of Ilocanos. Of the resident valley groups, Gaddang speakers are most represented in the Angadanan district, which included the Gaddang-speaking area of Cauayan, and in Santiago, that is, the Ganano river valley. Speakers of the Yogad dialect, which is closely related to Gaddang, or one of its variants, in terms of a classification by Beyer (1917, p. 24), are seen to be concentrated in the Echague region. The 1948 census, in a statistical review of all Philippine languages, gives a later total of 7,485 speakers of Yogad. Some 6,000 persons reported in the tabulation above that they were speakers of Ibanag, but these probably included very few actual Ibanags; rather, they would appear to be members of the Gaddang, Yogad, and Ilocano ethnic groups who reported themselves as using, or able to use, the valley lingua franca. In the Cagayan headwaters the Ilongot were still surviving in sparse numbers, together with a few Negritos scattered along the Sierra Madre range. The 1939 census showed 1,355 in the category of "pagan and not belonging to any religious group"; of these, 1,093 were in Pinappagan.

Eastward in the old Paniquy section of the upper Magat, the modern districts are Bagabag, Solano, and Bayombong. The relevant language speakers as of 1939 were as follows:

Municipal unit	Total population	Gaddang	Isinai	Ifugao	Igorot (Ibaloi)	Ilongot	Iloko
Bagabag	10,702	1,602	217	177	1	144	9,408
Solano	17,878	1,597	14	316	6	619	15,139
Bayombong	12,146	3,396	18	34	3	1,183	10,720
Total	40,726	6,595	249	527	10	1,946	35,267

Apart from the typical Ilocano influx, the predominating ethnic element is Gaddang. Father Godfrey Lambrecht, in his modern study of this ethnic group, speaks of the Gaddang as counting themselves the *naturales* of these towns, and living in the central districts (*Philippine Studies*, VII, 194). The Ibanag speech is of no numerical significance here. The Isinai are not represented this far down the Magat in any large numbers. The considerable "Ilongot" group occupy the mountainous eastern parts of these districts between the Magat and Cagayan. From the western Cordillera heights there has been some migration of Ifugaos, together with a handful of Ibaloi "Igorots," into these towns; Barrows also spoke of this migration tendency at the beginning of the century (1903; Beyer Collection). The 1939 census showed 712 persons in the category of "pagan and not belonging to any religious group."

Higher up the Magat, in the old Ituy and the adjacent mountainous districts to east and west, there are seven municipal units: Bambang, Aritao, and Dupax in the valley, Kasibu in the rugged country to the east, Pingkian (the Santa Cruz river area) and Kayapa on the Cordillera side, and Imugan southward in the Caraballos near the Balete Pass. The significant groups of language speakers in 1939 were:

Municipal unit	Total population	Isinai	Gaddang	Igorot	Ifugao	Ilongot	Iloko
Bambang	8,545	1,408	63	17	4	258	1,104
Aritao	6,208	506	65	66	6	528	6,056
Dupax	6,767	1,659	57	—	3	418	6,664
Kasibu	1,591	128	—	—	—	1,516	537
Pingkian	4,894	10	—	4,641	—	1	327
Kayapa	3,808	—	1	3,785	2	1,174	27
Imugan	2,043	—	6	1,614	—	13	547
Total	33,856	3,711	192	10,123	15	3,908	15,262

Here, at the head of the valley, Ilocano immigrants had not yet arrived in numbers comparable to their proportion in other Cagayan areas. They were notably few in the mountain districts, being themselves primarily valley dwellers. The major group in the valley areas continued to be Isinai, though they are surprisingly few in modern times. As of the 1948 census there were only 4,378 Isinai speakers in the whole Philippines. The Isinai, and also the small Gaddang group, were conspicuously few in the mountainous districts occupied by the non-Christians. To the east and the southeast were close to 4,000 scattered mountaineers classed as Ilongot. On the Cordillera and Caraballo heights to west and south, more than 10,000 Igorots were on the Nueva Vizcaya side of the boundaries with Pangasinan and Mountain Provinces, occupying communities in the Santa Cruz and Kayapa river systems. In the "pagan, etc." category, the 1939 figures were as follows: Pingkian 4,612, Kayapa 3,476, Imugan 1,437, Kasibu 1,287, other districts 199. As of 1948 there were 51,028 Ifugaos in Mountain Province.

REVIEW

Discussion of this interesting patchwork of valley and mountain peoples can await analysis in the final chapter to follow. It need merely be said here that continuity has been established across the southern Cordillera heights and the Caraballos Sur with the peoples seen in the early chapter on Pangasinan. The greatest problem offered by the records is the apparent dissipation around the beginning of the seventeenth century of the extensive population reported in the Magat valley areas. The question must arise whether the wet-terracing Ifugao of later times trace back to this population.

XIII. Review and Conclusions*

GENERAL CONSIDERATIONS

The preceding chapters put into a coherent record the ethnohistory of the lowland and mountain zones of northern Luzon so far as documents located by the writer can show it. While perhaps more problems have been opened up deserving new research than have been firmly solved, numerous vistas of ecological, demographic, and cultural dynamics have been explored. No explanatory frame regarding migrations, distributions, and relationships of people in such an area, it has been seen, could afford to be over-static.

The materials do not disturb the current theory that the Negritos represent the oldest human stratum among the Luzon populations. For the Malay-type peoples, however, it becomes unnecessary to postulate separate migrations wherever very distinctive ethnic elements exist in later times. Groups are seen reformulating their cultures to meet new situations or because they gain access to new materials and ideas. Changes have come not only voluntarily but also in some respects from outside compulsions.

It can readily be granted that more than one movement of Malay-type peoples into northern Luzon may have occurred prior to the opening of the written record. Yet even a single original migrant element could conceivably have been parent to the differentiated peoples and customs of later times. Adding to the local dynamics the contacts with technologically more elaborated Malay traditions in other zones of Southeast Asia, with

---

* This chapter is a revised and expanded version of one written by the author in an early draft of the manuscript. In that draft detailed interpretations, rather than brief summaries, were placed at the end of each area chapter. The attempt has been made to incorporate these sections into the present chapter in such a way as to provide the "general summary" the author intended in the final manuscript. However, he had planned to thoroughly revise and greatly expand his analyses. The conclusions and interpretations given are thus less complete, less integrated, and less satisfying than those the author would have provided had he lived to complete the manuscript. R. M. K.

Chinese and other Asian groups, and then with Europeans, the northern Luzon of today could build up from the early human baselines. Vanoverbergh seems to have had this possibility in mind when, in a study of dress and adornment in the Mountain Province, he stated: "The various so-called non-Christian tribes in [the Cordillera], . . . while differing one from another in numerous details, are *actually essentially one*. Whether they were originally one or have become so in the course of time is another question" (1929, p. 240). The historical records, of course, cannot answer questions of original migration, but they do show a rich texture of change over nearly four centuries.

From the vast body of data presented in the preceding chapters, certain consistent themes emerge. This review and synthesis will begin with an attempt to draw together such threads of consistency and to outline briefly the picture of lowland and mountain peoples which the early records provide. This general review will be followed by an analysis of the economy and settlement patterns in lowland and mountain areas, which will examine the degree to which cultural variations in northern Luzon reflect ecological factors.

The specific problems of ethnic variations, distributions, and origins raised in the area chapters will then be analyzed in some detail. Alternative hypotheses will be advanced, traditional theories examined, and questions raised which challenge further research. The chapter will conclude with a brief discussion of northern Luzon in terms of population genetics and linguistics, and with an examination of the wider comparative implications, both methodological and substantive, of this study.

THE LOWLAND POPULATIONS

The earliest documents give some important leads to conditions and events in the time period most immediately preceding Spanish entry, e.g., patterns of settlement along the coast, penetration by Chinese and Japanese merchants, the gold trade. A fair picture also emerges of the lowland groups at the period of initial contact, not least of all as regards their leadership and apparatus of defense and aggression. Mission records, especially for Pangasinan and Cagayan, add a surprisingly rich body of information on social structure, religious beliefs and activities, material equipment, and other matters. Even so, there is nothing like the detail of custom such as some later writers were to attribute confidently to the pre-Spanish heritage, and based on what appeared to be conservative or traditional elements of later days, e.g., de los Reyes, on the Ilocano "prehistoric" period.

Local groups are then seen responding to the first Spaniards, variously remaining or retreating, accepting or resisting innovations, being converted and resettled, and often drawing back after initial change. A continuity is notably apparent from the first moves of armed opposition and withdrawal, through numerous "rebellions" and "apostasies," to the politically oriented autonomy movements of later times. The records, indeed, present a veritable mine of materials exemplifying the phenomena of so-called acculturation. Also seen vividly are the early civil and ecclesiastical policies that gave cultural reformulations much of their special shape.

The ethnic leveling of the lowland cultures through Hispanization and Christianization, together with the spread of lingua franca verbal media, is fairly well shown. Widening contacts and numerical expansion, too, affected the genetic character of the lowland populations. But this is only seen at a few obvious points: the emergence of Spanish and Chinese mestizo elements; intermarriage with and absorption of mountain groups has been more or less preserved. People today count themselves to be Pangasinan, Ilocano, Ibanag, Itavi, Gaddang, Yogad, Isinai, or Palanan, and claim the languages concerned as their mother tongues. Here not only Spanish pressures, but also the expansion of Ilocano, Ibanag, and to a lesser degree Pangasinan colonists into other ethnic areas, have helped to conserve as well as to break down ethnic self-consciousness.

Even so, the background of these groups is by no means clear. The smaller, more localized units—Itavi, Yogad, Isinai, and Palanan—come fairly late into the records by name, but evidently, having differentiated dialects, they go well back in time. The Gaddang grouping is a shadowy one at best, with apparently various subdivisions over the large section of the Cagayan concerned, and with "Irraya" and other labels also appearing. The original bounds of the Pangasinan group are never made clear except near the coast. The processes of expansion and consolidation in this ethnic unit seem to have been especially complex in the little-documented northeast section of Pangasinan Province that has been of concern in this study. The great extension of the Ibanag southward up the Cagayan floor in historic times has been discussed, and particularly merits further study.

Above all, the vast group calling itself Ilocano needs to be understood, not least of all in order to better interpret the adjacent mountain groups. Particularly important, as has been noted, is the degree to which linguistic and other variations existed at the time the Spaniards arrived. The problem of Ilocano identity will be examined in the analysis to follow, as will similar questions regarding the Pangasinan and Ibanag.

THE MOUNTAIN POPULATIONS

The records of the mountain peoples were seen to have a kind of inverse relation to those concerned with lowland affairs. Once the lowlands were under Spanish control, they became by and large no longer newsworthy except as revolts or other stresses brought them into print. For the mountain peoples the beginning records have little substance, and only as military expeditions and mission workers make their sporadic penetrations does the picture start to fill out.

It has been an assumption of the study that the major river systems debouching from the high country—the Agno, the Abra, the Chico, and others—played a key role in the settlement of the northern Luzon mountains. The coastal people were boatmen and fishermen, and the long navigable course of the Cagayan river clearly served to take Malay-type peoples into the upper reaches of the Cagayan valley. For the terracing peoples, accessibility to streams that could provide a dependable flow of water for irrigation has been essential. The dry-gardening Isnegs of the north kept close to waterways that could carry rafts and plank boats, and even those dry cultivators preferring high defensive points such as were described in the Benguet records were not far from streams. Sluicing of gold where rivers reached the flats turned eyes upstream.

The hunter of wild game, the woodcutter, and the gatherer of wild honey and wax would rove more widely. Doubtless many of the trade and war trails used later between mountain and lowland communities followed tracks open for such initial exploitation of upland resources. These, it may be noted, tend to run along the tops of ridges and wind around slopes rather than seeking out flats: because of the mountain rains, any level ground tends to become swampy and is often impassable. Both the desire to prevent enemies from controlling water above one's settlement and the skill of feet and backs in getting loads up and down slopes could have carried people quickly into the higher mountains.

This speculative exercise begins to take historic shape in the early records of trade in gold, hides, wax, and other mountain products. While the records leave vague the question of how far the mountains had been permanently settled prior to Spanish times, it seems a plausible hypothesis that the first upland residence came about in the gold-working areas. As suggested earlier, the mining and smelting techniques could have been taught by Chinese traders. Other mountain groups might have been refugees from lowland wars, though such groups would probably not have gone, at first, beyond the inner valley and foothill pockets. It needs no reiteration here that under Spanish pressure retreat into the mountains became a major theme of historic times in all nine of the sectional studies. Of the Pangasinan, Sawyer could say even in 1900 that one of their main characteristics was "their propensity to *remontar*." The ethnohistory of the Cagayan is rendered embarrassingly complex by the escapings of valley peoples not only to the west, east, and south, but even to the north by sea to the Babuyan and Batan islands, and possibly beyond to Formosa. The Ilocos peoples were seen as largely defining their destiny at the time of Spanish arrival: those who stayed on the coast became trapped there, so to speak, between the sea and the hostile mountain populations, at least many of whom seem to be descendants of refugee kinsmen.

By the time military expeditions and mission workers were able to make effective enough contacts with the upland peoples to give factual reports of substance, the varied patterns of mountain living appear to have become well established. The materials of Manuel de la Vega and Quirante in 1609 and 1624, respectively, give particularly vivid characterizations of the Benguet people, and there are many other records of the moving frontiers of penetration on both the Ilocos and the Cagayan sides. Such portmanteau names as "Igorot" and "Kalinga" give place to a whole series of local names having geographic, ethnic, or other significance: "Adan," "Mandaya," "Busao," "Jumangi," "Silipan," and others. It remained, indeed, for Worcester, Cole, Beyer, and other modern scholars to reduce them in turn to the recognized ethnic groupings given in modern classifications. Here as in the lowland records there are rich materials illustrative of cultural dynamics. There are also hiatuses: for example, the lack of early references to mountain peoples in northern Ilocos; the absence of descriptions of the great rice-terracing systems until the nineteenth century.

The documents show that, throughout the historic period, mountaineers have been migrating in varying numbers to the lowlands. They have been seen both as forming separate communities of "new Christians" and as being assimilated into the existing lowland communities. Unfortunately, little is told beyond the fact of their acceptance of the Christianized and Hispanized way of life. It would still be possible, for any student wishing to study these countermovements, to find localities in which such dynamics could be investigated either in process or further along in the course of subsequent change. This problem would then merge with the much larger one of documenting more fully than has been done to date the local history and ways of life of the lowland populations in this area.

LOWLAND ECONOMIC PATTERNS

When the Spaniards arrived in 1572, the coastal populations of Pangasinan, Ilocos, and the lower Cagayan were growing rice, along with sugar cane, root crops, and tropical vegetables and fruits. They were also fishermen, and they raised livestock and engaged in hunting and gathering. It was inferred from demographic materials that they probably had already acquired the lowland wet rice technology familiar in later times. There is, however, a surprising dearth of reference to irrigation techniques.

This last point is true, interestingly enough, not only of the records of northern Luzon, but also of those for the Philippines as a whole. In the great Blair and Robertson collection of documents, for example, the first mention of irrigated fields occurs in a description of "Customs of the Tagalogs" by Juan de Plasencia in 1589, that is, more than thirty years after the arrival of the Spaniards in the Manila area. Only two other early references appear, also dealing with Tagalog agriculture (B&R, VII, 174; VIII, 252; XII, 210).

Of Ilocos, the Augustinian Medina wrote in 1630 of the close supervision that the fathers had to exercise over the mission-created settlements. Any neglect, he states, meant that the people "return to their natural way of life." His nineteenth-century editor, Coco, spoke of the fathers "bringing to completion" the network of irrigation canals there, and preserving them by "watchfulness." Aduarte in 1640 describes the Dominican pioneers in Pangasinan as "walking about among these little villages and fields," and also tells of the neglect of the sick "because their kinsmen are obliged to go out to their fields"—presumably at a distance from the homes. In the Cagayan records, the mission fathers are directly described as giving initial instruction in wet cultivation, and supplying tools and work animals. In the middle Cagayan zones, at least, the missionaries were agents for the diffusion of the wet rice techniques. Earlier Cagayan cropping seems to have featured dry rice.

The Tagalog, Pampanga, Pangasinan, and Ilocos wet rice cycles have traditionally involved planting the seedbeds around midyear when the wet summer season (southwest monsoon) sets in. Water then becomes available to prepare the sometimes parched fields, and transplanting follows along. The several dozen types of lowland rice mature for harvesting at different times through October to December, when drying weather brings more sunshine. Reference has been made already to the typical walling of the fields, and to the gravity system of irrigation with its flumes, dams, and gates. The wet rice farmer must work long hours in cooperating groups around July to repair and maintain the water system, and this is a special time of ritual and festive observances.

Seasonal vegetable and fruit crops, and the annual harvesting of sugar cane, were built conveniently into this precipitation and work cycle. Cultivated and wild roots indigenous to southeast Asia had been augmented by the sweet potato. Maize and tobacco also became important crop accretions in many areas. As seen, root crops have a place in all the economies of northern Luzon cultivators, and even the Negritos included wild roots in their diet. A contrast appears, however, between the peoples of the Ilocos side, featuring root crops along with wet rice, and those of the Cagayan side, featuring dry rice alone or along with wet rice, and also maize, with tobacco as a large compulsory commercial crop.

The provinces of the Ilocos coast, together with Abra, were seen as producing very little dry rice. It was suggested that a selective factor operated in this zone of seasonal extremes, namely, that dry rice, or more specifically the dry rices, of which a number of varieties exist, could be grown in the wet season only. Such cultivation would then compete for labor with wet rice cropping, which gave a much higher proportionate yield. Moreover, on hilly lands limited to shifting (swidden) cultivation, the sweet potato had a greater seasonal range and was a much surer crop needing less care than dry rice. How far dry rice may have had a larger place in the economy of the western coastal peoples prior to the adoption of wet rice is a question beyond the scope of the historic records; it is bound up with the longer-term problems of migration sequences and of diffusion, as will be seen shortly.

The very different precipitation pattern in the Cagayan region, with its short drier season around February-March, its spring (northeast monsoon) rains, and its summer and fall cyclonic storms, opens the way to a greater time range of cropping. Rainfall diminishes up the Cagayan floor, and the upper valleys are high, with cool and overcast winters. Dry rice could thrive here, with the swiddens being cleared and burned during the drier period, planting being done when rains came to soak the ground, and the crop ripening in the warm late summer. This is the dry- to rainy-season cycle familiar throughout southeast Asia, and was seen to be still followed among the mountain groups of the Cagayan region. When the wet rice techniques were introduced, with a June to November-January cropping timetable according to the types of rice, there was no conflict with the upland dry rice in terms of labor, and the water runoff was plentiful for irrigation in that period.

The dual cropping system of growing both dry and wet rice is also characteristic of central and eastern Luzon, where the seasonal variation in rainfall is less extreme than on the mountain-edged sections of the west coast; e.g., the 1903 census describes this system in Pampanga Province ("Agriculture," IV, 96 ff). The modern practice in northeast Pangasinan of growing considerable dry rice along with the massive production of wet rice appears therefore to be part of an old continuity of the dual cropping system through central Luzon northward into Cagayan. By growing more rice over a longer portion of the year, and having less climatic stricture on the growth of seasonal vegetables, fruit, and maize, the peoples concerned do not need to feature the generally low-prestige root crops as along mountainous stretches of the west coast.

This apparently older pattern was seen to have been drastically changed in the Cagayan when tobacco planting came to dominate during the official monopoly period. Subsequently, with population increase and especially the vigorous spread of Ilocano colonists through the Cagayan flats, wet cropping was resumed there. The modern double cropping of wet rice has also been emphasized where ecological conditions permit, in the Cagayan as elsewhere.

The long-term interpretation of these general facts and hypotheses about lowland cultivation must carry far back of the Spanish period, and its earlier phases are obviously beyond the scope of the historic records. Scholars dealing with migrations to the Philippines have tended to take the easy way of considering that the three food-staple elements seen here—roots and fruits, dry rice, and wet rice—were brought in that order by successively entering groups. It is plausible that roots and fruits were the first plants to be cultivated, not least of all because such cropping is basic to the vast zone of Oceania, further east in the Pacific. With the rices, however, the techniques could have spread through diffusion at least as much as by population movements, and there is no compulsive reason for considering that an outer section of Malaysia such as northern Luzon received dry rice ahead of wet rice. From the assumption that both might have arrived together, ecological factors such as those viewed here could then have operated selectively in shaping their spread, and also the emphasis given to them along with the older crops. Studies of these matters would need to consider whether pathways of diffusion were from south to north or vice versa; but the expectation in the case of dry rice, from the evidence examined here, would be that the continuity is from the Pampanga area northward into Cagayan.

LOWLAND RESIDENTIAL PATTERNS

The residential patterns of the lowland peoples at the time of Spanish entry are shown fairly clearly. Some at least of the settlements penetrated by Salcedo in 1572 along the Pangasinan-Ilocos coast appear to have been permanent villages of substantial dimensions. Yet near them were evidently rancherias of hamlet size, as with those brought together to give San Jacinto and Manaoag, both somewhat back from the Pangasinan coast, enough population to justify giving them each a resident missionary. Consolidation of small, scattered residential groups continued for decades, as with the eighteen new pueblos listed by de los Reyes as being founded in Ilocos around the last quarter of the seventeenth century. Habitual trading with Asian merchants evidently gave special prominence to a few communities at river mouths or sheltered anchorages (e.g., Agoo, the "Port of Japon"), adumbrating the urban developments of Spanish times.

On the Cagayan side, descriptions of large communities appear in the first Magat valley records, though how far the housing groups were concentrated or scattered out is not made clear. Some settlements around the Cagayan mouth and at the junctions of large tributaries may also have been sizable. In general, however, the typical Cagayan residential pattern found by the Spaniards seems to have been one of scattered hamlets. The relation of these settlement types to the differing economic systems will be analyzed when the corresponding materials for the mountain groups have been reviewed. It may be added that the widespread modern pattern of having a "población," or administrative, religious, and marketing center, with adherent "barrios," "rancherias," and possibly individual homesteads, around it, combines both old and new elements.

MOUNTAIN ECONOMIC PATTERNS

The dynamic frame of reference developed in reviewing critical features in the lowland economies has equal application when the mountain groups are examined. As seen in the nine area studies, different climatic, terrain, and other natural conditions exist which have favored differentiation and local patterning. Yet contacts of peace and war could distribute goods and ideas even over the highest mountain barriers. Trails from lowland to mountain were also busy with the passage of goods: the upland peoples particularly wanted metal, salt, livestock, ceramic wares, and other articles that were absent or in short supply in their own settings.

In the western and southern zones of the Cordillera, the Ibaloi, Kankanai, Lepanto, Bontok, Ifugao, and Tinguian peoples emphasized, along with wet rice terracing so far as it was practiced, root staples, which also marked the adjacent west coastal zones. Above all, the sweet potato, which was easily grown and, with the green leafage eaten as well as the tuber, was likely to have a position in the aggregate diet even exceeding that of the higher-prestige food, rice. Root staples, along with sugar cane, vegetables, and fruits suited to the heights, appear indeed to have provided the agricultural base up to the early nineteenth century among the Ibaloi of the Benguet area, and perhaps also the neighboring Kankanai. The records of Martinez de Zuñiga and la Gironière quoted in the discussion of Abra suggest that this was also true of the Tinguians.

By contrast, dry rice has had a negligible place in the economy of these people in recorded times. The only exceptions show in the modern agricultural statistics, where a few marginal mountain districts were seen to produce moderate amounts of dry rice. These lie mainly on the Pangasinan-Ilocos side, along the southwest and south face of the Cordillera, and in the Ilocos range between the coast and the Abra valley, where the growers indeed may be Ilocano colonists rather than mountaineers. Additionally, some dry rice is grown by marginal groups in northeast Ifugao, as will be seen shortly.

A climatic-economic stricture could have operated in the rice terracing zones, comparable with that suggested for the coastal areas, namely, that dry rice would compete for labor with the traditional wet rice crop, since both would have had to be planted in the winter in order to ripen in the warm summer. But in the high southern parts of the Cordillera another important ecological limitation could have been the great elevation above

sea level of so many occupied areas. The writer has no botanical data defining the maximum elevations at which the dry rices will grow efficiently
in the northern Luzon mountains, hence no way of knowing whether human choices rather than ecological limitations shaped its use. In practice,
however, for such an area as the Chico valley, dry rices are cultivated upriver to a little above Tinglayan, that is, to perhaps 3,000 feet above sea
level, some 2,000 feet below the top range of the mountain wet rices.

In great contrast to this western and southern economic scene, the Isneg
and northerly Kalinga populations of the northeast slopes of the Cordillera
were seen to have dry rice as the featured staple. The elevations here are
lower, and there is a short drier season suited to burning off the gardens,
followed by usually ample rainfall to keep the soil damp. The same is true
of the sparsely scattered Gaddang populations along the eastern Cordillera
adjacent to the middle Cagayan, some of the isolated "Kalinga" or Gaddang groups in the upper river fastnesses east of the Cagayan, and the
Ilongot peoples of the Cagayan headwaters and southern Caraballo Sur
slopes. These peoples also grow roots, sugar cane, vegetables, and fruits.
Particularly (as with the Isnegs) they may count maize a more satisfactory
crop and higher in prestige than the sweet potato, favored in the high
mountains. Moreover, their generally forested territories, threaded by numerous streams, have wild-food resources in much greater quantity than
the rugged and open Cordillera heights, so that extensive time is spent in
hunting, gathering, and fishing. In the case of northeast Kalinga, which
is somewhat drier and less forested than the other regions, a special resource, the banana, was emphasized to an unusual degree in the diet.

At this point some comments may be made upon the ecological and
historical perspectives back of the modern distribution of dry cultivation
in these areas. First, a plausible picture may come to mind of miners
reaching the southern or southwestern heights to work the gold sources.
Probably staying at first for part of the year only, they could be visualized
as trying out the viability of lowland plants in order to supplement the
foodstuffs they carried with them. Taro, yam, sugar cane, and some vegetables such as the widely used *mongo* (a lentil-like pea) became established.
Rice growing might have been tried, though without success. From this
kind of beginning could have come the plant base of later times. With
the addition of livestock (dogs, pigs, chickens) and products of hunting and
gathering, permanent settlement became possible. Although these happenings can be regarded as being of pre-Spanish occurrence, the records of
early trading with Pangasinan and Ilocos communities include interesting
references to the further dependence of mountain gold-mining groups on
the lowlands even for basic foodstuffs.

With this ready hypothetical start, the problem next opens out of how
far the high mountains further north in the Cordillera (the Kankanai,

Lepanto, Bontok, Ifugao, and Abra zones) had root-cropping populations in early times, especially prior to the development of wet terracing. The records do not contribute direct answers to this question. Mountaineers are seen to be coming down to trade and to hunt heads, but this occurs after the initial period of Spanish contacts during which some of the coastal peoples appear to have taken to the mountains. The later ethnological record which shows taro as having religious importance in Lepanto and Bontok communities has led some scholars to believe that groups with an economy based on roots occupied those areas. Cole was noted as suggesting that, although the Tinguians of Abra may be refugees from the coast in beginning Spanish times, the valley could have been populated earlier by root-cropping "Igorots." In turn, further questions arise. Did any such central Cordillera dry cultivators enter the area from the Benguet heights to the south, from the west coast either directly or via the Abra valley, or even from the Cagayan side? Furthermore, were such hypothetical groups ancestral to the terracing populations, or were they absorbed or ousted by separately migrating terracers? More will be said of these matters shortly.

On the Cagayan side, the affiliations of the dry-rice-producing mountaineers to the old Cagayan lowland populations appear generally obvious. But here, too, unsolved problems remain, such as the relation of the Isnegs to the early northwest coastal people, and to the Itavi ethnic group of the lower Chico; the relation of the latter group in turn to the Kalingas; the northward and southward affiliations of groups subsumed under the name "Ilongot"; and the larger question of how far the foothill and mountain zones were occupied prior to the retreat of groups from the pressures of Spanish times.

Even in the matter of dry rice cropping, there is room for considering more specific questions of diffusion and emphasis. The spread of dry rice cultivation up the Chico as far as the Tinglayan area could have had a complex history. Again, though hardly a reliable source ethnographically, Buzeta's mid-nineteenth-century description of the Isnegs as eating "maize and roots primarily" is a reminder that this people may not have been such devotees of dry rice cropping in earlier times as they are today. The extensive use of the banana in northeast Kalinga communities, a source of amusement to neighboring groups, illustrates the development of local variants. There is also the problem of the apparent decline of dry rice cropping in many Cagayan lowland zones, as along the northwest coast where Ilocanos moved in to form the predominant group.

The only zone on the Cagayan side where the dry rice pattern is sharply broken is along the southeast slopes of the Cordillera, west of the Magat river fork. The Ifugao peoples in the northern part of this zone were seen to be growing huge quantities of root crops, particularly sweet potatoes, although they considered dry rice cropping to be threatening in a religious sense to successful wet terrace cropping. Only a little dry rice, therefore, is grown, along with some maize, generally on marginal slopes that are at lower elevations and away from the terrace systems. Barton, in his *Ifugao Economics* (1922), speaks of the growers as being mostly "recent Silipan immigrants," that is, people from the northwest margins of Ifugao—probably former Christian converts who had been settled during the nineteenth century in the Magat gorge country. Further south, the all-too-little-described "Igorots" of the western Nueva Vizcaya mountains (the Pingkian, Kayapa, and Umingan districts) also stress root crops to the virtual exclusion of dry rice, as could be expected from their Ibaloi affiliations.

In both the Ifugao and west Nueva Vizcaya zones, the ecological factors of undue elevation and lack of time for tending and harvesting the less productive dry rice crop in the warm summer season could have been operating selectively, as was suggested for the heights further west. But the Ifugao's religious antagonism indicates a marshaling of ethnic preferences that have become deeply seated in the value system of these peoples. Moreover, the emphasis on root crops suggests migration or diffusion links with areas and populations outside the Cagayan, that is, either to the south or to the west, of which more below.

Wet rice terracing is practiced in modern times between elevations of approximately 1,500 feet (the Naneng area of Kalinga) and 5,000 feet (parts of western Ifugao and Benguet). Water is run down in a controlled manner through a steplike series of walled fields built along a stream bed or upon a hill slope. The essential principle different from the gravity irrigation and walled fields of lowland wet cultivation is that instead of the hardly visible gradient of the field systems on flat lands, the walls are built up to conform with the slope. The mountain pockets and stream beds occasionally have flats, where a series of fields adjoin without stepping. In Ifugao, at the other extreme, terrace walls 20 feet high are common, and a few run up to a maximum of about 50 feet (Barton, 1922). In advance of a discussion of the origins of terracing, it can be pointed out that such stepped walls could have developed directly out of the lowland field system. Yet they might also have been adapted from the dry-cultivator practice described above of walling swiddens or gardens, occasionally in terraced formations; in this case, the principle of artificial irrigation would have been independently invented, or have come through stimulus diffusion.

For ethnohistorical analysis it has been seen as necessary to distinguish different regional types of the wet rice terracing economy, and for such information modern ethnographic records have to be the source. There appear to be four principal variants:

The Lepanto-Bontok type. The terraces here have almost vertical stone faces, so as to utilize the enclosed field space to the maximum extent possible. Carabao are used to trample the flooded field, along with working by human hand and foot, to prepare it for the transplanting, and pig manure and vegetable material are added for fertilizer. Prior to modern double cropping, the field could be used for dry cropping of sweet potatoes or vegetables between the rice cycle. The cultural context was seen to be one of often large village aggregations, and there are distinctive ritual and other features.

The Ifugao type. The terrace walls have a somewhat greater slope, and are more carefully sculptured to the terrain. They are usually kept flooded through the year, though rice straw and soil are heaped up in mounds between rice crops for the growing of vegetables; this keeps weeds from growing and circumvents the need for fertilization. Fields are prepared by hand, using long wooden spades. The cultural context is one of scattered hamlets, linked by an elaborate local cooperative system and with overarching bodies of distinctive law and ritual.

The southern Kalinga type. The terraces, while generally resembling those of the Bontok area in their stone technology, have a low wall which is usually capped with an inward lean of earth, reducing the space of the enclosed field. Carabao trampling and fertilization are characteristic of field preparation. The cultural context is one of fairly large villages, again with a distinctive body of custom. Dual cropping of dry rice along with wet rice is characteristic of much of Kalinga. The plow and other lowland techniques have also been introduced very recently in new areas of settlement, including government-sponsored agricultural colonies, in the Tabuk district, where the Chico river sprawls over flats after descending from the mountains.

The Tinguian type. The Tinguian terraces are low, and at least in lowland areas they have no stone walls. Seedbeds generally resemble those of the Lepanto-Bontok area, but lowland techniques were seen to be strongly represented: use of the plow and harrow, absence of fertilization, harvesting with a rice knife rather than by hand plucking, and storage in Ilocano-type granaries. The cultural context is one of villages, sometimes very large in size, and of a highly elaborated ritual cycle combining mountain and lowland elements.

The dynamic extensions of these terracing systems in later historic times were discussed in the appropriate chapters. The Benguet Ibaloi terracing, mostly with hamlet-sized settlements, gives a strong impression of a less meticulous use of Ifugao techniques, perhaps combined with older swidden walling habits. The early-nineteenth-century records also appear to show it as coming first into Benguet by way of the Kabayan area adjacent to southwest Ifugao. In some contrast, the Kankanai, or southern Kankanai, terracing appears to be of Lepanto, or northern Kankanai, derivation, though this needs more study. The Tinguian type seems to predominate in the Balbalasang area of the upper Saltan. Scott documents very fully the modern spread of terracing into northern Kalinga, with the construction largely done by "hired labor from the higher Cordillera," that is, by expert southern Kalingas, Bontoks, or others. He says: "If it is not true that every stone-walled terrace north of Lubuagan was built by someone from south of Lubuagan, it is almost true. . . . Only the people of Mabaca claim to have built all their own walls—and, a loyal Bontoc or Ifugao might say, they look it" (1958, pp. 90–91).

Such boundary extensions of wet terracing are notably important for showing that the lines between dry and wet cultivation have not been the sole product of rainfall and other ecological determinants. Historical circumstances and cultural choices have also been shaping distributional patterns. In the twentieth century, the building of new rice terraces has been going on, with government and other encouragement, throughout nearly all sections of the Cordillera. At the same time, there are still vast areas where excessive elevation and slope, unsuitable soil, or excessive precipitation make terrace cropping impossible, even if the local people had enthusiasm for it. This is particularly so in the northern subprovince of Apayao, where in spite of prolonged official encouragement only a few terraced and irrigated fields have been tried, mainly by immigrant Ilocanos or Tinguians. The very heavy and almost year-round precipitation, and frequent flooding of streams, would appear to make walled fields a liability. Cole had said likewise of parts of Kalinga: "The steep mountain sides, largely of clay formation, and the long rainy season, which continually cuts away the soil, make [terraced] rice fields impossible" (1909, p. 345).

In such places the roughly cleared swidden, or natural-rainfall garden, was the favorable, and sometimes the only feasible, adjustment. Clearly, more study is needed of the realistic limitations set by the growth requirements of cultivated plant varieties, soil conditions, rainfall variations, and similar factors. Scott (1958) has broken some ground in this direction by delineating three "basic terrain types" of the northern Cordillera in which swidden cultivation occurs. Another useful survey, covering not only recent Philippine literature but also literature from other parts of the world, has been provided by the New Zealand geographer R. F. Watters (1960).

MOUNTAIN RESIDENTIAL PATTERNS

Dry gardeners have their choices of residence patterns rather tightly limited by ecological factors. It is not feasible for a large group to settle in a permanent community, since seasonally shifting fields would take most of the people too far away for much of the year. Such an economy, however, can sustain what have been referred to in the study as hamlets, ranging at their largest to perhaps 150 to 200 persons. Usually such populations spread even more, so that a few households or even single farmsteads form the local group. Where war and headhunting were the rule, as in the northern Luzon area, security factors militated against too much scattering, so that the pull and push of subsistence and security produced a hamlet system with perhaps typically from 60 to 120 people per unit.

Such peoples had a choice between shifting their hamlets frequently to follow their gardens, and setting up a permanent hamlet settlement and then ranging out from it to their shifting fields. In the latter case, temporary structures could be built in more distant gardens for use when the crop was being tended. Semi-migratory dry gardeners, viewed in the larger world scene, are likely to be content with unpretentious house structures, readily abandoned and easily replaced. Those who set up a permanent hamlet are likely to be more choosy about sites, and they may, if they wish, engage in architectural elaboration and build up palisades and other means of defense. They also must face longer-term problems relating to the disposal of the dead, property rights in orchards and other local resources, and similar matters concerned with residence over generations. As regards defense, one notable method used in northern Luzon was to build high tree houses for night occupation, though this could be done under either residential pattern. Such tree houses were described among the Tinguian in the early nineteenth century, and have been used in modern time by the Gaddangs of the eastern Cordillera and some of the Ilongots of the Sierra Madres.

In northern Luzon, the dry rice gardeners of both lowlands and mountains appear to have favored the pattern of having a permanent hamlet base. This was illustrated by the long-term occupation of many named hamlets in Apayao, and the descriptions of the well-architectured Isneg houses. Though the evidence is less clear, it would appear from records such as those of the Quirante and Galvez expeditions in the Benguet area that the root-gardening peoples were more mobile, and housing was kept more casual. The greater technical demands of the seasonal dry rice crop for care and storage as compared with root crops may have been one of the important shaping factors here.

With a wet-cropping system, and the construction of permanent fields, the lowland and highland peoples had opened out to them additional choices in residential patterns. They could, of course, continue to scatter out in hamlets or farmsteads, as with the small barrios and rancherias of many rural lowland zones, and also the Ifugao hamlets dotted among the terrace systems. But having an immediately accessible food supply in dependable quantity enables such groups, if they wish, to form larger communities. Such a high-yield grain crop as wet rice, with supplementary crops and flesh foods, can sustain village units, or even small-town units, depending on the favorableness of the terrain. The measure of a village here as against a hamlet or town is not exact, but the terms are used in their popular connotation, which perhaps puts villages in a range from around 150 persons to 1,500 persons. It was seen in the middle Ilocos chapter that in terms of this measure the Amburayan, Lepanto, and Bontok residential patterns favor large village units.

OTHER CULTURAL FEATURES

This general summary of lowland and mountain peoples can usefully conclude with a brief description of cultural features other than economy and settlement patterns, which will help to place the present ethnic diversity in proper perspective and will aid in unraveling the complexities of the ethnohistory of northern Luzon.

Once groups had established themselves in particular localities, and had hived off to form a series of settlements, the way was open for the distinctions of later times to develop: characteristic house forms, clothing styles, art tastes, social and religious behavior, and other cultural variants. Along with this differentiation, neighbors would tend to trade and exchange ideas in spite of the endemic hostilities which made inter-group contacts precarious. One of the most interesting indicators of background identity, not yet fully worked out, relates to the evidently old usage of considering certain mountains sacred (see Beyer, 1912). Different regional groups trace their origins mythologically back to one of a number of sacred mountains where their primal ancestors are supposed to have survived a flood.

The essential cement of ethnic identity, however, has been the fact that every living group, whether hamlet or village, was the center of an outward extending system of marriage and kinship ties, and of considerable cooperation in war and ritual. With these marched the need for communication in the form of shared speech. Such circles of interaction extended in overlapping rings from central to marginal communities in each ethnic area. The ethnic boundaries, as, for example, between Bontok and Ifugao, Tinguian and Kalinga, were seen to be usually marked by a mountain ridge or change from open to forested terrain. Alternatively, they were zones where migrating groups met more or less directly, as with Ibanag and Itavi, northern Tinguian and Ilocano in the Laoag valley, and Bontok and Kalinga in the upper-middle Chico.

Marginal groups had then the special problem of setting up boundary-preserving mechanisms. These boundary behaviors signalized their continuing allegiance to their ancestral heritage, while still being prepared to accept whatever advantages might accrue from trading and perhaps intermarrying with their adjacent but ethnically different neighbors, and even in selective respects adopting their customs. The zones concerned may even be marked by considerable merging or syncretization, as in the Saltan valley headwaters of Kalinga, and also the Tinglayan communities between Bontok and Kalinga. Such boundary phenomena, it may be noted, have not been well studied by anthropologists, since the latter have been generally absorbed with the delineation of the type phenomena of ethnic or culture areas. The northern Luzon mountains, with their dozen or so principal ethnic groups, some with important subgroups, provide a particularly effective field for such studies.

Beyond these ethnic divisions, numerous additional vistas of cultural comparison and dynamic development open out, partially illuminated from the records. The early records showed a distribution from Pangasinan in the south to the north Cagayan coast of the exercise of religious leadership by female shamans, in contrast to the male priesthoods of later times, in the wet terracing areas. In the western and southern districts of the Cordillera, as also everywhere in the Christianized lowlands, there has been increased stress on class distinctions, aristocratic leadership, and real property. The use of fermented rice "wine," along with or in place of the much wider and seemingly older use of sugar-cane wine, appears to correlate directly with the spread of wet rice terracing. The same appears to be true of the use of pigs rather than dogs in religious sacrifices and offerings, the emphasis upon elaborate community ritual rather than individualized magic, and the measure of prestige in terms of wealth rather than bravery in war. Betel chewing has been yielding to tobacco as a narcotic, and is favored today only among northern dry cultivators. The same is true of artificial tooth blackening, which was widely practiced earlier, as seen in the references to the strangeness of the white teeth of early mission fathers. Many further specific artifacts, usages, and ideas deserve to be traced in distributional and developmental terms through additional research.

ETHNOHISTORY OF NORTHERN LUZON: HYPOTHESES AND INTERPRETATIONS

Analyzing ethnohistoric relationships in northern Luzon requires fitting elements together as in a puzzle. When a lowland area and the adjacent mountains were examined in each chapter, a recurrent problem emerged: beyond these mountains were more mountains, and beyond these, lowlands again. What about influences or even large population movements from the other side? Having examined the Ilocos and Cagayan sides of the Cordillera, we can now see these complexities in better perspective, and can, so to speak, view each segment in three rather than in two dimensions.

The key piece in this puzzle is the central Cordillera heights, the zone of wet rice terracing. On the interpretation of this zone hinge the answers to many of the specific problems that have been raised. Moreover, the origin of rice terracing has evoked much speculation, and clarification of this matter has been a major aim of the ethnohistorical research on which this work is based. For here theories of separate migration run squarely against a theory of local development and differentiation from a common base. After the origin of rice terracing has been discussed in detail, the analysis will follow roughly the lines of the area chapters in considering lowland and mountain groups.

At this point, the reader should again be warned that the historical records seldom provide sufficient evidence for a clear-cut and definitive interpretation. Rather, they permit a careful assessment of alternative hypotheses, and frequently a cautious statement of probabilities. This study has been, among other things, an exercise in ethnohistorical method, and it is clear that this line of research must be supplemented by others—archaeological, linguistic, and ethnographic—if its full worth is to be derived.

1. *The Origin of Rice Terracing*

The conventional view has been that rice-terracing techniques were brought by a distinctive migrant group (e.g., Blumentrit, 1882; Beyer, 1918, 1947; Cole, 1922; Keesing and Keesing, 1934). Opinion has varied about whether such hypothetical terracers arrived before or after the coming of lowland wet rice techniques to the adjacent coast. Speculations of their place of origin usually refer to "somewhere" across the China Sea in the mountains of east Asia, but other zones in which terraces are constructed have also been suggested, notably the Java area to the south and Japan to the north. Certain cultural parallels have been noted, especially between the Lepanto-Bontok groups and the terracing Naga mountain peoples of Assam, e.g., elaborate stone construction, men's houses.

Beyer (1947) has suggested that as many as five post-Negrito migrations must have occurred to account for the racial and cultural characteristics of the Luzon peoples, with most or all of them affecting this northern zone. Earlier he had offered an explicit hypothesis for the entry of terracing into the Cordillera. This developed from a "detailed" study of the terracing systems throughout Mountain Province, which was made as part of a general survey of the "non-Christian peoples" for the 1918 Philippine census. Beyer says:

The general results of this study seem to indicate that the culture in question originally came to the Gulf of Lingayen and the west coast of northern Luzon from Southern China, and that it spread up the Agno and Kayapa river valleys and across certain relatively low watersheds into the upper ends of the Ifugao valleys. Here it became firmly established and underwent a period of development and gradual expansion through tortuous valleys and devious routes in a general northward direction,—eventually spreading over the greater part of Bontok, Lepanto, and western Kalinga to the borders of the province of Abra. . . . The culture of southern Benguet may have been an offshoot directly from the Agno valley, while that of northern Benguet may have come over from Lepanto or from western Ifugao. (Philippine Census, 1918, II, 936.)

Beyer lists a number of other cultural elements which he judged to be associated with this terracing tradition, including a four-post house with rat guards, weaving on a particular type of loom, use of rice wine, a cult of ancestors, and a calendar. Beyer was at the time an Ifugao specialist, and his emphasis on the Ifugao role here, together with reference to the Ifugao house form rather than the house forms of other groups, could have resulted from his greater familiarity with that people.

In 1941, Eggan opened up a new line of thought in a paper that pointed to a series of cultural gradients in the central zone of the Cordillera, suggestive of dynamic changes and localized developments that took "definite directions." He noted that social and political organization is least elaborated among the Ifugao, and then increases in complexity through the Bontok, Lepanto, and Tinguian areas to the Ilocano in the west. Conversely, terracing has its highest development among the Ifugao, and then decreases in its technical efficiency in a westerly gradient. An emphasis on both wealth and class differentiation increases in the east-to-west direction as features of the elaborating social organization. Eggan interpreted these variations as partly a product of "long continued contacts with Asiatic and European peoples," and as partly representing local "cultural drift" resulting from ecological and behavioral factors. On the basis of "both archeological and linguistic" evidence, Eggan has subsequently suggested that, even taking account of such dynamics, the "wedge" of Lepanto-Bontok groups represents a separate migration, possibly entering northern Luzon "between 1500 and 500 B.C." (1941, 1954).

It was one of the stated purposes of this study to see if the records could shed light on the question of whether the wet rice terracing techniques might have been a local Cordillera development. No direct answer has been forthcoming, though the lack of reference to the great terracing systems until so late might appear offhand to indicate that they were a product of comparatively recent innovation. Here it will be useful, without discounting the separate migration possibility, to argue the hypothetical case for local development, especially taking into account the vistas of lowland-mountain contact, which the records do show.

As a general frame of reference, it could be postulated that some group, moving into the mountains from a lowland area where wet rice cultivation was already practiced, worked out the problems of stepping the walled fields, engineering the water runoff to service a greater slope, and selecting rice to fit higher elevations. Alternatively, a group already in residence in the mountains but in contact with lowland communities that adopted wet rice, developed the innovations. They might already have worked out the key idea of terracing in their handling of taro and other root crops. The irrigated fields of root crops seen by Galvey in Benguet in 1829 and the occurrence of terraced root-crop cultivation in such places as New Caledonia and Hawaii should remind us that there is no necessary connection between wet rice and the basic terracing innovations.

The writer sees no reason why the wet-terracing adjustments could not have been worked out independently in a number of the east and southeast Asian areas where they are found, as well as in other zones of the world where terracing is practiced. At least migration and diffusion theories should be postulated only in cases where direct contacts were highly probable. In view of the total circumstances, this middle Cordillera zone does not appear to the writer to fit well the latter criterion, except possibly as some itinerant Javanese, Chinese, Japanese, or indeed a Spaniard might have triggered off the basic idea of constructing terraces. It requires a considerable stretch of the imagination to picture some mountain terracing group of east or southeast Asia leaving its home area for northern Luzon, and if it did, not influencing other mountainous zones of the Philippines. If one's taste does not run toward granting the possibility of some local innovator getting the requisite insights, it would be easier to visualize, say, some Japanese runaway sailor with a bag of rice that originated in cool upland terraces and showing mountain families how to grow it!

Once terracing was developed, whether by migration, local adaptation, or demonstration by an itinerant outsider, a paramount need would be to control the irrigation water sources above the fields, particularly protecting them from enemies. This, the writer has previously suggested (1934), may have motivated the pioneering groups to move to the heights. Unless a major waterway incapable of diversion serves as the irrigation source, the modern residential pattern among Lepanto and Bontok villagers rarely allows a community to tolerate another controlling water to exist above it. An absorption with ensuring the security of water is also one of the principal themes of the legal and ritual systems of terracers. War and headhunting also tied into the economic complex, as heads were needed in the agricultural rituals. It seems part of the hypothetical picture, therefore, that the early terracers would have had the stimulus to move upward into the river headwaters, both for continuity of irrigation and for defense.

The existence of the rugged grass and pine forest terrain on what might be called the Cordillera cap has clearly favored the terracing technique. Terraced rice production, supplemented by root cropping and a limited range of other plant food sources and of flesh foods, is essentially an open-country economy. It marches with montane climate, the traditional rice crop being planted in the cool, drier winter when the water run is more controllable, and harvested in the warm summer. Indeed, its characteristics suggest that it could have been developed by peoples already living above the humid forest line on a root economy, as noted earlier, or at least living high enough to range into this cap area.

When the Ilocos side of the Cordillera was being described, the hypothesis of a western development of wet rice terracing was to the fore, especially considering the large terracing villages of Amburayan, Lepanto, and Bontok. In the upper Cagayan chapter, however, the enticing vista opened up of possibly tracing the terracing techniques back to wet rice cultivators who might have moved into Ifugao from the Magat valley, particularly as a result of pressures by the initial Spanish expeditions of 1591–94. In this case, as Beyer recognized in his reconstruction of terracing dynamics, where two such groups have only a mountain ridge crossed by trails between them, it certainly seems unrealistic to postulate two independent instances of the working out of the basic terracing innovations. The criterion discussed earlier, of having opportunities for diffusion through contact, seems more than met.

Various alternative possibilities open out here when these two leads are being explored. First, all these inner mountain groups eastward to the Ifugao could have reached the heights from the west coast. Conversely, they could all have moved up from the Magat river area in the east and spread westward over the Cordillera. Or the ancestors of the Amburayan, Lepanto, and Bontok peoples could have been migrants from the west coast, and the Ifugao separate migrants from the Magat area. The terracing techniques could correspondingly have become established initially on one or the other side of the Cordillera backbone, and then spread across it. The problem discussed earlier, of whether root-gardening populations preceded wet rice terracers, is relevant here, and so is the matter of early (pre-Spanish) or late (early Spanish) dating of the terracing development.

Following up the southern Ilocos chapter, a case could be made for considering at least the Amburayan, Lepanto, and Bontok populations as having their origins on the west or Ilocos coast side. Correspondingly, the Lepanto-Bontok type of terracing village life might be hypothesized as drawing heavily upon cultural elements characteristic of the lowland life in early Spanish times.

Taking the shorter perspective, refugee lowlanders were seen as moving back before Salcedo and his successors from 1572 on. Ilocos coastal communities, too, provided examples of Spanish concentration of scattered units, which might have suggested the cooperative and defensive advantages of building tightly knit villages. The community organization of the Lepanto and Bontok, based on a series of wards or neighborhoods (*ato*), each with its own ceremonial center of "men's house," could derive from consolidation of any formerly scattered hamlets. Among other elements of modern Lepanto and Bontok custom lending themselves to possible interpretation as being Spanish-inspired are an emphasis upon male priesthoods rather than the old religious leadership of women shamans, the emergence of their aristocracies of wealth, and elaborated concepts of landed property with a focus on ownership of rice fields. On the west coast, trade goods, including metal to make tools, and carabao for use as work animals, were available in quantity. Contacts occurred much more frequently here with Asians or Europeans (if they had any role in triggering off the essential terracing innovations) than were possible in the upper Cagayan valley area.

The alternative possibility of an eastern or Cagayan origin could be argued, particularly in the case of the hamlet-living, hand-cultivating Ifugao. If, as seems likely, this group has a Magat river origin, the most plausible hypothesis is that they were refugees from the initial Spanish pressures. Leaving the then heavily settled valley floor, described by the first Spanish expeditions, they could have moved up the Matung, Lamut, or other river courses into present Ifugao territory, working out the terracing technique in order to conserve their wet rice system of production. From here on, Beyer's suggested pattern of distribution of the terracing innovations westward into Bontok, Lepanto, and other zones could have followed along.

More complex sequences need also to be taken into account in exploring this phase of the problem further. For example, it could be pictured that Ifugao already had by that time a root-eating population from the west or south who were joined by such Magat refugees. The presence of closely related dialects, sharply distinct from those of the Ifugao, on the eastern and southern fringes of Ifugao territory, may be significant in this connection. Or again, if the Ifugao ancestors were from the Cagayan side, they could have been dry cultivators when first settling the mountains, and then adopted the terracing techniques through contacts with the Bontok or else the Magat wet cultivators. Such features of Ifugao life as the scattered-out residential system and the elaboration of an overarching law and ritual may trace back to old Cagayan usages. The use of hand spades rather than work animals appears symbolic of the fact that until later times the Ifugao did not have access to elaborate trade goods by way of lowland settlements as the Lepanto had on the west coast.

The argument followed here has purposely emphasized the possibility that the terracing system developed as late as the beginning Spanish times, and hence challenges the migration hypotheses which give it a much greater antiquity. Unfortunately, the documents relating to the middle Cordillera are too scanty and late to throw light upon the chronological problems involved. Other methods such as archaeological surveys, comparative ethnological probing, and glottochronological analysis will need to be extended to see whether further clarification can be achieved. One striking point does stand out, however, after scrutiny of the records: the lack of reference by observers prior to the nineteenth century to the rice terrace systems. As said earlier, some of the stepped hillsides are so spectacular that they could be placed in modern lists of the "great wonders" of the world. Yet military commanders, mission fathers, and other visitors fail to give them even passing mention. In consequence, it seems reasonable to consider at least the more elaborated terraces on steeper slopes to be relatively modern.

The Monforte expedition of the 1660's recorded "Cayang" and "Lubing" (Kayan and Lubon) as having about 150 houses each. Communities of this size, it has been said already, seem to imply terraced fields. Yet with perhaps half as many people at the time as are in these communities today, their fields could have been located relatively unobtrusively in hill pockets and along the waterways. In Ifugao, particularly, the startling density of population found in the twentieth century could be a later development, resulting in extension of terraces to steeper hillsides and in higher step formations.

Most observers of the terrace systems, however, have been convinced that a great time span has been needed for their construction. Pseudo-archaeological guesses have claimed a timetable of as much as four thousand years for building some of the largest terrace systems, as at Banaue in Ifugao. As mentioned in the Benguet study, however, the whole Loo valley terrace system was built, according to government reports, in about two years. In 1932, the construction of a new irrigation ditch in the Mainit area of Bontok opened the way for "several hectares of new rice terraces" to be built. Even a hundred years of active building, for such people, could undoubtedly accomplish an amazingly extensive series of new or extended terraces.

At the same time, neglected terraces rapidly deteriorate for want of repair to walls and working of the soil. The terraces of the Kayapa valley, apparently not abandoned by its "Igorot" population until late in the nineteenth century, were overgrown and breaking down when Barrows visited the area early in the American regime. This valley, it was seen, was considered by Beyer to be one of the initial routes of entry for terracing, along with the Agno valley further west. Additional archaeological work on the age of terraces, particularly at any datable former settlement sites, would be of great aid in clarifying the chronological problems referred to here.

Another feature of wet rice terracing in nearly all parts of the Cordillera concerned is the starting of the traditional crop cycle in the drier winter season, around December to January. The exception is the Tinguian practice in Abra, conforming to the lowland cycle which starts with the onset of the summer rainy season, around June. Two factors have been suggested as favoring a winter cropping timetable in the mountains: first, the greater control which can be exercised over water during the drier winter months compared with the often torrential runoff in the late summer period; and second, the placement of the harvest time in the warmer summer, which favors ripening the grain. Barton states of the Ifugao that the reason for their winter cropping is that "during the period from June to December, the usual rice growing period in the lowlands, there is not enough sunshine to mature the rice well"—from July to January the weather is rainy and cloudy, then becomes "foggy, cold, and disagreeable." Barton also says of the Kalinga that the traditionally cropped type of rice will not grow in the summer cycle. The rices that are double cropped by the mountain peoples in modern times are later introduced varieties (Barton, 1922, p. 388; 1949, p. 9).

The seasonal reversal of the wet rice timetable could be made an argument for postulating that the mountain terracing was brought in from outside the Luzon area by a people with winter cropping habits. But it could also represent the successful application of some local innovator's ideas. The writer also calls to mind here that the upper Magat valley has cool and cloudy winters, located as it is at an elevation of around 1,500 feet. If a theory of a Cagayan side origin of the Ifugao and of wet terracing is favored, this valley might have been a staging area, so to speak, for varieties of rice suited to mountain conditions. Possibly, too, it could have been the locale where the January to June cycle was worked out. Whether modern Isinai tradition, subject as this ethnic group has been to later mission influences, could provide clues in these matters would have to be investigated. It may be, too, that in the end the crux of this and related problems will lie in a comprehensive study of the rices of both lowland and mountain areas: their characteristics and relationships, and especially their climatic and other ecological needs and limitations.

2. Pangasinan

Initial descriptions of the Pangasinan lowlanders prior to their conversion do not mark them off in such basic ways from the mountain Ibaloi to justify a hypothesis of disparate origins and migrations. Their tendency to a scattered settlement pattern, their hunting, their gear, and their political, social, and religious ideology and organization seem to have been generally similar. It will be recalled, however, that the Ibaloi appear to have based their economy upon root cropping until comparatively modern times, while the Pangasinan had wet rice apparently prior to the Spanish entry.

As seen in Chapter III, old trade trails connected the Benguet heights of the Ibaloi with the Pangasinan plains to the south, with the southern Ilocos coast to the west, and with "Ituy," the upper Magat river flats, to the east. To evaluate the possible origins of the Ibaloi, the peoples of the Cagayan side, particularly the Isinai of the upper Magat, must be considered. Data on the Isinai are sketchy, however, and their possible past connections with the Pangasinan populations must remain highly problematical. All in all, it seems most likely that the lowlands of old Pangasinan are the zone from which the ancestors of the Ibaloi moved upward to the heights.

An unknown factor is how far what was to be called in historic times the Pangasinan ethnic group was consolidated out of formerly diversified population elements. It could easily be pictured that the coming of rice production and of external trade, whether brought by a new migration of people or diffused into the area, brought about a leveling out of custom and language. It could be suspected particularly that groups living inland in what became northeast Pangasinan were culturally variant, and had also bred differences in their genetic heritage through hybridization with Negritos as well as through localized inbreeding. Unfortunately, these eastern areas break into the historical records considerably later than the coastal peoples. But their populations then appear under differentiated names: Igorots, Italons, Alaguetes, Ilongots, and, in the upper river in Cagayan, Isinais.

The coming of the Spaniards not only brought extensive changes in the life of those people who chose to stay on in the lowlands, but also threw up new barriers of separation between them and the mountain populations. Trading relations of convenience continued. Yet the mountaineers became "infidels," and if former lowlanders retreated from Spanish control they were branded as "runaways" and if at first Christianized, "apostates."

An obvious feature of early culture change was the acceptance of the sweet potato as a staple food. Later, apparently in the nineteenth century, root crops gave place progressively to wet cultivation of rice on terraces. The resemblances in technology between Ibaloi and Ifugao suggest that rice terracing spread to the Benguet heights from the northeast.

3. The Problem of Ilocano Identity

The major problem that emerges from the Ilocos side of northern Luzon concerns the identity of the Ilocano. In 1609, that is, nearly forty years after the initial Spanish occupation, Morga referred to the western coastal people as "the Ylocos": this the first reference to them as a single unit. In 1630, Medina spoke of them as "Ilocans." There is also some implication in Loarca's 1582 description that a common language was spoken, but the first specific reference to the use of a single language throughout Ilocos is that by Latona in 1662, long after the mission fathers had put Iloko into writing. Even here, the reference could be to the use of Iloko as a lingua franca, with older languages, if any, still used locally.

Much speculation has gone on, it was said in Chapter II, about how far linguistic and other variations existed among the Ilocos coastal populations at the time the Spaniards arrived. The modern northern Ilocos people, by some views, appear to show Negrito hybridization, and this is projected back as indicating genetic differences. So, too, are language variations of today, especially distinctions between northern and southern Iloko. Political fragmentation, spiced by feuding and war, was evidently characteristic of the region prior to the imposition of Spanish peace. In the northwest Luzon sections, particularly, the question of ethnic unity versus a "congeries of peoples" hypothesis emerged for discussion.

It has been seen that the records do not solve these questions of early Ilocano identity: they will need to be followed up through archaeological, linguistic, and other relevant investigations. The materials suggest, however, that whatever differences were developed up to the early Christian centuries through the coming of separate Negrito and Malay-type migrants, the adjustment of groups to their local habitats, and other dynamic happenings, a leveling-out process had already started before the Spaniards arrived. Two factors come especially to mind: the apparent establishment of wet rice cropping at numbers of points along the coastal flats, and the coastal trading in which Asian merchants were participants. The major consolidating forces, however, seem to have been post-Spanish: the overarching governmental system; the ecclesiastical imprint not only in spiritual matters but also in technological improvement, literacy, and other secular fields; the making over of the indigenous leadership into an aristocracy of minor officialdom and wealth; money and commerce; the rise of urban centers; and, by no means least, the making of common cause in anti-Spanish movements. It has been suggested in the text that the principal model for Ilocanization in Spanish times was provided by the Vigan area. There have also been modern variants generated: the influential mestizo enclave in Vigan, the northern Ilocos irrigation societies, the Ilocano homesteader probing into lonely mountain pockets.

The Ilocos sections to follow will examine, rather briefly, ethnohistorical problems concerning the Kankanai, Lepanto, and Bontok (touched upon already in the discussion of rice terracing); the Tinguian; and the northern Ilocos coast and adjacent mountain populations.

4. Southern Ilocos: The Kankanai, Lepanto, and Bontok

As was noted in the discussion of the origin of rice terracing, the hypothesis that the Kankanai-Lepanto-Bontok groups are offshoots of an Ilocos coastal population seems highly plausible. The presence of valued minerals, copper and particularly gold, in the Suyoc-Mankayan region suggests that this area was the first to be permanently settled, again in pre-Spanish times under the stimulus of Chinese trading.

As has been seen, the Lepanto and the Bontok show the full elaboration of an intensive wet-terracing production of rice, with large, tightly knit villages, much use of stone construction, the "men's house" and "girls' house," and the *ato* system by which villages are subdivided into ward-like segments. Differences between Lepanto and Bontok in dialect and in house architecture, dress, and other cultural features are there, just as more minor differences show among subregions and down to the local community level. Yet an over-all similarity prevails which seems to indicate that the Lepanto-Bontok ways of life are built up from one prime reformulation of an old coastal culture. In this case it is by no means impossible that such a reformulation took place at beginning Spanish times rather than earlier, particularly in view of the similarities, noted earlier, between Bontok-Lepanto patterns and the post-Spanish "model" provided by mission centers.

The modern distinctions between the Kankanai and the Lepanto suggest that large-scale inland movement, whether at beginning Spanish times or before, originally took place to the north of the Suyoc-Mankayan area. The coastal districts around Candon would then have held the common population pool. From there, migrants would have moved up into the Kayan-Sagada-Bontoc zone and the Bauko-Sabangan zone, in both of which the Lepanto and Bontok peoples now border one another. Lepanto-type culture could then have diffused southward to envelop the Suyoc-Mankayan area, which comprises its southern flank today.

Any comprehensive interpretation of these rice-terracing groups of the high Cordillera inevitably hinges on the degree to which the highlands were permanently occupied in pre-Spanish times, and on the origin and antiquity of rice terracing. The inability of the historical records to resolve these questions must leave the ethnohistory of the high Cordillera to the realm of speculation pending further research.

5. Middle Ilocos: The Tinguian

The primary problem which emerged from the study of records of the middle Ilocos region was the relationship between the mountain populations, particularly the Tinguian, and the peoples of the adjacent coastal areas.

The records indicate that mission fathers penetrated the Abra gap in 1598 because the inner valley area held a resident population, which was their target. It is not made clear, however, whether they were following up refugees from the coastal zone, which could well have been the case on the valley flats, or they were hoping for converts among already well-established groups.

Such inland peoples of northern Abra, and also the northern sections of Kalinga subprovince on the Cagayan side of the Cordillera, have been up to modern times dry gardeners occupying sparsely scattered hamlets: the "mountain Tinguians," the Isneg or Apayao, and the northern Kalinga groups. Barring separate migration theories, the presence of these dry cultivators in areas where adjacent coastal groups practice wet cultivation can be interpreted in two ways. First, all of the peoples of the area could originally have been dry cultivators, with coastal groups later adopting wet rice techniques. Second, the mountain groups could represent offshoots from coastal populations practicing lowland double-cropping of wet and dry rice. The ecological strictures of rainfall, elevation, and terrain previously discussed could have militated against effective wet rice cultivation in these mountain areas, even after critical terracing innovations had been worked out to the south.

The distribution of the dry-gardening mountain Tinguian suggests that they were offshoots of pre-Spanish coastal populations that were later made over into the Ilocano, or northern Ilocano, mold. They could well have moved inland originally by way of the Abra gap from the Vigan coastal area, and then spread upland by way of the Abra tributaries. This could be visualized, in terms of the first hypothesis, as having occurred before Spanish times, and prior to the coming of wet cultivation to the coastal communities. Or it might have taken place after the wet techniques had been adopted, as in the second hypothesis. In the latter case, however, it could be expected that the flats along Abra valley floor back of the gap would have been developed immediately in terms of the familiar lowland cultivation methods. Instead, when wet cultivation took hold among the valley Tinguians, the techniques used were those of mountain terracing, which diffused northward, probably from the Lepanto. Furthermore, they appear to have come quite late into the Abra valley, possibly even since the beginning of the nineteenth century.

Although it seems likely that the Tinguians derive from lowland populations, their considerable contacts with mountain groups across the Cordillera and to the south and north introduce further complexities. The most notable of various old trade trails going eastward is the one the Spaniards improved in the nineteenth century as a military "road," leading across into the headwaters of the Saltan river in Kalinga subprovince. This trail, which the Spaniards attempted to control by establishing a post at Balbalasan, was the most direct and accessible route for movement from the Ilocos side to the Cagayan side of the Cordillera. In the Cagayan chapters of the study a northern Kalinga group called by the Spaniards "Calauas" were seen as trading tobacco regularly over this pass into Ilocos via Abra. In modern times, as Cole, Worcester, and others have shown, the Saltan river headwaters area is less of an ethnic frontier than a mingling place and a kind of no-man's-land in which Tinguian and Kalinga peoples and cultural influences conjoin.

Several other trails to the south leading into southern Kalinga and Bontoc are marked by sharper ethnic breaks: they involved crossing formidable terrain and taking greater risks of hostile attack. Further south, easier trails gave connections into Lepanto, both up the Abra valley and to the heights, especially in the Besao district. Here, trading and occasional intermarriage between Tinguians and Lepantos has made the boundaries less sharp. The same is true regarding the Tineg river zone of northeast

Abra, where mountain Tinguians have traded and mingled somewhat with the Isneg people of southern Apayao by way of old trails. Some small Isneg settlements were established in the Tineg area, apparently by "runaways," when Apayao was being brought under government control. Many earlier observers considered these dry-gardening mountain Tinguians of the north and the Isnegs of Apayao to be west and east parts of a single ethnic group, but Cole and other modern ethnographers were able to show them as having significant distinctions that suggest origins in different coastal zones.

6. Northern Ilocos

Two problems are of particular significance for this northern zone. The first, which is tied to the wider question of Ilocano identity, concerns the background of the coastal peoples, who appear to have been cultivating wet rice at the time of Spanish arrival. Second, the sharp contrasts between these wet cultivators concentrated in the southern lowlands and the sparsely settled dry-gardening mountain peoples to the east and north raise the question of whether they share common origins.

When the Spaniards arrived, they found a continuous series of lowland settlements from the Vigan area to the Laoag area. Their apparent cultivation of wet rice was inferred from demographic records. This distribution may have come about, on the one hand, from a northward spread in pre-Spanish times of the population that was to become the Ilocano. Or it could have been produced through different local groups along the coast, each adopting wet cultivation techniques, and so reformulating their customs in parallel ways. Such diffusion could have occurred through observing such innovation among neighbors, or through instruction by Chinese visitors. To the extent that differing dialects were in use, the latter interpretation also needs rounding out by postulating the subsequent adoption by the different groups of the Iloko language as a lingua franca.

The fact that the northern Ilocano of modern times has a degree of distinctiveness in language and customs does not throw definitive weight to one or the other interpretation. The dynamics either of a northward migration or of a local reformulation could equally have given scope for such distinctiveness to emerge. It was seen, for example, that some students of Iloko have claimed that the north preserves its "purer" or "more primitive" forms; if so, this could be explained either by the selective persistence of pre-Iloko forms, or else in terms of the greater geographic isolation and largely self-contained life. The considerable spirit of independence generated among its people in historic times, too, could be an older pre-Ilocano tendency, or it could be interpreted as a locally accentuated phase of Ilocano values.

With these problems in mind, the data relating to the mountain groups can be reviewed. A strong impression is gained from the records that most of the "infidels" of historic times were recent migrants from neighboring areas. This is particularly true of the sparse Isneg populations of the northern mountains. These groups seem to have drifted across from the Apayao river area in the course of trading with the Ilocos coastal settlement of Bangui and with eastern Laoag valley settlements. In the same way, the Tinguian settlements of the south appear to be northward extensions of the "mountain Tinguians" of neighboring Abra.

How far the latter people were already in the mountain environs of the Laoag river valley at the time the Spaniards arrived is not made clear by the records. There is the old story quoted by de los Reyes of the "Igorrotes of Dinglas" who were opposed to living in villages and "fled to the mountains" in the face of the terrors of the Spanish. The implication here, however, is that these were remontados, or "runaways," to the mountains rather than an original highland population. The mission records of work directed at the Tinguians indicate that it opened even later than that among the "Apayaos."

As seen, Negrito bands ranged here as elsewhere in northern Luzon. More interesting from an ethnohistoric standpoint are the somewhat shadowy "Adan" or "Adang." Judging from the records, the Adan were a small enclave of dry gardeners who were established in the fastnesses upriver from Bangui, perhaps before the Isneg drift from Apayao set in. They could have been refugees from settlements on or near the coast at the time Spanish ships began to range along it. Or they could have been in this mountain area prior to Spanish times.

Inevitably, in considering the Adan, the hypotheses raised above in relation to Ilocano origins come again to mind. If the lowland groups were migrants from the Vigan area, the Adan could be elements from an earlier population who chose to move into the northern fastnesses rather than be assimilated. If, instead, they were a local group who accepted wet cultivation techniques and were in time to become Ilocanized, the Adan could be descendants of their more conservative members who took to the mountains instead. In other words, reference to the mountain populations does not throw weight more to the one interpretation of lowland origins than to the other.

7. Northwest Cagayan and Isneg

The ethnohistory of the northwest Cagayan area centers around two questions: first, what was the ethnic and linguistic character of the coastal population in earlier times, and second, what is the origin of the Isnegs of interior Apayao?

A few writers have suggested that the Isneg language may be a dialectal variation of Iloko. This leads on to the wider question of whether the Isneg people, or the coastal people, or indeed both, might be continuations into northern Luzon of Ilocano ethnic elements. The documentary evidence examined lends no weight to any hypothesis asserting close linkages. Even apart from the questions posed earlier on the nature and timetable of Ilocano identity, this ethnic group apparently failed to move up the coast north of the Laoag-Bacarra region until historic times. In the mountains west of the Cordillera ridge the "Apayaos" or "Calanasas" were sharply differentiated from the lowland populations, and their presence there was not reported until the seventeenth century. At most, therefore, any theory that tries to link these northern peoples with the Ilocos coast peoples would need to see the connection as an early and indirect one. A hypothesis might be tenable that a congeries of locally differentiated ethnic groups inhabited this rugged northwest Luzon area in pre-Spanish times, all with a common origin. Of these, the western groups became Ilocanized.

A quite different line of speculation suggested in early ethnographic literature is that the northern coast and Apayao mountains were settled by people from the offshore Babuyan and Batan islands. This view illustrates well the need for careful ethnohistorical study, since the informants of the time were almost surely mixing into their older folklore the oral memories of the Babuyan and Batan islanders who were resettled along the margins of Apayao. This occurred not only in the lower Abulug, where most early ethnographic observations were made, but also, as will be seen later, in southeast Apayao, where a few Babuyan islanders took up residence in the eighteenth century.

The language and culture of the offshore islands, usually called "Ivatan," does not appear to have any closer relation to Isneg than would be warranted by their respective geographic positions in the northern Philippines. The nearest of the Babuyan islands to this section of the Luzon coast, it may be noted, is the small island of Fuga some 20 miles to the north of the Sanchez-Mira area. Beyer classed the Ivatan language tentatively as an offshoot of the Iloko language group. At most, the relationship between the northwest Cagayan area groups and the offshore island groups seems to be an indirect and old one, and it would of course fit a "congeries of peoples" theory.

On the Cagayan side, the question poses itself of whether the coastal population at the time Spaniards arrived comprised western extensions of the Ibanag. If this were so, the Isneg might be descendants of a prior population forced inland, or else mountain offshoots of the Ibanag settlements, possibly refugees of beginning Spanish times.

The Ibanag group, it will be recalled, appears to have had its original home in the lower Cagayan river valley. But as with Iloko on the west coast, the Ibanag language became the lingua franca of most of the valley peoples, used first in trade and later in governmental and mission work. This led to the Ibanagization, so to speak, of many groups, who were formerly of other ethnic affiliation, at the same time that they were being Christianized and Hispanized. This could also have happened along this northwest Cagayan coast if the original people were not Ibanags. An impression is gained from the records that this latter is what happened, especially as the old population that formerly spread westward to Pata and Cabicungan became concentrated in the Abulug-Pamplona region. It seems hardly likely that a vigorous and high-prestige Ibanag population would have been displaced so easily from such living sites. Moreover, the lack of Ibanag settlements along the coast between Abulug and the Cagayan river mouth was also seen as lending weight to the view that the coast further west was not a continuation of Ibanag territory.

The argument here has purposely been given a negative slant, since obviously the hypothesis that the coastal peoples were Ibanag seems to be the most tenable one. Because the records do not settle the matter, it becomes a problem which would need to be investigated through archaeological surveys, together with ethnological and linguistic probing below the surface of modern changes among the Abulug-Pamplona *naturales* and the Ibanags of the Cagayan mouth area. The Isneg culture and language would also be taken appropriately into account to test out possible relations between them and the Ibanag.

Provided the old coastal populations were not directly related to Ilocano, Babuyan-Batan, or Ibanag, it might be hypothesized that they were a more or less distinct ethnic entity. Taken alone, their smallness numerically would make this a dubious view. If, however, the Isnegs are thought of as an inland extension of their group, the idea becomes more plausible. What was called above a "congeries of peoples" theory could tolerate a more or less separate ethnic and linguistic grouping in this isolated coast and mountain zone.

Such a hypothesis rules out the need for postulating a separate migration to explain the Isneg. But it should be noted immediately that in the case of this interior group, there exists another alternative possibility. Southern Apayao, it was noted, is drained by a separate river system called the Matalag, which flows into the lower Chico. In the lowlands here the Christianized Itavi, differentiated somewhat from the Ibanag in culture and language, form the original population. The Isnegs, therefore, could have been mountain kinsmen of the Itavi, entering Apayao from this southeast side and spreading northward in turn to the Abulug-Apayao river districts.

Vanoverbergh, whose extensive works provide the principal sources of ethnological information on the Isneg, has gone so far as to suggest that their original affiliations do lie with the Itavi. He bases this view particularly on linguistic closeness between Itavi and Isneg (1932, pp. 55–57). The distribution of the Isneg, who live mainly on the northern rivers of Apayao and leave most of the Matalag tributaries to another ethnic group, seems to weigh against such a thesis. If it were to be true, however, the further question is raised on the possible relations between the Itavi in the southeast and the northern coastal populations. On the one hand, Itavi-Isneg migrants might have spread northward through Apayao to the north coast. On the other, north coast Isneg migrants might have spread overland into the lower Chico. This possibility of a still larger ethnic grouping having originally existed, although it seems dubious, also merits archaeological, ethnological, and glottochronological investigation. On the archaeological side, Vanoverbergh's reference given above to finds of pottery remains in uninhabited areas may be relevant to this problem.

The dry gardening practiced by the Isneg, and the ecological factors that militate against rice terracing even where it has been introduced in recent years, have already been reviewed in some detail. The records are not clear whether the coastal populations had wet cultivation in beginning Spanish times. If the north coast flats did have wet rice cultivation, there was undoubtedly, under the double-cropping system, a dry rice crop as well. People moving inland, it could then be assumed, abandoned the first technique and came to emphasize the one that represented an ecological fit. Correspondingly, they would have needed to spread out in more scattered hamlets. The adoption of maize, which thrives in Apayao, diversified the economic base and resulted in less dependence on root crops, which do not store well in such a humid climate. By contrast, if the coastal people were originally dry gardeners, less cultural reformulation would have been called for. The Itavi people in the lower Chico, it was seen, appear to have been dry gardeners when the Spaniards arrived.

The remaining question is the timetable of Isneg entry. This could have occurred long before Spanish times, with people first hunting and gathering forest products in the high country, and then either electing to settle permanently there or being forced in as a result of intergroup warfare.

The more tempting hypothesis is that they moved up the river valleys as refugees from the initial Spanish contacts and pressures, as suggested already. The richness of their trade goods, the place given to maize and tobacco growing, their use of the wooden boat, which looks to be of Spanish origin, and their substantial and distinctively architectured housing are among cultural elements which suggest that they could have brought into Apayao a Spanish-influenced tradition. It must be recognized, however, that such elements could have been adopted or adapted in the later centuries. At least the apparent great falling away of population along the north coast in the decades prior to 1610, when the Fotol mission was started, seems to indicate that many people had moved back into the mountain fastnesses. Such "running away" was also seen in the records in the Matalag-Chico river area.

8. *Lower Cagayan: The Ibanag*

The ethnohistory of the lower Cagayan appears to have been less complex than in most northern Luzon areas. The group known as the Ibanag
were seen as of prime concern in this zone. Probably, as Malumbres suggests, the lower Cagayan river flats were the original residential zone of
the Ibanag, even though populations speaking Ibanag and calling themselves such have come to predominate from the Tuguegarao area southward to the Cagayan-Magat junction.

At the time the Spaniards arrived, the Ibanag probably were already
cultivating wet rice on the flats, as well as dry rice in hilly areas. They had
been trading with Chinese and Japanese. Prior to Spanish concentration
policies, their settlements appear to have been small and scattered, except
possibly at trading points near the Cagayan mouth, e.g., Camalaniugan.
In later times, as seen, the development of Tuguegarao, which in the nineteenth century became the capital of the province, caused the initial urban
focus at Lal-lo to wane. The swampy lower Cagayan coast and river flats
correspondingly tended to lose population to that area.

The original population of northeast Cagayan was evidently Negrito.
After penetration by Malayan peoples, the Negritos took refuge in swamp
and foothill country to both the east and the west of the river. Spanish
pressures and thwarted uprisings led many Ibanag to retreat to these eastern and western fastnesses, either prior to Christianization or as "apostates."
The shadowy accounts of the Vangag and Aripa missions and of the Dummun and Paret-Paranan river "infidels" seem to be the stories of such runaway groups. But these episodes in lower Cagayan ethnohistory became
almost wholly matters of the past, since such isolated groups were converted and resettled in the later nineteenth and early twentieth centuries.
By today virtually the only remaining non-Christians in this northeast
Luzon area are the remnants of the Negritos.

The possible relation of the Ibanags to the Isnegs of Apayao has been
discussed in the last section. Here it need merely be said that the great
swamp and forest area west of the Cagayan seems hardly likely to have
provided the original migration routes for the peopling of Apayao.

9. *Chico River Area*

The possibility that the Isneg may trace back to the Itavi of the lower
Chico, although it seems unlikely in terms of present distributions, must
be borne in mind in assessing the Chico materials. Of more immediate
importance here are the affiliations of the Kalinga groups, since their geo-
graphical position suggests ties with the Itavi.

Seen in terms of all possibilities, the Kalingas could have come to occupy
their present home areas not only by going up the Chico but also by coming
down it, by crossing east from what is now Abra Province, or by moving

westward over rugged country from the middle Cagayan. As a convenient means of analysis, the last three possible migration routes may be considered first.

The upper Chico waterways were seen to be homes for the Bontok and Lepanto ethnic groups, who share many close cultural likenesses. The Bontok area meets the Kalinga area in a little-recorded zone called Tinglayan, where several communities draw upon elements from both cultures. Further down the Chico, the Kalingas of the Lubuagan and Tanudan districts, although still having villages based on a terracing economy, show a very marked shift in culture. From here the terrain becomes lower, and north of Naneng the settlements are small and at most have recently built terraces to supplement a traditional dry-gardening economy. On the west side, in the upper Saltan valley adjacent to Abra, there is also wet terracing, and this gives way similarly to dry gardening as the elevation falls away.

Whether the Lubuagan-Naneng terracing and that of the upper Saltan go far back in time or may be fairly recent, which is apparently the case with the Tinguian wet cultivation system, is not clear from the works of Barton and other writers of Kalinga. The moving front of modern terracing, however, is well reported by Scott (1958). On the eastern side, it will be recalled, the slopes that fall away to the middle Cagayan valley are homes for sparse dry cultivating Gaddang groups, but away south of them are terracers *par excellence*, the Mayoyao subgroup of the Ifugaos.

In the light of this quick review, it might at first seem feasible to consider the Kalingas as extensions of one or other of these neighboring mountain groups instead of referring their origins to the lower Chico. The dry-cultivating systems of lower Kalinga zones could then be seen as ecological adjustments to terrain and rainfall by groups migrating northward and so downward. The Kalingas, however, show particularly marked physical and cultural contrasts to the Bontoks, Tinguians, and Ifugaos. The breaklines in the Tinglayan and Saltan headwaters, although somewhat blurred by the minglings of people and the diffusions of custom, are so distinctive in terms of dress, housing, color preferences, social structure, religion, and other matters that historic continuities appear tenuous. On the eastern side, the Gaddang are also markedly different even from the Kalinga dry cultivators.

Although these leads to possible relationship must properly continue to be open to further testing through appropriate research, the soundest frame of ethnohistorical reference seems to correspond to the most obvious geographic one, namely, to look to the lower Chico area as the departure place for Kalinga entry into the mountains. First mobile ranging parties, and then permanent settlers, can easily be visualized as entering the upland valleys of the Matalag, Saltan, Mabaca, and Bananid, and also working their way higher up the Chico itself.

The materials presented in the middle Cagayan chapter show the degree to which the lower-middle Cagayan was kept turbulent by fighting, which evidently drew in Ibanag, Itavi, Gaddang, and perhaps other groups. The foothills and secluded valleys of the Chico could, therefore, have been refuges for weaker or defeated groups long before the Spaniards arrived. At lower elevations dry rice would then have been their staple crop, provided it had penetrated the Cagayan by then. If very high elevations were reached, yams and taro could alternatively have served as the plant food staples. Other refugees could then have joined them, particularly as the Spaniards penetrated the lower Chico. This time span, together with the addition of later groups, could have produced the diversity that Beyer describes when he was led to say in 1916 of the Kalingas: "[They consist] of several distinct peoples who are now so exceedingly mixed in physical type, language, and culture that it is difficult if not impossible in the state of our present knowledge to separate the constituent groups and define their distinguishing characteristics" (1917, pp. 49–50).

Fortunately Barton has subsequently provided considerable material on the Kalingas of the Lubuagan district (Barton, 1949). Edward Dozier, too, has pending publications comparing this group with the Saltan and Mabaca valley Kalingas. Yet much remains to be done in this part of the Cordillera before the ethnohistorical problems raised here can be fully answered. One interesting example of Kalinga distinctiveness is a great stress on ceremonial costumes, so that they have been called the "peacocks" of the Philippines. Their emphasis on gaudy color and elaborate ornament might lend itself to interpretation as one way of assertion by mountaineers of their sense of superiority over their drab fellows in the adjacent Christian lowlands.

10. *Middle Cagayan*

The ethnohistory of the middle Cagayan area shows some broad parallels to that of the lower Cagayan. The groups remaining along the main river course were Christianized. But in the face of Spanish pressures many retreated to fastnesses in the east, west, and south, either prior to conversion or as "apostates." The same happened in miniature at Palanan, with runaways taking to the mountains. Those "infidels" who were not converted and resettled earlier came within the spheres of governmental and mission influence in the later nineteenth and early twentieth centuries, so that by today only small pockets of non-Christians remain in the least accessible strongholds.

In ethnic and linguistic terms, however, the story of the middle Cagayan is considerably more complex than that of the lower Cagayan. The records also leave obscure some rather vital points concerning the pre-Spanish identity and distribution of population elements. The first fathers did note a linguistic breakpoint at Tuguegarao. Later materials also show the Iguig area north of Tuguegarao to be predominantly Itavi speaking, though this could have been a result of population shifts in Spanish times. From Tuguegarao south, the name "Irraya" comes vaguely into the picture as an ethnic term, in addition to its firm early use as a regional term. In later times "Irraya" was to be applied along with "Kalinga" for some of the more or less inimical non-Christians on the rivers east of the Cagayan, as in the German scholar Semper's account. The most definite and lasting ethnic term, however, for peoples other than Ibanag speakers in the middle Cagayan has been Gaddang or Gaddan.

The modern Gaddang speakers were seen as being in recent times very small in numbers. This is true of the Christianized valley Gaddangs as well as of the non-Christian Gaddangs left in the eastern Cordillera region. Beyer and others also class the modern pockets of non-Christians in the upper river valleys east of the Cagayan as Gaddangs. Some districts above the Cagayan-Magat fork, including Cauayan as already seen, still have Gaddang-speaking majorities, though there, too, in the aggregate their numbers are relatively few.

Beyer, discussing this group, says that their language is "closely related to Ibanag and is divided into a number of dialects" (1917, p. 43). An impression is gained from the records, too, that the Gaddang of different areas had developed various subethnic and dialect groupings. The point has also been stressed that many former Gaddang speakers had adopted the Ibanag lingua franca, so that their descendants in modern times counted themselves as belonging to the higher-prestige Ibanag ethnic group. How far this can explain the great preponderance of Ibanag speakers southward to the Ilagan and Gamu areas, as against considering the Ibanags as actual migrants from the north, will perhaps always be a matter of speculation.

In general, however, it would appear that the Tuguegarao area was actually settled extensively by Ibanags, submerging what were perhaps the northernmost of the original Gaddang speakers. Some Ibanags undoubtedly migrated further upriver. But the great majority of the people in the southerly districts are probably Ibanagized Gaddang groups. Careful research, especially in rural settlements, would probably turn up plentifully persisting Gaddang-type usages, along with linguistic elements from Gaddang dialects.

The early records give no indication that wet cultivation had reached the middle Cagayan prior to Spanish times. The old settlement pattern of scattered hamlets, and the mobile nature of the population which could so easily move out from Spanish control, suggests an economy of shifting dry cultivation. This type of economy, it was seen, has persisted up to modern times among the Mountain Province Gaddang and some of the "Catalangans" east of the Cagayan. It will also be noted as continuing southward into large zones of the upper Cagayan.

11. *Upper Cagayan*

The possibility that the ancestors of the modern Ifugao may have been migrants from the Magat valley, perhaps even as refugees from Spanish domination, has been suggested in the discussion of the origin of rice terracing. Here this hypothesis, as well as other possible origins of the Ifugao, can be considered more closely. The Gaddang, Ilongot, Isinai, and other ethnic groups of this zone will also be briefly examined in the light of the documentary record.

The primary puzzle posed by the records is what happened to the large villages in the upper Magat reported by the 1591 expeditions. It was seen from eighteenth-century mission records that instead of the old figure of "fifteen thousand tributes," seven new "churches" could list only 970 baptisms in six years.

Some of the nearly six thousand "Ilongots" living in the mountains to the east and south of the valley flats could be descendants of refugee groups that were seen even in the records of 1591–94 to have deserted their villages in the face of Spanish expeditions. Some of the old inhabitants, too, may have moved westward into the Cordillera heights to become part of the modern "Igorot" populations of Pingkian, Kayapa, and eastern Benguet. Here they would have joined with peoples similarly retreating from the low zones of Pangasinan via the Kayapa, Agno, and other river valleys.

The most tempting hypothesis here, however, is to consider that the Magat population may have provided the original ethnic pool from which the numerically largest group of Mountain Province people, the Ifugao, took form. It could be pictured that in the period following the first Spanish military penetrations, and perhaps before Fray Tomás Gutiérrez started mission work in 1632, many at least of these wet-cropping people had moved back into mountain country. This could account for the otherwise strange fact that the mission fathers reported only dry cultivation in Ituy by the date mentioned. Because the heights immediately to the west were occupied by dry-gardening Ibaloi groups, notably in the gold-mining areas, any such migrations would be likely to skirt this zone and so move to the northwest. The Matung-Cadaclan river system could have provided a route directly from the Bambang area of Ituy into southern parts of the present Ifugao territory around Hungduan and Kiangan. Alternatively, the heights could have been scaled via the Lamut and Ibulao river systems further north from Paniquy. Any well-organized group entering the mountains here at the time would have had no significant competitors for territory—at most some sparsely settled dry cultivators comprising mountain Gaddang occupants or refugees who might have moved southward from Spanish-occupied zones.

Whether or not such a hypothesis of a post-Spanish origin for the modern Ifugao could hold up on the basis of further evidence, it seems a fair hypothesis that this ethnic group had its prior cultural base in the Pani-quy-Ituy area of the Cagayan lowlands. The Ifugao cropping system, with its terrace walls, and also other facets of Ifugao life, such as the scattered hamlet system, could then represent cultural reformulations appropriate to mountain living of elements from the former lowland culture. This interpretation could account for the fact that the Ifugao are so distinct from the Bontok and Lepanto, with their large village clusters, who appeared to have their origins in lowland populations on the Ilocos side. Archaeological surveys, especially in the Matung and other river courses between the upper Magat and Ifugao subprovince, together with ethnological probing in the mountain settlements of the region, could well solve these problems. Glot-tochronological comparisons of Isinai and Ifugao, together with other languages of this part of northern Luzon, could also suggest relationships and time horizons.

In such studies, possible connections between southern Gaddang groups and the Ifugao also merit attention. The "Paniquy" valley area around Bagabag, into which the Lamut river system drains directly from Ifugao subprovince, together with the adjacent Ibulao system, is at least equally a logical choice as the departure point for the original migrations into Ifugao. The lower Magat, below the rugged gorge country, is a third zone from which people could have moved into the high country. In both these valley areas the early populations appear to have been of Gaddang affiliation, though in the second they have become largely Ibanagized.

Beyer, in his 1916 survey of the Philippine population, classes the Yogad speech as one of the dialects of Gaddang (1917, p. 24). Generally, however, it has been placed as a separate though closely related speech type, as in the recent censuses. For the Ganano valley and the upper Cagayan river, as for the Magat, there is need for archaeological, ethnological, and linguistic investigation to unravel so far as possible the relationships between the Gaddang, the Yogad, and the so-called "Ilongot" populations. Here the ecological-cultural perspectives do not seem to have been complicated prior to Spanish times by any contact with wet cultivation techniques. The scattered groups of the higher country now subsumed under the term Ilongot, although given varied names as seen in the records, are known moderately well, notably through the early twentieth-century work of Jones on the "Italon" subgroup, still largely unpublished since his death in the field (see Rideout, 1912). A popular description of the Ilongot way of life has been written by Wilson (1947). Almost no Negritos are left in this eastern zone, while the Tagalog-speaking peoples of Casiguran and Baler have their contacts with areas further south rather than into the Cagayan.

The ethnohistorical continuity of the Cagayan headwaters with the Pangasinan region to the south and west has been discussed in reviewing that region. It will be recalled that the southern faces of the Cordillera and Caraballo Sur heights were crossed by trade routes evidently used in pre-Spanish times.

In the analysis of patterns of agriculture in northern Luzon, it was noted that the wet rice techniques practiced in the Magat valley seem to have diffused northward from Pampanga or Pangasinan. How close were cultural affinities in pre-Spanish times between the populations of eastern Pangasinan and those of the Magat is not clear. In the first place, as seen, the eastern Pangasinan populations do not break into the records until fairly late, when the area had already become a refuge for runaways; in the second, the picture in the Magat area changed extensively in early Spanish times, and comparatively little is known about the Isinai, who now inhabit the lowlands. This zone is another in which further research is needed if we are to assess in proper perspective the ethnic variations of modern times.

GENETIC AND LINGUISTIC PERSPECTIVES

The discussion to this point had dealt almost exclusively with ecological and cultural dynamics. An additional brief review is needed of genetic and linguistic dynamics, although technical treatment of these matters would need to be carried much further than seems relevant here. Such technical discussion, too, will have to await the availability of more data from future research.

Even early observers, it was noted, tried to describe the physical differences they saw or had heard about among the northern Luzon peoples. The dark pygmy Negritos, of course, stood out distinctively, and were generally grouped together as they still are, with virtually no attempt to distinguish regional or individual types. Negritoid strains were also postulated as underlying the Malay-dominant northern Ilocanos and some other groups. Some writers also tried to account for what were thought to be Oriental-like characters among the Cordillera peoples by claiming that Chinese or Japanese refugees had moved into the mountains.

A number of scholars—Blumentritt, Worcester, Folkmar, Cole, Beyer, Sullivan, and others—have reviewed the physical differences among northern Luzon groups. The number of metric observations offered, however, has been even in the aggregate few, and types rather than the range of variants in characters have been stressed. Although knowledge of breeding processes in human populations is imperfect, a general picture could be constructed for northern Luzon of small groups scattering out, and their original gene pools then being subjected variously to genetic drift, to selection, possibly to the establishment of mutant changes, and in certain localities of interaction to hybridization. In some regions, marked contrasts in type would tend to develop, whereas in others there would be an intergradation or low cline of characters, as up a river valley where the populations were continuous. Such a habitat factor as the presence or absence of malaria would exemplify selective forces that have been at work, although in ways that can only be speculated upon. The possible effects of malaria in shaping ethnic distributions in the mountains and, where endemic in foothill zones, of separating lowland and mountain populations, have been usefully suggested by Eggan. On the social side the shared bilateral kinship system, presumably old in the area, together with marriage beyond immediate cousins, would usually have forced mating out beyond the hamlet, though not beyond the wet cultivation village, and so cumulatively affected these dynamics. The concentric circles of kin and alliance based on each living group would have in general an intergrading effect up to each ethnic boundary. Adding to these hypothesized processes the factors of original migration into mountain areas of groups from differing lowland zones, and subsequent expansion in the numbers of people and settlements, the likenesses and differences among peoples seen in modern times should come as no surprise. A degree of hybridization with Asians, and later with Europeans and a few Negroes who accompanied them, adds the final genetic touches to this hypothetical picture.

Linguistic studies in the area are more extensive, as in earlier works by mission fathers, and later writings by Scheerer, Seidenadel, Vanoverbergh, and others. They are currently being sharpened by field investigators, including Summer Institute of Linguistics workers. Some glottochronological analyses have also been done in connection with the Philippine Studies program of the University of Chicago. The range of diversity represented in the modern language and dialect situation would appear to present no difficulties of interpretation in terms of well-known dynamics of linguistic change. For glottochronological comparisons in the Cordillera, however, account must be taken not only of internal developments within the mountains but also of the possible origins of the groups concerned in separate language pools of the lowlands.

To summarize quickly: the Lepanto and Bontok dialects are relatively alike, and so apparently are the Kalinga and Gaddang dialects on the east side. Pangasinan, Ibaloi, Isinai, Ifugao, Tinguian, and Apayao all appear to be specialized along distinctive lines. The writer is not sure of the relation of Kankanai, or southern Kankanai, to the adjacent Ibaloi and Lepanto speech forms. The linguistic problems associated with the widely distributed Iloko and Ibanag languages have been discussed in the appropriate sections. Ilongot has at least three main dialects, according to Beyer, and Palanan has been seen as apparently a northern outlier of Tagalog-type dialects. The so-called Negrito language of modern census classifications is really not a separate language but rather a racial identification. Except for archaic elements, which may represent surviving fragments of the old forms of speech, the Negrito groups have taken over the language coin of Malay-type neighbors.

WIDER CONSIDERATIONS

It was suggested in the opening chapter that this study of lowland and mountain relationships in northern Luzon could have significance for ethnohistorical research in other parts of the world. It seems to need no laboring at this point that for any region under scrutiny the available historical records merit careful study for light they may shed on ecological, demographic, and cultural dynamics.

The basic or minimal theoretical case or model of such relationships involves migrants from a lowland group moving into an adjacent mountain area. Ethnohistorical research may then be able to establish more or less the common human baseline at the time of such migration, the subsequent reformulations in the life of each group, and hence the significance of likenesses and differences in later times. To the extent that trading and other contacts continue between the highland and lowland groups, the ethnohistorical picture becomes further elaborated. Not least of all, such perspectives provide a dynamic frame of reference within which further ecological, archaeological, linguistic, and ethnological studies can operate effectively. In this study, the Pangasinan-Ibaloi and Ilocano-Tinguian relationships appear to have approximated this minimal theoretical model.

In mountain zones widely over the world, populations have entered a highland area from two or more sides. Here a theoretical case or model of dyadic type can be constructed minimally with two groups that have moved up to an identical mountain habitat from lowland settings on opposite sides. Coming from different milieus, they are then subjected to similar ecological influences, so that reformulation should involve convergent phenomena. When the factor of contact is then introduced, the opportunity opens out for diffusionistic and acculturative influences to operate, possibly carrying beyond the mountain groups themselves into the lowland groups by way of continuing interaction. The dynamic frame of reference opened out to the archaeologist, linguist, and ethnologist becomes much more complicated. In the study, the problems of relationship between the Lepanto and the Ifugao, and the Bontok and the Kalinga, exemplify the implications of this dyadic model.

It would be possible to carry further such exercises in a case or in a model construction in order to cover various additional type situations, including the multiple interplay of groups such as has obviously marked most zones of the northern Luzon Cordillera. Only two, however, show basically different dimensions. One concerns the possibility that one or more of the mountain groups came originally from some zone or zones other than the adjacent lowlands, which could have been true of parts of the northern Luzon mountains. The other delineates the migration of a mountain group back to the lowland milieu, such as was discussed earlier in the chapter.

One of the striking features of the northern Luzon record, of importance not only for comparative study in other areas but also for cultural theory generally, is the repetitive nature of certain phenomena of persistence and change. Most obvious, in zone after zone, are patterns of response to Spanish penetration and pressures: the initial resistance and retreat; the subsequent expectancies of benefits to be gained; the later violent reversionary tendencies and continuing, more sophisticated revolts; the flights to available hinterlands where self-conscious conservatism could flourish; the development of no-man's-lands between the pacified and the unpacified, where the stranger's life was unsafe, yet through which essential commerce could move.

Both war and peace stimulated dynamic population movements, and along with disease, technological change, and other factors, modified the earlier demographic patterns. Widened contacts called for increased verbal interaction, so that a bilingual self-education flourished, and the key languages spread as lingua franca media and served as agencies of linguistic and ethnic leveling. The availability of any special resource such as gold or terrain for tobacco growing tended to bring about increased economic specialization.

For both lowlander and mountaineer, a selective merging of old and new elements occurred to make up a reformulated way of life. Although the lowland groups leaned much more to new things, partly because of great accessibility and ecological flexibility, and partly by force of the alien control, economic, familial, religious, festive, and other usages continued to give an indigenous stamp to their cultural milieu. In all such matters, the northern Luzon record presents rich stores of case material capable of being analyzed further than has been done for the purposes of this particular study.

Appendix

Agricultural Census 1948: Crop Production in Census Year

RICE (in *cavanes**)

| | Irrigated (wet) | | Upland |
Province	First crop	Second crop	(dry)
Pangasinan	3,009,862	262,621	171,815
La Union	291,908	34,501	29,853
Ilocos Sur	318,680	62,006	25,310
Abra	176,016	39,181	13,706
Ilocos Norte	377,609	31,068	7,509
Mountain	348,441	167,652	56,846
Cagayan	560,191	177,921	28,917
Isabela	1,398,083	49,677	132,695
Nueva Vizcaya	475,874	35,087	8,194

OTHER CROPS

Province	Corn (maize) (*cavanes*)	Camote (sweet pot.) (*kilos*)	Gabe (taro) (*kilos*)	Ubi (yams) (*kilos*)	Tuguet† (*kilos*)	Tobacco (*kilos*)
Pangasinan	267,368	2,483,033	325,463	103,590	187,374	1,220,453
La Union	19,445	1,224,675	102,921	68,691	98,819	718,239
Ilocos Sur	60,671	1,365,875	52,959	11,691	35,879	271,820
Abra	74,281	572,623	93,307	39,072	6,123	204,313
Ilocos Norte	36,182	634,169	93,849	57,029	63,144	327,160
Mountain	41,367	67,490,327	1,873,821	278,133	180,435	115,141
Cagayan	429,025	645,230	261,794	128,881	101,032	2,009,809
Isabela	562,619	980,293	532,526	56,596	44,796	6,546,235
Nueva Vizcaya	35,991	5,229,726	144,736	3,007	4,169	149,470

* One *cavan* equals 75 liters.
† *Dioscorea sativa*, L., a wild root rather like a wild potato.

Bibliography

Alcazar, José de. 1895. Historia de los Dominios Españoles en Oceania: Filipinas. Manila.

Algué, Juan. 1899. Atlas de Filipinas. Manila.

Anderson, Barbara. 1960. "Report on Some Lexico-Statistical Counts on Languages of the Mountain Province, Philippines." Unpublished paper, University of Chicago.

Barrantes y Monero, V. 1869. Apuntes Interesantes sobre las Islas Filipinas. Madrid.

Barrows, David P. 1903. A Preliminary Report on Explorations among the Tribes of the Cordillera Central of Northern Luzon. Manila. (Seen in the Beyer Collection, History and Ethnography of the Igorot People, Vol. 4, Paper 12.)

Barton, Roy F. 1922. Ifugao Economics. University of California Publications in Anthropology, Archaeology and Ethnology, Vol. 15, No. 5, pp. 385–446.

———. 1946. Ifugao Religion. Memoir 65, American Anthropological Association.

———. 1949. The Kalingas, Their Institutions and Custom Law. Chicago.

Bautista, B. R. 1937. "The General Practice of Lowland Rice Farming in the Philippines." Philippine Journal of Agriculture, VIII, No. 1, 105–19.

Beyer, H. Otley. 1912. "Origin Myths from the Philippine Mountain Peoples." Philippine Journal of Science, VIII, No. 2, 85ff.

———. 1917. Population of the Philippine Islands in 1916. Manila.

———. 1948. Philippine and East Asian Archaeology, and Its Relation to the Origin of the Pacific Islands Population. Quezon City.

———. 1955. "The Origin and History of the Philippine Rice Terracers." Proceedings, 8th Pacific Science Congress, I, 380–98. Quezon City.

——— (Ed.). Collection of Papers on Philippine Ethnology. (Many volumes of manuscripts, including translations from Spanish sources, seen up to 1932 in Manila by the writer.)

———, and Jaime C. de Veyra. 1947. Philippine Saga. A Pictorial History of the Archipelago Since Time Began. Manila.

Blair, Emma H., and James A. Robertson (Eds.). The Philippine Islands, 1493–1803. 54 vols. Cleveland, 1903–9. (The standard published record of Philippine historical documents, primarily translated from Spanish sources.)

Blumentritt, Ferdinand. 1882. Versuch einer Ethnographie der Philippinen. Gotha.

Buzeta, Manuel. 1850–51. Diccionario Geográfico, Estadístico, Histórico, de las Islas Filipinas. 2 vols. Madrid. (Includes an alphabetical description of geographic features and settlements, and a review of known ethnic data.)

Catholic Truth Society, Manila. 1936. A Short History of the Filipino People. Manila.

Cavada y Mendez de Vigo, Augustin de la. 1876. Historia, Geográfica, Geológica y Estadística de Filipinas. Manila.

Censuses of the Philippines. 1903, 1918, 1939, 1948.

Christie, E. J. 1914. "Irrigation in Ilocos Norte." *Philippine Journal of Science,* IX.

———. 1914. Notes on Iloko Ethnography and History. Manila. (Seen in the Beyer Collection on Philippine Folklore, Social Customs and Beliefs, Vol. 10, Paper 392.)

Cole, Fay-Cooper. 1909. "Distribution of the Non-Christian Tribes of Northwestern Luzon." *American Anthropologist,* XI, 329–47.

———. 1922. The Tinguian: Social, Religious and Economic Life of a Philippine Tribe. Chicago.

———. 1945. The Peoples of Malaysia. New York.

Concepcion, Juan de la. 1788–92. Historia General de Filipinas. 14 vols. Manila.

Conklin, Harold C. 1961. "The Study of Shifting Agriculture." *Current Anthropology,* II, 27–59.

Crawford, John. 1820. History of the Indian Archipelago. Edinburgh.

Eggan, Fred. 1941. "Some Aspects of Culture Change in the Northern Philippines." *American Anthropologist,* XLIII, 11–18.

———. 1954. "Some Social Institutions in the Mountain Province, Northern Luzon, and Their Significance for Historical and Comparative Studies." *University of Manila Journal of East Asiatic Studies,* III, No. 3, 329–35.

Flormata, Gregorio. 1901. Memoria sobre la Provincia de Pangasinan. Manila.

Gemelli Careri, Giovanni Francesco. 1699. Giro del Mondo (A Voyage Round the World). Napoli.

Gironière, Paul P. de la. 1854. Twenty Years in the Philippines. New York.

Hanke, Lewis (Ed.). 1943. Cuerpo de Documentos del Siglo XVI sobre los Derechos de España en las Indias y las Filipinas. Mexico.

Iwao, Sei-ichi. 1943. Early Japanese Settlers in the Philippines. Tokyo.

Jenks, A. E. 1905. The Bontoc Igorot. Manila.

Keesing, F. M. 1938. "Population and Land Utilization among the Lepanto, Northern Philippines." *Comptes Rendus du Congrès International de Géographie,* II, No. 3C, 458–64. Amsterdam.

———. 1949. "Notes on Bontoc Social Organization, Northern Philippines." *American Anthropologist,* LI, 578–601.

———. 1962. "The Isneg: Shifting Cultivators of the Northern Philippines." Southwestern Journal of Anthropology, XVIII, 1–19.

———, and M. Keesing. 1934. Taming Philippine Headhunters: A Study of Government and of Cultural Change in Northern Luzon. London and Stanford.

Kroeber, Alfred L. 1943. Peoples of the Philippines. Rev. ed. New York.

Lambrecht, Francis. 1929. "Ifugao Villages and Houses." *Publications of the Catholic Anthropological Conference,* I, No. 3, 117–41.

Lambrecht, Godfrey. 1959. "The Gadang of Isabela and Nueva Vizcaya: Survey of a Primitive Animalistic Religion." *Philippine Studies,* VII, No. 2, 194–218.

Laufer, Berthold. 1908. "The Relations of the Chinese to the Philippine Islands." Smithsonian Institution, Miscellaneous Collection, Vol. 50, pp. 248–84.

Le Bar, Frank M., and Milton D. Graham (Eds.). 1955. The Philippines. 4 vols. New Haven.

Leitz, Paul S. (Ed.) 1956. Calendar of Philippine Documents in the Aver Collection of the Newberry Library. Chicago.

Lopez, Francisco. 1627. Arte de la Lengua Iloca. Manila.

Mallat de Bassilan, Jean B. 1846. Les Philippines, Histoire, Géographie, Moeurs, Agriculture, Industrie et Commerce. 2 vols. Paris.

Malumbres, Julian. 1918a. Historia de Cagayan. Manila. (Covers early materials on the Cagayan valley as a whole, as well as later materials on Cagayan Province; among important records quoted are a survey by Captain Varona y Velazquez in 1746, another by Antonio Mora in 1805, and various chronicles of Cagayan towns.)

———. 1918b. Historia de la Isabela. Manila. (Continues the record of the middle Cagayan, principally from 1740 on.)

———. 1919. Historia de Nueva Vizcaya y Provincia Montañosa. Manila. (Two parts, the first dealing with Nueva Vizcaya, mainly in the nineteenth century, the second with what is now Mountain Province, mainly in the same period.)

Martinez de Zuñiga, Joaquín. 1814. An Historical Review of the Philippine Islands. 2 vols. London. (Translated from the Spanish work by John Maver.)

———. 1893. Estadismo de las Islas Filipinas. 2 vols. Madrid. (Extensively translated by W. E. Retana.)

Meyer, Hans. 1885. Die Igorroten. Appendix of Eine Weltreise. Leipzig.

Millan y Villanueva, Camilo. 1891. Ilocos Norte. Descripción General de dicha Provincia por Pero Nuño. Manila.

Montero y Vidal, José. 1886. El Archipiélago Filipino y las Islas Marianas. 2 vols. Manila.

Moss, C. R. 1920a. Nabaloi Law and Ritual. University of California Publications in Archaeology and Ethnology, Vol. 15, No. 3. Berkeley.

———. 1920b. Kankanay Ceremonies. University of California Publications in Archaeology and Ethnology, Vol. 15, No. 4. Berkeley.

———. 1924. Nabaloi Tales. University of California Publications in Archaeology and Ethnology, Vol. 17, No. 5. Berkeley.

Nydegger, William F. 1960. Tarong: a Philippine Barrio. Unpublished Ph.D. dissertation, Cornell University.

Pardo de Tavera, T. H. 1901. Etimología de los Nombres de Razas de Filipinas. Manila.

Perez, Angel. 1902. Las Igorrotes: Estudio Geográfico y Etnográfico sobre algunos Distritos de Norte de Luzon. Manila.

———. 1904. Relaciones Agustinianas de las Razas del Norte de Luzon. Ethnological Survey Publications, No. 2. Manila.

Phelan, John L. 1959. The Hispanization of the Philippines, Spanish Aims and Filipino Responses 1500–1700. Madison.

Philippine Commission of 1900, Report. 4 vols. Washington. (Also further reports of the Commission to 1915.)

Pittman, Richard S. 1952. Notes on the dialect geography of the Philippines. Summer Institute of Linguistics. 2d ed. Grand Forks, N.D.

Puya y Ruiz, Adolfo. 1885. Filipinas. Descripción General de la Provincia de Cagayan. Manila.

Reyes y Florentino, Isabelo de los. 1890. Historia de Ilocos. 2 vols. Manila. (Volume I deals with pre-Spanish times; Volume II with the history of the Spanish period.)

Rideout, Henry M. 1912. William Jones—Indian, Cowboy, American Scholar, and Anthropologist in the Field. New York.

Robertson, J. A. 1914. The Igorots of Lepanto. Manila.

Sawyer, F. H. 1900. The Inhabitants of the Philippines. New York.

Scott, William H. 1958. "A Preliminary Report on Upland Rice in Northern Luzon." Southwestern Journal of Anthropology, XIV, No. 1, 87–105.

Scheerer, Otto. 1905. The Nabaloi Dialect. Manila. (An appendix gives a translation of the "Diary" of Galvey's 1829 expedition.)

Thèvenot, Jean de. 1673. Relation d'un voyage fait au Levant. Paris.

Vanoverbergh, Morice. 1929. "Dress and Adornment in the Mountain Province of Luzon, Philippine Islands." Publication of the Catholic Anthropological Conference, I, No. 5.

———. 1932. "The Isneg." Publication of the Catholic Anthropological Conference, III, No. 1, 1–80. (This author has a number of further works on specialized subjects relating to the Isneg.)

———. 1955. Iloko Grammar. Baguio.

———. 1956. Iloko-English Dictionary. Baguio. (This is a revision of Andrés Carro's Vocabulario Iloco-Español.)

Vega, Manuel de la. 1609. Expeditions to the Province of Tuy. Manila.

Villaverde, Juan F. 1909. "The Ifugaos of Quiangan and Vicinity." Philippine Journal of Science, IVa, No. 4. (Translated by Dean C. Worcester.)

Watters, R. F. 1960. "The Nature of Shifting Cultivation: A Review of Recent Research." Pacific Viewpoint, I, 59–99.

Welsh, Doris V. 1959. A Catalogue of Printed Materials Relating to the Philippine Islands in the Newberry Library, 1519–1900. Chicago.

Wilson, O. O., 1947. Ilongot Life and Legends. Baguio.

Worcester, Dean C. 1899. The Philippine Islands and Their People. New York.

———. 1906. "The Non-Christian Tribes of Northern Luzon." Philippine Journal of Science.

———. 1912. "Headhunters of North Luzon." National Geographic Magazine, XXIII, 833–930.

———. 1913. "The Non-Christian Tribes of the Philippines." National Geographic Magazine, XXIV, 1157–1256.

———. 1914. The Philippines, Past and Present. New York.

Yabes, Leopold Y. 1936. A Brief Survey of Iloko Literature from the Beginnings to Its Present Development. Manila.

Zaide, Gregorio F. 1949. The Philippines since Pre-Spanish Times. Manila.

Index

Index

Lago, Fray Bernardo, 137
Lakaaden, 82
Lal-lo, *see* Nueva Segovia
Lambrecht, Father Godfrey, 299
Langangan, 203
Languages: in 1948 census, 115 n.; study of, 12–13, 341–42. *See also individual dialects*
Laoag, 9, 26, 159, 160–61, 166 n.; as capital of Ilocos Norte, 44
Laoag River, 8, 144
Lapog, 142
La Union Province, 9, 10, 48, 88; census data on, 46, 90 n., 114–15; formation of, 44, 83
Lavezaris, Governor, 15, 17, 18
"Layug na Caboloan," 30
Lepanto (northern Kankanai), 4, 8, 11, 111, 319, 320, 321, 326–27, 335; origins of, 92, 339; terraces of, 117, 312–13
Lepanto, Comandancia of, 45, 110
Lepanto language, 93, 341
Letona, Fray Bartolomé de, 282
Leyrat (Sarrat), 159
Limahon (Limahong), 18–19, 137, 170; in Sinay, 125–26
Limos (Remus), 231
Loarca, Miguel de, 20, 21, 22, 147, 148; on Abra, 123; on Pangasinan, 53
Lobato, 292
Lobo, *see* Taban
Lower Cagayan area, *see* Cagayan, lower
Lowlands: residential patterns of, 308–9; settlement of, and cultural theory, 342–43
Lubuagan, 235
Lullutan (Batavag), 248
Lumabang (Solano), 294
Luna, *see* Namagpacan
Lungao, 160
Lupao, 75
Luppo, Don Ambrosio, 245
Lutab, 85–86

Macao, trade with, 32
Macasiag, 68, 129, 131, 132
Madamba, Don Felipe, 132
Madriaga, Fray Manuel, 157
Magalat, 242
Magaldan (Mangaldan), 54, 59
Magat River, 8, 267, 322, 338, 340
Magdalena, Fray Bernabé de la, 233
Magic, 317. *See also* Religion
Magogao (Magaogao), 235
Magsanop, Don Juan, 151–53
Magurig, *see* Dudulique
Maguin, 207
Maize, 10, 11, 52, 96, 122, 207, 306, 310,

333; in Chico River area, 221; in Middle Cagayan, 169, 239
Malagueg, 242, 243
Malaguey, 241
Malaria, 341
Malaueg, 230, 234. *See also* Rizal
Malayans, in northern Luzon, 2, 301–2, 304
Malaysia, piracy of, 13
Maldonado, Juan Pacheco, 62–63
Malionlion (Maliongliong, San Bartolomé), 72, 77, 283, 287
Malong, Don Andrés (King): revolt led by, 33–34, 67–68, 100–101, 130, 132; in Ilocos Norte, 151–4
Malumbres, Julian, 5, 103–4, 181, 207; on Abra, 140; on Santa Cruz mission, 227, 228; on Tuga mission, 232–33
Manacu, 207
Manaoag (Mauazug), 27, 54, 89 n.
Mandayas, revolts of, 194, 196–98
Manila: councils in (1676–78), 36; "delusion" concerning, 33; 1646 earthquake in, 70–71
Manila Bay, 33
Mankayan, 108, 109, 112
Mangaldan, 87, 89 n.
Maricdin, Don Dionisio, 68
Marin, Fray Esteban, 26, 28
Marin, Fray José Tomás, 158, 199
Marriage customs, 59, 69, 73, 190, 316
Martin, Fray José, 262
Martinez de Zuñiga, Joaquín, 14–15, 19, 20, 63, 77, 291–92; on Pangasinan rebellion (1764), 42–43; on Tinguians and Igorots, 135
Massi, 185, 201, 202
Masingal, 142
Matatanga, 229
Medina, Juan de, 27, 32, 100, 164–65; on Abra, 129; on Laoag, 151; on missions in northern Pangasinan, 67
Mena, Fray Benito de, 157
Mendoza, Fray Andrés de, 293
"Men's houses," 95
Mercado, Captain, 189
Metals, in trade, 13. *See individual metals*
Meyer, Hans, 140–41
Middle Cagayan area, *see* Cagayan, Middle
Migration theory, of mountain settlements, 2–3
Millan y Villanueva, Camilo, 165
Minanga, 233
Minaio, Fray Francisco, 248–49
Mining, *see* Copper, Gold
Miranda, Captain Toribio de, 275
Mirandaola, 18
Missions: in Abra, 124, 126–28; "active," 36;